THE ROBBERY OF NATURE

Capitalism and the Ecological Rift

The Robbery of Nature

John Bellamy Foster and Brett Clark

MONTHLY REVIEW PRESS

New York

Library of Congress Cataloging-in-Publication Data available
from the publisher.

ISBN 978-158367-839-8   paper
ISBN 978-158367-778-0   cloth

Typeset in Minion Pro and Brown

MONTHLY REVIEW PRESS, NEW YORK
monthlyreview.org

5 4 3 2 1

Contents

Preface

*As long as human beings exist, the history of nature and the
history of human beings mutually condition each other.*
—KARL MARX

THE ROBBERY OF NATURE draws on the classical historical-
materialist critique associated with Karl Marx and Frederick Engels
to explain how capitalist commodity production robs human society
and life in general of the conditions of natural and social reproduction,
generating a planetary rift that today knows virtually no bounds.[1] The
result is an existential crisis in the human relation to the earth that
can only be overcome through a long ecological revolution.

In Marx's classical critique of capitalism, human production alters
the material form of physical existence, but can do so only in con-
formity with natural laws and processes—if it is not to create an
"irrevocable rift in the interdependent process of social metabolism, a metabolism prescribed by the natural laws of life itself."[2] This
insight forms the basis of Marx's famous theory of metabolic rift.
In this perspective, the labor process constitutes the vital "social
metabolism" mediating the relationship between humanity and "the
universal metabolism of nature," that is, natural processes as a whole.[3]

Capitalist commodity production, however, introduces an "alienated mediation" of this essential ecological relationship through its one-dimensional pursuit of the "value form" (exchange value) at the expense of the "natural form" (use value).[4] The result is the metabolic rift. This requires a revolutionary reconstitution of society as a whole in order to restore a viable socioecological metabolism—one that will sustain the elemental conditions of life for the "chain of human generations."[5]

In this book, we seek to elaborate on Marx's theory of metabolic rift by employing his notion of the "robbery" or "expropriation" of nature—which, since human beings are inherently a part of nature, is undermining the natural-material bases on which humanity's existence rests.[6] This degradation of the human relation to the earth results from treating "Nature" as a "free gift to . . . capital," and from the violation of the basic "conditions of reproduction" and ecological sustainability, including those of the Earth System as a whole.[7]

The expropriation of nature is at one and the same time the expropriation of land/ecology and the expropriation of human bodies themselves. Much of this book is therefore concerned not simply with the robbing of nature but also the robbing of the physical bases of human existence, through various forms of oppression, associated with class, race, gender, and imperialism. In extreme cases, this manifests itself as what Engels called "social murder."[8] The ecological rift is thus also a *corporeal rift*, reflecting the interdependent character of the social metabolism, which connects human beings with nature and their own corporeal organization. Capitalism's degradation of the earth depends ultimately on an "alienated speciesism," according to which to be "an animal," or indeed a "living thing," means to be an object of expropriation. Yet, for Marx, following Thomas Müntzer, "all living things must also become free."[9]

We first articulated the notion of the *expropriation of nature*, around which the present argument revolves, in our article "The Paradox of Wealth: Capitalism and Environmental Destruction," appearing in *Monthly Review* in November 2009, now revised and updated in this book as chapter 6, "Capitalism and the Paradox of Wealth."

The Introduction and most of the other chapters (chapters 1–5 and 8)—"The Expropriation of Nature," "The Rift of Éire," "Women, Nature, and Capital in the Industrial Revolution," "Marx as a Food Theorist," "Marx and Alienated Speciesism," and "Marx's Ecology and the Left"—were all written, beginning in 2016, as extensions of this notion of the expropriation or robbery of nature, as perceived from a historical-materialist perspective, and with this book explicitly in mind. Exceptions to this are chapter 9, "Value Isn't Everything," written by John Bellamy Foster and Paul Burkett in response to attacks on the labor theory of value by ecosocialists; chapter 7, "The Meaning of Work in a Sustainable Society," which was part of a debate on the role of work in a future green society; chapter 10, "The Planetary Emergency, 2020–2050," addressing the question of a climate change exit strategy, which is extensively revised and updated for this book; and chapter 11, "The Long Ecological Revolution," emerging out of a debate on ecology, technology, and ecosocialism. These chapters have all been included to round out the argument and to give more concrete meaning to the long ecological revolution to which the entire argument necessarily leads. All of the previously published essays have been adapted to form integral components of this book. Chapter 2, "The Rift of Éire," appears here for the first time.

This book is focused on putting forward a critique of capitalism's catastrophic degradation of the environment. But in the process, we are often compelled to question other left-environmental views that approach these issues in partial, one-sided ways. In doing so, our intention is not to create further divisions within the left, but rather to unite the movement by insisting that the age-old revolutionary principle of the masses, "I am nothing and I should be everything," be extended to the world of life itself, merging the calls for substantive equality with ecological sustainability in a universal struggle for sustainable human development.[10] This demands a much deeper and more revolutionary materialism, one that only an ecohistorical materialism can provide.

The multifaceted analysis provided in the following chapters would not have been possible without the help of those with whom we have (between the two of us) written on these topics over the years, including Daniel Auerbach, Kelly Austin, Paul Burkett, Rebecca Clausen, Hannah Holleman, Stefano B. Longo, Fred Magdoff, Brian Napoletano, Pedro Urquijo, Richard York, and Karen Xuan Zhang.

We are also deeply indebted to our colleagues at *Monthly Review*, including, in addition to Hannah and Fred, Susie Day, R. Jamil Jonna, John Mage, Martin Paddio, Al Ruben, John J. Simon, Intan Suwandi, Camila Valle, Colin Vanderburg, Victor Wallis, and Michael Yates. Ian Angus, editor of Climate and Capitalism, has given us continual support and encouragement.

Our friend Desmond Crooks generously helped in the design of the book's cover.

In the process of developing our ideas, we have benefited from interactions with a wide range of thinkers. We would particularly like to acknowledge in this respect Lazarus Adua, Elmar Altvater, Samir Amin, Robert J. Antonio, Shannon Elizabeth Bell, Amanda Bertana, Jordan Besek, Ted Benton, Natalie Blanton, Paul Buhle, Alex Callinicos, Michael Carolan, Matthew Clement, Julia B. Corbett, Michael Dawson, Peter Dickens, Ricardo Dobrovolski, Sue Dockstader, Liam Downey, Adam Driscoll, Wilma Dunaway, Riley Dunlap, Eric Edwards, Martin Empson, Andrew Feenberg, Jared Fitzgerald, Joseph Fracchia, R. Scott Frey, Michael Friedman, Paul Gellert, Martha E. Gimenez, Jennifer Givens, Patrick Greiner, Ryan Gunderson, Gregory Hooks, Leontina Hormel, Alf Hornborg, Cade Jameson, Andrew K. Jorgenson, Naomi Klein, Peter Linebaugh, Delores (Lola) Loustaunau, Andreas Malm, Philip Mancus, Jeffrey Mathes McCarthy, Robert W. McChesney, Julius McGee, István Mészáros, Marcello Musto, Kamran Nayeri, Kari Norgaard, Frank Page, Marcel Paret, Mauricio Betancourt De La Parra, Thomas C. Patterson, David Pellow, Paul Prew, Camilla Royle, Kohei Saito, Ariel Salleh, Jean Philippe Sapinski, Keith Scott, Helena Sheehan, Eamonn Slater, Richard Smith, Christian Stache, Joanna Straughn, Stephen Tatum, Howard Waitzkin, Kyle Powys Whyte, Chris Williams, Ryan Wishart, and Christopher Wright.

Our ideas on ecology and society are inextricably interwoven with those of the two people with whom we share our lives on a daily basis, and without whose support and encouragement these pages would be blank. We therefore dedicate *The Robbery of Nature*, with deep humility, to our earthly "muses," Carrie Ann Naumoff and Kris Shields.

Introduction

THE CHAPTER on "Machinery and Large-Scale Industry" in the first volume of Karl Marx's *Capital* closes with this statement: "All progress in capitalist agriculture is a progress in the art, not only of robbing the worker, but of robbing the soil. . . . Capitalist production, therefore, only develops the techniques and the degree of combination of the social process of production by simultaneously undermining the original sources of all wealth—the soil and the worker." "Robbing the worker" referred to the theory of exploitation, which entailed the expropriation of the worker's surplus labor by the capitalist. But what did Marx mean by "robbing the soil"? Here robbery was connected to his theory of the metabolic rift arising from the expropriation of the earth. As he stated earlier in the same paragraph, "Capitalist production . . . disturbs the metabolic interaction between man and the earth, i.e. it prevents the return to the soil of its constituent elements consumed by man in the form of food and clothing; hence it hinders the operation of the eternal natural condition for the lasting fertility of the soil."[1]

The same basic logic was present in the other famous passage on the metabolic rift, at the end of the chapter on "The Genesis of Capitalist Ground Rent" in the third volume of *Capital*. There Marx referred to "the squandering of the vitality of the soil" by large-scale capitalist enterprise, generating "an irreparable rift in the interdependent process of social metabolism, a metabolism prescribed by the natural laws of life itself."[2]

In both instances, Marx's notion of the robbery of the soil is intrinsically connected to the rift in the metabolism between human beings and the earth. To get at the complexities of his metabolic rift theory, it is useful to look separately at the issues of the *robbery* and the *rift*, seeing these as separate moments in a single development. This is best done by examining how Marx's ecological critique in this area emerged in relation to the prior critique of industrial agriculture provided by the celebrated German chemist Justus von Liebig. Of particular importance in this context is Liebig's notion of the "robbery system" (*Raubsystem*) or "robbery economy" (*Raubwirtschaft*), which he associated with British high farming, a high-input, high-output, capital-intensive form of large-scale industrial agriculture.[3]

For Marx, as for Liebig, this robbery was not of course confined simply to external nature, since humans as corporeal beings were themselves part of nature.[4] The expropriation of nature in capitalist society thus had its counterpart, in Marx's analysis, in the expropriation of human bodily existence. The robbery and the rift in nature's metabolism was also a robbery and a rift in the human metabolism. This was visible in the many forms of bonded labor, in the conditions of social reproduction in the patriarchal household, and in the destructive physical impacts and the loss of the vital powers of individual human beings.

LIEBIG: INDUSTRIAL AGRICULTURE AND THE ALIENATION OF THE SOIL

Beginning in the late 1850s and early 1860s, Liebig, who had long advocated the use of scientific methods in agriculture, began to argue that British high farming's systematic "alienating [of] the crops" of the fields was irrational from a long-term perspective, since it ultimately despoiled the earth of its nutrients. "A farmer," he declared, "may sell and permanently alienate all that portion of the produce of his farm which has been supplied by the atmosphere [but not the constituents of the soil]—a field from which something is permanently taken away, cannot possibly increase or even continue equal in productive power." He stressed that "the axiom thus enunciated is simply a natural law."[5]

The "natural law" at issue here was what Liebig called the "law of compensation" or law of replacement (*Gesetz des Ersatzes*), whereby nutrients removed from the soil had to be restored.[6] This was in turn based on the recognition of the metabolic interaction (*Stoffwechsel*) governing the exchanges of matter and energy between life-forms and their environments. Metabolism was a fundamental concept of natural science, and Liebig was one of its nineteenth-century pioneers.[7] In essence, it raised the question of the material interchanges and processes governing the complex interrelations between organic and inorganic nature.

"All plants, without exception," Liebig wrote, "exhaust the soil, each of them in its own way, of the conditions for their reproduction." To sell the food and fiber to populations in cities hundreds and thousands of miles from the land prevented the return of these essential nutrients to the soil, resulting in a system of "spoliation." Attempts to compensate for this—for example, through Britain's imports of guano from Peru, and bones from the battlefields and catacombs of Europe—were temporary and makeshift solutions, almost inherently insufficient, which plundered other countries of their earthly resources.[8]

Liebig's emphasis in the late 1850s and early 1860s on the alienation and robbery of the soil can be seen as a product of developments that began in the 1840s and extended to the time that Marx was writing *Capital* in the 1860s. Responding to the deterioration of soil conditions and the commercial demands for higher agricultural productivity—what historians have called the Second Agricultural Revolution—English farmers in 1841 began importing massive amounts of guano from Peru.[9] Meanwhile, the Irish potato famine, beginning in 1845, led to the abolition of the Corn Laws in England, allowing for the importation of cheaper grain and forcing new, competitive market conditions, which in turn gave rise to what

Marx called a "new regime" of the international food system.[10] This period saw the development of high farming or intensive agriculture in England (itself symbolized by the importation of guano, bones, oil cakes, and other natural fertilizers), and the shift to an increasingly meat-based agricultural system grounded in practices such as the famous Norfolk rotation, establishing a mixed animal-crop system.[11] In this context, concerns were raised about the loss of soil nutrients from new, intensive forms of agriculture and the waste of nutrients in human sewage resulting from massive food and fiber imports to the cities.[12] In Germany and other parts of Europe, there were growing worries among agronomists and soil scientists about England's voracious importation of bones from the Continent. The entire period of the Second Agricultural Revolution was thus one of crisis and transformation in the socioecological metabolism of British soil cultivation, associated with the Industrial Revolution.

To underscore the enormity of the crisis of soil ecology, Liebig made a point of attacking entrenched notions propounded by some agriculturalists and the classical political-economist David Ricardo that the "power of the soil" on any given plot of land was "indestructible" and hence "inexhaustible."[13] The development of modern chemistry had discredited such views. Plant growth, Liebig contended, depended on "eight substances." (Today we know this to be eighteen, sixteen of which, excluding carbon and oxygen, are chemical elements that for most plants—with the partial exception of nitrogen converted into organic nitrogenous compounds from the air by legumes, such as clover, peas, and beans—are derived from the soil and not the atmosphere.) All of these elements had to be replenished for the soil to remain fertile.[14] Of these, the nutrients needed in the largest quantities were nitrogen, phosphorus, and potassium. Liebig's famous "law of the minimum," moreover, indicated that there was a complex balance of soil nutrients such that, to enhance the productivity of the soil in a given area, it was necessary to supply the nutrient in which the soil was most deficient, to the point at which that nutrient was once again in proportion with the next-most deficient soil mineral. Growth rates were determined by the most limited factor. Soil "exhaustion" meant that the mineral composition of the earth had been so compromised that nutrients needed to be massively imported by "the hand of man" from outside the farm. "In this sense," Liebig declared, "most of our cultivated fields are exhausted," requiring massive infusions of chemical nutrients from outside.[15]

Liebig was not alone from the 1850s through the 1870s in addressing the issue of the destructive relation to the soil. Other major natural scientists, agronomists, and political economists raised the same questions, including George Waring, Henry Carey, James F. W. Johnston, Carl Fraas, and Wilhelm George Friedrich Roscher—all of whom (except Waring) Marx studied closely.[16] It was Liebig, however, who advanced the most critical and global concerns with respect to large-scale industrial agriculture. In doing so, he focused in particular on the extraordinary ascent of the guano trade as a measure of the extent of the European soil crisis.

By far the richest deposits of guano were to be found on the Chincha Islands off the coast of Peru, where it was the product of cormorants, boobies, and pelicans feeding since time immemorial on huge shoals of fish in the coastal currents and depositing their excrement in what became mountains of natural fertilizer. Peruvian guano was rich in nitrogen, ammonia, phosphates, and alkaline salts. Historian Gregory Cushman writes that "all told, from 1840 to 1879, Peru exported an estimated 12.7 million metric tons of guano from its islands," the great bulk of it destined for British fields.[17]

Between 1841 and 1855, according to Liebig, "upwards of 1,500,000 metric tons" of Peruvian guano had been imported into Great Britain, and two million tons into Europe as a whole. This was enough, based on the figures for Europe in this period, to produce an additional 200 million cwts (or hundredweights—an imperial hundredweight is 112 pounds) of grain, compared to what would have been produced without the guano. This was "sufficient to feed perfectly 26¾ million human beings [more than the population of England, Wales, and Scotland at that time] for one year." Liebig indicated that "one cwt. of guano was, in terms of the effective mineral constituents it contained, the equivalent of 25–80 cwt. of wheat."[18]

A sense of the deficiency in English agricultural fields in relation to their full productivity could thus be found in the immense quantity of guano imported at great cost and applied to fields—as well as in the importation of bones (bonemeal), nitrates, oil cakes, and other fertilizers and feeding stuffs for farm animals. Reflecting on this situation, Liebig charged that if England were to continue with its high farming system, it would so despoil the soil and become so dependent on increasing inputs that it would need quantities of guano "of about the extent of the English coal fields." No wonder that "British and American ships have searched through all the seas, and there is no small island, no coast, which has escaped their enquiries after guano."[19]

All this reinforced Liebig's argument that the much-vaunted industrial agriculture of British high farming was simply a more intensive, modern "robbery system" undermining the conditions of reproduction for future generations. To be sure, this was a more "refined" form of robbery, where "robbery improves the art of robbery." But the resulting impoverishment was the same. Indeed, the system's new techniques often effected an even more thoroughgoing impoverishment of the constituents of the soil. Rather than a "mark of progress," under these circumstances, an increase in crop production was likely a sign of long-term regression—the more so if examined on a global scale.[20] The English importation of bones from the Continent to be used as fertilizer, and its effect on the growth of individuals, could be seen in the greater height of British military conscripts relative to their Continental counterparts. "Great Britain," Liebig declared, "robs all countries of the conditions of their fertility; she has already ransacked the battle-fields of Leipzig, Waterloo, and the Crimea for bones, and consumed the accumulated skeletons of many generations in the Sicilian catacombs. . . . We may say to the world that she hangs like a vampire on the neck of Europe, and seeks out its hearts-blood, without any necessity and without permanent benefit to herself."[21]

Such a modern robbery culture, based on the total alienation of the soil, was the antithesis of a rational agriculture rooted in the application of science. Liebig did not hesitate to point out the structural

reasons for this contradiction. As he wrote in the conclusion to the
introduction of the 1862 edition of his *Agricultural Chemistry*, the
entire rapacious system associated with industrial agriculture could
be attributed to "the folly and ignorance . . . which private property
interposes" in the way of the "recovery" of the constituents of the soil.
The natural law of compensation was being violated by a production
system that knew no bounds, operating as if "the Earth is inexhaustible in its gifts."[22] Moreover, attempts to compensate for the loss of
soil nutrients by using only particular fertilizers might yield still more
irrational results in the form of an "excess of nutritive substances," as
opposed to "rational husbandry."[23]

MARX: THE ROBBERY OF NATURE AND THE METABOLIC RIFT

Marx's conception of the robbery or expropriation of nature was
necessarily much broader than that of Liebig, though the latter's natural-scientific researches had a decisive impact on Marx's thought. Marx
emerged as a materialist thinker in his early twenties through a long
and intense struggle with the Hegelian system of German idealism, in
which his doctoral dissertation on Epicurus's ancient materialist philosophy of nature played a central role (together with his encounter
with the work of Ludwig Feuerbach). Epicurean materialism, which
exerted a powerful influence on the scientific revolution of the seventeenth century, would remain a crucial reference point in Marx's
critical outlook, even as he developed his own historical-materialist
approach.[24] As a thinker concerned centrally with the human relation
to the earth through production, his analysis already displayed, in the
early 1840s, a broad ecological outlook, though his sharper critique of
the environmental contradictions of capitalist development was only
developed in his mature works. Still, in the 1840s, he addressed such
issues as the expropriation and alienation of the land; the division
between town and country; the pollution of air, water, and food in
the cities; and the corporeal reality of humanity, since human beings
remained inherently "a part of nature," albeit increasingly alienated
from their natural environments.[25]

By the 1850s, due to the influence of his close friend Roland Daniels—physician, natural scientist, communist organizer, and author of *Mikrokosmos*, which Marx read and commented on, but which, due to Daniels's premature death, was not published until the late twentieth century—Marx took up the concept of metabolism, integrating it into his system.[26] No doubt he also drew upon Liebig. During this period, he introduced the concept of "social metabolism," representing the real material relation between nature and humanity formed by the labor and production process.[27] The "social metabolic process," he wrote, constituted "the real exchange of commodities," including the productive exchange with nature, encompassing both matter and form, "use-value and . . . exchange-value." The labor process itself was defined as the "eternal natural necessity which mediates the metabolism between man and nature, and therefore human life itself."[28]

Marx's analysis of the social metabolism was thus never conceptually divorced from what he called the "universal metabolism of nature"—of which the human social metabolism was simply a part.[29] His entire dialectical framework rested on what would today be called an ecological (or socioecological) systems theory, connecting the materialist conception of history to that of nature—and requiring continuing study not only of changing developments in human history, but also in natural history (which in Marx's work took the form of extensive inquiries into geology, agronomy, chemistry, physics, biology, physiology, mathematics, and more).[30]

While writing *Capital* in the late 1850s and 1860s, Marx famously paused twice, not only to absorb Charles Darwin's evolutionary theory and its implications for the human relation to the environment, but also to study Liebig's analysis of the robbery system characterizing modern agriculture. In taking up Liebig's critique, he was to develop this more fully than Liebig had, forging a dynamic theory of the alienated social metabolism based on the exploitation of human labor. For Marx it was clear that socioecological contradictions were embedded in the process of capital accumulation in historical ways that went far beyond Liebig's natural-scientific perspective.[31] The result was a much deeper and richer sense of the structural imperatives underlying the expropriation of nature in the modern system of commodity production, informed by developments in natural science while also connecting these processes to the inner contradictions of capitalism as a historical social system.

To understand Marx's ecological critique, it is necessary to recognize that the contradiction between natural-material use values and economic exchange values lay at the core of his entire system. Inspired by Georg Wilhelm Friedrich Hegel's contradiction between matter and form, Marx's critique of the capitalist political economy rested in large part on the contradiction between metabolic interchange and the economic value form of commodities. The circuit of exchange value ultimately depended on the production and exchange of commodities embodying natural-material use values. "The chemical process, regulated by labour," Marx wrote, "has everywhere consisted of an exchange of (natural) equivalents," whose violation meant the expropriation of nature, with disastrous consequences.[32] The capitalist valorization process could thus never free itself from the conditions of "metabolic interaction [*Stoffwechsel*] between man and nature."[33] All attempts to do so, as in industrial agriculture or the exploitation of labor power, generated a metabolic rift, a crisis of social metabolic reproduction.

Marx's concern with the break in social metabolic reproduction of capitalism was undoubtedly deeply affected by the growing public discussions in the 1850s, during the Second Agricultural Revolution, of soil nutrients, the impact of the guano trade, and the enormous waste of human sewage. These developments all derived from English high farming and what Marx called the "new regime" of international food production following the abolition of the Corn Laws. He stressed in the *Grundrisse* how "self-sustaining agriculture" had broken down and been replaced by an industrial agriculture that required "machinery, chemical fertilizer acquired through exchange, seeds from different countries etc.," while guano was being imported from Peru in exchange for the export of other products.[34] In the new regime of food production, 25 percent of the wheat consumed in Britain in the mid-1850s was imported. Meanwhile, "large tracts of arable land in Britain" were being transformed into pasture. The derangement of the British food trade in the period, including competitive price instability, which interfered with securing the necessary foreign supplies, was such as to make "even an abundant harvest, under the new regime, [appear] relatively defective."[35]

These concerns regarding the contradictions of capitalist agriculture and its material impacts were further heightened by Marx's reading of the 1862 edition of Liebig's *Agricultural Chemistry*, especially its long incendiary introduction, on which Marx took extensive notes in 1865–66 while struggling to complete the first edition of *Capital*. "One of Liebig's immortal merits," Marx declared in *Capital*, was "to have developed from the point of view of natural science, the negative, i.e. destructive side of modern agriculture." Nevertheless, he followed this immediately by pointing out that Liebig's work contained the most egregious errors whenever its author ventured beyond the laws of natural science to comment on the laws of political economy.[36] Only by integrating these new natural-scientific developments with the critique of capital would it be possible to understand the wider implications for the human-nature metabolism. Thus, in *Capital*, Marx argued that "all progress in increasing the fertility of the soil for a given time is a progress towards ruining the more long-lasting sources of that fertility," and that "the more a country proceeds from large-scale industry as the background of its development, as in the case of the United States, the more rapid is this process of destruction."[37] Here he emphasized that capital accumulation, through its rapacious expropriation of nature, inevitably promoted ecological destruction. Hence, in his *Economic Manuscript of 1864–65*, he expressly raised the question of "the declining productivity of the soil when successive capital investments are made."[38]

At the heart of the contradiction was the reality that the social metabolism with nature under capitalism was mediated by value. Thus "the cultivation of particular crops depends on fluctuations in market prices and the constant changes in cultivation with these price fluctuations." This reflects the fact that "the entire spirit of capitalist production, which is oriented toward the most immediate monetary profit—stands in contradiction to agriculture, which has to concern itself with the whole gamut of permanent conditions of life required by the chain of human generations."[39] Writing in *Theories of Surplus Value*, Marx observed that

> even manure, plain muck, has become merchandise, not to speak of bone-meal, guano, potash, etc. That the [natural] elements of production *are estimated* in terms of money is not merely due to the formal change in production [as compared with pre-capitalist forms of agriculture]. New materials are introduced into the soil and its old ones are sold for reasons of *production*. . . . The seed trade has risen in importance to the extent to which the importance of seed rotation has been recognised.[40]

Yet the mediation of value, the high inputs and high outputs required by capitalist agriculture, long-distance trade, and the pressures on the soil all pointed to the intensification and long-term instability of the agricultural metabolism.

Marx argued that more intensive forms of agriculture, even as they produced a record harvest, could so deplete the soil that famine followed, requiring years for the soil to recover.[41] Ireland, he noted, was even forced to "export its manure [soil nutrients]" across the sea to England in a dramatic instance of ecological imperialism.[42] In the East Indies, "English-style capitalist farming . . . only managed to spoil indigenous agriculture and to swell the number and intensity of famines." This was part of a colonial "bleeding process, with a vengeance!"[43]

The deeper significance of Marx's analysis became clear as he developed the implications already present in his concept of social metabolism in order to conceptualize the systemic nature of the ecological contradictions of capitalism. Hence, in *Capital*, he brought the natural-material or ecological side of his social metabolic reproduction to the fore, in an attempt to understand the wider ramifications of the capitalist robbery system and its disruptive, indeed destructive, impact on natural systems. It was in this context that he raised the critical issue of the "irreparable rift in the interdependent process of social metabolism."[44] By "irreparable rift," he did not of course mean that a restoration of a rational and sustainable metabolism between human beings and the earth was impossible—indeed, he was to define the need for socialism ultimately in these terms.[45] Nevertheless, the destructive aspects of capitalism's alienated metabolic relation to the earth were not to be denied.

Here Marx's deep understanding of Epicurean materialism is evident. Central to his materialist ontology was the Epicurean conception of mortality, to which he often made reference.[46] Thus, in *The Poverty of Philosophy*, he referred to "*mors immortalis*" (death the immortal), an allusion to Lucretius's "Immortal death has taken away mortal life."[47] Both in Epicurean materialism and in Marx's own philosophy, this referred to the transitoriness of things as the only permanent material reality.

In evoking the enormity of capitalism's destructive impact on the "metabolism prescribed by the natural laws of life itself," nothing would have been more characteristic for Marx than to recall Lucretius's epic poem *De rerum natura*. In Thomas Charles Baring's classic 1884 translation, we read: "A property is that which ne'er can cut itself adrift; / Nor can be sundered anyhow, without a fatal rift."[48]

It is quite conceivable that Marx, confronted with capitalism's growing ecological contradictions, turned back to Epicurus (and Lucretius) to call up the notion of a "fatal rift" (or "irreparable rift"), reflecting the disruption and destruction of nature's properties and processes. In this perspective, capitalism, by robbing the elements of reproduction on which future generations depended, undermined not only external nature, but also the basis of human life itself.

THE CORPOREAL RIFT

The metabolic rift generated by capitalism is not confined to the alienated relation to external nature but affects the human metabolism itself, the bodily existence of human beings—a phenomenon we can call the corporeal rift. This is related to what socialist ecofeminist

Ariel Salleh has called "metabolic value," that is, struggles around social reproduction focused on the household and the reproduction of humans themselves, as both physical and social beings.[49] It is also connected to what Howard Waitzkin called "the second sickness"— the social-epidemiological effects of capitalist development.[50]

A key component of Epicurean materialism, one that distinguished it from later Cartesian dualism, was the fundamentally corporeal nature of human beings, who are part of and dependent on nature. As Norman Wentworth DeWitt explained, "To Epicurus body and soul are alike corporeal; they are coterminous."[51] Following this approach, Marx consistently integrated his materialist conception of history with the materialist conception of nature, as developed within modern science, while also incorporating physiological developments. Human beings, like other animals, have specific bodily needs essential to their survival, such as hydration, sufficient calories, sleep, and clean air. Marx argued that in meeting these physiological imperatives, human beings actively make history, transform the world, and produce a social metabolism interconnected with the universal metabolism.[52] Yet while humans can make history, there are real constraints on this potential, given the limits associated with "inherited socio-cultural conditions," the corporeal structure related to evolutionary descent, and the biophysical characteristics and processes of the Earth System.[53] With these considerations in mind, Marx offered a rich historical examination of the numerous ways that the capital system degraded, undermined, or disrupted the corporeal metabolism, thwarting human social development.

During the long transition from mercantilism to industrial capitalism, the expropriation of nature also involved the extreme expropriation of human bodily existence. Marx wrote that "this history," which involves the outright seizure of title to property from immediate producers, "is written in the annals of mankind in letters of blood and fire."[54] Peasants were forcibly removed from the countryside when the customary rights associated with land tenure were abolished. British soldiers carried out evictions by burning villages, as well as individuals who refused to leave. Bourgeois property laws helped steal the land, ushering in a revolutionary transformation, whereby the human population was progressively removed from access to the means of subsistence. As a result, landowners "conquered the field of capitalist agriculture, incorporated the soil into capital, and created for the urban industries the necessary supplies of free and rightless proletarians," who had to sell their labor power to earn wages to purchase the means of subsistence.[55] This is a relationship of force and deprivation, because, as Marx remarked, "if the workers could live on air, it would not be possible to buy them at any price."[56]

With colonial expansion and European settlement of distant lands, the violation of corporeal existence took the form of the expropriation associated with the genocide against the indigenous peoples of the Americas and the enslavement of Africans.[57] Violence and coercion were integral components of the bonded labor system: confinement, flogging, beating, and rape were commonplace. In this living nightmare, slaves were beasts of burden, regularly deprived of the conditions that allowed for adequate sustenance. Escaped slaves were hunted, tortured, and killed, so long as there was a steady supply of more bonded workers.[58]

With the demise of slavery, the British devised the infamous "coolie" trade. Large numbers of Chinese bonded workers were forced to dig in the guano islands off the coast of Peru, to provide the fertilizer to spread on English fields. As one contemporary English observer described the conditions of these workers:

I can state that their lot in these dreary spots is a most unhappy one. Besides being worked almost to death, they have neither sufficient food nor passably wholesome water. Their rations consist of two pounds of rice and about half a pound of meat. This is generally served out to them between ten and eleven in the morning, by which time they have got through six hours' work. Each man is compelled to clear from four to five tons of guano a day. During the last quarter of 1875, it is reported that there were 355 Chinamen employed at Pabellon de Pica alone, of whom no less than 98 were in the hospital. The general sickness is swelled legs, caused, it is supposed, by drinking condensed water not sufficiently cooled, and by a lack of vegetable diet. The features of this disease are not unlike those of scurvy or purpura.

The bodily metabolism of these workers was thus being sacrificed to obtain the guano to compensate for the impaired soil metabolism on English fields. The suicide rate of the Chinese bonded workers digging the guano was so high that, as a U.S. consul to Peru noted in 1870, guards had to be placed "around the shores of the Guano Islands, where they are employed, to prevent them [the Coolies] from committing suicide by drowning, to which end the Coolie rushes in his moments of despair."[59]

Throughout their critique of capital, Marx and Frederick Engels exhaustively assessed the system's effects on corporeal conditions. They were horrified by the extent to which it failed to meet bodily needs, resulting in disease, suffering, and shortened lives. Marx stressed that capitalist production "squanders human beings, living labour, more readily than does any other mode of production, squandering not only flesh and blood, but nerves and brain as well."[60] This contradiction exists at the heart of the capital system, whose "purpose is not the satisfaction of needs but the production of profit."[61]

Drawing on firsthand experience, fieldwork, and official reports and studies, Marx and Engels detailed changes in corporeal existence. In 1839, when Engels was eighteen years old, he wrote a vivid description in his "Letters from Wuppertal" of corporeal and ecological conditions in his birthplace, Barmen, Germany, then the most industrialized city in the region. He observed that the river was red due to pollution from cotton factories using "Turkey red" as a dye. He linked many of the city's problems, such as the lack of a "vigorous life" and degraded health, to working conditions, both in factories and at home. "Work in low rooms where people breathe in more coal fumes and dust than oxygen—and in the majority of cases beginning already at the age of six—is bound to deprive them of all strength and joy in lives," he wrote. "The weavers, who have individual looms in their homes, sit bent over them from morning till night, and desiccate their spinal marrow in front of a hot stove."[62]

For *The Condition of the Working Class in England*, his pioneering study in urban sociology and environmental injustice, Engels, accompanied by his partner Mary Burns, went door to door conducting interviews and collected official medical and public health reports, documenting and analyzing the social and ecological conditions in Manchester, whose dominance in spinning and weaving cotton had made it the center of the Industrial Revolution. The city was ominous, due to the black smoke that blocked out the sun. Charles Dickens described this ceaseless smoke pollution as "black vomit, blasting all things living or inanimate, shutting out the face of day, and closing in on all these horrors with a dense dark cloud."[63] Engels detailed how the conditions within factories further robbed workers of their health, "The atmosphere of the factories is, as a rule, at once damp and warm, unusually warmer than is necessary, and, when the ventilation is not *very* good, impure, heavy, deficient in oxygen, filled with dust and the smell of the machine oil, which almost everywhere smears the floor, sinks into it, and becomes rancid."[64] These workers spent long hours, day after day, tending to machines. As a result, they were physically exhausted, yet only slept a couple hours a day, preventing rest and restoration of their bodies and making them more susceptible to diseases.

Engels documented how specific types of work contributed to distinct corporeal problems.[65] Working in mills caused curvatures in the spine and bowing of leg bones. Women suffered pelvis deformities. Winders, who wound thread onto bobbins, suffered from eye problems, such as diminished eyesight, cataracts, and, in time, blindness. Dressmakers were confined in small rooms with "almost total exclusion from fresh air," breathing in "foul air." These girls also experienced skeletal deformities at a young age, and their growth was stunted. Exposure to dust, toxins, and air contaminants was a major problem. Workers in the combing rooms of spinning mills breathed in "fibrous dust," causing "chest affections," such as asthma, constant coughing, and difficulty breathing. These health problems also resulted in a loss of sleep.[66] Metal workers laboring at grinders inhaled sharp metal particles, often developing Grinder's asthma, which included shortness of breath, spitting blood, and coughing fits. The conditions were worse for those who worked with a dry stone versus a wet stone; the average life span was thirty-five years for the former and forty-five years for the latter.[67] Workers bleaching textiles were exposed to chlorine. Potters who dipped the wares were exposed to lead and arsenic. Their clothing was contaminated with these dangerous materials, to which their family members at home were thus also exposed. These workers in particular experienced stomach and intestine disorders, epilepsy, and paralysis.[68] Using medical reports, Engels considered how miners, which included adults and children, were exposed to "the inhalation of an atmosphere containing little oxygen, and mixed with dust and the smoke of blasting powder, such as prevails in the mines, [which] seriously affects the lungs, disturbs the action of the heart, and diminishes the activity of the digestive organs." He noted that these miners developed "black spittle" disease when their lungs were saturated with coal particles, causing intense pain, headaches, and difficulty breathing.[69]

All these ailments and conditions disrupt corporeal existence, disturb metabolic bodily processes, and shorten workers' lives. Engels illuminated corporeal class differences, as machine operators looked decades older than their wealthy counterparts.[70] The bodies of workers were simply worn out due to the conditions of work. Reflecting on the consequences of factory conditions and their effects on the human metabolism, Marx wrote:

> Every sense organ is injured by the artificially high temperatures, by the dust-laden atmosphere, by the deafening noise, not to mention the danger to life and limb among machines which are so closely crowded together, a danger which, with the regularity of the seasons, produces its list of those killed and wounded in the industrial battlefield. The economical use of the social means of production, matured and forced as in a hothouse by the factory system, is turned in the hands of capital

into systematic robbery of what is necessary for the life of the worker while he is at work, i.e. space, light, air, and protection against the dangerous or the unhealthy concomitants of the production process, not to mention the theft of appliances for the comfort of the worker.[71]

Technological innovations, which could improve working conditions, were only employed if they reduced labor costs and increased production—or when there was enough social pressure that forced protection and regulation.[72] As Marx pointed out, "The decisive factor is not the health of the worker, but the ease with which the product may be constructed . . . which is on the one hand a source of growing profit for the capitalist [and] on the other hand the cause of a squandering of the worker's life and health."[73]

In addition to documenting how working conditions robbed workers of their health and shortened their lives, Marx analyzed extensively the ways in which the system of capital affected the nutritional intake and corporeal constitution of workers. This issue is especially important, given that nutrients provide energy and support vital bodily functions. Thus, an insufficient supply causes an array of corporeal problems. On this front, two of the major concerns for Marx included adequate food/calorie consumption and health risks associated with food adulteration.

Drawing on official reports regarding public health in the United Kingdom, such as those by John Simon, the Chief Medical Health Officer of the Privy Council, Marx considered how class and gender influenced calorie intake. He noted that agricultural families had diets deficient in protein and carbohydrates. "Insufficiency of food" among these families "fell as a rule chiefly on the women and children." Adult industrial workers consumed around nine pounds of bread each week, constituting almost their entire diet. Needlewomen consumed the least, at just under eight pounds, while shoemakers ate the most, at eleven-and-a-half pounds. In general, as far as consumption of butter, meat, sugar, and milk, "the worst-nourished categories were the needlewomen, silk-weavers and kid-glovers"—all

jobs predominantly occupied by women.[74] Historian Anthony Wohl
stresses that at the time of these studies, individuals performed physically demanding labor and had to walk long distances to work. Thus,
the caloric intake for the average working-class family was not sufficient. They ate few fresh green vegetables and drank little liquid,
water or otherwise. As a result, they received minimal protein and
were deficient in vitamins A and D. Families with children too young
to work suffered even greater food insufficiencies.[75]

"The intimate connection between the pangs of hunger suffered by
the most industrious layers of the working class," Marx explained, "and
the extravagant consumption, coarse or refined, of the rich, from which
capitalist accumulation is the basis, is only uncovered when the economic laws are known."[76] Capitalists attempted to "reduce the worker's
individual consumption to the necessary minimum," except in special
cases, such as in the mines in South America. Quoting Liebig, Marx
noted that "the men cannot work so hard on bread" alone while forced
by mine owners to carry almost 200 pounds of metals up 450 feet, so
the workers were compelled to eat beans as well.[77]

Using this documentation, Marx and Engels highlighted how
the capitalist system disrupted corporeal metabolic processes due
to insufficient or inadequate food, leading to various illnesses, ailments, and starvation diseases. In particular, Engels detailed how
working-class children were very vulnerable to rickets and scrofula
due to poor-quality food and inadequate nutrition.[78] In working-class
neighborhoods, sewage ran through the streets and no clean water
was available. When food prices increased, families reduced their
daily rations. All these conditions made them more susceptible to
contagious diseases and illnesses, as in the regular cholera epidemics
of the period.

To make matters worse, the adulteration of food, drink, and medicine was common. The working poor consumed dark bread rather
than the white loaves prepared for the wealthy. The former was made
with alum, sand, and bone earth, often with feces and cockroaches
baked into it.[79] Other common adulterations included adding mercury to pepper; white lead to tea; dirt and red lead to cocoa; clay and

sand to medicinal opium; copper in gin, bread, and butter; chalk in milk; and strychnine to beer. Regular consumption of these items resulted in chronic gastritis and food poisoning, which was sometimes fatal.[80] Many of the pigments used to color food were poisonous and would accumulate in workers' bodies.

Marx remained concerned about corporeal issues throughout his life. In "A Workers' Inquiry," a questionnaire Marx devised in 1880 at the request of *La Revue socialiste* that asked French workers to share details and stories of their labor conditions, he listed a hundred specific questions, many of which addressed bodily matters. In particular, he requested information connected to the sizes of workrooms, including details regarding ventilation and temperature; muscle strain; exposure to industrial effluvia and specific diseases related to the work; safety standards and actions in case of accidents; specific bodily dangers and detrimental health effects related to work; whether or not children were working at the site; duration of shifts; time it took to travel to and from work; prices of lodging and food, including types of food consumed; how many years workers average within specific trades; and "the general physical, intellectual, and moral conditions of life of the working men and women employed" in the trade.[81]

Just as the profit-driven capital system disrupts natural processes and cycles, it creates corporeal rifts, undermining general health, the bodily metabolism, and longevity. It violates an array of "biological needs whose satisfaction is an absolute prerequisite of human existence."[82] The satisfaction of basic bodily needs is central to humans' capacity to make history. Joseph Fracchia argues that Marx's materialist focus on bodily questions

> enabled him to decipher the exploitative character of capitalism and to expose the corporeal depths of capitalist immiseration. In this way, he wielded human corporeal organisation as a limited, but effective normative measure for social critique and as an attribute of freedom: labour practices which deform the body and atrophy its dexterities are indicators of exploitation [and

expropriation], while those that enhance its capacities and culti-
vate its dexterities are emancipatory.[83]

Marx and Engels sought to uproot the capital system, which "vampire-like, lives only by sucking living labour, and lives the more, the
more labour it sucks."[84] None of this was inherent in the human condition, nor had the human body been so systematically and intensively
exploited before; capitalist methods were designed to carry corporeal
exploitation, that is, expropriation of bodily powers, to its maximum.
Nothing could be more at odds with the ancient Epicurean materialists, who rejected the pursuit of wealth at the cost of the human being.
As Lucretius writes in the opening paragraph of Book II of *De rerum
natura*: "Therefore we see that our corporeal life / Needs little, altogether, and only such, / As takes the pain away."[85]

For Marx and Engels, a society of associated producers—socialism—is founded on mending this corporeal rift, along with the rift
in the metabolism between society and nature in general, to establish
a sustainable path for human social development, and to overcome
needless pain and suffering. It is necessary, as Salleh has argued, to
develop a society that moves beyond capitalist commodity value to
one that emphasizes "metabolic value," encompassing the entirety of
social and environmental needs.[86]

The Conditions of Reproduction of Nature and Humanity

For Marx, "It is not the *unity* of living and active humanity with
the natural, inorganic conditions of their metabolic exchange with
nature, and hence their appropriation of nature, which requires
explanation or is the result of a historical process, but rather the
separation between these inorganic conditions of human existence
and this active existence, a separation which is completely posited
only in the relation of wage labour and capital."[87] Likewise, we can
say that it is not the *universal metabolism of nature* (or even the
human-social metabolism) that requires explanation, but rather

the *metabolic rift*, the active estrangement of this universal/social metabolism with nature.

Human beings in Marx's conception are "corporeal" beings, constituting a "*specific* part of nature"—the "self-mediating beings" of nature.[88] With the development of class society, this crucial self-mediating characteristic that distinguishes human species-being, takes an alienated form. The expropriation of nature on behalf of the capitalist class becomes the basis for the further expropriation and exploitation of humanity and nature, in a vicious circle leading ultimately to a rupture in the metabolism of nature and society, including corporeal existence.

In the most important revelation to come out of Marx's doctoral thesis on ancient materialism, he wrote: "It was only with Epicurus that appearance is grasped as appearance, i.e. as an *alienation of the essence* which *gives practical proof of its reality through such an alienation*."[89] For Marx, the alienated social metabolism between humanity and nature provided the "practical proof" of the possibility of a new, more organic system of social metabolic reproduction, to be organized by the freely associated producers. Stripping away the alienation and destruction, it was possible to perceive the potential for more egalitarian, collective, and sustainable relations. In such a higher society, "socialized man, the associated producers, [would] govern the human metabolism of nature in a rational way . . . accomplishing it with the least expenditure of energy and in conditions most worthy and appropriate for their human nature."[90]

Should we see Marx's theory of metabolic rift as ecological by today's standards? Some have argued not. Sven-Eric Liedman, in his ambitious and in many ways enlightening 2018 biography, *A World to Win: The Life and Works of Karl Marx*, insists that Marx cannot be considered "an ecologically conscious person in the modern sense." True, he notes, "Marx found support in Liebig for his thesis that over the longer term capitalism was devastating in all aspects." But Marx, Liedman tells us, "also imagined that the society that would replace capitalism could also restore the balance between humanity and nature in agriculture." Hence "the pessimistic conclusions that Marx . . . drew from Liebig's book" were "not unconditional. In *another* society, agriculture would not drain nature of its resources, just as industry would not devastate the air, water, and soil. . . . The 'irreparable break' he spoke about is thus only irreparable in a capitalist society."[91]

By Liedman's yardstick, then, it is precisely because Marx offered a conception of a future society beyond capitalism, directed to sustainable human development, in which the associated producers would rationally regulate the metabolism between nature and society, that his views can be said to have fallen short of those who can be considered "ecologically conscious person[s] in the modern sense." The implication is that modern Green thinkers, by definition, see ecological devastation as "unconditional" and hence wholly insurmountable, and are inherently pessimistic and apocalyptic, conceiving of no way forward for humanity—at least if this requires a break with the existing social order. This is no doubt an accurate description of the views of most mainstream environmentalists today, who categorically refuse to consider any solution that involves going beyond capitalist relations of production.

For Marx, in contrast, it was essential to treat nature, as the Epicureans had, as "my *friend*," challenging the entire system of the alienation of nature and society.[92] If the classical historical-materialist ecological critique little resembles today's contemporary mainstream ecology, this is hardly because Marx's critique is somehow antiquated. Rather it is Marx's critique that has emerged in recent years as the theoretical and practical point of departure for the most advanced planetary movement of the twenty-first century: ecosocialism. In our time, the famous words of the "Internationale" take on new meaning: "The earth shall rise on new foundations / We have been naught, we shall be all."

1

The Expropriation of Nature

TWENTY-FIRST-CENTURY monopoly-finance capitalism constitutes what Karl Marx once called an "age of dissolution."[1] All that is solid in the current mode of production is melting into air. Hence, it is no longer realistic to treat—even by way of abstraction—the crucial political-economic struggles of our day as if they were confined primarily to the exploitation of labor within production. Instead, social conflicts are increasingly being fought over capitalism's expropriation and spoliation of its wider social and natural environment.[2] This historical shift and the deepening fissures that it has produced can be seen in the growth of what David Harvey has termed "anti-value politics," directed at the boundaries of the system and visible in such forms as the ecological movement, growing conflicts over social reproduction in the household/family and gender/sexuality, and global resistance to the expansion of imperialism/racism.[3] To understand these rapidly changing conditions, it is necessary to dig much deeper than before into capital's external logic of expropriation, as it was first delineated in Marx's writings during the Industrial Revolution.[4] Most important, because at the root of the problem, is the extreme expropriation of the earth itself and the consequent transformation in social relations.

Like any complex, dynamic system, capitalism has both an inner force that propels it and objective conditions outside itself that set its boundaries, the relations to which are forever changing. The inner dynamic of the system is governed by the process of *exploitation* of labor power, under the guise of equal exchange, while its primary relation to its external environment is one of *expropriation* ("appropriation . . . without exchange" or "without equivalent").[5]

Capitalism, or generalized commodity society, had its origins in the mercantilist age from the mid-fifteenth to mid-eighteenth centuries. Mercantilism was a period dominated by expropriation under the hegemony of merchant capital, including robbery, enslavement, and the outright seizure of the title to real property—a process misleadingly dubbed by the classical economists "previous [also primary or primitive] accumulation"—whereby vast numbers of human beings were separated from the natural conditions of their existence, through the alienation of both land (nature) and labor.[6]

This historic transformation required the forcible dissolution of all earlier property forms and relations of production via the enclosure of the commons and the expropriation of small peasant holdings, enforced by the "gallows, pillory and whip," and extended worldwide to the "extirpation, enslavement and entombment in mines" of indigenous populations.[7] The emerging "bourgeois order," as Marx put it, was "a vampire that sucks out its [small-landholding feudal peasants'] blood and brains and throws [them] into the alchemistic cauldron of capital," imposing new private property relations.[8] The reenslavement of women in the transition to capitalism took various forms, including the burning of witches and wife selling, both of which enforced capitalist patriarchy.[9] Nature, or what Marx termed the "universal metabolism of nature," was itself expropriated wherever possible by the emerging capitalist system, reduced to a mere "free gift . . . to capital" to be used and "abused" at will.[10]

But if capitalism thus came into being "dripping from head to toe, from every pore, with blood and dirt," in a violent process of expropriation that commercialized the soil, enslaved populations throughout the periphery, and created the modern working class, thereby making the systematic exploitation of labor possible, expropriation did not simply cease at that point.[11] Rather, it continued to define the external logic of the system, establishing, maintaining, and extending capitalism's boundaries through its relations to households, colonies, and elemental natural processes—all of which lay outside the circuit of capital. As Sven Beckert writes in *Empire of Cotton*, "war capitalism" in the mercantilist period rested on "the violent expropriation of land and labor in Africa and the Americas. From these expropriations came great wealth and new knowledge, and these in turn strengthened European institutions and states—all preconditions for Europe's extraordinary economic development by the nineteenth century and beyond."[12] Such "war capitalism" continually metamorphosed into new historic forms.

At various points in the development of the system, this dialectic of exploitation and expropriation, or the relation between the system's inner and outer dynamics, shifted in emphasis from one to the other, even though both invariably characterize the operation of capitalism. In its early period, under mercantilism and colonialism, expropriation principally defined the system. In 1770, at the outset of the Industrial Revolution, overall profits from slavery, according to Robin Blackburn in *The Making of New World Slavery*, were sufficient to cover a quarter to a third of British gross fixed investment needs.[13] However, by the mid-nineteenth century, at the height of the Industrial Revolution, capitalism had metamorphosed into a developed mode of production centered on impersonal value relations and based on the systematic exploitation of what Marx called "formally free labour."[14] In its descending phase of monopoly capitalism in the late nineteenth and twentieth centuries, distinguished by a tendency toward stagnation in the accumulation process, the overall thrust of the capital system shifted back toward profit upon expropriation, while maintaining the myth of a system based on (equal) exchange, or *quid pro quo*.[15] Monopoly profits became dominant while the imperialist expropriation of surplus under conditions of enforced inequality was extended to the entire global periphery, and given a systematic basis through alliances between multinational corporations and imperialist states.

In today's phase of globalized monopoly-finance capital—characterized by secular stagnation in the capitalist core, planetary ecological crisis, and the rise of neoliberalism as a system of financialized redistribution—relations of expropriation have further asserted themselves, to the point that the system seems at times to have entered a period of the forcible dissolution of everything in existence: an age of structural crisis and exterminism, extended to the web of life itself.

PROFIT UPON EXPROPRIATION

For Marx, as for Georg Wilhelm Friedrich Hegel in *The Philosophy of Right*, appropriation, that is, property, was an inherent feature of human life. It was present in all societies, constituting the material condition of human existence, making production possible.[16] Marx observed in the *Grundrisse* that "all production is appropriation of nature on the part of an individual within and through a specific form of society. In this sense it is a tautology to say that property (appropriation) is a precondition of production. . . . That there can be no production and hence no society where some form of property does not exist is a tautology. An appropriation that does not make something into property is a *contradictio in subjecto*."[17]

Particularly absurd, in Marx's view, was the attempt in bourgeois ideology to associate appropriation in general with the formation of private property, as, for example, in John Locke's political theory of appropriation in *The Second Treatise on Government*, or Daniel Defoe's *Robinson Crusoe*—both of which saw private property as emerging out of the state of nature in isolation from society. Seeking to justify the bourgeois economy, Jean-Baptiste Say wrote in his *Treatise on Political Economy* that property was originally a "gratuitous gift" of nature but that all men had "consented" to the appropriation of these gifts of nature as private property by a few individuals, "to the exclusion of all others."[18] In sharp contrast, Marx insisted that the appropriation of nature was a universal phenomenon of social life, of the social metabolism of humanity and nature, while the alienated "laws of capitalist appropriation" gave rise to bourgeois private property and capital accumulation. Few ideas were more grossly distorted than that of the liberal conception of the "free gift of Nature to capital"—or the subordination of the entirety of human metabolic interactions with nature through production to the narrow laws of capitalist appropriation.[19]

Although Pierre-Joseph Proudhon had declared in *What Is Property?* that all property, and hence all appropriation, was theft, Marx pointed to the illogic of such a position, since there could be no theft, that is, expropriation, without the prior appropriation or property. Proudhon's view, with its lack of historical analysis, failed to account for numerous, varied property forms, including common or communal property, and even small peasant holdings. Hence, in characterizing property or appropriation as theft, Proudhon mistakenly associated all property with bourgeois private property, particularly landed property.[20] Nevertheless, while Proudhon's analysis was much too crude, there was no doubt that bourgeois private property rested on the alienated appropriation or expropriation of the elemental conditions of production, and that since this was a product of the historical class struggle, it could be transcended.

Expropriation in Marx's conception is specifically identified with "appropriation . . . without exchange"—appropriation minus the equality in all actual exchange relationships.[21] Expropriation thus meant theft of the title to property. In pre-capitalist or tributary modes of production, including feudalism, the forced appropriation of the surplus product from the direct producers is transparently a form of expropriation.[22] Under mercantilism, expropriation was often direct, as in the enclosures, where common property was confiscated—and as in the enslavement and extirpation of populations and the looting of land and resources throughout the world.

In ordinary commercial transactions in the mercantilist era, this reliance on the forced confiscation of property was only somewhat more hidden. Thus, Marx quoted Benjamin Franklin's statement that "*war . . . is robbery, commerce . . . is . . . cheating*," as representative of the mercantilist view. The cheating that constitutes merchant capital in its normal commerce, Marx explained, occurs by means of "a long series of intermediate steps" in the circulation of commodities, including commercial capital's domination over production throughout the mercantilist period. It is not to be explained "merely by frauds practiced on the producers of commodities."[23] In the organization of "modern manufacturing" (capitalist handicraft), with its historical roots in the prior mercantilist form, expropriation could be seen as occurring at every step, "because a whole series of plundering parasites insinuate themselves between the actual employer and the worker he employs."[24]

In developed capitalist production, class-based expropriation is disguised by a system of formally equal exchange within the market, in which workers, via the wage contract, are said to be paid an amount equal to their labor. Workers in the "hidden abode" of production are, it is true, paid the value of their labor power, equal to the necessary, historically determined costs of their reproduction, during the portion of the working day necessary to cover this. Yet capital nonetheless extracts a surplus product from the unpaid labor in the remainder of the working day—during which there is only "apparent exchange," hence the labor is "appropriated without an equivalent"—a disguised form of "tribute."[25] But given the specific form in which this expropriation occurs within the value circuit in capitalist production, under the guise of equal exchange, Marx distinguishes the *exploitation* of labor power in developed capitalist industry as a specific type, *sui generis*, not to be confused with *expropriation* in its more general historical sense as robbery or theft outside the process of production and valorization.[26]

In the transitional stage represented by mercantilism up to the mid-eighteenth century, profit was often identified in political economy with buying cheap and selling dear. The most "*rational* expression" of the mercantilist view in this respect was to be found in the work of James Steuart, with whom Marx was to commence his *Theories of Surplus Value*. In his 1767 *Inquiry into the Principles of Political Oeconomy*, Steuart distinguished between the "real value" of commodities rooted in labor and production costs and what he called "profit upon alienation"—or what Marx preferred to call "profit upon expropriation." Profit upon alienation/expropriation derived from buying cheap and selling dear (what today is called arbitrage). This meant, in effect, appropriating without exchange a part of the surplus produced by labor by purchasing the commodity below its value (as determined by the costs of reproduction), and then selling the same commodity at what the market would bear, yielding exorbitant gains.[27]

The tendency to see profit upon alienation as an explanation of profits in general formed the principal economic fallacy of mercantilism, pointing to both its methodology and its limits. Insofar as profits are made simply by expropriatory gain, such profits are canceled out at the level of the economy as a whole by the losses elsewhere. Hence, no general theory of profits could be derived from the mere notion of profit upon expropriation, requiring rather an analysis of value and production. It was only the rise of value in the form of abstract labor, the crystallization of socially necessary labor time, that made the system of unlimited capital accumulation possible. Still, Marx saw profit upon expropriation as a particular form of profitability, distinct from profit upon production.

Marx drew on Steuart's profit upon expropriation (or profit upon alienation) again and again to explain the origins of capitalism and the outer boundaries that defined it as a system. In Marx's words, "to buy cheap so as to sell dearer is the law of commerce. Hence not the *exchange of equivalents*." Merchant capital, whenever it takes a dominant form ruling over productive capital, relies on "profit upon expropriation" and "fraud," constituting a "system of plunder."[28] Although productive capital's dominance over commercial capital was established by the Industrial Revolution, the wider process of expropriation of land and labor that brought industrial capital into being continued to define much of the system. Indeed, the concentration and centralization of capital pointed to the absorption of small capitals by bigger ones, and a socialization process that would eventually lead to the expropriation of the expropriators.[29]

In his overall analysis, Marx designated numerous forms of *appropriation without exchange* (or without reciprocity), some general, others more specific, encompassing widely differing levels of analysis

and spheres of operation. These included such broad terms as robbery, plunder, theft, looting, tribute, cheating, swindling, usurpation,
parasitism, spoliation, dissolution, confiscation, enslavement, colonialism, patriarchal domination, squandering, blood-letting, and
"vampire-like" relations—along with more specific concepts such
as rent, usury, monopoly profits, "free gifts of Nature to capital,"
impoverishment (in the formal sense of undermining "conditions
of reproduction"), profit upon alienation/expropriation, profit by
deduction, "secondary exploitation," "odious exploitation," the metabolic rift, and the alienation of land/labor.[30] Although the critique of
capital at its most abstract level in *Capital* necessarily assumed conditions of equal exchange with respect to the value of labor power
under the wage contract, thus focusing on exploitation, the reality of
expropriation on the boundaries of the system was never absent from
Marx's analysis and continually crops up in his more concrete historical discussions.[31]

Marx's general framework with respect to exchange and expropriation can be understood more fully by looking at the analysis of
economic anthropologist Karl Polanyi. Not only was Polanyi directly
influenced by Marx's critique of political economy, but he traced
out some of the same underlying logic in the development of concepts surrounding historic forms of "appropriational movements,"
or property transactions. For Polanyi, as for Marx, a fully developed
exchange system has exchange of equivalents as its basis, and thus
is rooted in "quantitativity." So significant is quantitative equivalence
in defining exchange, that unequal exchange as such is a contradiction in terms.[32] To confuse developed commodity exchange, which
operated under the guise of the exchange of equivalents, with non-
exchange economies, such as the feudal relations of lord and serf,
where the expropriation is direct and transparent, would, in Marx's
words, be like calling "the relation between the robber who presents
his pistol, and the traveler, who presents his purse, a relation between
two traders."[33]

To distinguish property transactions of the non-exchange variety, Polanyi usefully defined two other forms of "appropriational

movements of goods and services": (1) *reciprocity*, which demands a broad "adequacy of response," as in use values that are of commensurate importance and represent the fulfillment of needs on all sides; and (2) *redistribution*, which involves the movement of shifting proportions of surplus product in and out of a center to be apportioned in varying ways through an essentially political process. In modern society, the two forms of exchange of quantitative equivalents and redistribution dominate, while reciprocity, geared to substantive equality in the interchange (bartering) of use values—a form historically identified with communal modes of production—is largely absent.[34]

THE CAPITALIST EXPROPRIATION OF NATURE

The term *expropriation*, in English, originally meant the appropriation without equivalence of the title to real property, and hence the separation, removal, and alienation of human beings from the land. To expropriate more generally was "to dispossess (a person) of ownership" or right to a property. The term also took on the more general connotation of confiscation and robbery.[35]

It is in the sense of separation and removal of the workers from the land (the natural conditions of production), introducing a universal alienation and the dissolution of all prior property relations, that the concept of expropriation can be seen as dominating Marx's two major discussions of primary accumulation: in the *Grundrisse* and in volume 1 of *Capital*.

In what has traditionally been called *Pre-Capitalist Economic Formations* (the title given to this section of the *Grundrisse*, published in a separate volume edited by Eric Hobsbawm), Marx was principally concerned with what he conceived as the "age of dissolution," extending over centuries, involving the separation and expropriation of workers from the land.[36] The central theme of the dissolution of earlier forms of property, and hence of the human relation to nature through production, was set out early on in Marx's discussion of *Pre-Capitalist Economic Formations*, where he famously wrote:

It is not the *unity* of living and active humanity with the natural, inorganic [tool-mediated] conditions of their metabolic exchange with nature, and hence their appropriation of nature, which requires explanation or is the result of a historic process, but rather the *separation* between these inorganic conditions of human existence and their active existence, a separation which is completely posited only in the relations of wage labour and capital.[37]

Exploring this *separation* in the "conditions of [the] metabolic exchange with nature" or the double alienation of land and labor therefore became the major theme in Marx's analysis of primary accumulation.[38] At the same time, his conception of the separation and estrangement of land and labor—in conjunction with the development of nineteenth-century science and in response to the crisis of the soil—led to his mature ecological critique focusing on the metabolic rift.[39]

In Marx's analysis, the dual alienation of land and labor took the form of "a dissolution of the relation to the earth" for the majority of the population. Individuals were suddenly faced with the "objective conditions of production as *alien property*, as their own *non-property*," expropriated by others, creating a whole new "relationship of domination." It was this alienation that came to define the entire human metabolism with nature through production.[40] In this new social division of labor, characterized by universal estrangement, workers, the dispossessed, had no means of livelihood except through the alienation (selling) of their own labor power. "Closer analysis," Marx wrote, "will show that what is dissolved in all these processes of dissolution," as capitalism grows and spreads and the majority of humanity is separated from "the metabolic exchange with nature," are all those "relations of production in which use-value predominates; production for immediate use." This "age of dissolution" of pre-capitalist economic relations was made possible by the growth of a system ruled by "monetary wealth," giving rise to generalized commodity production. It had its logical culmination in "the genesis of the industrial capitalist."[41]

The great movement of expropriation of the mass of the people from the land through enclosures in England was part of an even greater age of global expropriation—often characterized in the dominant ideology as "the age of exploration"—in which land and labor were seized through colonization, enslavement, and the plundering of resources. Under mercantilist relations, profit upon expropriation, associated with commercial capital, dominated over profit upon production, associated with manufacturing capital. The hegemony of merchant capital over production was most clearly evident in English wool production and the "putting-out system," where merchants provided the raw materials and the instruments while household labor carried out the production—a process that gave merchants numerous opportunities for expropriatory gain.[42]

The amassing of monetary wealth in world trade constituted a crucial precondition for the transition to a developed capitalist economy. But the decisive transformation, leading to the rise of industrial capitalism, emerged only with the expropriation of human beings from the land, that is, from the natural-material conditions of their existence. As Polanyi wrote:

> What we call land is an element of nature inextricably interwoven with man's institutions. To isolate it and form a market for it was perhaps the weirdest of all the undertakings of our ancestors. . . . We might as well imagine his being born without hands and feet as carrying on his life without land. And yet to separate land from man and to organize society in such a way as to satisfy the requirements of a real-estate market was a vital part of the utopian concept of a market economy.[43]

In all of this, we can distinguish two general forms of expropriation: (1) expropriation in the form of private property, involving *appropriation without exchange*, and (2) expropriation in a more general sense, manifested in alienated human relations with the material world as a whole—the realm of use values or real wealth and what Marx called the "natural economy"—that is characterized

by *appropriation without reciprocity*.[44] Here "the conditions of reproduction" are not maintained, and expropriation takes the form of the
running down of the entire world outside the narrow realm of capital
accumulation. It is in this latter sense that Marx referred to the "spoliation," "squandering," and "robbing" of the earth, in his theory of
metabolic rift—according to which the extraction of soil nutrients
from the land in capitalist agriculture, and their shipment to the new
urban-industrial centers in the form of food and fiber, preventing
their recirculation to the fields, results in the rupture of elemental
natural processes. In this way, the German chemist Justus von Liebig's
"law of replenishment" was violated by the very nature of industrial-
capitalist metabolism, conceived as a "*robbery system*" (*Raubsystem* or
Raubbau).[45]

For Liebig, English industrialized agriculture gave rise to a "spoliation system" that undermined the "conditions of reproduction of the
soil." A rational agriculture therefore had to be based on the principle
of *restitution*, or "the restoration of the elementary constituents of the
soil."[46] Likewise, for Marx, it was necessary "to return to the soil...
its constituent elements consumed by man in the form of food and
clothing," ensuring the "systematic restoration of the earth," thereby
maintaining its *conditions of reproduction*. Such a rational agriculture
and a rational science, in Marx's conception, depended on a society
of associated producers. Seen in this way, the ecological depredations
of capitalism were obvious: "Instead of a conscious and rational treatment of the land as permanent communal property, as the inalienable
condition for the existence and reproduction of the chain of human
generations, we have the exploitation and the squandering of the
powers of the earth."[47]

With the growth of the system, capitalism's rapacious expansion
led to the expropriation of nature as a mere adjunct to capital, giving
rise to enormous unforeseen consequences, on an increasingly global
scale. Already in the mid-nineteenth century, the dire effects of this
were becoming apparent, with the social and ecological costs of
capitalist production reaching levels that were incalculable. This was
visible in colonial expansion and in the accompanying thoroughgoing

destruction of the conditions of reproduction of numerous species, even among those not appended directly to the market, and their resulting extermination. In an attempt to rationalize this process, Charles Lyell, in his *Principles of Geology* in the 1830s, wrote an extensive justification of this anthropogenic extinction of species in the interest of the advance of human commerce, seeing non-human species as provided in excess by providence. "If we wield the sword of extermination as we advance," he wrote, "we have no reason to repine at the havoc committed."[48]

In relation to indigenous populations, Locke, the Massachusetts Bay colonist John Winthrop, and other seventeenth-century colonial thinkers contended that Native Americans had failed to appropriate land through their labor, and hence had no real property—save for "moveable" property—and could therefore be removed from the land altogether as "savages" who lacked sovereign rights. Although Locke (an investor in the slave trade through his shares in the Royal African Company and a principal author of the slave-based Carolina Constitution) clearly favored indigenous populations in the Americas over slaves brought over from Africa, whom he depicted as inherently inferior, the privileges that he accorded to Native Americans did not go far. His contention that the indigenous populations merely occupied and did not improve the land, and so did not own it, and were thus subject to the laws of capitalist expropriation, amounted to an elaborate justification for their elimination as peoples and nations.[49]

Not just bourgeois political economy but also bourgeois natural science was enlisted in the abuse of nature's powers (and natural economies) on behalf of the accumulation of capital, without reciprocity or restraint.[50] Hence Marx's larger critique of capitalist expropriation focused not only on the dissolution of previous social relations, but also its attempted dissolution of all natural limits—in ways that led to the enslavement and extirpation of indigenous peoples and natural economies throughout the world, while undermining the conditions of reproduction.[51] In developing this wider critique of the system, Marx employed Hegel's dialectic of barriers and boundaries. Elemental natural processes constituted an objective limit on the system, given that production could change only the *form* of what nature created. Nevertheless, capital treated all such natural limits as mere barriers to be transcended, rather than boundaries or limits to be respected.[52]

The result was to generate systemic crisis tendencies—ultimately traceable to contradictions between use values and exchange values, and between elemental natural processes and the capital accumulation process. The "ruse" of conquering nature by supposedly following its laws, adopted by bourgeois science and famously presented by Francis Bacon, was duplicitous, Marx pointed out, insofar as it served to justify the shortsighted, instrumental expropriation of nature for capital accumulation without end, disregarding "the universal metabolism of nature."[53] Capitalism, he argued, systematically degrades the conditions of reproduction not only of external nature, conceived abstractly as separate from humanity, but also those of human beings—conceived as *metabolic*, and therefore natural, as well as social, beings. By means of its expropriatory processes of "externality and alienation," capitalism "squanders human beings, living labour, more readily than does any other mode of production, squandering not only flesh and blood, but nerves and brains as well"—along with the larger natural environment.[54]

THE GENESIS OF INDUSTRIAL CAPITALISM

As famed historian Peter Linebaugh writes in *Stop, Thief!*, "Expropriation is prior to exploitation, yet the two are interdependent. Expropriation not only prepares the ground so to speak, it intensifies exploitation, so together I call them x^2." The dialectic of exploitation and expropriation throws light on the preconditions that set the stage for the Industrial Revolution, as well as on the later development of the system. Taking their cue from Marx, Nancy Fraser and Michael C. Dawson refer to a system of "racialized expropriation," explaining that the "massive expropriation of bodies, labor, land, and mineral wealth," especially in what was called the "New World," took place prior to the emergence of large-scale capitalist exploitation of industrial workers.[55] It involved dividing the world into "racialized superior and inferior humans," with the "labor, property, and bodies" of the latter subject to robbery, violation, and murder. It created a hierarchy of nations, predicated on the global alienation of the earth. Echoing Marx in his chapter in the first volume of *Capital* on "The Genesis of the Industrial Capitalist," Dawson writes that "this division facilitated and justified the brutal colonizing of Africa, Asia, and the Americas; the genocide aimed at indigenous peoples; and the enslavement of Africans. These expropriations enabled the launching of the Industrial Revolution and the growth of both the United Kingdom and the United States as hegemonic economic powerhouses."[56]

The English Industrial Revolution would have been virtually impossible without cotton and the expropriation of populations and the land in Africa and the Americas with which the empire of cotton was built. The origin of the age of capital was thus intimately bound to a racialized system of accumulation that integrated the global economy and engendered a series of distinct ecological rifts.

In an article titled "The British Cotton Trade," written for the *New-York Daily Tribune* in September 1861, Marx highlighted the fact that cotton fiber and manufactured cotton textiles, along with the potatoes that helped feed a great part of the working population, were the two critical pivots—with respect to food and fiber—upon which the Industrial Revolution was laid (later, as we shall see, a new intensive food pivot was introduced, following the Irish potato blight and the repeal of the Corn Laws, of which guano was to be the symbol). "English modern industry, in general," Marx explained,

> relied upon two pivots equally monstrous. The one was the *potato* as the only means of feeding Ireland and a great part of the English working class. This pivot was swept away by the potato disease and the subsequent Irish catastrophe. A larger basis for the reproduction and maintenance of the toiling millions had then to be adopted. The second pivot of English industry was the slave-grown cotton of the United States. The present American crisis [the U.S. Civil War] forces them to enlarge their

field of supply and emancipate cotton from slave-breeding and slave-consuming oligarchies. As long as the English cotton manufactures depended on slave-grown cotton . . . they rested on a twofold slavery, the indirect slavery of the white man in England and the direct slavery of the black men on the other side of the Atlantic.[57]

The Industrial Revolution in this conception had one crucial *fiber*, taken from the earth, as a central pivot—cotton. This tropical and subtropical shrub had been cultivated for thousands of years in both the Old and New Worlds, flourishing in the drier regions of Asia, Africa, and the Americas. The Romans had imported cotton cloth from India as early as the first century. But cotton textiles were largely nonexistent in most of Europe in the subsequent feudal era, until the Italian city-states beginning in the twelfth century started to obtain cotton goods regularly through trade with Asia via the Arab world. By the early seventeenth century, European merchants aggressively competed over access to high-quality, colorful cotton goods from India and China, to sell in their home countries, to trade for spices in other parts of Southeast Asia, and to exchange in Africa for slaves to be shipped to the Americas. With the outward expansion of Europe in the long sixteenth century, merchants were able to gain control of transoceanic trade from which expropriatory gains were made, but were long unable to establish a hold on cotton production itself, which remained based in the East. As Beckert explains, "Three moves—imperial expansion, expropriation, and slavery—became central to the forging of a new global economic order" in which the empire of cotton was to play a central role, leading eventually to "the emergence of [industrial] capitalism."[58]

The languishing European cotton industry encountered a number of constraints at first, such as lack of adequate access to raw cotton, low-quality textiles in comparison with the products of India, and higher costs of production. Portuguese, Spanish, Dutch, English, and French merchants relied initially on purchasing Indian textiles for the acquisition of slaves from Africa to work the plantations of the

Americas. As Basil Davidson states in *The African Slave Trade*: "This pattern of trade and contact carried the coastal people [of western Africa] inextricably into a system of spoliation, and, in so doing, continually deepened their dependence on overseas partners whose own interests were to increase the spoliation, not to lessen it or transform it into productively creative forms."[59] Over eight million slaves were sent to the Western Hemisphere between 1500 and 1800, with five million of them shipped during the eighteenth century alone.[60]

The cotton system, based on the triangular slave trade, produced the "white gold" on which the Industrial Revolution was built—establishing a cheap source of raw cotton, initially imported from the British slave plantations in the West Indies. Nevertheless, cotton textile production in England in the eighteenth century could not have survived without trade protections introduced in the period against cheaper, higher-quality cotton textiles from India. This war on cotton textile imports from India was furthered by the evolution of British colonialism. By 1813, the British East India Company was deprived of its monopoly on trade in the subcontinent, marking the victory of industrial capital over mercantilism. This led to the forcible deindustrialization of Indian production, to the benefit of Lancashire cotton manufacturers. Meanwhile, the main source of raw cotton for British industry shifted from the West Indies to the United States around the time of the 1793 invention of the cotton gin, which greatly accelerated the processing of raw cotton, creating new economies of scale.[61]

The combination of these developments allowed England to increase production of cotton textiles, with the amount of cotton processed in its industries soaring from 2.5 million pounds in 1760 to 366 million pounds in 1837. In 1760, one-third of British cotton textiles were exported, but by 1850, 94 percent were sent to the Americas and Africa.[62] Cotton served as the thread that connected Asia, Europe, Africa, and the Americas, allowing the British to gain control over land and people, and to acquire immense expropriatory profits that helped establish a centralized and hierarchical capitalist system. The entire system rested on the triangular slave trade between Africa, the Americas, and Britain. In 1730, Marx observed, "Liverpool employed

15 ships in the slave trade; in 1751, 53; in 1760, 74; in 1770, 96; and in 1792, 132."[63] The profits of the slave trade, Eric Williams wrote in *Capitalism and Slavery*, "fertilized the entire productive system" of Britain at the time of the Industrial Revolution. Mercantilism and the slave trade were to create industrial capitalism, which subsequently destroyed them.[64]

The same system required for its expansion the expropriation of indigenous lands. In the *Grundrisse*, Marx noted that "at certain periods people lived exclusively by plunder. But to be able to plunder, there must be something to plunder, and this implies production. Moreover, the manner of plunder is itself determined by the manner of production, e.g. a stock-jobbing nation cannot be robbed in the same way as a nation of cowherds."[65] From the long sixteenth century to the mid-twentieth century, the Doctrine of Discovery decreed by European monarchs and adopted by the U.S. government in 1792, together with more sophisticated rationales such as Locke's political theory of appropriation, served as legal justifications for the expropriation of lands of Native Americans, who clearly possessed the land but were deemed to be without property rights.[66] The right to land was conferred on colonists, dissolving prior productive relationships, undermining indigenous trade networks and communal/gift economies, and imposing an alienated mediation with nature. War and terrorism were directed at Native American tribes. So murderous was this expropriation that, as Marx observed,

in 1703 those sober exponents of Protestantism, the Puritans of New England, by decrees of their assembly set a premium of £40 on every Indian scalp and every captured redskin; in 1720, a premium of £100 was set on every scalp; in 1744, after Massachusetts Bay had proclaimed a certain tribe as rebels, the following prices were laid down: for a male scalp of 12 years and upwards, £100 in new currency, for a male prisoner £105, for women and children prisoners £50, for the scalps of women and children £50. Some decades later, the colonial system took its revenge on the descendants of the pious Pilgrim fathers, who had grown seditious in the meantime. At English instigation, and for English money, they were tomahawked by the redskins. The British Parliament proclaimed bloodhounds and scalping as "means that God and Nature had given into its hand."[67]

According to U.S. Supreme Court Chief Justice John Marshall in the *Johnson v. McIntosh* decision of 1823, the "doctrine of discovery" established that the white settler-colonizers had acquired "the exclusive right to extinguish the Indian title of occupancy, either by purchase or conquest."[68] This gave legal cover to the Trail of Tears in the Jacksonian era, when, as W. E. B. Du Bois wrote, "The Indians [of the Southeast] were removed to Indian Territory, and settlers poured into these coveted lands.... [There] stretched a great fertile land, luxuriant with forests of pine, oak, ash, hickory, and poplar; hot with the sun and damp with the rich black swamp-land; and here the cornerstone of the Cotton Kingdom was laid."[69] Raw cotton accounted for over half of U.S. exports during the first sixty years of the nineteenth century. In 1858, the United States exported on average over 3.8 million pounds per day.[70]

Slaves were seen in capitalist accounting as work animals or as machines, hence mere capital stock. "The slave-owner," Marx wrote, "buys his worker in the same way as he buys his horse. If he loses his slave, he loses a piece of capital, which he must replace by fresh expenditure on the slave-market."[71] The destructive treatment was even more pronounced when there was an active slave trade, given the increased ability to replace those who prematurely died. John Elliott Cairnes, in his classic analysis of slavery, *The Slave Power* (1862), on which Marx drew, stated: "It is in tropical culture, where annual profits often equal the whole capital of plantations, that negro life is most recklessly sacrificed. It is the agriculture of the West Indies, which has been for centuries prolific of fabulous wealth, that has engulfed millions of the African race."[72] Once the international slave trade was abandoned in Britain and the United States in 1807–1808, U.S. plantations became dependent on the reproduction of slaves in border states.[73]

The rise of industrial capital also promoted encroachment on natural limits, such as robbing the earth of necessary soil nutrients—a form of expropriation without replenishment, or earth robbery. The economics of slavery led to large-scale plantations growing monoculture crops. In the United States, slave production was carried out with crude, inferior tools, further increasing the hardships of this work.[74] All available land was devoted to growing cash crops, without crop rotation. Constant, intensive cotton and tobacco production violated the law of replenishment, as soil nutrients were taken up by the plants and shipped elsewhere.

The slave labor system, while profoundly destructive and inefficient—except when judged by the narrowest capitalist productivity criteria, encompassing the brutal superexploitation of slaves through what Edward Baptist has called a "torture system"—was nonetheless a historic necessity of cotton plantation agriculture. It was heavily supported by the state and supplied necessary raw materials and capital for the Industrial Revolution, both in England and later in the United States.[75]

What cannot be ignored or downplayed in all this is the dehumanization and degradation of the "racialized chattel slaves" themselves—the expropriation of their bodies and their lives. "Production based on slavery," Marx noted, was "more expensive," including its long-term effects on the conditions of production and reproduction:

> Under slavery, according to the striking expression employed in antiquity [Varro, *Rerum Rusticarum, Libri Tres*, I, 17], the worker is distinguishable only as *instrumentum vocale* [speaking instrument] from an animal, which is *instrumentum semi-vocale* [semi-mute instrument], and from a lifeless implement, which is *instrumentum mutum* [mute implement]. But he himself [the slave] takes care to let both beast and implement feel that he is none of them, but rather a human being. He gives himself the satisfaction of knowing that he is different by treating the one with brutality and damaging the other *con amore* [with zeal].[76]

Marx went on to refer to the work of Frederick Law Olmsted, with whom he was personally acquainted, and who had attributed the heavy, clumsy tools that slaves were given, compared to farmers in other parts of the United States, to the fact that they would destroy anything else as a result of their conditions of labor. Slaves were likewise made to use mules instead of horses, because only the former would endure the utter brutality that pervaded all aspects of the system of slave labor.

As Eugene Genovese pointed out in *The Political Economy of Slavery*, "The South's inability to combat soil exhaustion effectively proved one of the most serious economic features of its general crisis."[77] Competitive pressures to serve domestic and international markets stimulated efforts to increase yields, exacerbating the spoliation of the soil and driving a westward movement for new lands for slave production. Monoculture impeded the rotation of crops, and the low prices for raw cotton and vast amount of land under cultivation in need of enrichment contributed to the lack of investment in fertilizers, given the costs of such actions. Improvements to the land were not made and the destruction of the soil was soon caught in a vicious circle, violating the laws of replenishment of nutrients and organic matter, leading also to soil erosion and thus generating an ecological rift in the nutrient cycle.[78]

Nevertheless, the extreme expropriation of the earth, in combination with the slave system and imperialism, provided the wealth and raw materials that spurred the development and expansion of industrial capitalism, especially in Britain. In effect, the slave colonies were indirectly exporting their soil via cotton fiber to England, in what Marx characterized as a "brutal spoliation" of the soil. As Olmsted put it, production in the tobacco plantations in Virginia generated not so much legitimate profits, but rather a kind of profit upon expropriation. Such gains resulted from "transmuting the soil of the country into tobacco—which was sent to England to purchase luxuries for its masters—and into bread for the bare support of its inhabitants [the slave workforce], without making any [real] return."[79]

Cotton manufacturing in Britain went from "2.6 percent of the value added in the economy as a whole" in 1770 to 17 percent in 1831, above the percentages associated with iron, coal, and wool. In 1830, "one in six workers in Britain labored in cottons," with most of these workers being women and children. By this point, British colonialism had finally succeeded in deindustrializing and destroying the cotton textile industry in India, with which it had been unable to compete on a free trade basis, with the result that India became a major destination for English cotton textiles.[80] All of this aligned with Britain's larger plundering of the subcontinent.

Writing to the Russian economist Nikolai Danielson in 1881, Marx commented on the enormous expropriation of India's surplus product and the devastation that this "bleeding process" had wrought on the society:

> In *India* serious complications, if not a general outbreak, is in store for the British government. What the English take from them annually in the form of rent, dividends for railways useless to the Hindoos, pensions for military and civil servicemen, for Afghanistan and other wars, etc., etc.—what they take from them *without any equivalent* and *quite apart* from what they appropriate to themselves annually *within* India, speaking only of the *value of the commodities* the Indians have *gratuitously* and annually to send *over* to England, it amounts to *more than the total sum of income of the 60 millions of agricultural and industrial labourers of India*! This is a bleeding process, with a vengeance! The famine years are pressing each other and *in dimensions* till now not yet suspected in Europe![81]

The expropriation of the earth brought on by the new, rapacious system was also evident in the rise of industrialized agriculture in Britain, which introduced a Second Agricultural Revolution in the midst of the Industrial Revolution.[82] Following the 1846 repeal of the Corn Laws, prompted in large part by the Irish potato blight, which required the elimination of agricultural protection and an increase in the importation of foodstuffs, a new, more intensive food regime emerged in British agriculture. The recourse to Peruvian guano as a way of enhancing the productivity of the soil symbolized the rise of a new *food pivot* for industrial capitalism, while also constituting a temporary fix for the metabolic rift arising from the expropriation of the soil in capitalist agriculture.[83] In addition, many slave plantation owners in the U.S. South saw guano as a key to restoring the fertility of their own exhausted fields.[84]

In the 1840s, agricultural chemists and agronomists discovered that the new, intensive, industrial agricultural practices and the town-country divide were depleting the soil. Soil nutrients (such as nitrogen, phosphorus, and potassium) contained in food and fiber were being shipped hundreds and even thousands of miles from farms to the new urban-industrial centers, only to end up as waste polluting the cities. In an extensive analysis of industrial agriculture and soil nutrients, Liebig highlighted the problems associated with violating the law of replenishment, preventing essential nutrients from being returned to the soil to support the growth of plants.[85] As Marx argued, citing Liebig:

> Large landed property reduces the agricultural population to an ever decreasing minimum and confronts it with an ever growing industrial population crammed together in large towns; in this way it produces conditions that provoke an irreparable rift in the interdependent process of social metabolism, a metabolism prescribed by the natural laws of life itself. The result of this is a squandering of the vitality of the soil, which is carried by trade far beyond the bounds of a single country.[86]

Liebig claimed that this system of robbery led Great Britain to expropriate resources from other nations: "Like a vampire it hangs on the breast of Europe, and even the world, sucking its lifeblood without any real necessity or permanent gain for itself."[87] In an attempt to compensate for lost nutrients, "the battle-fields of Leipsic, Waterloo, and the Crimea" and the "catacombs of Sicily" were plundered for bones to pulverize for phosphorus fertilizer. But so long as the law of replenishment was being violated, through appropriation without reciprocity, evermore inputs of fertilizer were required to maintain intensive production. The spoliation of soil plagued capitalist agriculture throughout the world. Marx noted that England had turned Ireland into "an agricultural district" that "provides corn, wool, cattle and industrial and military recruits." Hence, "England has indirectly exported the soil of Ireland, without even allowing the cultivators the means for replacing the constituents of the exhausted soil."[88]

While a variety of manures were incorporated into farming operations, from 1840 to 1880 guano was the most prized fertilizer in the world. Off the coast of Peru, the Chincha Islands were the site of the world's largest deposits of high-quality guano, hundreds of feet deep. Peruvian guano, rich in the nutrients plants need, particularly nitrogen, phosphorus, and potassium, was the product of thousands of years of seabirds eating anchovies and other fish rich in nutrients from the ocean. Their dung accumulated and retained the nutrients, given that it rarely rained on the islands. Peruvian farmers had long harvested relatively small quantities to support agricultural production on less fertile soils.[89] As the soil crisis deepened in Britain and other parts of the Global North, a scramble to secure access to guano ensued. Peru was in debt to Britain for monies that were borrowed in the fight for independence from Spain. The government in Lima entered into trade negotiations regarding guano. In the 1840s, Antony Gibbs & Sons, a British commercial firm, secured a series of monopolistic trade agreements, giving it exclusive rights to the sale of Peruvian guano on the global market.[90]

Gibbs & Sons paid the Peruvian government per ton of guano shipped. In 1846–47, these sales supplied only 5 percent of the state revenues, but the proportion increased to 80 percent by 1869.[91] During the heyday of the nineteenth-century guano trade, in 1870, over 700,000 tons were shipped from Peru alone. Between 1850 and 1860, Gibbs & Sons dispatched over 3,000 ships, transporting guano throughout the world to fertilize agricultural fields, including thousands of tons to the United States to enrich the exhausted fields along the east coast and the South.[92] Marx pointed out that the "blind desire for profit" had "exhausted the soil" of England, forcing "the manuring of English fields with guano." But neither guano nor the new commercial synthetic fertilizers that began to appear at this time offered lasting solutions to the ecological problems associated with the capitalist expropriation of the earth.[93]

Whereas the original workforce on the guano islands consisted of male convicts, army deserters, and slaves, it was eventually switched over to Chinese "coolies," who started to arrive in Peru in 1849. As Gaiutra Bahadur, author of *Coolie Woman*, has stated, "coolie" was "the bureaucratic term the British used to describe [primarily Asian] indentured laborers" (though it was later to take on the character of a racial slur). The infamous "coolie trade" consisted of the nineteenth-century transportation of East Asian contract workers under force or deception, as a substitute for the earlier slave trade, constituting still another form of racialized expropriation. The British first introduced the coolie labor system in the early nineteenth century, when 200 Chinese laborers were transported to Trinidad. By 1838, some 25,000 South Asian "coolies" had been exported to the British colony of Mauritius. Although the British mainly transported Indian workers inside the British colonies, between a quarter of a million and half a million Chinese "coolies" were shipped to various British, French, Dutch, and former Spanish colonies in the Americas, Southeast Asia, and Africa between 1847 and 1874, as well as to the United States. So merciless was this trade that Marx declared that the conditions of these "bonded emigrants" sold to work "on the coast of Peru" was "worse than slavery."[94]

Between 1849 and 1874, over 90,000 Chinese workers were contracted to be shipped to Peru. Around 10 percent of those transported died during the voyage across the Pacific. Most worked on plantations or on railroads. The most unfortunate were sent to work in the guano pits, where they were forbidden to leave the islands. The total workforce fluctuated between 200 and 800 Chinese workers—new workers simply replaced those who died, given the extensive coolie labor system.[95] This work was done exclusively by men. It involved grueling physical labor, using picks and shovels to extract the guano from the mountainous deposits, loading wheelbarrows and sacks, and transporting the manure to chutes for loading boats. Each worker was expected to load five tons of guano each day. Behavioral infractions and failure to meet daily quotas were met with physical punishment. The work was exhausting; the stench was overwhelming; and guano dust coated everything, penetrating the eyes, noses, and mouths of the workers. Opium was imported in an attempt to prevent further revolt and suicides among the workers.[96] Alanson Nash, a contemporary witness, reflecting on these conditions, explained, "once on the islands a Chinaman seldom gets off, but remains a slave, to die there."[97] They were seen as expendable beasts, forced to "live and feed like dogs."[98] An account in the *Christian Review* noted that "the subtle dust and pungent odor of the new-found fertilizer were not favorable to inordinate longevity." Guano labor involved "the infernal art of using up human life to the very last inch."[99] An 1856 article in the *Nautical Magazine* reported that "few probably are aware that the acquisition of this [guano] deposit, which enriches our lands and fills the purses of our traders, entails an amount of misery and suffering on a portion of our fellow creatures, the relation of which, if not respectably attested, would be treated as fiction."[100]

Here the "hidden abodes" related to the expropriation of land and people, the rift in the soil nutrient cycle, and racialized expropriation were evident.[101] Guano played a pivotal role in maintaining the expansion of industrial capitalist agriculture, despite the deepening of the ecological rift. This remained the case until the large historic deposits in Peru were greatly diminished, compounded by the practice of driving away or killing birds on the islands, as they were deemed a nuisance. With guano in short supply, there was a shift to nitrates as a fertilizer source, and eventually the production of synthetic fertilizers.

Reflecting upon Liebig's understanding of the robbery system, environmental historian Joachim Radkau writes: "In his eyes, British agriculture was . . . the pinnacle of destructive agrarian exploitation, and guano covered up the ecological crisis that had long since begun."[102] The spoliation of the soil continues today, despite the development and application of synthetic fertilizers, given that the inner dynamic of the capital system continues to rob the earth of its conditions of reproduction.

"Progress Here, Regression There"

One of Marx's most profound ecological insights, unique among political economists of his time, was his observation that with increasing economic development, ecological limits become more serious impediments to the system. Progress in capitalist accumulation and expansion thus normally results in ecological regression. As he wrote in volume 3 of *Capital*:

> The productivity of labour is also tied up with natural conditions, which are often less favorable as productivity rises—as far as that depends on social conditions. We thus have a contrary movement in these different spheres: progress here, regression there. We need only consider the influence of the seasons [climatic changes], for example, on which the greater part of raw materials depend for their quantity, as well as exhaustion of forests, coal and iron mines, and so on.[103]

By the time he wrote *Capital*, Marx was not only acutely aware of the seriousness of the metabolic rift between humanity and nature that emerged with capitalist expropriation of the earth, but argued that this was related to the expropriation of human beings themselves:

> From the standpoint of a higher socio-economic formation, the private property of particular individuals in the earth will appear just as absurd as the private property of one man in other men [human slavery]. Even an entire society, a nation, or all simultaneously existing societies taken together, are not the owners of the earth. They are simply its possessors, its beneficiaries, and have to bequeath it in an improved state to succeeding generations, as *boni patres familias* [good heads of the household].[104]

Marx of course was not alone in his day—or even before—in perceiving these intersecting contradictions. Among English thinkers at the time of the Industrial Revolution, none captured the dialectic of worldwide expropriation more fully than William Blake in his attacks on the entire system of the British Empire. In his 1793 engraved, allegorical poem *Visions of the Daughters of Albion*, Blake simultaneously evoked the sexual oppression of English women (daughters of Albion), the enslavement of Africans, "the extirpation . . . of the indigenous population" of the Americas (as Marx was later to put it), and the ecological destruction of the New World. Grimly inspired and deeply enraged by John Gabriel Stedman's searing *Narrative of a Five Years Expedition Against the Revolted Negroes of Surinam* (1790), for which he provided around sixteen engravings, Blake produced in his *Visions* perhaps the most powerful lyrical protest against the intersecting expropriations of his time—giving a glimpse of the other, even more terrible, side of "the dark satanic mills." As Kevin Hutchings writes, "*Visions* explicitly correlates the villainous [slave-trader] Bromion's brutal appropriation and rape of Oothoon's body with a figurative but nonetheless violent 'rape' of the natural world" as "Oothoon represents both a person and a landscape." Indeed, "nothing can happen to her human portion that does not also affect the environmental aspect of her identity." As the despicable Bromion boasted post-rape: "Thy soft American plains are mine, and mine thy north & south: / Stampt with my signet are the swarthy children of the sun: / They are obedient, they resist not."[105]

It is perhaps a commentary on our own time that this revolutionary, dialectical criticism of settler colonialism and the empire of the earth, connecting the various forms of extreme expropriation, which figured so largely for both Blake and Marx, is now being revisited in recent scholarship. As Fraser emphasizes, today's financialized capitalism constitutes an age of "the racialized interplay of expropriation and exploitation."[106] In our epoch of crisis and dissolution, capital now seeks to overcome all social and ecological boundaries to its expansion, extending to the biogeochemical cycles of the planet itself, treating all of these as mere barriers to be overcome. According to economist Riccardo Bellofiore, the present structural crisis of the capital system threatens not simply "housing, education, pensions, health and care services . . . as well as . . . the aggression to the body and life of male and female workers . . . [extending] to the spoliation of nature itself. . . . What is at stake by now are the conditions of existence and reproduction of human beings in their entirety."[107]

All of this points to the pressing need for an "anti-value politics" aimed at resisting capitalism's expropriation of all that exists.[108] Nevertheless, today's widening struggles cannot be fought simply on the boundaries of the system, that is, in the realm of *expropriation*, but require a return as well to the implicit issue of appropriation without equivalent within capitalist production itself, the realm of *exploitation*. In the present age of dissolution, in which everything solid within production seems to be melting into air, to be replaced by we know not what, and with the planetary climate heating up due to anthropogenic rifts generated by a system of unrestrained accumulation, there is no alternative in the end for humanity other than the *expropriation of the expropriators*—opening the way to a new more sustainable and egalitarian, socialist future.

2

The Rift of Éire

A NUMBER of critics of Karl Marx's metabolic rift analysis have argued that despite his crucial ecological observations, his "views on nature are not exactly systematic" and have little importance for his critique of capitalism as a whole.[1] Similarly, Marx's analysis of Irish history has often been characterized as overly empirical and episodic and lacking a "comprehensive treatment." It is significant therefore that the last decade has seen a revolution in ecological studies of nineteenth-century Ireland highlighting the unity and complexity of Marx's historical analysis in this area, in which his theory of metabolic rift has played the central role.[2] Based in part on the recent pathbreaking work of Irish scholars, including Eoin Flaherty, Terence McDonough, and Eamonn Slater, we argue that Marx's (and Frederick Engels's) analysis of nineteenth-century Irish history revealed what is referred to here as "the rift of Éire" in the colonial period.[3] Indeed, it is in relation to the analysis of the systematic disruption of the Irish environment that Marx's ecological inquiries can be seen as taking on a concrete and developed form, encompassing the ecological as well as economic robbery that characterized the Irish colonial regime.

Marx and Engels were strong critics of English colonialism in Ireland and supporters of Irish revolutionary movements throughout their adult lives. Their writings on Ireland, including newspaper articles, speeches, letters, and unpublished and unfinished manuscripts, come to around 500 pages in print.[4] Marx's most important analyses on the Irish question, however, occurred in November and December 1867, shortly after he had completed the first volume of *Capital*. On September 11, 1867, three days before the first thousand copies of *Capital* were to be published in Hamburg, two Fenians, Irish nationalists, were arrested in Manchester: Colonel Thomas Keely, who had organized an abortive Fenian uprising the preceding March, and Captain Thomas Deasy. A week later, on September 18, the prison van was ambushed by the local Fenian organization, liberating both men. However, in the process a shot was fired into the van, perhaps intended to break the lock, and a police sergeant, Charles Brett, was killed. Keely and Deasy escaped, making their way eventually to the United States, but three Fenians were arrested on the spot and many more men were arrested indiscriminately in Irish communities in Manchester. Five men were charged with the murder of Sergeant Brett.[5]

Marx wrote to Engels on November 2, 1867, that he was seeking "in every way" to back the English workers supporting Fenianism. On November 13, all five men were found guilty and condemned to be executed. On November 19, Marx called for a full discussion of the Fenian question at a meeting of the General Council of the International Working Men's Association. The meeting was held on November 26, three days after three of the convicted men were executed (one of the five was pardoned and the other had his sentence commuted). Marx had prepared five-and-a-half pages of notes for a talk on the occasion, but feeling that his broad historical analysis of the Irish question was inappropriate so soon after the executions, he yielded the floor to the Englishman Peter Fox. Marx's full address was given to the German Workers' Educational Association in London on December 16, when he presented a 90-minute talk based on a further set of thirteen-and-a-half pages of notes. Although he did not write out his entire speech on that occasion, we have in addition to his notes, a two-and-a-half-page summary of his talk, taken down in the meeting by Johann Georg Eccarius. In addition, Marx wrote a detailed summary of his analysis of the Irish situation in a letter to Engels on November 30.[6]

These four documents from November–December 1867, together with supplementary material from *Capital*, his *New York Tribune* articles going back to the 1850s, and other related writings, along with some of Engels's correspondence and unfinished *History of Ireland*, form the basis for the present analysis of Marx's systematic treatment of the Irish question, including what Slater has called a "more severe form of the metabolic rift" than exists under capitalism per se—reflective of the colonialism that was imposed on Ireland by the English, both before and after the Great Famine.[7] Marx provided a long historical perspective on the colonization of Ireland, though concentrating on nineteenth-century conditions separated by the Great Famine: the Period of Rack-Renting, 1801–46, and the Period of Extermination, 1846–66.[8] The rift of Éire, he was to argue, culminated in the expulsion of the population and the destruction of the soil, presenting a choice between ruin and revolution.

THE PERIOD OF RACK-RENTING (1801–1846)

For centuries, the British Crown waged a campaign of conquest on Ireland, which involved murder and expropriation. Throughout the sixteenth and seventeenth centuries, the native population of Ireland was pushed onto marginal lands, at best, particularly in the western region of the country. Protestant Penal Laws ensured that Catholics were not allowed to hold office, own land, or receive inheritance. The English, Marx pointed out, effectively robbed the land and became the "land-owning aristocracy."[9] Westminster came to directly rule Ireland, which was formalized in 1801, when the United Kingdom of Great Britain and Ireland was established. In his historical analysis of the rack-renting period, Marx devoted much attention to assessing how the property, technical, and food-regime relations took distinct forms, which created the foundation for the emerging colonial metabolic rift.

During the 1800s, the manufacturing industries of Ireland were dramatically diminished or eliminated, unable to compete with British operations. As detailed by the famous Irish nationalist leader and lawyer Isaac Butt (1813–79), in 1800 in Dublin, there were 91 wool manufactures, with over 4,000 workers. By 1840, there were only 12 manufactures, employing 682 people. The same trend was evident in industries associated with the production of silk, flannel, hosiery, and blankets across the country. There were 1,000 looms in County Wicklow in 1800, however, by the 1860s there were none.[10] As deindustrialization advanced, Ireland was turned almost exclusively into an agrarian nation.[11]

As a result, during this period, the power of the landlords increased. There were a few English and Anglo-Irish families, as part of the "ascendancy class," who controlled the only means of survival and wielded expansive influence.[12] The landlords, many of whom were absentees, often employed "middlemen" as intermediaries who handled the subletting of holdings to tenant farmers in the expanding "rack-renting" system.[13] Named after the instrument of torture, rack-renting stretched these farmers to the margins of existence, as they paid excessive rents, as part of year-to-year contracts that gave them access to agricultural lands. The tenant farmers, depending on the size of the land they rented, would in turn lease out small plots of land to cottiers (rural laborers living in cabins) in exchange for labor in the fields.[14]

Under this rack-renting arrangement, tenant farmers paid for the use of the land and any improvements they made. In other words, if they invested in the means to enhance the productivity of the crops, such as enriching the soil, their rents increased, eliminating any additional earnings they generated. To make matters worse, the owners regularly demanded "higher rents on the expiration of the existing lease," exacerbating the insecurity of tenants.[15] Either tenant farmers renewed leases under "less favourable conditions" or they were evicted. If the latter situation arose, the new tenants paid higher rents, associated with improvements from the previous occupants. Marx explained that the consequences of "the system of *rack-renting*" were extremely clear, as "the people had now before them the choice between the occupation of land, *at any rent*, or *starvation*." In this situation, he indicated, "middlemen accumulated fortunes that they *would* not invest in the improvement of land, and *could* not, under the system which prostrated manufactures, invest in machinery, etc. All their accumulations [and those of the owners] were sent therefore to England for investment."[16]

For the small famers and cottiers as "tenants-at-will" of the owners, there emerged a tendency to maintain the general conditions of the soil just enough to support the production of desired crops, with little to no added investment in drainage and irrigation, as this would have resulted in even higher rents and losses for the farmers. These rack-renting conditions, Marx assessed, created a situation that "left the Irish, however ground to the dust, holder of their native soil."[17]

The farms generally consisted of the tenants and cottiers. The latter lived in modest cabins, generally with access to a few acres of land for tillage that the tenant leased, which was known as the conacre system. The cottiers commonly did not receive wages, as they agreed to provide a specific number of days of labor to the tenant farmers in exchange for housing and access to small parcels on which they raised their food—potatoes. Marx noted, "The great mass of agricultural wages were paid in kind, only the smallest part in money."[18] Cottiers, if possible, raised a few pigs, which were fed surplus potatoes, or spun linen in their cottages, in order to sell locally to make a small amount of cash to cover any shortfalls related to the agreed-upon hours worked in relation to rents.[19]

Beginning in 1815, the Corn Laws in Britain generated high prices for grains, encouraging an expansion of tillage in Ireland, in order to serve the needs and interests of the English. Marx documented the increase through the years—in the three years following passage, "300,000 qrs" (quarter of a hundredweight) were exported to Britain, followed by over a million in 1820, and two and half million in 1834.[20] In the early 1840s, the Irish were producing grain yields per acre that were just below the English, and potato yields twice that of the French.[21] This situation intensified the plundering of Ireland of its resources, in a colonial metabolic transfer that increased the vulnerability of the country, its people, and the soil.

In *The Rural Economy of England, Scotland, and Ireland* (1855), Léonce de Lavergne pointed out that it was widely recognized in the late eighteenth and early nineteenth centuries, in the writings of figures like Arthur Young, that the soil of Ireland was far "superior to England," given that it was richer in nutrients.[22] These conditions dramatically changed as a result of the colonial relationship, the rack-renting system, and the practices on farms. Tenant farmers in Ireland primarily practiced a rotation consisting of growing two grains, such as wheat and oats, in succession, and then potatoes. The grains served as cash crops for export to Britain and as the basis to cover the costs of leasing the land. Potatoes provided a basis for subsistence. Farmers moved through this rotation, without letting the fields lay fallow or growing clover in order to rest the land and help restore fertility. In an attempt to replenish the soil, farmers added much manure when it was time to plant potatoes.[23]

"The ridge system of cultivation," Slater explains, was used to grow potatoes via a method of deep cultivation, whereby a spade was utilized to access the nutrients in the subsoil and mix them with the top soil. Earthing (hilling) potatoes was a labor-intensive process. The cottiers "laid the manure directly on the surface of the sod. The seed potato was then placed upon the surface and covered with an inverted sod dug with the spade from the trench paralleling the seed row. This was repeated across the width of the field to create a series of troughs and ridges."[24] As the potatoes grew, cottiers used spades to dig up even more soil from the trench, in order to cover the stems of the plants, which encourages tuber growth. Through this process, not only was the subsoil mixed with the top soil, but minerals from the iron pan—the hard layer that forms under soil due to the deposit of iron salts, which prevents adequate drainage—were brought up, as it was broken up.[25]

In his discussion of how distinctions "in the chemical composition of the soil" influenced variations in the "natural fertility" of land, Marx specifically focused on how various techniques brought "different types of soil into cultivation," which could enhance or diminish available nutrients. For example, he explained, "artificially induced improvements in the composition of the soil or of a mere change in the hierarchy of soil types" could take place "when various subsoil conditions come into play, once the subsoil also begins to be tilled and turned over into top layers," as was the case in the spade production of potatoes in Ireland. It "turn[ed] the subsoil into the top layer or mix[ed] the two together."[26]

The practices associated with the ridge system of potato production in Ireland helped increase the amount of nutrients available to support plant growth. Nevertheless, further enrichment was needed, as potatoes required more nutrients than the other crops.[27] Cottiers devoted much work to gathering additional fertilizers, including dung, sand, seaweed, shells, and ashes, in order to enrich exhausted soils. While manure from farm animals was used, it was in short supply, as much of the land during this period was devoted to tillage, rather than pasture. Thus, some cottiers collected manure-soaked grasses where animals were concentrated to integrate these nutrients into the soil to grow potatoes. In the winter, the animals were sheltered and fed potatoes within the small family cabins, allowing cottiers to collect 10 to 15 tons of manure in the spring. The sand, seaweed, and shells were carted from the sea to markets in towns for sale. For ash fertilizer, the top five inches of the land were dug up and dried before being burned. The resulting ash was then mixed with the soil. This was not a sustainable practice, however, since it led to the loss of organic matter.[28]

Given that manuring by cottiers was reserved for the potato rotation, the ridge system improved the drainage of the fields and brought up necessary nutrients and minerals from the iron pan and subsoil. The incorporation of additional fertilizers further enriched the soil. These practices supported the potato crop as well as the rest of the grain portion of the rotation. The metabolic rift in the soil nutrient cycle remained present, however, manifesting in a number of socioecological challenges. After a full rotation of crops, the soils were generally exhausted. Planting and manuring potatoes played an important role in trying to help improve soil conditions.

Slater points out the differing roles of the potato. For tenant farmers, it was necessary for helping restore soils to support cash crop production. For cottiers, it provided them with food. Nevertheless, the crops were still taking up more nutrients than were being incorporated into soil. Cottiers thus had the demanding task to devote even more time and energy through the years to restoring these depleted fields, given that under the conacre system the potato crop was their responsibility. The mining of nutrients from the subsoil and the gathering of additional fertilizers, by cottiers, helped temporarily support this arrangement, but lands were often rendered unproductive for years.[29]

The property relations, the rack-renting arrangement, and the conacre system created a "constant drain of rent," which "was shown in the continual export of agricultural produce" of grains to Britain. Lavergne indicated that this drain "created a void which was not filled up by any return."[30] Irish families subsisted on a diet consisting of potatoes, along with some milk and fish. During this period, the average male, doing physically demanding work, reportedly consumed up to 12 to 14 pounds of potatoes per day.[31] The lack of other nutrients, and marginal existence, created according to Marx a "state of popular starvation."[32] Lavergne proposed that the potato was "one of the most valuable gifts . . . but only on condition that it is not too greatly extended, as then it becomes a scourge, for it exhausts without renewing the means of production."[33] For Marx, this situation was bound to the larger colonial metabolic rift, associated with the conquest of Ireland and the period of rack-renting. "The landowner," Marx remarked, "who does nothing at all here to improve the soil, expropriates from him [the tenant] the small capital which he incorporates into the soil for the most part by his own labour, just as a usurer would do in similar conditions. Only the usurer would at least risk his own capital in the operation. It is this continuous robbery that forms the object of the dispute over Irish land legislation."[34] During this period, the intensification and expansion of the rack-renting and conacre systems created a fragile agroecology, with an underlying metabolic rift in the nutrient cycle, which was extremely vulnerable to the famine that followed.

THE PERIOD OF EXTERMINATION (1846–1866)

In 1845, the potato blight caused by *Phytopthora infestans*, a fungus-like pathogen, which first appeared in the United States and the European Continent, broke out in Ireland. By 1846, it generated a general famine, known in Ireland as the Great Hunger or Great Famine, which lasted for three to four years, with failures of the potato crop occurring partially in 1847 and then more generally in 1848–49. A million people died and more than a million people emigrated. Ireland at the time was especially vulnerable to the effects of the blight because of the destitute condition of the population, given that its subsistence diet was based entirely on the potato and the reliance on a monoculture consisting of only one variety, the "lumper" potato. The British government, based in Westminster, responded to the famine inconsistently and inadequately. Grain continued to be exported from Ireland to feed England.[35]

The actual cause of the blight was unknown at the time that it appeared. Perhaps the most prominent theory then was offered by the respected scientist John Lindley, editor of the *Gardeners' Chronicle and Agricultural Gazette*. He argued that the blight was the result of a deluge whereby potatoes had sucked up water through their roots and had become saturated, leading to their tissues becoming swollen and rotting away. However, Miles J. Berkeley, a mycologist who worked closely with Charles Darwin, proposed in 1846 that it was a fungus operating as a plant pathogen, calling the pathogen *Botrytis infestans*. The pathogen was more definitively isolated by Anton DeBary in 1876, building on Berkeley's work, and renamed *Phytopthora infestans*.[36] Engels was aware of the scientific debates and discoveries, indicating in a letter to Marx in 1858 that it was "single-celled fungi" that were "causing disease in potatoes."[37]

Yet, for Marx, in seeking to explain the conditions in Ireland in 1867 and why the Irish peasantry remained in a perilous state, the primary issue was not the plant pathogen itself, viewed as a natural cause, but the social conditions that had paved the way to the Great Famine, that is, the entire history of the rack-renting system and the

subsequent transformation in the socioecological food regime beginning in 1846. As he wrote to Engels on November 30, 1867, "The
system of 1801–46, with its rack-rents and middlemen, collapsed
in 1846."[38] Underlying it all, he explained in his talk the next month
to the German Workers' Educational Association, was "the exhaustion of the soil" due to a social structure that failed to replenish and
improve the land.[39]

The "barren fields" resulting from the potato blight caused people
to emigrate, resulting in the pooling of small holdings and the replacement of tillage with pasturage. But what was at first a natural tendency
initially soon "became a conscious and deliberate system." Chief here
was the Repeal of the Corn Laws as "one of the direct consequences
of the Irish disaster."[40] As Ireland lost its grain monopoly and cheap
grain poured in from abroad, bread prices fell, and tenant-farmer and
cottier rents could not be paid. Meat and wool prices had been rising
for some time and the demand was great. "Meat and wool," Marx
wrote, "became the slogan, hence conversion of tillage into pasture."[41]
In 1847–48, an Act of Parliament was passed that the Irish landlords
had to support their own paupers. As a result, the Irish landlord class,
already deep in debt, sought to clear their states of the impoverished
population. Worsening the conditions of the old ascendancy class, the
Encumbered Estates Act was passed in 1853 that forced "the debt-
ridden old Irish aristocrats to the hammer of the auctioneer or bailiff,
thus driving them from the land just as starvation drove away their
small tenants, subtenants and cottagers."[42] The entire Irish situation
in this period was thus summed up by the forcible eviction *en masse*
of the population, the consolidation of farms, and the deterioration
of the soil. Between 1851 and 1861, the total decrease of farms was
120,000, mainly affecting farms of less than fifteen acres.[43]

At the center of Marx's argument was the dramatic decline in
estimated yield per acre of every major crop. In his December 1867
speech, he provided data indicating that, in 1851–56, wheat had
declined by 9.6 percent, potatoes by 43 percent, and flax by 35 percent.[44] Although Ireland had previously exported vast quantities of
wheat, it was now said by the ruling British colonial interests to be

good "only for cultivating oats." Indeed, by 1866, Ireland was exporting only an amount equivalent to a little more than a quarter of the
wheat that it was importing. Becoming a net importer of grain was of
course partly a product of the competition presented by cheap foreign grain following the Repeal of the Corn Laws. But a more critical
problem was the deterioration of the land itself, which was only compounded by the expulsion of the cottiers. In the conacre/rack-renting
system, "the farmer," Marx noted, had "in a great measure trusted to
his labourers to manure the land for him."[45] With the breakdown of
that system following the Great Famine, the clearing of the estates,
and the consolidation of farms, the process of manuring, hitherto carried out by the peasants with their spade agriculture and ridge system
of cultivation, was undermined. The law of replacement regarding soil
nutrients, as identified by Justus von Liebig, was violated, generating
a new, hardly less extreme modality of the metabolic rift, attributable
to the "new regime" of food production.[46] "Since the exodus," Marx
remarked, "the land has been underfed and overworked." The resulting decline in agricultural productivity, he hastened to add, was not
necessarily reflected in value terms, since under consolidation and
the shift from tillage to pasturage "rents and profits . . . may increase,
although the produce of the soil decreases. The total produce may
diminish, and still [the] greater part of it be converted into surplus
produce, falling to the landlord and (great) farmer. And the price of
the surplus produce has risen." None of this, however, altered the fact
that less food was being produced per acre.[47] The upshot was the "*ster-
ilisation* (gradual) of the land, as in *Sicily by the ancient Romans*."[48]

The rack-renting system in which the laborers were "ground
to the dust" was replaced by a "regime since 1846, [which] though
less barbarian in form, [was] in effect [hardly less] destructive, leaving no alternative but Ireland's voluntary emancipation by England
or life-and-death struggle."[49] The most visible manifestation of the
new agricultural regime, was, Marx pointed out, that "in 1855–56,
1,032,694 Irishmen were replaced by 999,877 head of livestock
(cattle, sheep and pigs)."[50] Marx wrote in *Capital*: "Having praised the

fruitfulness of the Irish soil between 1815 and 1846, and proclaimed it loudly as destined for the cultivation of wheat by nature herself, English agronomists, economists and politicians suddenly discovered that it was good for nothing but the production of forage."[51] Or as Engels satirically put it, in 1812:

> England was at war with the whole of Europe and America, and it was much more difficult to import corn—corn was the primary need. Now America, Rumania, Russia and Germany deliver sufficient corn, and the question now is rather one of cheap *meat*. And because of this Ireland's climate is no longer suited to tillage. . . . Today England needs grain quickly and dependably—Ireland is just perfect for wheat-growing. Tomorrow England needs meat—Ireland is only fit for cattle pastures. The existence of five million Irish is in itself a smack in the eye to all the laws of political economy, they have to get out but whereto is their worry![52]

The solution that the English and the Anglo-Irish landlord class imposed on colonial Ireland in the period after 1846 was what Marx called a "fiendish war of extermination against the cott[i]ers."[53] In employing the term extermination to describe the Irish condition, Marx and Engels, along with their contemporaries, such as Butt and Lavergne, had in mind its twofold meaning as both *exclusion* and *annihilation* of the Irish peasantry.[54] The result of this "quiet business-like extinction," as Marx called it, was the forced emigration, death, pauperization, and "physical deterioration" of the great mass of the Irish people. For the Irish, Marx observed in 1867, it is a question of a "life-and-death struggle." The "*absolute increase* in the number of deaf-mutes, blind, insane, idiotic, and decrepit inhabitants," what could be called a corporeal rift, was a natural result of these conditions. In such circumstances, the Irish were forced to choose between "ruin and revolution."[55] Hence, the Fenian upsurge.[56] Hence, the Land War that was to follow. Each generation of Irish was forced in their own way to rise up against English rule.[57]

Colonial Ireland and the Metabolic Rift

In discussing the absolute general law of accumulation in relation to
Ireland in the first volume of *Capital*, Marx observed that the depop-
ulation of Ireland had reduced the amount of cultivated land and
hence the production of the soil, with a greater area given over to
pasture. However, in referring to the decreasing production of grain
that resulted, he noted that this was also accompanied by a decreased
production per acre, which could not be separated from the fact that
"for a century and a half England has indirectly exported the soil of
Ireland, without even allowing its cultivators the means for replacing
the constituents of the exhausted soil."[58] The failure to maintain the
soil metabolism was central to Marx's understanding of the extreme
ecological degradation of colonial Ireland and was also emphasized in
his December 1867 speech on Ireland, in which he indicated that the
nutrients necessary to fertilize the Irish soil "were exported with the
produce and rent."[59]

Marx's analysis here coincided with what Jonathan Swift in *Maxims
Controlled in Ireland* and Thomas Prior in *A List of the Absentees of
Ireland* had both in 1729 called the "drain" of wealth from Ireland to
England.[60] The full extent of this drain was made clear in the 1804
treatise *An Essay on the Principle of Commercial Exchanges*, written
by John Leslie Foster (later appointed Baron of the Exchequer of
Ireland), which documented the enormous payments of the Irish to
the English in the form of rents to absentees. The great drain of value
to absentee landlords was financed by the export of grain to England
for which the Irish themselves received nothing in return. The loss of
the produce Ireland exported to pay the rent of absentee landlords
forced it to seek increased imports. This, however, necessitated a vast
borrowing of foreign funds (primarily in England) to finance Irish
imports, leaving the country deeper and deeper in debt.[61] As Foster
said, "It is Ireland paid by Ireland to work for England. It is the part of
England to enjoy, and of Ireland to labour."[62] As Marx noted, referring
to a later report, Ireland was "forced to contribute cheap labour and
cheap capital" to further the industrialization of England.[63]

But the drain, as Marx so astutely emphasized, was not simply a question of economic values but of natural-material use values. In the case of Ireland, an agrarian nation under colonial rule, what was being drained away was the most important use value of all—the nutrients that were vital to the replenishment of the soil. Ireland was thus the site of an extreme metabolic rift, caught in the vice grip of economic and ecological imperialism, from which arose the necessity of "ruin or revolution."[64]

3

Women, Nature, and Capital in the Industrial Revolution

THE REMARKABLE RISE in recent years of "social reproduction theory" within the Marxist and revolutionary feminist traditions, identified with the studies of such figures as Tithi Bhattacharya, Johanna Brenner, Heather Brown, Paresh Chattopadhyay, Silvia Federici, Susan Ferguson, Leopoldina Fortunati, Nancy Fraser, Frigga Haug, David McNally, Maria Mies, Ariel Salleh, Lise Vogel, and Judith Whitehead—to name just a few—has significantly altered how we look at Karl Marx's (and Frederick Engels's) treatment of women and work in nineteenth-century Britain.[1] Three conclusions with respect to Marx's analysis are now so well established by contemporary scholarship that they can be regarded as definitive facts: (1) Marx made an extensive, detailed examination of the exploitation of women as wage slaves within capitalist industry, in ways that were crucial to his overall critique of capital; (2) his assessment of women's working conditions was deficient with regard to housework or *reproductive labor*;[2] and (3) central to Marx and Engels's outlook in the mid-nineteenth century was the severe crisis and threatened "dissolution" of the working-class family—to which the capitalist state in the late nineteenth century was compelled to respond with an ideology of protection, forcing women in large part back into the home.[3]

Although all of the above points are now conclusively established, still lacking is a larger synthesis integrating these results with one another and with what decades of intensive historical research have taught us about women and work in the Industrial Revolution. By examining the historical specificity of the condition of women in England in the early to mid-nineteenth century, we can better understand the assumptions regarding gender, family, and work influencing the writing of Engels's *The Condition of the Working Class in England* and Marx's *Capital*.[4] This synthesis would throw light on such difficult problems as: (1) why did Marx not extend his critique to reproductive work within the household, which at times he seemed on the threshold of doing?; and (2) how, if we follow Marx's argument that capital denies (commodity) value to housework and subsistence activity, is it possible to speak of the *expropriation* of reproductive labor?[5]

Furthermore, since both nature and women's reproductive work are treated by classical political economy and by Marx in his critique of capital as "a free gift . . . to capital," a historical and theoretical synthesis of the kind that we propose here opens a wider conception of the robbing of both women's reproductive work and nature—as realms external to the value circuit of capital in its ideal conception.[6] This analysis enables us to understand more fully the connections between social reproduction feminism and socioecological reproduction theory, associated in particular with Marx's theory of metabolic rift, in which natural cycles and flows are disrupted or even ruptured and species are depleted.

Ultimately, the crucial issue today is how capital as a system engages in the creative destruction of the entirety of the social and ecological conditions sustaining human existence—including the family, the constitution of human beings (identity, the body), culture, the economy, and the environment—and how this makes the revolutionary expansion of human freedom through the reconstitution of society at large an absolute necessity for present and future generations.

The "Woman Question" in Marx's Day

As Federici points out, "the 'woman's question' of the time" in which
Marx was writing had to do primarily with "the conditions of wom-
en's factory work in the Industrial Revolution."[7] In contrast to popular
conceptions of a male-dominated factory workforce, the Industrial
Revolution in England was initially founded on the labor of women
and children. Symbolic of this, the spinning jenny was originally
invented for use by a young girl, with its horizontal wheel placed in
a way that made it extremely difficult for an adult worker to use it
for any length of time.[8] From the late eighteenth century through the
mid-nineteenth century, nearly all working-class women—daughters,
mothers, wives, and widows—were compelled to enter the paid labor
force. As historian Maxine Berg observes, "When we talk of industry
in the eighteenth and early nineteenth centuries, we are talking of a
largely female workforce." Women workers were so dominant in the
cotton, wool, silk, flax, lace, and other textile sectors at the core of
industry, that up until the mid-nineteenth century they constituted
the main source of surplus value for the emerging industrial capitalist class. "It was the female, and not the male, workforce," Berg notes,
"which counted in the most important high productivity industry of
the period—textiles." Many of these women workers were concentrated in proto-industrial occupations, where the female labor force
outnumbered the male by four to one or even eight to one.[9]

In the early nineteenth century, more than 60 percent of married working-class women in Britain had a recorded occupation or
positive earnings, primarily in industry or domestic service. These
numbers were extremely conservative with respect to female labor
participation in the workplace since enumerators frequently under-
reported the occupational designations of married women, while the
employment of young girls and women in such proto-industrial sectors as "modern domestic industry," occurring in homes of employers
or so-called mistresses' houses, were quite clearly seriously under-
counted. Additionally, unmarried adult working-class women were
not able to live without employment.[10] As Joyce Burnette has shown,

based on the 1833 factory report of Dr. James Mitchell, who collected
data from over two hundred factories across England, 56.8 percent of
all factory workers on average in the industries sampled (cotton, wool,
flax, silk, lace, potteries, dyehouse, and paper) were female. Women
also dominated domestic service in the homes of the middle class
and the wealthy by a very wide margin.[11] Indeed, the available data
suggests that working-class women in the late eighteenth and early
nineteenth century were employed as wage workers on as high or on
an even higher level than working-class men—once rural industries
such as agriculture and mining and the urban trades (constituting
a relatively privileged sector of the labor force still engaged in traditional crafts) and general commerce were excluded.[12] Given that
female workers received much lower wages, one-third to one-half of
that of males, they were hired preferentially in the new industries as
factory operatives and in proto-industrial sectors.[13] In fact, for a while
women's wages were so low that it was cheaper to pay them to pull
barges along canals than to have horses do it, given the costs of maintaining the latter.[14]

The reality that both sexes in proletarian families were equally part
of the labor force was a mere given in Marx's day, and was not normally considered something that needed to be established. When the
subject came up, it mainly had to do with contemporary demands to
force women workers out of industry. Thus John Stuart Mill, writing
in the *Examiner* in 1832, argued that "we should wish to see a law
established, *interdicting altogether* the employment of children under
fourteen, and *females of any age*, in manufactories." Marx and Engels
always strongly opposed restrictions on employment for adult women,
an idea nonetheless supported by parts of the male workforce.[15]

But though the general reality of women's employment in industry
was not in doubt in Marx's day, he did, with his usual thoroughness,
carefully examine the available statistics on the gender division within
industry. Relying on the 1861 census for England and Wales, he fac-
tored out the upper classes; urban workers in skilled trades; commercial
workers, "unproductive" workers generally (using scare quotes to indicate that this was by capitalist criteria); "groups, such as members of

the government, priests, lawyers, soldiers, etc."; those too old or young to work; and the pauperized part of the population.[16] He was thus able to make rough estimates of the gendered division of the working class among those employed as productive workers in core industries or as domestic servants—both of which were central to proletarianization. Looking at textiles, the largest sector by far within manufacturing, he showed that only 27.6 percent of the workers were adult males. (Although not directly indicated by Marx, the 1861 census revealed that female workers greatly predominated over male workers in the textile industry *at every age*, including children.)[17] Likewise, among domestic servants only 11.4 percent were adult males. In contrast, in metal works and metals manufacturing, a considerably smaller sector, women were only about 8 percent of the total. Marx's figures thus suggested that overall the industrial (manufacturing) workforce in the urban centers was predominantly female. Moreover, this was also true of domestic servants (considered unproductive workers in capitalist accounting since paid out of surplus value), who clearly constituted part of the proletarianized workforce. In emphasizing the severe oppression of young women in domestic service, Marx angrily observed that they were referred to "in common parlance" as "little slaveys"—indicating that this was indeed close to the truth.[18]

Although the Victorian censuses have been criticized in contemporary scholarship for underestimating the overall level of female employment and exaggerating the total number of domestic servants, none of this seriously undercuts Marx's main conclusions, which point to: (1) the greater number of working-class women than working-class men employed in urban industry, excluding the trades and commerce; (2) the much higher employment of women than men in textiles, the most important industry (and leading source of surplus value) in the Industrial Revolution; (3) the huge proportion of the nation's labor force dedicated to domestic service in the houses of the well-to-do, where women servants enormously outnumbered men; and (4) the slave-like conditions imposed on these female servants, who typically worked eighteen-hour days for almost no pay, under the most degrading conditions.[19]

As recent literature has confirmed, Marx devoted substantial portions of *Capital* to describing the brutal working conditions of women in industry, whom he saw as far more heavily exploited than men. Women workers predominated in modern domestic industry, often working in "mistresses' houses," which Marx associated with what he called the "stagnant" portion of the industrial reserve army, because of the precariousness of the labor.[20] Modern domestic industry, like "modern manufacturing" or modern handicraft, was largely unregulated, even after the passage of the Factory Acts and the Ten-Hour-Day Bill. Pointing to "the horrors" in this sector of production, Marx highlighted the death of the twenty-year-old Mary Anne Walkley, who had been employed in one of the better seamstress establishments or mistresses' houses. She had been forced to work continuously for 26.5 hours in a room packed with thirty other young women, making dresses for a ball in honor of the new Princess of Wales. They had only one-third of the necessary air in cubic feet per person—not unusual at the time. Looking at data on over six hundred female patients treated in Nottingham General Dispensary, all of them lacemakers and most between the ages of seventeen and twenty-four, Marx found that the numbers of those contracting tuberculosis had increased phenomenally in less than a decade, from one in forty-five workers in 1852 to one in eight in 1861—a measure of rapidly deteriorating working conditions and the severe compromising of workers' health.[21]

Given that male workers (often husbands and fathers) were generally unable to earn wages sufficient to meet the subsistence needs of the family (including the social reproduction of labor power), and that adult women workers were often paid only a third of male wages, capitalism in the mid-nineteenth century, Marx emphasized, was increasingly propelling all members of the proletarian household into the workforce, simply to keep a single family afloat: "In place of the man who has been dismissed by the machine the factory may employ, perhaps, three children and one woman! . . . [Hence] four times as many workers' lives are used up as there were previously, in order to obtain the livelihood of one working family."[22] The consequence was the abolition of disposable time (even time for consumption and for sleeping) on the part of *all* the members of the family, who frequently worked six or even seven days a week, often for twelve or more hours a day. These conditions contributed to the almost complete disintegration of the working-class family.

This situation was especially evident in the condition of women, who, then as now, were considered the main caretakers in the household. According to one contemporary account, reported by a factory inspector in 1844 as a typical case, a married factory operative had

> half an hour to dress, suckle her infant and carry it out to nurse; one hour for household duties before leaving home; half an hour for actually travelling to the mill; twelve hours' actual labour; one and a half hours for meals; half an hour for returning home at night; one and a half hours for household duties and preparing for bed, leaving six and a half hours for recreation, seeing and visiting friends and sleep; and in winter, when it is dark, half an hour extra time on the road to the mill and half an hour extra on the road home from the mill.[23]

In the mid-nineteenth century, as Margaret Hewitt observes in *Wives and Mothers in Victorian Industry*, "the married textile operative was absent from her home before six o'clock in the morning till after six o'clock at night—sometimes later if she was working for an unscrupulous employer." The effect on children was horrendous. "'What do they do,' asked Charles Dickens of the Rector of a parish in a large English town, 'what do they do with the infants of the mothers who work in the mills?' 'Oh,' replied the clergyman, 'they bring them to me, and I take care of them in the churchyard [cemetery]!'"[24]

In some localities, the mortality rate among infants under age two whose mothers were factory operatives was reported to be 50 percent or higher.[25] The major industrial districts, such as Manchester, Stockport, and Bradford, as Marx explained based on the *Sixth Report of Public Health* (1864), had average annual mortality rates for children alive and less than one year of age of over 25 percent. "The high death rates . . . apart from local causes" were "principally due to the employment of mothers away from their homes, and to the neglect and maltreatment arising from their absence," including frequent poisoning of the infants with opiates.[26] In Lancashire in the mid-1850s, the portion of all married women operatives with children less than one-year old averaged 21 percent. According to the 1851 census, 50 percent of women in their prime (many of whom were also mothers) had no husband to support them, and hence were part of the active labor force. As a result, even in the second half of the nineteenth century, when conditions improved somewhat, overall infant mortality in industrial districts ranged from around 19 to 25 percent. Wet-nursing of infants was unaffordable for the working class, and cow's milk was prohibitively costly and frequently contaminated. Instead infants in the working class were most often spoon-fed a pap made with bread soaked in water and sometimes sweetened with sugar. As Hewitt writes (and Marx had noted), "To soothe the distressed cries of the infants," who were undernourished and suffering, often seriously, from an inappropriate diet, "nurses were in the habit of administering gin and peppermint and certain other nostrums, such as Godfrey's Cordial, Atkinson's Royal Infants' Preservative, and Mrs. Wilkinson's Soothing Syrup," along with opium (or laudanum, or morphine), which was "an ingredient of all."[27]

The poor care of infants reflected the deficient diet and outright poverty of the urban working class in general, as well as the almost complete elimination of time for necessary tasks of recuperation and social reproduction within the working-class family. The working-class diet consisted mainly of "tea and bread, bread and tea," sometimes supplemented by potatoes and various condiments. Milk and meat of any kind were rarities, as were most vegetables. Adult workers ate about ten pounds of bread a week on average, all of it purchased from bakers, and all of it seriously adulterated.[28] Domestic cooking facilities and implements were limited, and fuel was expensive. Water, often extremely polluted, had to be carried into the household, generally for long distances, and most frequently by women. There were no sanitary facilities. Sickness was widespread and epidemics frequent. The workers in industrial centers lived in overcrowded rented rooms and hovels, consisting usually of a single room, with only the barest of furniture, a bed, a table, and several chairs.[29] Most significant was the expropriation of nearly all the time necessary for the social reproduction of the proletarian family even at a bare level of existence—a condition that could scarcely continue. "The women who worked 14-hour days in the Midland factories during the 1830s," Caroline Davidson grimly writes in *A Woman's Work Is Never Done*, "could survive without doing much housework at all. They and their families existed off wheaten bread and potatoes, washed down with tea or coffee, and lived, for the most part, in filthy houses."[30]

Working-class families, Marx and Engels observed, were in a severe state of crisis and "dissolution," with the old patriarchal family structure collapsing amid the breakdown of the home as the center of production, followed by the massive entry of women into the labor force. The hope among early English radicals was that a new more egalitarian family structure based on equality between the sexes would emerge within the working-class struggle, a political aspiration that had appeared in the Owenite movement, but had largely subsided in the Chartist era.[31] In the meantime, it was clear that the working-class family needed protection, given the murderous conditions with which it was then confronted. Though eventually some protection was provided on bourgeois terms by the factory legislation and the Ten-Hour-Day Bill, the larger answer for Marx remained the worker's self-organization and equality in the workplace, constituting the seeds of the new society. As Marx wrote in 1880, "The emancipation of the producing class involves all human beings without distinction of sex and race."[32]

One reason for Marx's silence on the subject of women's reproductive work in the household, Federici suggests, was the "near absence" of such reproductive work "in proletarian homes at the time of Marx's writing, given that the entire family was employed in the factories from sun-up to sun-down." She adds: "Marx described the condition of the industrial proletariat of his time as he saw it, and women's domestic labor was hardly part of it. . . . Although from the first phase of capitalist development, and especially in the mercantilist period, reproductive work was formally subsumed to capitalist accumulation, it was only in the late nineteenth century that domestic work emerged as the key engine for the reproduction of the industrial workforce."[33] Commenting on the shutting down of U.S. cotton mills during the Civil War, Marx observed that this at least had some positive effect for the women, who now "had sufficient leisure [that is, time away from the factory] to give their infants the breast, instead of poisoning them with 'Godfrey's Cordial,'" an opiate.[34] For Marx, "the collective working group," which

> is composed of individuals of both sexes and all ages[,] must under the appropriate conditions turn into a source of humane development, although in its spontaneously developed, brutal, capitalist form, the system works in the opposite direction, and becomes a pestiferous source of corruption and slavery, since here the worker exists for the process of production, and not the process of production for the worker.[35]

Most of these conditions were to abate in later years. The late eighteenth to mid-nineteenth century proved to be a "major discontinuity" with respect to women's work roles, distinct both from earlier household-based production and the later "separate spheres" regime of the Victorian era. The share of "occupied women" fell by an average of 0.7 percent a year in the second half of the nineteenth century. "From levels recorded as high as the 67.5 per cent of married women working in Cardington in the 1780s, participation rates of married women in the whole country fell to 10 per cent in 1911."[36] Much of this change was due to factory legislation, the ten-hour day, rising wages, and the now official bourgeois ideology of the male breadwinner and the female housewife. The last served to strictly define gender roles in the newly emerging era of monopoly capitalism, in which relative surplus value, as opposed to absolute surplus value, was dominant.[37] Having run up against "insuperable natural obstacles" in its annihilation of time for the entire working-class family, capital subsequently introduced a new regime of a family wage, whereby an adult man alone could theoretically earn enough to support his whole household. This wage was kept down, however, by women's increased social reproductive work in the household, which served as a free gift to capital. Moreover, the family wage was only applicable to male "breadwinners" in a privileged sector of the working class.[38]

By 1884, in *The Origin of the Family, Private Property, and the State*, Engels argued that women's emancipation required a new push to free women from confinement to the household, and the revolutionary "re-introduction" of women into the labor force, to break down the new bourgeois patriarchy and to establish the conditions for a more equal family:

> Today, in the great majority of cases, the man has to be the earner, the breadwinner of the family . . . and this gives him a dominating position which requires no special legal privileges. In the family, he is the bourgeois; the wife represents the proletariat. . . . The peculiar character of man's domination over woman in the modern family, and the necessity, as well as the manner, of establishing real social equality between the two, will be brought out into full relief only when both are completely equal before the law. It will then become evident that *the first premise for the emancipation of women is the re-introduction of the entire female sex into public industry*; and that this again demands that the quality possessed by the individual family of being the economic unit of society be abolished.[39]

REPRODUCTIVE WORK, NATURE, AND VALORIZATION

However necessary it is to acknowledge Marx's understanding of the crisis and dissolution of the working-class family of his day, it cannot entirely account for the absence in his work of a detailed examination of social reproduction in the household. A deeper explanation lies in the very structure of his critique of capitalist political economy. Here it is crucial to understand that Marx's *Capital* was a *critique*, meant to uncover the inner logic and contradictions of the capitalist mode of production. The categories used, such as those associated with the labor theory of value—which Marx adapted and developed from classical political economy, and which he believed allowed for the scientific examination of capital as a system—were not, for him, universal, but rather historically specific categories to be transcended along with the revolutionary transcendence of the capital system itself. Moreover, Marx, as is well known, structured his critique of bourgeois political economy in the form of successive approximations, moving from the more abstract analysis in volume 1 of *Capital* to increasingly concrete levels of analysis in the unfinished second and third volumes.[40] *Capital* itself was originally conceived as simply the first of what would have been five different books, including volumes on landed property, wage labor, the state, international trade, and the world market and crisis.

The incomplete nature of Marx's project, given that even *Capital* was unfinished, has constituted a major problem for later Marxian theorists attempting to build on his dialectical social science. As Michael Lebowitz has brilliantly argued, the unwritten book on wage labor would necessarily have been devoted to what Marx called "the political economy of labor," as opposed to the critique of "the political economy of property."[41] Logically, this would have required the incorporation of a detailed analysis of the social reproduction of labor power—of a kind which Marx seemed at times to be on the threshold of providing—but which lay analytically beyond the immediate critique of capital.[42]

At the root of this analysis was Marx's understanding of the capital relation itself, as depicted in classical bourgeois political economy. The inner logic of capital as a system of valorization and accumulation, as he explained in the *Grundrisse* of 1857–58, runs roughshod over all other inherited social and natural relations and conditions of production, which remain external to its own mode of production.[43] The development of the state is itself in part a product of the need to manage the "alienated mediations," not only internal to the class system, but also between capital and the larger realm of existence, of which it is a part.[44] Capital, in its process of unlimited expansion, is presented with "insuperable natural obstacles," including those imposed by the limits of the human body itself, resulting in "the sheer robbery of every normal condition needed for working and living."[45] Constantly seeking to overcome but never able to transcend such natural obstacles, the system is periodically confronted with crises of accumulation, which, though seemingly resolved at each step of its progress, forever increase in scope.

This aspect of Marx's critique, related to the boundary conditions of the system, is seen most readily in what he referred to—in a qualified deference to classical bourgeois political economy—as "so-called primitive [primary] accumulation," which he preferred to treat as the problem of *expropriation*.[46] This stood for capital's necessary and continuing attempt to transcend or readjust its boundaries with respect to its external conditions of production, to further enhance the accumulation process.[47] Industrial capitalism requires as its initial basis the expropriation and monopolization of the land, essential for the generation of a proletarian labor force and for the development of capitalist landed property and farming. While, in a wider sense, the constant need for expropriation to create and re-create the basis of its rule, making the continuing exploitation of labor possible, stands for the reality that the capital system exists invariably in nature's midst and emerges out of prior household-based modes of production.[48] Driven to transcend its external and natural conditions of production, and treating them not as boundaries but as barriers to overcome, capital constantly seeks to expropriate what it can from its natural and social environment while also externalizing its costs onto realms outside its inner circuit of value. Especially in his theory of metabolic rift, but elsewhere as well—for example, his later ethnological studies of the family—Marx moved more and more toward embracing the contradictions of the inner and outer determination of capital as a system.[49] This reflected capitalism's own course of development, which increasingly raised the question of "the activation of capital's absolute limits"—in relation to the family, the nation-state, and the environment.[50]

Nevertheless, the critique of capital as a social relation had to be approached initially from the standpoint of its own ideal conception and intrinsic process, as presented in classical political economy, and in terms of its inner logic of (commodity) value generation or valorization. This ideal conception of capital had to be subjected to a full critique at the outset, on an abstract level (as in the first volume of *Capital*). It was only then in Marx's project that the reality of concrete, historical capitalism could be approached, moving to lower levels of abstraction and hence a more comprehensive historical analysis. At the concrete level of historical capitalism, it became clear that the system required as a product of its own internal logic, and in order to maintain its drive to capital accumulation, the control of the boundaries—represented by the terms of expropriation of the wider conditions of production—that defined the overall system. In this sense, Rosa Luxemburg's emphasis on the dependence of capitalism as an imperial system on the constant expropriation of external areas reflected this same logic.[51] Capital's formation of the nation-state and its control of immigration and emigration were likewise means of controlling and managing the boundaries of its labor force, along with its natural and social boundaries in general.

Still, from the system's own standpoint of the generation of value through commodity production, those areas outside commodity production, including both the reproduction of labor power and what could be expropriated from nature, were considered "free gift[s] ... to capital" and were excluded from the value (and income) calculus—a reality *of the system* that is as true today as when Marx was writing.[52] Hence, as Marilyn Waring has noted, "the treatment of Mother Earth and the treatment of women and children in the system of national accounts have many fundamental parallels"—and significantly, neither is included in "value added."[53]

Marx defined wealth in terms of the production of use values; however, bourgeois political economy, in what he characterized as its greatest contradiction, is interested only in exchange value, and increasingly reduces wealth merely to value generated in commodity production.[54] Use values derived from nature, natural processes, and the costs of the social reproduction of the household are therefore treated by the system as merely *gratis*, to be freely expropriated in its expansion. Here, in contrast to exploitation, there is no equal exchange, even on a formal basis, but actual robbery—usurpation, expropriation, dependence, and enslavement.[55]

This contradiction between capital accumulation and its conditions of production underlies Marx's entire analysis. The exploitation at the heart of the system, whereby surplus value is extracted from labor (variable capital), can ultimately proceed only through the destruction of the life and body of the laborer—either in absolute or relative terms—as well as the removal of the worker from the means of production (in particular the earth). The annihilation of time and the damage to workers' physical and mental health, coupled with the outright "robbery system" through which nature itself is expropriated, with no concern for its reproduction, have devastating effects on the household and the wider metabolic relation to the environment.[56] Exploitation and expropriation thus have a dialectical relation in Marx's analysis—neither can be understood without the other. Capturing this succinctly, Eleanor Marx wrote that "women . . . have been expropriated as to their rights as human beings, just as the labourers were expropriated as to their rights as producers. The method in each case is the only one that makes expropriation at any time and under any circumstances possible—and that method is force."[57] As Karl Marx put it, capital, in its process of self-valorization "usurped [expropriated] the family labor necessary for consumption."[58]

The logic of Marx's critique of political economy thus strongly suggests that necessary unpaid reproductive work forms the basis for the necessary paid labor (the wage) provided to the worker. The use values produced in the household and the time used up in their production—where reproductive work is not simply annihilated, threatening the dissolution of the family as in Marx's day—become appended to the system of capitalist exploitation. This expropriation of social reproductive work within the household helps decrease the value of labor and, particularly under monopoly capitalism, also promotes the realization of surplus value. Not only is this consistent with Marx's whole argument, and foreshadowed (but not actually analyzed with respect to housework) in *Capital*, but more important, it constitutes the *reality* of capitalist production. Industrial capitalism splits the old preindustrial, patriarchal household economy, in which all work was regarded as essential and on a more or less equal footing, and divides it into a sphere of invisible household labor and "public" commodity-producing labor, both exploiting labor in industry and expropriating social reproductive work in the household. The actual division of labor between these two spheres—the capitalist work-place proper and housework—has historically been affected by the needs of capital accumulation as a whole, the size of the industrial reserve army of labor at a given time, the regulatory apparatuses of states, social inequalities, and social movements. Any understanding of reproductive-productive labor in capitalism must consider these dialectical relationships.

Marx at various times indicates that capitalism's definition of *pro-ductive* labor as that which contributes to the production of value/surplus value, which is historically specific to the capital system itself, and should not be confused with the wider productivity of human labor in general. For Marx, there is no doubt that non-commodity-producing labor (contrary to capital's own accounting) is also *social labor*—or else social labor historically would simply be confined to capitalist commodity relations. Moreover, it is only insofar as social labor generates *use values* (and not exchange values) that one can speak of *real work*, in Marx's terms. He was absolutely clear (though unfortunately too brief) about the main contradiction related to the family and production in his time—that capital usurped the "free labor for family sustenance" by turning women into wage slaves within industry, while also subject to the patriarchal head of the household.[59]

In the mid-nineteenth century, as we have seen, it was women workers who generated both the highest rates of surplus value for capitalists and the maximum absolute amount of surplus value. This is in fact implicit throughout Marx's analysis. As Chattopadhyay writes: "Throughout the discussion of value determination by the quantity of abstract labour time going into a commodity, Marx refers to '*human* [*menschliche*] labour and not male [*männliche*] *labour*.' In other words, commodity-producing (abstract) labour, for Marx, is gender-neutral."[60] Marx is clear that women are more exploited within commodity production than men; but additionally, given the dynamics of the capital system and social mores, their social reproductive work in the household is expropriated (through the expropriation of time used for the production of use values and/or in consumption work for the realization of surplus), perpetuating much of the dependent condition imposed on women in the patriarchal family. The expropriation of nature and social reproductive labor lying in the "other hidden abodes" outside the sphere of commodity production, as Fraser puts it, becomes crucial to Marx's entire understanding of capital as a system.[61] Engels later observed that capital in Germany was able to maintain lower wages for workers because larger portions of the cost of reproducing labor power were carried out unpaid in the household—in effect producing higher rates of exploitation and higher profits by indirectly expropriating non-commodity labor.[62]

REGIMES OF SOCIAL REPRODUCTION

Building on the foregoing analysis, a comprehensive account of the capital system necessitates addressing the "background conditions of possibility," which includes the underlying relationships and conditions associated with social reproduction and ecological reproduction. As Fraser writes, "Social reproduction is an indispensable background condition for the possibility of economic [commodity] production in a capitalist society," where social reproduction and economic production are constituted as separate spheres.[63] Likewise, "Nature's capacity to support life and renew itself constitutes another necessary background condition for commodity production and capital accumulation."[64] Fraser stresses that these background conditions of capitalist valorization have a distinct "character of their own," but they interact and change with the historical development of the capital system, which manifest in distinct regimes of social reproduction.

István Mészáros, drawing upon Marx, illuminated the alienated relationships that emerge with these historic transformations of capital. As Marx explained, human beings, by necessity, mediate their relationship to nature through labor. In this metabolic relationship, in which substances are exchanged and in the process changed, humans both confront the nature-imposed conditions of the processes operating in the material world and influence these circumstances through labor and the associated structure of production. Capitalist class society, however, produces a set of second-order mediations—what Marx called "alienated mediations"—connected to commodity exchange, which result in the estrangement of humanity, labor, and nature.[65] According to Mészáros: "The *primary* social metabolic functions without which humanity could not possibly survive even in the most ideal form of society—from the biological reproduction of the individuals to the regulation of the conditions of economic and cultural reproduction—are crudely equated with their [alienated] capitalist varieties [second order mediations], no matter how problematical the latter may be." The specific forms of domination associated with these second-order mediations—for example, the double day imposed on women and the pervasive destruction of ecosystems—are then misrepresented as "'natural' and insurmountable," defying the mounting hardship and crises they entail.[66]

All this is associated with the splitting of production and reproduction, and operates through the twin processes of exploitation and expropriation. For Fraser, "expropriation is an ongoing, albeit unofficial [in terms of capitalist accounting], mechanism of accumulation, which continues alongside the official mechanism of exploitation."[67] This process is evident in the historic transformation of social reproduction and the patterns of expropriation.

As detailed earlier, during the Industrial Revolution in England, the conditions for social reproduction within the working-class family, which enabled the operation of the capitalist economy, were collapsing. "So dire was this situation," Fraser notes,

> that even such astute critics as Marx and Engels mistook this early head-on conflict between economic production and social reproduction for the final word. Imagining that capitalism had entered its terminal crisis, they believed that, as it eviscerated the

working-class family, the system was also eradicating the basis of women's oppression. But what actually happened was just the reverse: over time, capitalist societies found resources for managing the contradiction—in part by creating "the family" in its modern, restricted form; by inventing new, intensified meanings of gender difference; and by modernizing male domination.[68]

The splitting of reproduction and production becomes part of the constitution of the capital system—producing an alienated second-order mediation. While production depends on social reproduction, the latter is pushed to the boundary—the background—and serves as a realm of expropriation, on which the general system of capital accumulation depends.[69] The potential dissolution of the working-class family becomes a severe contradiction at the boundary of the system, as the social reproduction of workers is undermined. Fraser contends that efforts to address this key contradiction within the capital system led to three successive regimes of social reproduction following the early Industrial Revolution in England. "In each regime . . . the social reproductive conditions for capitalist production have assumed a different institutional form and embodied a different normative order: first 'separate spheres,' then 'the family wage,' now the 'two-earner family.'"[70]

The second half of the nineteenth century, in Fraser's account, saw the rise of a regime of "liberal competitive capitalism," in which the "separate spheres" of social reproduction and production are firmly established for the first time. The dissolution of the working-class family served as a boundary, creating a problem for the capital system, which was then in a volatile phase. A series of social and political changes took place to try to "protect" families, while securing further accumulation. Middle-class reformers, disturbed by what they saw as the "de-sexing" of working-class women and the societal "leveling" of the sexes caused by women's employment as factory operatives, pushed for legislation to protect women and children. During this period, social reproduction and economic production were defined by the system as separate spheres. Fraser explains that in "splitting off reproductive labor from the larger universe of human activities, in which women's work previously held a recognizable place," it was reduced to "a newly institutionalized 'domestic sphere,' where its social importance was obscured."[71] These efforts were accompanied by ideological justifications of male domination, in which it was asserted that men were the breadwinners and women were housewives. This position further amplified the fact that "women had to share a subordinate position in every social class without exception."[72]

Legislation such as the Ten-Hour-Day Bill and various Factory Acts made attempts to mitigate the exploitation of women and children in industry, which also played into the patriarchal ideology of the time. However, state legislation for protection was fraught with contradictions, given the larger context of economic production and the fact that the whole regulatory apparatus needed to establish a fully developed family-wage system had not yet been developed.[73] The establishment of "separate spheres" was problematic given racial, ethnic, gender, and class divisions. Wages for industrial workers (men and women) remained low, and the absence of additional wages undermined social reproduction, which was further exacerbated by industrial pollution and poor-quality food. Lost wages were not replaced by additional support from the state, limiting actual changes in the conditions families confronted. The regime of liberal competitive capitalism was thus defined in part by the formal, but not real, subsumption of reproductive work to the needs of the capitalist system.[74]

For ecofeminist Mies, whose analysis in *Patriarchy and Accumulation on a World Scale* provides a global counterpart to the same argument, the "housewifization"—the creation of the separate spheres of "breadwinner" and "housewife"—in this period was intimately connected to the emergence of imperialism and super-exploitation on a truly global scale, traditionally associated with the transition from competitive to monopoly capitalism. This involved expropriating additional wealth to be concentrated at the center of the system, part of which was used to support a better-paid labor aristocracy and the whole emerging family-wage system. These changes included destroying the integrated reproductive-productive relations of indigenous peoples, decimating the productive capacities of colonies to create new markets for British textiles, maintaining systems of slavery as long as possible to enrich European capitalists, and establishing a system of unequal ecological exchange to continue the robbing of the Global South.[75]

What Fraser calls the regime of "state-managed capitalism," which is better understood in terms of monopoly capitalism, mainly arose after the Great Depression and Second World War and was characterized by the family wage.[76] During the monopoly-capitalist period, the state in the Global North played a larger role in regulating economic production and social reproduction, creating or expanding an array of "social welfare" programs and other forms of public spending (frequently in response to pressure from labor and other social movements), which institutionalized the "male-breadwinner/female-homemaker model of the gendered family." These reforms were directed toward bolstering the conditions of social reproduction, following a long period of mass unemployment, extreme labor exploitation and conflict, poor education, and familial hardships. It involved distributing some of the surplus generated during a period of unusually high rates of economic growth and business unionism. At the same time, an overarching concern of monopoly capitalism was the realization of surplus value, especially given the increasing scale of commodity production and the mechanization of production in general.[77] This was the context in which the family wage became the norm, at least in relatively privileged, largely white sectors of the working class, particularly in the United States.

During the mid-twentieth century, monopoly capital greatly expanded and developed the sales effort.[78] Figures like Harry Braverman and Susan Strasser highlighted how monopoly capitalism, in the words of the former, transformed households, as it "penetrated into the daily life of the family and the community."[79] The expansion of the capital system created the universal market, whereby household provisioning and food production—and eventually recreation, entertainment, elderly care, clothing, services, etc.—were increasingly obtained through the marketplace. Batya Weinbaum and Amy Bridges explain that with the separation of spheres and the establishment of a family wage, "the reproduction of labor in *capitalist* societies requires that the products and services produced with a view to profit be gathered and transformed so that they may meet socially determined needs." In this way, capital sought to qualitatively transform social reproductive work to aid in the realization of surplus value, adding "consumption work for women."[80] Given the gendered division of labor in households, the increased "free" time allotted to women for social reproduction ended up realizing surplus value, serving the needs of a system of capital faced with saturated markets, rather than fulfilling human needs. Fraser emphasizes that "social-reproductive activity is absolutely necessary to the existence of waged work, the accumulation of surplus value and the functioning of capitalism as such."[81] Yet under monopoly capitalism, socially reproductive work is much more geared to the realization of surplus value than toward meeting the elemental needs of the family.

Here there is a shift toward the real subsumption of social reproductive work made possible by the institutionalization, for a time, of the family wage for relatively privileged sectors of the working class.[82] Clearly, for many families of color in the United States, this condition never really applied: "Women of color found low-waged work raising the children and cleaning the homes of 'white' families at the expense of their own."[83] The resources that helped support the family wage and social entitlement programs were also reliant upon the "ongoing expropriation from the periphery (including the periphery within the core)." The lands of indigenous peoples throughout the world were expropriated to support "development projects," such as the construction of dams. Additionally, throughout the Global South, capital engaged in the superexploitation of labor and the extreme expropriation of social reproductive work, relying on the position of "semiproletarianized" households, such as families with access to small parcels of land to grow food, to help meet the reproductive needs not met by wages—essential to many migrant labor systems.[84]

The most recent social reproduction regime depicted by Fraser, the two-earner family, emerged in relation to "globalized financialized capitalism." This period of global monopoly-finance capital and neo-liberalism is marked by privatization of public goods and the erosion or elimination of many of the social programs that supported social reproduction. It has involved the reincorporation and recruitment of relatively privileged working-class women into the paid workforce, in part due to inflation, declining real wages for working-class families, and increasing household debt, as well as to shifts in social norms inspired by feminist movements. Less privileged working-class women, who always had to work, find additional jobs in the expanding service and care sectors.

More hours of paid work are thus required to support families, causing a pinch on the time available for domestic labor. Fraser notes that a consequence of this "is a new, *dualized* organization of social reproduction, commodified for those who can pay for it and privatized for those who cannot, as some in the second category provide care work in return for (low) wages for those in the first."[85] Rather than closing the care gap, this situation creates a deficit, reminiscent of mid-nineteenth-century capitalism. Working-class women are caught in the double day, whereby they bear the responsibility both for earning wages and for unpaid household work.[86]

Efforts to address this "care gap" have been heavily racialized, as migrant workers "take on reproductive and caring labor previously performed by more privileged women. But to do this, the migrants must transfer their own familial and community responsibilities to other, still poorer caregivers, who must in turn do the same," and so on throughout the global hierarchy of nations.[87]

All these processes are "intensifying capitalism's inherent contradiction between economic production and social reproduction."[88] In contrast to the previous social reproduction regimes, whereby the state was used as a means of social protection, the state is firmly under the thumb of neoliberal monopoly-finance capital. Social reproduction is being transgressed in a way that is "systematically expropriating the capacities available for sustaining connections." Hence Fraser stresses that "the boundary dividing social reproduction from economic production has emerged as a major site and central stake of social struggle"—leaving open the question of what may emerge from this current care crisis.

SOCIAL AND ECOLOGICAL METABOLISMS

The logic of capital accumulation is that of a system that systematically expropriates its natural and social conditions of production while externalizing its costs on everything outside the circuit of capital— including its own conditions of production.[89] This is manifested in a continual, if shifting, *care crisis* in the realm of social reproduction and a deepening *metabolic rift* with respect to ecological reproduction. Moreover, both increasingly take on more global-imperial dimensions. This is recognized by Fraser, who sees the "boundary struggles" of capitalism entailing not only the expropriation in various ways in different periods of social reproductive labor, but also "the free-riding on nature." As she puts it:

> Structurally, capitalism assumes—indeed, inaugurates—a sharp division between a natural realm, conceived as offering a free, unproduced supply of "raw material" that is available for appropriation [expropriation], and an economic realm, conceived as a sphere of value, produced by and for human beings. . . . Capitalism brutally separated human beings from natural, seasonal rhythms, conscripting them into industrial manufacturing, powered by fossil fuels and profit-driven agriculture, bulked up by chemical fertilizers. Introducing what Marx called a "metabolic rift," it inaugurated what has now been dubbed the Anthropocene, an entirely new geological era in which human activity has a decisive impact on the earth's ecosystems and atmosphere.[90]

These struggles over social as well as ecological reproduction— along with those over global-imperial hegemony—are what Mészáros was primarily concerned with in raising the question of the system of social metabolic reproduction. Today this problem is brought to the fore by the "activation of capital's absolute limits," with respect to the system's fundamental boundaries: the microcosm of the household, the imperial system, and the Earth System. As a creatively destructive metabolic order, the capital system expropriates its own conditions of production, externalizing the costs onto its social and natural environment. In this way, progress turns into retrogression. Both social reproduction theory and Marxian ecology have discovered this in different ways. Both point to the fact that, as Mészáros emphasized, we need to replace the current alienated system of social metabolic reproduction with an entirely different one aimed at substantive equality.[91] A similar view is offered by Salleh, who argues that crises of social reproduction and the metabolic rift are intrinsically related, and that working-class women's struggles over social reproductive labor, when joined with what might be called the emergence of an "environmental proletariat"—a broad, unified coalition of working humanity in revolt against ecological degradation and social exploitation—constitutes the key to constructive revolutionary change. Here we can see an emerging synthesis in Marxist and revolutionary feminist theory, centering on "the human-nature metabolism."[92]

Conclusion

In the normal operations of capitalist production, according to Marx,

> every sense organ is injured by the artificially high temperatures, by the dust-laden atmosphere, by the deafening noise, not to mention the danger to life and limb among machines which are so closely crowded together, a danger which, with the regularity of the seasons, produces its list of those killed and wounded in the industrial battle. The economical use of the social means of production, matured and forced as in the hothouse by the factory system, is turned in the hands of capital into systemic robbery of what is necessary for the life of the worker while he

is at work, i.e. space, light, air and protection against the dangerous or the unhealthy concomitants of the production process,
not to mention the theft of the appliances for the comfort of the
worker.[93]

This robbery of the male and female worker's health within the
workplace naturally carries over into the realm of the household and
the social reproduction of labor power. In Marx's day, the demands
put on the workers in industry tended to annihilate whatever time
there was for the reproduction of labor power. By the late nineteenth
century, however, capital had at least formally created separate, alienated spheres of housewife and breadwinner—firmly establishing the
two realms of housework and paid work outside the home—thereby
altering the conditions in both spheres. This transformed the family
itself under monopoly capitalism, resulting in the relative rather than
absolute expropriation of time within the household—though giving
way in the most recent neoliberal period to new forms of absolute
expropriation. Likewise, capital dealt with its first ecological crises
(the degradation of the soil and rapacious deforestation) by means
of new alienated mediations (synthetic fertilizers), which in the long
run were to reappear as crucial aspects of a global metabolic rift that
degrades nature even further.

What is required in these circumstances is a struggle that will
challenge capital's subjection of reproductive labor, its colonization
of the people of the planet, and its degradation of the earth itself.[94]
In this view, if the revolutionary struggle for socialism in the past
failed, it is because it was not revolutionary enough, and did not take
on the capital system and its particular social metabolic reproduction as a whole. It did not demand the reconstitution of human labor
based on a society of associated producers and a world of creative
labor—aimed at the fulfillment of human potential, while rationally
regulating the human metabolism with nature so as to protect the
earth for future generations. It did not embrace the full diversity of
human life and of the natural environment.[95] In our age, the revolutionary Anthropocene, such a mistake cannot be repeated.

4

Marx as a Food Theorist

Hunger is hunger; but the hunger that is satisfied by cooked meat eaten with a knife and fork differs from hunger that devours raw meat with the help of hands, nails and teeth.

—KARL MARX

FOOD HAS BECOME a core contradiction of contemporary capitalism.[1] Discussions of the economics and sociology of food and food regimes seem to be everywhere today, with some of the most important contributions made by Marxian theorists.[2] Amid plentiful food production, hunger remains a chronic problem, and food security is now a pressing concern for many of the world's people.

Yet despite the severity of these problems and their integral relation to the capitalist commodity system, it is generally believed that Karl Marx contributed little to our understanding of food beyond a few general comments on subsistence and hunger. In their 1992 introduction to *The Sociology of Food*, Stephen Mennell, Anne Murcott, and Anneke H. van Otterloo declared that "food as such is only of passing interest to Marx," quipping that the only mention of "'diet' in an index of Marx's writings" referred "to a political assembly."[3]

To be sure, the capitalist food regime at the time of the Industrial Revolution was far less developed than our own, and hence had only just begun to be theorized, by Marx and others. Nevertheless, Marx was such a keen observer of the political economy of capitalism and the metabolism of nature and society that lack of an analysis of food would represent a surprising and significant gap in his work. We will show that Marx in fact developed a detailed and sophisticated critique of the industrial food system in Britain in the mid-nineteenth century, in the period that historians have called "the Second Agricultural Revolution."[4] Not only did he study the production, distribution, and consumption of food; he was the first to conceive of these as constituting a problem of changing food "regimes"—an idea that has since become central to discussions of the capitalist food system.

As will become clear, food for Marx was far more than a "passing interest": in his work one finds analyses of the development of agriculture in different modes of production; climate and food cultivation; the chemistry of the soil; industrial agriculture; livestock conditions; new technologies in food production and preparation; toxic additives in food products; food security; and much more. Moreover, these issues are not peripheral, but organically connected to Marx's larger critique of capitalism.

Since Marx's analysis of food production and food regimes was not developed in a single text but integrated into his larger critique, which remained unfinished, and in some cases unpublished, it is understandable that many commentators have missed this aspect of his work altogether. Yet these issues were far from marginal to Marx, as he based his materialist conception of history on the notion of humans as corporeal beings, who needed, as "the first premise of human existence," to produce their means of subsistence, beginning with food, water, shelter, clothing, and extending to all of the other means of life.[5] "All labour," he wrote in *Capital*, "is originally first directed towards the appropriation and production of food."[6]

In outlining Marx's analysis of the commodification of food in capitalist society, we will proceed from food consumption to food production and food regimes, and finally to fundamental problems of the soil and the social metabolism of human beings and nature. The object here is to overturn the prevailing view, which focuses simply on questions of the cheapness of food and the irrational forms of food consumption prevalent in contemporary society, and to replace this with a deeper perspective that locates the contemporary food regime in the underlying material conditions of capitalist production, understood as an alienated metabolism of nature and society.[7]

THE FOOD COMMODITY

In his discussions of food consumption under capitalism, Marx is directly concerned less with consumption by the upper classes than with the nutritional intake of the great majority of the population, namely the working class, both urban and rural. Now, as in Marx's day, our knowledge of the diet of the Victorian working class relies primarily on official studies commissioned by John Simon, the Chief Medical Health Officer of the Privy Council, and the leading medical authority in England. Simon, whom Marx much admired, organized the first major investigations into British public health, and this research was the main source for Marx's epidemiological knowledge of the English working class in the 1860s.

In his 1983 book *Endangered Lives*, Anthony Wohl describes what Simon and his medical teams discovered about the working-class diet:

> As in the country, so in the town, the staples were bread, potatoes, and tea. . . . If the rural poor ate birds then the urban poor ate pairings of tripe, slink (prematurely born calves), or broxy (diseased sheep). . . . Stocking weavers, shoe makers, needle women and silk weavers ate less than one pound of meat a week and less than eight ounces of fats. Bread formed the mainstay of their diet with a weekly consumption which varied from almost eight pounds a head in the case of the needlewomen to over twelve pounds per adult among the 2,000 or so agricultural labourers in [Edward] Smith's survey. Large numbers of workmen were getting their carbohydrates and calories mainly in bread—over two pounds of it daily! Dr. Buchanan, another of John Simon's team at the Privy Council's medical department, sadly concluded that

there were "multitudes of people . . . whose daily food consists at every meal of tea and bread, bread and tea." . . .

While the total calorific intake might have been generally adequate, the Victorian working-class diet was heavy in carbohydrates and fats, low in protein, and deficient in several vitamins, notably C and D. Nearly all the diets investigated reveal a serious lack of fresh green vegetables, a low protein intake, and very little fresh milk. . . . For approximately one-third of the entire population there would be a ten-year period or so when the children were too young to contribute significantly to the family income, during which the family would be underfed. This must be put within the context of Victorian life-long working hours, often arduous physical labour, and long walks to and from work. Modern nutritional studies show that adults walking a distance to work and engaged in strenuous activity may use 3,700 or more calories a day [compared to an intake of "only 2,099 calories *per capita* for the working-class family"], and that the body uses up far more calories when recovering from sickness.[8]

It is in this context of a class-based Victorian system and its effects on the working class that Marx's discussions of food and nutrition should be viewed. In *Capital*, he reproduced tables compiled by Simon and his associates showing the inadequate nutritional intake of workers in the industrial towns, noting that employees of Lancashire factories barely received the minimum amount of carbohydrates, while unemployed workers received even less, and both employed and underemployed received less than the minimum quantity of protein. More than a quarter of the factory operatives surveyed consumed no milk in an average week. The weekly quantity of bread per worker varied from around eight pounds for needlewomen to eleven and a half pounds for shoemakers, amounting to an average of almost ten pounds of bread. The average meat intake per worker, in contrast, was just 13.6 ounces per week. Agricultural workers were likewise deprived of the minimum "carbonaceous food" (carbohydrates, high in energy) and "nitrogenous food" (protein rich). Of all agricultural workers in the United Kingdom, those in England were the worst fed.[9]

"The diet of a great part of the families of agricultural labourers," Marx wrote, "is below the minimum necessary to 'avert starvation diseases.'" Drawing on a study by one of Simon's researchers, Dr. Smith, that surveyed the nutritional intake of convicts, Marx constructed a statistical table on the nutrition of various workers, and the results were startling: agricultural laborers received only 61 percent as much protein, 79 percent as much non-nitrogenous nutrients, and 70 percent as much mineral matter as convicts did, while laboring twice as much. Marx considered the findings so important that he devoted the first two pages of his 1864 "Inaugural Address of the International Working Men's Association" to presenting some of these results.[10]

Frederick Engels was equally concerned with nutrition. In 1845 he had pointed in *The Condition of the Working Class in England* to the artificial food scarcity and inflated prices that contributed to the poor nutritional intake of urban workers, along with problems of contamination and spoilage. He treated scrofula as a disease related to nutritional deficiencies—an observation that, as Howard Waitzkin explains in *The Second Sickness*, "antedated the discovery of bovine tuberculosis as the major cause of scrofula and pasteurization of milk as a preventive measure." Likewise, Engels discussed the skeletal deformities associated with rickets as a nutritional problem long before the medical discovery that it was due to deficiencies in vitamin D.[11]

Marx went beyond looking simply at the quantity and type of food and nutrients workers consumed; he also dealt with questions of food degradation, additives, and toxins, all associated with the transformation of food into a commodity. In the nineteenth century such discussions fell under the heading of "adulteration," which classically carried a wider meaning than it does today, referring not only to mixing something else into a food, but more pejoratively to the "corruption or debasement by spurious admixture."[12] The questions of what goes into food and why—basic problems of contemporary food analysis—arose here. Engels had raised these issues in *The Condition of the Working Class in England*, where he argued that the frequent adulteration of food was a key problem in nutrition. He cited an article from the *Liverpool Mercury* that explained that sugar was often mixed with a chemical substance from soap; cocoa was adulterated with dirt and mutton fat; and pepper was "adulterated with dust from husks."[13]

Marx's critique of adulteration in *Capital* transcended Engels's earlier work, reflecting the more detailed data and improved science of the 1860s, which made clear the degradation of commodified food being fed to workers and even to the middle class. Factory owners, food manufacturers, and shopkeepers took advantage of working-class customers by adulterating food products—not simply by watering them down, but by incorporating deceptive, dangerous, and even toxic ingredients into their production, and reducing their nutritive value, all to save costs and enhance their saleability. In researching this problem, Marx relied especially on the work of Arthur Hill Hassall, the pioneering Victorian scholar of food adulteration. Marx also drew on a report of H. S. Tremenheere, a Royal Commissioner charged with studying the conditions of journeymen bakers, as well as two parliamentary reports on food adulteration, published in 1862 and 1874, and the work of the French chemist Jean-Baptiste-Alphonse Chevallier.[14]

Hassall, a London physician, was the first to use a microscope effectively to detect food adulteration. He had already made a pioneering contribution in 1850 with *A Microscopic Examination of the Water Supplied by the Inhabitants of London and the Suburban Districts*, showing "for the first time," in the words of Mary P. English, "the mass of organic refuse and living animalcules in the drinking water of the metropolis." It was Hassall's technique that would be employed by surgeon Edwin Lankester (the father of E. Ray Lankester, Charles Darwin and Thomas Henry Huxley's protégé, and Marx's friend) in his investigations of the 1854 cholera outbreak in Soho—during which Lankester played a key role in the discovery of the waterborne source of the disease.[15] Hassall himself was invited to deliver a report to Parliament on the 1854 cholera epidemic, resulting in his dramatic *Report on the Microscopical Examination of Different*

Waters (Principally Those Used in the Metropolis) During the Cholera Epidemic of 1854, which included twenty-seven enlarged engravings of microscopic samples of the city's water supply.

Hassall soon turned to the study of food adulteration, and, with the encouragement of *Lancet* editor Thomas Wakley, published a series of articles on the topic. In 1851–54, he made a microscopic analysis of 2,500 food and drink samples. Hassall was able to detect alum—toxic in large doses, used for whitening—in bread; iron and mercury in pepper; copper in bottled pickles and fruits; and iron oxide in potted meats, fish, and sauces. Inspired by Hassall, Lankester published a 103-page book titled *A Guide to the Food Collection in the South Kensington Museum*. In it he presented the details of food adulteration, listing over eighty common substances used to adulterate various foods and drinks. Lankester's list included over forty mineral substances, such as lead carbonate (or white lead) and carbonate of copper, used in tea; red lead (or lead chromate) used in cocoa; and chalk used in sugar. Hassall's work, including his 1857 *Adulterations Discovered; Or, Plain Instructions for the Discovery of Frauds in Food and Medicine*, which was utilized by Marx, led to the various parliamentary inquiries into adulteration.[16]

Hassall defined adulteration as "the intentional addition to an article, for purposes of gain or deception, of any substance or substances the presence of which is not acknowledged in the name under which the article is sold." He noted that such practices were often excused on the basis that customers wanted them, as in the use of "various pigments" to color food. The public was kept ignorant of the fact that these colors were "produced by some of the most poisonous substances known." In estimating the "effects of adulteration on health," Hassall emphasized "that some of the metallic poisons used are what are called *cumulative*"—that is, they accumulate in the body. Moreover, "the great cause which accounts for the larger part of the adulteration which prevails," he wrote, "is the desire of increased profit."[17]

Marx traced such food adulteration to class. He quoted Tremenheere to the effect that "the poor man, who lives on two pounds of bread a day, does not now get one-fourth part of nourishing matter, let alone the deleterious effects on his health." The bread, particularly of the poor, was commonly "adulterated with alum, soap, pearl-ash [potassium carbonate], chalk, Derbyshire stone-dust and other similar . . . ingredients."[18] As Marx noted, "the bread of the poor" was quite different from that of the rich. Produced in "holes" underground, as opposed to the "finest bakeries," loaves bought by the poor were far more likely to be subjected to "the adulteration of the flour with alum and bone earth."[19] By the early years of the Industrial Revolution, according to Marxian historian E. P. Thompson, bread production was characterized by three kinds of loaves: the finer white loaf for the wealthy, the intermediate "'household' loaf" for the middle class, and the brown loaf, full of waste, for the poor: "Dark bread was suspect as offering easy concealment for noxious additives." All but the finest bread, available only to the rich, was adulterated, and even in high-end bakeries the quality of the bread and the conditions under which it was produced were suspect.[20] As Marx put it:

Englishmen, with their good command of the Bible, knew well enough that man, unless by elective grace a capitalist, or a landlord, or the holder of a sinecure, is destined to eat his bread in the sweat of his brow, but they did not know that he had to eat daily in his bread a certain quantity of human perspiration mixed with the discharge of abscesses, cobwebs, dead cockroaches and putrid German yeast, not to mention alum, sand and other agreeable mineral ingredients.[21]

Here Marx was suggesting, based on his knowledge of the work of Tremenheere and Hassall, that some of these artificial additives such as alum and potassium carbonate, might be toxic in cumulative amounts.

Of course, much of this dangerous adulteration—the contamination from people, cobwebs, cockroaches, and rodents—arose from the unsanitary conditions in which bread was produced, particularly for the poor. In his study "Bread Manufacture," Marx stressed that the labor process compelled workers, in this case journeymen bakers, to begin work before midnight and complete their weekday shifts at 3 PM the next day, while on weekends they worked continuously from 10 PM on Thursday evening until Saturday evening without a break. The underground vaults where they worked were full of "pestilential vapors" and "noxious gases" that not only harmed the workers but entered the food.[22] The average life span of a working-class journeyman baker was just forty-two years.

The work of Chevallier provided another source for Marx's writings on food adulteration. Chevallier had shown that for each of 600 items he studied there were, in Marx's words, "10, 20, 30 different methods of adulteration"—not only in food and drink, but also medicine. The most widely used medication of the time, opium, was adulterated with "poppy heads, wheat flour, gum, clay, sand, etc." Some samples did not contain any trace of the drug at all.[23] The unhealthy and even poisonous contents of the Victorian working-class diet was thus a key concern of Marx's food analysis.

Wohl summed up the adulteration of food in Victorian England as follows:

> Much of the food consumed by the working-class family was contaminated and positively detrimental to health. . . . The list of poisonous additives reads like the stock list of some mad and malevolent chemist: strychnine, cocculus indicus (both are hallucinogens) and copperas in rum and beer; sulphate of copper in pickles, bottled fruit, wine, and preserves; lead chromate in mustard and snuff; sulphate of iron in tea and beer; ferric ferrocyanide, lime sulphate and turmeric in chinese tea; copper carbonate, lead sulphate, bisulphate of mercury, and Venetian lead in sugar confectionary and chocolate; lead in wine and cider; all were extensively used and were accumulative in effect, resulting, over a long period, in chronic gastritis, and indeed, often fatal food poisoning. Red lead gave Gloucester cheese its "healthy" red hue, flour and arrowroot a rich thickness to cream, and tea leaves were "dried, dyed, recycled again and again." As

late as 1877 the Local Government Board found that approximately a quarter of the milk it examined contained excessive water, or chalk, and ten per cent of all the butter, over eight per cent of the bread, and over 50 per cent of all the gin had copper in them to heighten the colour.[24]

Quoting Simon extensively, Marx argued that the dietary conditions of the working class were part of a larger dialectic of poverty, a symptom of the entrapment of the poor in capitalist society. As Simon wrote, "privation of food is very reluctantly borne . . . as a rule, great poorness of diet will only come when other privations have preceded it."[25]

Mennell, Murcott, and Otterloo's dismissal of Marx on food notwithstanding, diet clearly played an underappreciated role in Marx's analysis. Indeed, the issues that concerned Marx, including the nutrition of workers, and the profit-driven adulteration and contamination of food, still concern us today. Food security remains an urgent problem in the United States, affecting some 15.8 million households in 2016—around one in eight.[26] Only stringent federal regulations have kept the food supply relatively safe. But chemicals added to enhance color, flavor, or storage properties remain ubiquitous, and toxins in food, resulting from the introduction into the environment of some 80,000 new synthetic chemicals, not the product of evolution, are a major concern.[27] All of these problems are best understood in terms of the logic of capitalism, including its effects on food production and consumption, which Marx was already grappling with in the mid-nineteenth century.

FOOD REGIME CHANGE

Contemporary food-regime analysis as a formal subject of inquiry grew out of the Marxian and world-system traditions, particularly the work of Harriet Friedmann and Philip McMichael, in the late 1980s.[28] From the start, it centered on the notion of global food "regimes," based on specific and unequal distributions of power and resources, in contradistinction to mainstream analyses that depicted the history of food systems as a process of linear, continuous development and expansion.[29] The concept of the food regime thus stood for the historical specificity of given arrangements of production, exchange, distribution, and consumption. Friedman and McMichael focus on two regimes: the first, which in their analysis began in the 1870s, depended on colonial tropical imports to Europe, and on imports of grain and livestock from the settler colonies—in other words, a global system dictated by the needs of the metropolitan countries. The second food regime, emerging after the Second World War with the rise of U.S. hegemony and a postcolonial, if still imperialist, world, was organized around the export of surplus food, mainly grain, from the United States, and by the Green Revolution, dominated by agribusiness. Also important in the development of this second global food regime were exports to the wealthy countries of tropical fruits, especially bananas, and later of orange juice concentrate (mainly from Brazil), coffee, cacao for chocolate, spices, and so on. Other scholars have since tried to define a third, current food regime, in which globalization and emerging economies play an increasing role. Marx's theory of metabolic rift has been incorporated into some of these theories as a way of explaining disjunctures in food regimes.[30]

The biggest weakness of food-regime analysis has been its approach to agriculture during the Industrial Revolution, including its response to Marx's analysis. In 1996, Colin Duncan, a Canadian scholar with a background in Marxian theory, published *The Centrality of Agriculture*, in which he contended that mid-nineteenth-century agriculture in Britain remained in essence "preindustrial," or at most "light-industrial," and represented an "ecologically balanced age" in farming—rooted in the famous Norfolk four-course system of crop rotation.[31] Duncan strongly rejected Marx's critical analysis of British agriculture in this period, claiming that he had seen only its flaws, and failed to recognize its preindustrial, self-sufficient, and ecologically sound character. In advancing these ideas, Duncan rejected not only Marx, but also set aside the work of contemporary economic and agricultural historians who had reached conclusions that largely supported Marx's critical view.[32]

Duncan began his book by contending that Marx was "alarmist" about the ecological effects of capitalism in his time. In particular, he argued that Marx's adoption of the German chemist Justus von Liebig's notion of the "robbing of the soil," was "quite untenable in general and indeed . . . probably nowhere less appropriate than in the case of England the ostensible case study for *Capital*." Duncan insisted that the English model of high farming in the mid-nineteenth century, based on new scientific methods of cropping, was the "most ecologically benign among all the highly productive farming systems the world has seen." Innovations in British high farming remained preindustrial or protoindustrial, in his view, since they relied very little on mechanization and artificial chemicals, instead focusing on the development of biological or ecological technique. Notably, Duncan sought to glorify English agriculture of this period while ignoring the rest of the British Isles, including a colonized Irish agriculture—as if these could be separated. Nor did he give any real attention to English livestock raising, or the provision of fertilizer and what he called the "crypto-industrial" aspects of oil cake manufacture. Duncan considered the mechanization of agricultural technology "negligible"—a view that hardly took into account the changing reality.[33]

Such an obviously deficient analysis might well have been ignored by subsequent scholars. But Duncan's vision of the "ecologically benign" character of English agriculture, including his criticisms of Marx, have been enthusiastically and uncritically adopted by Marxian food-regime analysts and world-system theorists, such as Friedmann and McMichael. In her 2000 essay "What on Earth Is the Modern World-System?" Friedmann argued, following Duncan, that "English High Farming demonstrates that under specific conditions . . . capitalist agriculture was ecologically sustainable." In terms of energy, she contended, English high farming "achieved the most productive and sustainable wheat farming ever known." (The source cited in support of this statement, however, was a study of agriculture in England in the 1820s, *prior* to the advent of high farming.) What destroyed English high farming, she argued, was not its internal ecological contradictions but its struggle to compete on the world market, especially

with the advent of what was then known as the Great Depression in
Europe, in the final quarter of the nineteenth century. This exposure
to "alien ecosystems," that is, competition from ecosystems outside
England, along with the intrusion of the world-market system, meant
that "high farmers [were] prevented from continuing their ecologically benign mix of domestic species."[34]

Duncan's criticisms of Marx on English high farming were likewise
taken up by Mindi Schneider and McMichael, who repeated the claim
that it was the most ecologically sustainable form of high-productivity agriculture in history, and that its four-course rotation efficiently
recycled nutrients. In the Norfolk rotation, wheat was grown in the
first year, turnips in the second, barley, with clover and ryegrass
undersown, in the third, and the clover and ryegrass grazed in the
fourth. Turnips were fed to the cattle in the winter. The clover fixed
nitrogen in the soil. Schneider and McMichael cited the existence of
such a rotation as evidence of the ecological soundness of English
high farming.

Marx's analysis of agriculture under capitalism, Schneider and
McMichael argued, following Duncan and Friedman, was therefore
flawed and distorted, even in relation to his own time. Marx, they said,
mistook the problems of soil for universal conditions, and "failed to
understand soil formation as a historical process"—though here they
overlooked the fact that Marx was a close student of the geology of soil
formation and referred throughout his works to soils as *historical* products, unlike most earlier classical political economists. Schneider and
McMichael consequently dismissed the historical relevance of Marx's
theory of metabolic rift, drawn from the work of Liebig, in which the
soil was depleted of its nutrients as food and fiber were sent to the
cities. As they put it: "The success and relative ecological sustainability
of England . . . challenge Marx." They charged that he "neglected to
include agriculture as a primary driver of the mechanisms of the metabolic rift." Rather, he made the error of focusing on the *industrialization*
of agriculture as a disruptive force, turning a blind eye to the "centrality
of agriculture" and its almost complete independence from industry in
this period, as was later propounded by Duncan.[35]

It is worth digressing somewhat to note that the Norfolk four-year rotation, the basis for most of the foregoing claims for the ecological superiority of English agriculture, did have some advantages, but still generated problems, and in any case was never universally applied, and was only one of multiple agricultural methods in use at the time. First, the benefits: (1) Only in two of the four years (in the cases of wheat and barley) did large quantities of products—and therefore nutrients—leave the farm. (2) The rotation facilitated pest control, including weeds, diseases, and insects. (3) Nitrogen fixation by legumes was what made the system sustainable; otherwise lower levels of available nitrogen would have decreased yields of the other crops. It is true, then, that a mixed animal-crop system can be more ecologically sound than a cropping system by itself.

But there were also drawbacks: (1) Nutrients were still being exported from farms in two of the four years, and they needed to be replaced. Of course, not that many nutrients per hectare were exported in animal products in such a system, because most passed right through the animal in the form of manure and urine, which, if captured and returned by farmers to the fields, could significantly limit this loss of nutrients. (2) The whole system was not motivated by sustainability but by increasing production and capital accumulation. It thus gave way, especially after the abolition of the Corn Laws, to a high-farming system governed by the massive inputs of fertilizers. As economic historian Mark Overton has written, "The development of chemical fertilizers and other external inputs" undermined the system, creating an agriculture that "depended on energy-intensive inputs."[36]

Indeed, rather than identifying high farming of the mid-nineteenth century with the Norfolk rotation, which had already long been in use, it should be seen as an overlay of intensive energy imports on the crop rotation system, culminating in the decline of grain production itself. As agricultural historian E. L. Jones explained, the main innovation of high farming, or more accurately "high feeding," was

intensity of operation, the feeding of purchased oilcake to the livestock on a lavish scale, to produce both meat and dung; the latter, with purchased agricultural fertilizers, in turn lavished on the arable land to promote high yields of grain, and fodder crops for the stock. The greater the scale of feeding farm-grown and bought-in fodder, and the heavier the applications of farm-produced and purchased fertilizer, the more the saleable produce and the more manure for the next round of cropping, that is, the higher the farming. This was the "expanding circle" that [John Joseph] Mechi [the most famous proponent of high farming] advocated.[37]

The disappearance of anything like food self-sufficiency was implicit in the increased emphasis on meat and dairy production over cereal production after 1846, leading to the growth of pasturage, particularly in Scotland and Ireland, and marked the decline of the more sustainable, mixed animal-crop system. Although the growth of pasturage and of an agriculture centered on meat production in some ways alleviated the soil nutrient problem, since a ruminant-based system of food production can recycle nutrients more efficiently, it was only possible as a result of a shift to imports of wheat and other grains. In effect, a large part of the British metabolic rift was transferred abroad, to the main exporters of grain to Britain—Germany, Russia, and the United States—depleting their own soils and permitting the British to concentrate on sheep and cattle.[38]

By the 1870s, imports of guano and nitrates began to drop, while imports of bones, oil cakes, and seeds for domestic oil cake production continued to skyrocket. The decreased reliance on guano and nitrate imports reflected England's shift during the "golden age" away from domestic grain production. However, imports of bones continued to increase, primarily as inputs for the superphosphate industry, the first chemical fertilizer. Likewise, oil cakes and seeds for their production were increasingly imported as high-energy imports fed to cattle to spur growth and yield a richer manure.[39] At the same time, as part of the same logic, Britain was importing more and more of its wheat, to be consumed primarily by the working class.

The historical sequence is thus clear. Following the repeal of the Corn Laws in 1846, wheat imports soared, and by the end of the century the share of wheat in Britain produced domestically had fallen from 90 percent to less than 25 percent. In the 1860s while Marx was at work on *Capital*, British wheat imports had already risen to more than a third of domestic consumption.[40] The writing was already on the wall for English agriculture, which would be done in by an unbalanced emphasis on livestock, a vastly expanded land area devoted to pasturage, and the massive infusion of grain, fertilizer, and energy inputs from abroad. With this history in mind, it becomes clear that the criticisms of Marx by Duncan, Schneider, and McMichael not only missed the larger context of Marx's analysis but also ignored the wider body of research on the history of British agriculture. Although the notion of a "golden age" of English agriculture in the third quarter of the nineteenth century was common in the work of economic historians in the early twentieth century, subsequent scholarship overturned this idea well before Duncan wrote his book.

Far from ignoring the question of food regimes, Marx can be credited with introducing into political economy the concept of what he himself called the "new regime" of industrial-capitalist food production, connected to the repeal of the Corn Laws and the triumph of free trade after 1846. He associated this "new regime" with the conversion of "large tracts of arable land in Britain," driven by the "reorganization" of food production around developments in livestock breeding and management, and by crop rotation, coupled with related developments in the chemistry of manure-based fertilizers. In the mid-1850s, these trends were already apparent: close to 25 percent of wheat consumed in Britain was imported, 60 percent of it from Germany, Russia, and the United States.[41] The 1830s and 1840s had been characterized by a soil fertility crisis, due to the lack of fertilizers to replace the nutrients shipped as food and fiber to the cities and thus lost to the soil. Hence, in addition to new forms of stock management and breeding and the system of crop rotation, the "new regime" was characterized by intensified efforts to augment fertilizers, partly by chemical means, partly by imports of guano and other natural fertilizers. Guano imported from Peru was not only rich in phosphates, but also had as much as thirty times the nitrogen of most manures.[42] The use of legumes as part of the rotation system helped provide at least some of the needed nitrogen for grains and turnips. On top of all this was the increased use of machinery in agriculture. Marx also emphasized that British agriculture, even within the British Isles, was an imperial system, particularly in English control of Irish agriculture; he noted that Irish "manure was also [in effect] exported" to England, and Ireland gained little or nothing in return—an early form of unequal ecological exchange.[43] In Marx's view, the industrialization of agriculture led initially to a period of progress, but carried with it deep ecological and economic contradictions, threatening the future of British agriculture.

Marx did not of course deny the initial economic advances achieved under the new regime of high farming. As he wrote in *Capital*:

> The repeal of the Corn Laws gave a marvelous impulse to English agriculture. Drainage on the most extensive scale, new methods of stall-feeding and the artificial cultivation of green crops, the introduction of mechanical manuring apparatus, new treatment of clay soils, increased use of mineral manures, employment of the steam-engine and all kinds of new machinery, more intensive cultivation in general, are all characteristic of this epoch. . . . The actual productive return [to capital] of the soil rose rapidly. Greater outlay of capital per acre, and as a consequence more rapid concentration of farms, were essential conditions of the new method. At the same time the area under cultivation increased from 1846 to 1856.[44]

Nevertheless, Marx was deeply concerned with the contradictions and dangers of the new regime of food production. Two central issues, beyond the more general problem of the metabolic rift, stood out in his critique. The first was the shift in British agriculture from cereal and grain production for human consumption to increased pasturage and forage crops to supply an agriculture increasingly geared toward meat and dairy. Cereal or grain production was clearly aimed at feeding the working population, which, as described above, lived largely on bread; meat production, and to some extent dairy, primarily fed the upper classes. Nor was there any doubt, even then, which use of land—grain or meat and dairy—was most efficient in the overall production of food for human consumption.

Second, Marx also worried about the abuse of animals under new methods of breeding for meat and fat content, introduced by Robert Bakewell and others. Sheep and cattle breeds were developed to be rounder and broader, carrying larger loads of flesh and fat relative to bone structure, to the point that animals could often barely support their own weight. The growth rate of animals bred for meat production accelerated, with sheep and cattle subject to butchering after two rather than five years. Calves were weaned earlier, in order to increase dairy industry production. English bullocks in the period were increasingly stall-fed and kept tightly confined. Cattle were fed a concoction of ingredients to speed up growth, including imported oil cakes, which produced a richer manure. Each bullock was fed some ten pounds of oil cake a day, and slaughtered the moment it reached maturity.[45]

Sheep still grazed on pastures in the high-farming system, forming a major part of the Norfolk system of crop rotation, in which legumes and cover crops replaced fallow fields. Legumes partially enriched the soil by fixing nitrogen from the atmosphere (a process that was not yet understood when Marx was writing). This, however, encouraged the growth of pasturage over grain production. The population working the land was further replaced by sheep—part of the process of the enclosure of communal land that was by then well developed in England and expanding elsewhere in the British Isles.

Marx's analysis of this new regime focused especially on the French agriculturalist Léonce de Lavergne's 1854 study *The Rural Economy of England, Scotland, and Ireland*. Lavergne was a strong supporter of the meat-based, dairy-based English high-farming model, with its Norfolk rotation, use of forage crops, and its enhanced and accelerated feeding, breeding, and butchering—all described in great detail in his work, which Marx studied closely, along with Walter Good's

1866 *Political, Commercial, and Agricultural Fallacies*. Lavergne contended that Bakewell, in showing how to speed the growth of meat and fat in animals, had established himself as an innovator on the level of Richard Arkwright and James Watt. Agriculture had decisively changed in the British Isles, Lavergne wrote, "from a natural [process into] more and more a manufacturing process; each field will henceforth be a kind of machine . . . the steam-engine sends forth its columns of smoke over the green landscapes."[46]

However, Marx rejected many of Lavergne's claims for the superiority of English high farming. Among these were Lavergne's assertions about soil nutrition and his emphasis on the advantages of meat and dairy-based food production. Marx noted the extreme deformities in animals, stall-feeding, earlier weaning of calves, and high levels of pasturage initiated by this new regime, in contrast to cereal and grain production for the general populace. While Lavergne argued that France should follow the English example and shift from grain to meat, Marx took the opposite view. He also emphasized the reliance of English agriculture on energy-intensive inputs from abroad, and stressed, based on the works of Good and Lavergne, that the English high-farming system shortened the turnover time for cattle, violating natural processes.[47]

The treatment of animals under the new regime was another critical issue for Marx. "The cattle, usually of the short-horned Durham breed," Lavergne observed, "are there shut up loose in boxes, where they remain till ready for the shambles. The flooring under them is pierced with holes, to allow their evacuations to fall into a trench below." In 1851 *The Economist* trumpeted the superiority of "box-feeding" of bullocks, which confined them almost completely to stalls.[48] All of this struck Marx, as he wrote in an unpublished notebook, as "Disgusting!" Feeding in stables, he declared, created a "system of cell prison" for the animals:

> In these prisons animals are born and remain there until they are killed off. The question is whether or not this system connected to the breeding system that grows animals in an abnormal way

by aborting bones in order to transform them to mere meat and a bulk of fat—whereas earlier (before 1848) animals remained active by staying under free air as much as possible—will ultimately result in serious deterioration of life force?[49]

This question, as Marx posed it, was more ecological than economic, and capitalist agriculture, with its emphasis on commodity value and purely instrumentalist orientation, could offer no answer. Nor was there room in the dominant attitude toward food production for sympathy toward animals, which were treated as mere machines or raw materials for human use.[50]

The new regime of industrial-capitalist agriculture, Marx suggested, led to further expropriation of land, since meat-based agriculture required fewer laborers than grain-based systems. This could be seen most dramatically in Ireland where, between 1855 and 1866, "1,032,694 Irishmen [were] displaced by about one million cattle, pigs, and sheep."[51] He noted similar developments in Scotland.[52] After the repeal of the Corn Laws, Ireland lost its grain monopoly within the English colonial tariff system, and hence grain was imported from outside the British Isles, while Irish fields lay waste. Marx dryly observed that Lavergne and his fellow bourgeois agronomists had suddenly discovered that Ireland, once thought fit only for growing grain, was destined by providence for pastures.[53] Marx's ultimate concerns in all of this were the food and nutrients available to the working class under the new system of industrialized agriculture.

As we have seen, Marx recognized that the new regime of high farming was initially characterized by significant growth, and that it contained deep internal contradictions that would lead to its eventual demise. Both insights anticipated the subsequent analyses of economic historians of British agriculture, who more than a century later arrived at the same conclusions. Since the high-farming system's contradictions were first highlighted, in 1968, by F. M. L. Thompson in his essay "The Second Agricultural Revolution," historians have largely repudiated the notion of a "golden age" of agriculture in England in the third quarter of the nineteenth century. As E. J. T.

Collins, co-editor of Part 7 (1850–1914) of the multivolume *Agrarian History of England and Wales*, wrote in 1995:

> By the early 1900s, Britain was importing over three quarters of its bread grain and nearly one half of its temperate foodstuffs, where a century before she had been almost self-sufficient. . . . In a number of important respects nineteenth century agriculture failed, not just in the Great Depression [the last quarter of the nineteenth century in Europe], but in the prior "Golden Age." . . . The High Farming period, 1850–73, is [conventionally] depicted as one of unprecedented technical progress. . . .
>
> Recent research [however] is now suggesting that agricultural growth rates were significantly higher in the second quarter of the century under the Corn Laws than in the third quarter, the Golden Age, suggesting that after an impressive start, the Second Agricultural Revolution and its new scientific husbandry quickly lost momentum. The trend is similar to that inferred from the national accounts, with one estimate suggesting an average annual growth rate of upwards of 1.5 percent between the 1830s and 1850s, falling to 0.5–0.7 percent over the following two decades, and another more recent one, a mere 0.2 percent between 1856 and 1873, compared with 2.0 percent for the whole economy. . . .
>
> After a strong performance in the second quarter [of the century], wheat yields levelled off from the later 1850s, and declined slightly between 1868 and 1880. . . . Not just the arable sector but . . . the livestock sector appears to have underperformed. Indeed, the agricultural evidence suggests only a modest improvement in meat output, of at best one per cent per annum, and between the early 1850s and later 1860s only a fraction of that. . . .
>
> By this reading the "Second Agricultural Revolution" would appear to have run out of steam long before the onset of the Great Depression [beginning in 1873]. Agricultural growth rates between 1850 and 1875 averaged, according to Collins, 0.8 percent per annum at most.[54]

Collins's explanation for the failure of English high farming was similar to Marx's: the inability to rapidly increase the productivity of the soil per hectare as required by the accumulation process, despite growing amounts of imported nutrients, a problem referred to as a "technological plateau."[55] The shift of food production from grains to sheep and cattle, which appeared to circumvent the metabolic rift, only exported it elsewhere, to those countries now feeding Britain with imported grain. High-energy inputs could not keep the new meat- and dairy-oriented economy from stagnating. Meanwhile, despite the Corn Law repeal, persistent high prices for grain plagued the economy in the mid-1850s, as Marx stressed. Collins writes that concerns about "food security in the third quarter of the century," were rampant. "Grain prices in the mid-1850s were higher than at any point since the 1810s and very little lower in the early and mid-1870s than in the 1840s. . . . The Golden Age, indeed, saw a resurgence of food riots. An unruly mob looted bakers' shops in Liverpool in February 1855, and disturbances broke out subsequently in London and Liverpool."[56] Hence, nothing could be further from the truth than the claim that British high farming represented a "golden age," a worldwide peak of self-sufficient, ecologically sustainable, high-productivity agriculture.

The Metabolic Rift and the New Regime of Food Production

At the root of food production for Marx was the question of the soil, and thus of soil chemistry, geology, agronomy, and other natural sciences. A given means of production, he argued, could be judged in part by the "means of nourishment" it derived from the soil.[57] Capitalism, while promoting increased productivity in agriculture, also caused a metabolic rift by robbing the soil of its nutrients.[58]

It is precisely here, however, that some on the left have faulted Marx's analysis. Ecosocialist Daniel Tanuro has criticized Marx for being "very ironical" regarding Lavergne's declaration that, in the latter's words, all the "principal elements" needed for the growth of forage plants could be obtained by them "from the atmosphere," suggesting that Marx, despite his close attention to soil chemistry, had made an error here—a fault that Tanuro oddly attributed to Marx having privileged Liebig's science over traditional knowledge.[59]

Here it is important to take a close look at the facts. In Lavergne's view, only cereal crops exhausted the soil, while forage crops that fed livestock were self-renewing.[60] Yet we now know that for almost all plants it is only carbon (via CO_2) that is derived from the atmosphere. This means that the other sixteen essential chemical elements have to be derived from the soil—except in the case of legumes, such as clover, alfalfa, peas, and beans, which can obtain *one* of the nutrients they need, nitrogen, by the symbiotic bacteria living in their root nodules, thereby drawing nitrogen gas (N_2) from the atmosphere and converting it to a form that plants can use. But legumes too are dependent on the soil for the other fifteen essential nutrients, and like all plants—as Marx following Liebig argued—they rob the soil of its nutrients.[61]

Given these basic conditions of soil chemistry, a strictly grass/legume system organized around ruminants could circumvent this by exporting fewer nutrients per unit of land. But this means that grains would need to be imported, because the system would no longer be self-sufficient in the production of food, and particularly the grains that fed the nineteenth-century working class. Moreover, the actual attempts constantly to *expand* production in the high-farming period within a livestock-based system required energy-intensive fertilizer inputs. When agriculture became a capitalist enterprise it needed to try to increase output and value added continuously just as in any other sector. Capitalism, as Marx emphasized, is the opposite of an ecologically self-sufficient system.

Criticisms of Marx's metabolic rift analysis by other leftist food-regime theorists are typically more wide-ranging and less precise, with no more basis in reality. Duncan wrote that "Marx thought guano was applied to English fields because their fertility had been exhausted. There is no evidence for this view. There is ample evidence, however, that English farmers were enthusiastic about getting more out of their land"—and for this reason alone they desired guano.[62]

But the fact is that the soil *had* been exhausted from its natural state. Normally during the first years following conversion of forest to agriculture, sufficient nutrients are available from nutrients stored in the soil for high crop yields. "It is only about twenty years," Marx noted in *The Poverty of Philosophy* in 1847, "since vast plots in the eastern counties of England were cleared; they had been left uncultivated from the lack of proper comprehension of the relation between the humus and the composition of the sub-soil." Thus farmers were often "enthusiastic" simply to return the fertility of soils to something close to its original level. Further, Duncan's point here ignores that Marx was writing about a system governed by capital accumulation, in which the failure to expand engenders crises. Farmers not only desired, but were required by the sanctions of the market, to extract more from the soil in each successive cycle of production, on pain of economic failure. This meant that a metabolic rift, caused by the intensive robbing of soil nutrients and a boom-and-bust cycle, was built into industrial-capitalist agriculture.[63] The system's underlying logic was to draw more and more energy inputs from outside the economy. This was well captured by the Doncaster Agricultural Assembly, which declared in 1828 that "one ton of German bone dust saves the importation of ten tons of German corn."[64]

The reality is that England imported 88,540 tons of guano in 1847–50, and 209,460 tons in 1868–71, showing a huge growth in intensity of the application of this natural fertilizer, far exceeding the growth rate of agriculture. The same could be said for bones and oilseed cakes, imports of which increased by similar proportions. This was a necessity driven by the intensive extraction of nutrients from the soil. It is for this reason that Good was to declare in 1866: "We have scoured the globe for raw bones" and guano.[65]

In this context, it is difficult to know what to make of Schneider and McMichael's claim, against Marx, that "English high farming was a sophisticated form of self-renewing agriculture."[66] It was, as we have seen, and as Marx indicated, a system that required massive net energy inputs in the form of fertilizers and material inputs from abroad that increased far more rapidly than did productivity in agriculture. It also required, even in the heyday of high farming, the massive and rapidly increasing import of wheat, the main staple of the populace. English agriculture in the "golden age" was geared more and more to meat production.

For Marx, the new regime of food production was *industrial*, in the sense that it relied heavily on the application of science to agriculture (in this case geology, chemistry, and physiology), heavy use of energy inputs, factory-like production, and a simplified, degraded division of both labor and nature.[67] Machinery, too, was increasingly applied, and while that machinery was initially powered by farm animals, not fossil fuels, the use of steam engines in agricultural production was beginning. Duncan's claim that English high farming was "pre-industrial" hence makes as little sense as it does to describe it as a self-sufficient and benign ecological system.[68]

All of this points to the power of Marx's theory of metabolic rift, which captures the reality of changing food regimes and ever shifting ecological crises. As Michael Carolan argues in *The Sociology of Food and Agriculture*, the key to theorizing "the ecological footprint of food systems" is Marx's "metabolic rift thesis." "Disconnecting people from the land," he continues,

> caused major disruptions in the soil nutrient cycle in the form of too few nutrients in the countryside and far too much in the cities, often in the form of sewage. . . . And the "solution" to this problem—was it to repair the rift by bringing agricultural practices in line with ecological limits? No; the solution was to exacerbate the rift through artificial fertilizers. This solution may have relieved certain tensions in the short term but it failed to deal with the root of the rift—namely, producing food in ways that ignore ecological limits.[69]

Marx's analysis of the new regime of food production in mid-nineteenth-century industrial Britain therefore takes us in a full dialectical circle. An examination of the conditions involved in the consumption of food nutrients leads to the question of the whole regime of industrial-capitalist food production, and from there to the issue of the soil and capitalism's alienated social metabolism. In Marx's own words: "Capitalist production . . . only develops the techniques and the degree of combination of the social process of production by simultaneously undermining the original sources of all wealth—the soil and the worker."[70]

5

Marx and Alienated Speciesism

FEW CONTEMPORARY scholarly controversies on the left are more charged than those surrounding Karl Marx's view of the status of animals in human society. Some left animal-rights scholars allege that Marx was *speciesist* in his early writings. Moreover, it is contended that, despite their later adherence to Darwinian views, Marx and Frederick Engels never fully transcended this deeply embedded speciesist outlook, which therefore infected historical materialism as a whole. These critics concentrate their objections primarily on the *Economic and Philosophical Manuscripts of 1844*, claiming that Marx presented an anthropocentric and dualist perspective of a chasm, rather than a continuity, between nonhuman and human animals, thereby justifying an exploitative and instrumentalist approach to human-animal relations that ignored or denied animal suffering and was blind to the basic conditions of animal existence.

Pioneering ecosocialist Ted Benton offered the classic criticism of Marx in this respect, arguing that Marx's predominant approach to human-animal relations, particularly in his early writings, was not only "speciesist," but, by virtue of its anthropocentric humanism, constituted "a quite fantastic species-narcissism." Marx's views, he added, were rooted in Cartesian dualism, which radically separated the human being (mind) from the animal (machine). Marx, Benton told his readers, saw animals as permanently "fixed" in their capacities. In describing how the alienation of labor reduced human beings to an animal-like condition, Marx was said to have downgraded non-human animal life altogether.[1]

Other animal-rights critics of Marx have followed suit. Renzo Llorente claims that a "certain speciesism [was] constitutive of Marx's . . . thinking," and that his whole theory of alienated labor was "predicated on a division between human and nonhuman animals."[2] John Sanbonmatsu alleges that Marx advanced the "extermination in the realm of thought of the *sensuous existence, and experiences, of billions of other suffering beings-in-the-world* on earth."[3] Katherine Perlo insists that Marx committed "ideological violence" against animals, while David Sztybel contends that Marx considered animals "merely instrumentally valuable," like any machine.[4]

The term *speciesism* was coined by Richard Ryder in 1970, and is defined in the 1985 *Oxford English Dictionary* as "discrimination against or exploitation of certain animal species, based on an assumption of mankind's superiority."[5] But while speciesism is formally defined as differentiation between humans and animals *leading to discrimination against and exploitation of other species*, some animal-rights scholars have sought to expand this to apply to *any* differentiation between the human species and other animal species, whether or not this is actually used to justify discrimination or abuse.[6]

Thus Benton declares that Marx draws a sharp "contrast between the human and the animal [that] cuts away the ontological basis for . . . a critical analysis of forms of suffering shared by both animals and humans."[7] Here the charge is *not* that Marx ever directly sought to justify the suffering of animals, for which there is no evidence, but simply that his *humanist* ontology undermines the whole ontological basis for the recognition of animal suffering. Hence, Benton declares that "humanism equals speciesism," in direct opposition to Marx's notion that a "fully developed humanism equals naturalism."[8]

What is most remarkable about these criticisms of Marx as a speciesist thinker is that they typically rely on taking a handful of sentences from one or two texts out of context, and ignore Marx's wider arguments and his intellectual corpus as a whole. Coupled with this is the neglect of the larger historical conditions, intellectual influences, and debates out of which Marx's treatment of the human-animal dialectic arose—even though this is crucial to any meaningful understanding of his thought in this area. This includes: (1) his studies of Epicurus and Lucretius; (2) his knowledge of the German debate on animal drives and animal psychology, most notably the work of Hermann Samuel Reimarus; (3) his critique of René Descartes on animals and mechanism; (4) his use of Ludwig Feuerbach's notion of species being; (5) his incorporation of Charles Darwin's evolutionary theory; and (6) his development of the concept of socioecological metabolism based on Justus von Liebig and others. In addition, claims that classical historical materialism was speciesist necessarily downplay Frederick Engels's explorations of animal-human ecology.

It is important to recognize that Marx's discussions of animals were primarily historical, materialist, and natural-scientific in orientation. Marx and Engels's examinations of the position of animals in society were therefore not directed at issues of moral philosophy, as is the case for most of their critics. By the same token, the value of classical historical materialism in this area is what it teaches us concretely with regard to the changing relations between human beings and other animals, particularly with respect to evolving ecological conditions, including what Marx called the "degradation" of animal life under capitalism.[9]

Although it was obviously not the major focus of his work, which was devoted to developing a critique of the capitalist mode of production, concern for and affinity with animals is not absent from Marx's analysis.[10] Overall, his consideration of the human-animal dialectic was affected by a conception of the historical specificity of human-animal relations, associated with different productive modes. This gave rise to Marx's critique of what political scientist Bradley J. Macdonald has called the "alienated speciesism" arising from the capitalist alienation of nature.[11]

Epicurus and the Human-Animal Dialectic

Marx's historical-materialist thinking was deeply affected by his explorations of Epicurean materialism—the subject of his doctoral thesis.[12] Central to Epicureanism is a protoevolutionary perspective and an emphasis on the close material relationship of humans and other animals, as all life emerges from the earth. Animals, like humans, are viewed as sentient beings that experience pain and pleasure.[13] Epicureanism addresses environmental destruction, including the death of species.[14] As Marx put it, for Epicurus, "the world is my *friend*."[15]

Ironically, given the emphasis of Epicurean materialism on a strong human-animal connection and the influence of this on Marx, both Benton and Sztybel in their criticisms chose to quote, out of context, a statement from Marx's Epicurean notebooks, in which he declares: "If a philosopher does not find it outrageous to consider man as an animal, he cannot be made to understand anything."[16] For Benton, this is clear and compelling evidence of an "extreme and unequivocal human/animal dualism" on Marx's part.[17] Similarly, for Sztybel, it is an indication that Marx at this early stage lacks a naturalist perspective and takes an overall instrumentalist approach to animals.[18] Neither critic, however, examines the actual context in which this sentence appeared—that is, Marx's critique of Plutarch's attack on Epicurean materialism for rejecting a religion based on fear. Thus, in the immediately preceding sentence, which neither Benton nor Sztybel quote, Marx conveys what he takes to be Plutarch's view: "For in fear, and indeed an inner, inextinguishable fear, man is determined as animal [that is, devoid of reason and freedom], and it is absolutely indifferent to the animal how it is kept in check."[19] In this passage, Marx is objecting to Plutarch's anti-Epicurean polemics in *That Epicurus Actually Makes a Pleasant Life Impossible* and *Against Colotes*.[20] In these works, particularly the former, Plutarch, following Plato, claimed that the religion of the masses should be based on fear, including the fear of the afterlife ("The Hell of the Populace").[21]

Marx's fierce conflict with Plutarch, in the context of the latter's attack on the Epicurean critique of religion and immortality, is the basis of an appendix to his dissertation—titled "Critique of Plutarch's Polemic Against the Theology of Epicurus," only a fragment of which survives—where the same critical observations on Plutarch are put forth. Marx's argument is that reason allows human beings to transcend what Plutarch sees as animals' "inner fear that cannot be extinguished."[22] Here, Marx, following Epicurus, acknowledges the kinship between animal suffering and human suffering. He also highlights, in opposition to Plutarch, the "corporeal" basis of human beings, linking them to other animals—since humans have immortal souls no more than animals do—while stressing the potential of humanity to raise itself by practical reason, that is, self-conscious material existence.[23]

Nevertheless, a close examination of the passage that Benton and Sztybel quote and the surrounding text indicates that Marx here is less concerned with nonhuman animals than the question of human beings shorn of reason. This makes any attempt to see this passage as a denigration of nonhuman animal life as misleading to an extreme.

Lack of knowledge of Epicurean materialism by animal-rights critics affects the criticisms of Marx in other ways as well. In an attempt to demonstrate that Marx sees animals purely instrumentally, Sztybel quotes Marx's statement in the *Economic and Philosophical Manuscripts* that "nature too, taken abstractly, for itself, and rigidly separated from man, is *nothing* for man." Unaware that this is an allusion to one of Epicurus's principal doctrines, Sztybel concludes that Marx means that nature, including animal life, is "at best of *instrumental* value."[24] Yet, no classically educated individual in Marx's own day could have failed to recognize in Marx's statement Epicurus's famous declaration (which Marx quoted throughout his life): "Death is nothing to us. For what has been dissolved has no sense-experience, and what has no sense-experience is nothing to us."[25]

Hence, in writing that nature separated from humanity, that is, outside sensuous, material interaction, was nothing to humanity, Marx was highlighting that human beings were objective, corporeal, sensual beings—the very point of his critique of Georg Wilhelm Friedrich Hegel in this part of the *Economic and Philosophical Manuscripts*.

Removed from sensual connections to the earth, which define human beings—just as they define all corporeal beings—as living, suffering beings, it was obvious that nature in Marx's (as in Epicurus's) terms was "*nothing* for man." Divorced from nature, human beings, like nonhuman animals, have no existence at all. Far from promoting an instrumentalist approach to animals, what Marx is emphasizing here is the material relation that governs the existence of humans and all species. Rather than representing a separation of humans from other animals or a moral justification for the utilitarian use of the latter, this statement was an expression of their shared existence as physical beings. As Joseph Fracchia argues, for Marx, it was "human corporeal organization" that both identified human beings as animals and served to distinguish them from all other animals.[26]

Indeed, far from denying the connection between human beings and other animals, Marx wrote in *On the Jewish Question* in 1843, prior to his *Economic and Philosophical Manuscripts*, that "the view of nature which has grown up under the regime of private property and of money is an actual contempt for and practical degradation of nature. . . . In this sense Thomas Müntzer declares it intolerable that 'all creatures have been made into property, the fish in the water, the birds in the air, the plants on the earth—all living things must also become free.'"[27]

THE CRITIQUE OF CARTESIAN ANIMAL MACHINES

Seeking a broad philosophical foundation for what he sees as Marx's dualistic view of humans and animals, Benton repeatedly suggests that Marx's so-called speciesist approach to the human-animal relation is trapped in the "paradigm[atic] dualist philosophy of Descartes."[28] In his 1637 *Discourse on Method*, Descartes associated human beings with the mind, while animals were relegated to the status of machines or natural *automata*—a view that was to have an enormous impact on the development of Enlightenment thought.[29] However, missing from Benton's description of Marx's alleged Cartesian dualism is any recognition of the eighteenth- and early nineteenth-century critique of the Cartesian animal-machine notion within German philosophy and psychology, of which Marx was the heir. German Romantic, Idealist, and Materialist thinkers alike challenged the Cartesian animal-machine hypothesis and, in the process, generated a new revolutionary understanding of animal (and human) psychology.[30] Marx based his own criticisms of Descartes's animal-machine notion on this long-standing anti-Cartesian tradition within German philosophy.

The central figure in the German philosophical revolt against the Cartesian notion of the animal machine was the deist (and virulently anti-Epicurean) philosopher Reimarus, whose discoveries in animal psychology (and animal ethology) in the mid-eighteenth century influenced thinkers such as Immanuel Kant, Johann Gottfried Herder, Johann Gottlieb Fichte, Hegel, and Feuerbach.[31] Reimarus adamantly rejected the Cartesian reduction of animals to machines. He also objected to the French philosopher and psychologist Étienne Bonnot de Condillac's notion that nonhuman animals had a consciousness and an ability to learn from the environment, essentially identical to human beings. In response to such conceptions, Reimarus in his *Drives of Animals* (1760) introduced the concept of *Trieb* or drive (generally translated until the twentieth century as *impulse* or *instinct* since there was then no clear English equivalent). In what was gradually to emerge as the basic explanatory category in psychology, Reimarus argued that there were innate drives in animals (including human beings) that interacted with sensations.[32] Drive (*Trieb*) for Reimarus thus stood for the capacity of the animal to pursue a beneficial end "without any individual reflection, experience, and practice, without any training, example, or model, from birth onward, with an artfulness ready from birth that was masterful in achieving its end."[33]

Reimarus developed a taxonomy of ten classes and fifty-seven subclasses of drives, of which the most important were "*skillful drives*" (*Kunsttriebe*)—more specifically, artifice or skillful activity in the form of innate rule-governed capacities for certain actions—which he used to describe the surprising productive proficiency of bees, spiders, and other animals. His notion of a skillful drive was that of an innate drive that was also agential, that is, an "elective drive," incorporating an element of choice.[34] It was this analysis that strongly influenced Marx, who was fascinated with Reimarus's notion of skillful drives.[35]

For Reimarus, nonhuman animals lacked access to the more abstract, *generic* (related to genus) conceptions of things, and therefore to the higher levels of reasoning, such as conceptual relation (metacognition), inference, reflection, and language.[36] Nevertheless, animals had, to a degree, consciousness and imagination responding to sense stimuli, which interacted with their basic drives. In his philosophy of history, Kant argued on this basis that the human species was defined by its freedom to transcend innate drives and to develop conscious ends based on the perception of general human psychological and ethical needs.[37] Herder added that the broader, more generic concepts that characterized human consciousness, in comparison to nonhuman animals, were a product of a much wider, more universal set of experiences reflecting relatively undetermined human interactions with the environment, allowing them to rise above some of their stronger animal drives.[38]

In *An Advanced Guide to Psychological Thinking*, Robert Ausch indicates that, following the publication of Reimarus's *Drives of Animals*, the concept of drive (*Trieb*) was incorporated into the analysis of animal psychology and "students of animal behavior were forced to work within Reimarus's frame."[39] Animals of various kinds were seen as exhibiting complex, innate drives that were unlearned, uniform, and too intelligent to be reduced to Cartesian mechanical terms. If the human species was distinct, in Reimarus's theory, it was due to its capacity to work with generic concepts, while the Cartesian relegation of animals to the status of machines was considered philosophically and psychologically bankrupt.

Marx's attempt to develop a social ontology of labor arose on this basis, relying on the most advanced animal (and human) psychology of his day. He was very impressed by Reimarus's conception of animals' skillful drives and evoked it throughout his work, for example, when comparing the production of nests and dwellings on the part of "the bee, the beaver, the ant, etc." to the more conscious production exercised by human labor. "A spider," Marx wrote in *Capital*, in accordance with Reimarus's notion of skillful drives, "conducts operations which resemble those of the weaver, and a bee would put many a human architect to shame by the construction of its honeycomb cells. But what distinguishes the worst architect from the best of bees is that the architect builds the cell in his mind before he constructs it in wax."[40] Like other animals, Marx stated in the *Economic and Philosophical Manuscripts*, that the human being "is on the one hand,"

> equipped with *natural powers*, with *vital powers*, he is an *active* natural being; these powers exist in him as dispositions and capacities, as *drives* [*Triebe*]. On the other hand, as a natural, corporeal, sensuous, objective being he is a *suffering*, conditioned and limited being, like animals and plants. That is to say, the *objects* of his drives exist outside him as *objects* independent of him; but these objects are objects of his *need*, essential objects, indispensable to the exercise and confirmation of his essential powers. To say that man is a *corporeal*, living, real, sensuous, objective being with natural powers means that he has *real, sensuous objects* as the object of his being.[41]

What stands out here is the strong materialism and naturalism of Marx's analysis, which unites human beings with nonhuman animals through the concept of drive related to various dispositions and faculties.[42] If the human species has more developed social drives, needs, and capacities compared to other animals, as reflected in human production and social labor, these arise through a corporeal organization that unites humanity with the rest of life. It follows that even though nonhuman animal species lack the *self-conscious* social drives characteristic of human beings as *Homo faber*, they nonetheless remain objective, sensuous beings, with their own distinct forms of species life, which reflect their own corporeal organization, drives, needs, and capacities.

Benton and others have strongly criticized Marx's concept of "species being," which he took from Hegel and Feuerbach, for setting humanity an order above nonhuman animals, thus exhibiting speciesism. Here too misunderstandings abound. "Species being" (*Gattungswesen*), sometimes translated as *generic being*, stood, in Marx's analysis, for distinctively human-species drives and capacities leading to a higher level of consciousness or self-consciousness, connected to generic consciousness (objectification) and the "universal" character of human production.[43]

Feuerbach, building on Reimarus, Kant, Herder, and Fichte, had argued that it was the self-consciousness of human beings that allowed them to see themselves as part of a generic or species being, that is, as social beings, and this constituted the "essential difference" between them and other animals. "Strictly speaking," he wrote, "consciousness is given only in the case of a being to whom his *species*, his *mode of being*, is an object of thought. Although the animal experiences itself as an individual—this is what is meant by saying that it has a feeling of itself—it does not do so as a species. . . . The inner life of man is constituted by the fact that man relates himself to his species [generically], to his mode of being."[44]

Marx took over some aspects of Feuerbach's conception of species being, particularly the notion that distinctively human consciousness was a generic consciousness or developed species consciousness.[45] Marx, however, connected this both to the postulate of animal drives underlying nonhuman and human psychology, and to the notion of human beings as laboring beings (*Homo faber*).[46] In Marx's materialist conception, human beings actively and self-consciously transform their relation to nature and thus their own needs and potentials through their production. Hence, if, in his theory of alienation, Marx saw this capacity for self-conscious development as characterizing human rather than nonhuman animals, this was not conceived as an invidious distinction aimed at justifying the domination of the latter, but merely a recognition of human needs, powers, and capacities for active self-development in history, exercised through the labor and production process.

Benton, Llorente, and Sanbonmatsu all censure Marx for contending that human beings, when alienated from their labor, are reduced to those dispositions they have in common with nonhuman animals—eating, drinking, procreating, and, at most, fashioning their dwellings and dressing up—while being estranged from their specifically human *species being* as creative, laboring producers.[47] In this, the early Marx is supposed to have advanced a speciesist ontology. However, Marx's classical historical-materialist analysis does not deny that human beings share a close kinship with other animals biologically and psychologically, including numerous common drives. Rather, he suggests that the human species is distinctive in its capacity to produce more "universally" and self-consciously, and thus is less one-sidedly limited by specific drives than other animals. Humanity is therefore able to transform nature in a seemingly endless number of ways, constantly creating new human needs, capacities, and powers.[48]

This character of human beings as self-conscious species beings also generates the capacity of self-alienation through the development of the division of labor, private property, class, commodity production, etc. Alienation is seen by Marx as a uniquely self-imposed human problem, not to be confused with animal suffering (in which human beings also partake), which is not the product of such self-alienation. This self-alienation of humans, the product of human history, is also an estrangement from nature and other natural beings, resulting in an alienated speciesism in capitalist society, as in the Cartesian designation of animals as machines.[49]

Marx was acutely aware of the ecological conditions of animals and of the destruction and pollution wrought on them by capitalism. Hence, in the *German Ideology*, Marx and Engels famously commented: "The 'essence' of the fish is its 'being,' water. . . . The 'essence' of the freshwater fish is the water of a river. But the latter ceases to be the 'essence' of the fish and is no longer a suitable medium of existence as soon as the river is made to serve industry, as soon as it is polluted by dyes and other waste products and navigated by steamboats, or as soon as the water is diverted into canals where simple drainage can deprive the fish of its medium of existence."[50]

Marx was a strong critic of Cartesian metaphysics, for its removal of the mind/soul from the realm of the animal and the reduction of the latter to mere mechanical motions.[51] In Marx's words, "Descartes in defining animals as mere machines, saw with the eyes of the period of manufacture. The medieval view, on the other hand, was that animals were assistants to man."[52]

MARX, DARWIN, AND EVOLUTION

Benton compares the early Marx unfavorably to the early Darwin, who indicated in 1839 in his notebooks that humans had similar facial expressions to that of the orangutan in the zoo, thereby indicating the relatedness of humans and animals.[53] However, Marx, nine years Darwin's junior (and who might not have seen an orangutan), argued only a few years later, in 1843, that the commodification of animals was an example of the "degradation" of nature by human society—a point that Darwin himself hardly grasped at this or any other stage.[54] A year later, in the *Economic and Philosophical Manuscripts*, Marx explicitly noted the close relationship between human beings and other animals as objective natural beings.[55]

Such an emphasis on strong human-nonhuman animal connections were hardly the dominant view of the time. Charles Lyell, in his pathbreaking *Principles of Geology* (1830–33), with which Marx as well as Darwin were familiar, devoted four chapters to the extinction of species, much of which justified the killing off of animal species by humans. "If we wield the sword of extermination" against animals, "as we advance," Lyell wrote,

we have not reason to repine at the havoc committed, nor to fancy, with the Scotch poet [Robert Burns], that "we violate the social union of nature"; or complain, with the melancholy Jacques [Shakespeare, *As You Like It*], that we

Are mere usurpers, tyrants, and, what's worse,
To fright the animals, and to kill them up
In their assign'd and native dwelling-place.

We have only to reflect, that in thus obtaining possession of the earth by conquest, and defending our acquisitions by force, we exercise no exclusive prerogative. Every species which has spread itself from a small point over a wide area, must, in like manner, have marked its progress by the diminution, or the entire extirpation, of some other.[56]

Marx and especially Engels took careful note of the human destruction of local ecologies and species through the worldwide expansion of capitalism. Yet, in contrast to Lyell, there is no moral justification of these actions and consequences to be found in their analysis. Instead, there is a critique of how the system of capital generated an alienated speciesism. For example, Engels made references to the effects wrought by invasive species (goats) introduced by European colonists onto the island of Saint Helena. Here, one sees a concern over the resulting destruction of indigenous ecology.[57]

Evolutionary ideas in a general sense had long preceded the publication of Darwin's *Origin of Species* in 1859 and its theory of natural selection.[58] Therefore, it should not surprise us that, as a consistent materialist, Marx incorporated evolutionary ideas into his perspective from the beginning, as early as 1844, insisting, against the religious view, on the spontaneous generation of species sometime in the distant geological past. He saw nonhuman and human animal species as sharing an evolutionary and morphological kinship.[59] If Marx metaphorically said in 1857 that "human anatomy contains a key to the anatomy of the ape," the metaphor was nonetheless rooted in a genuine morphological kinship between humans and the higher primates.[60]

Marx would have been well aware of Carl Linnaeus's classification of *Homo sapiens* as among the primates in close proximity to the ape.[61] He had studied in the gymnasium in Trier under the famous German geologist Johann Steininger. Later, at the University of Berlin, Marx attended lectures in anthropology given by Heinrich Steffens, a natural philosopher as well as an important geologist and mineralogist. Marx was familiar with Georges Cuvier's *Discourse on the Revolutionary Upheavals on the Surface of the Globe*.[62] His interest in geology was to continue for the remainder of his life. As late as 1878, he was copying into his notebooks excerpts from the prominent English geologist Joseph Beete Jukes's the *Student's Manual of Geology*, paying careful attention to geological extinction of species resulting from shifting isotherms (climate zones) due to paleoclimatic change.[63]

In July 1858, just two weeks after the famous presentation of papers by Darwin and Alfred Russell Wallace, establishing them as codiscoverers of natural selection as a basis for evolution, Engels wrote to Marx that "comparative physiology gives one a withering contempt for the idealistic exaltation of man over the other animals. At every step one bumps up against the most complete uniformity of structure with the rest of the mammals, and in its main features this uniformity extends to all vertebrates and even—less clearly—to insects, crustaceans, earthworms, etc."[64] Marx and Engels both strongly admired Darwin's *Origin of Species*, referring to it as "the book which, in the field of natural history, provides the basis for our views."[65] And no wonder, because, as Fracchia indicates, "Marx's positing [in *The German Ideology*] of human corporeal organization as the first fact of human history amounts to a Copernican upheaval—precisely because . . . it is the human complement to Darwin's approach to animal organisms in general."[66]

In response to the new knowledge that was developing in the natural sciences, Marx and Engels went even further in their critique of the Cartesian notion of animal machines. Thus, Engels provided in "The Part Played by Labour in the Transition from Ape to Man" what Stephen Jay Gould called "the best nineteenth-century case for gene-culture coevolution," which is the form that all theories of human evolution, accounting for the development of the human brain and language, must take.[67] In that same work, Engels dealt with the complex evolution of animals in relation to their environments, not simply by adapting to their environments but as dialectical subjects-objects of evolution.[68] "It goes without saying," he wrote, "that it would not occur to us to dispute the ability of animals to act in a planned, premeditated fashion."[69] In notes to the *Dialectics of Nature*, which he obviously intended to develop further, he wrote:

We have in common with animals all activity of the understanding: *induction*, *deduction*, and hence also *abstraction* (Dido's [Engels's dog] generic concepts: quadrupeds and biped), *analysis* of unknown objects (even the cracking of a nut is the beginning of analysis), *synthesis* (in animal tricks), and, as the union of both, *experiment* (in the case of new obstacles and unfamiliar situations). In their nature all these modes of procedure—hence all means of scientific investigation that ordinary logic recognises—are absolutely the same in men and the higher animals. They differ only in degree (of development of the method in each case). . . . On the other hand, dialectical thought—precisely because it presupposes investigation of the nature of concepts themselves—is only possible for man, and for him at a comparatively high stage of development.[70]

Likewise, Marx suggested in his *Notes on Adolph Wagner* that animals were capable of distinguishing "theoretically" everything that pertained to their needs. In the paragraph immediately following, he noted ironically (and grimly) that "it would scarcely appear to a sheep as one of its 'useful' properties that it is edible by man," drawing broad parallels between the expropriation (and suffering) of animals and the exploitation of workers. Marx believed his three small dogs displayed an intelligence akin to humans.[71] Marx and Engels thus adopted a view identical with Darwin in the *Descent of Man*—that "the difference in mind between man and the higher animals, great as it is, is certainly one of degree and not of kind." Indeed, like Darwin, they can be said to have subscribed, in general, to the view that the "immense superiority" of human beings when compared to even the higher animals can be attributed to human "intellectual faculties," "social habits," and "corporeal structure."[72]

ALIENATED SPECIESISM AND THE METABOLIC RIFT

Given his historical-materialist approach, which actively incorporated evolutionary and scientific insights, Marx was able to assess how the development of capitalism transformed animal relationships, created an alienated speciesism, and fostered widespread animal suffering. Along these lines, John Berger, in his essay "Why Look at Animals?," warns that viewing nonhuman animals as simply the source of meat, leather, or milk is ahistorical and involves imposing a nineteenth-century conception "backwards across the millennia."[73] He indicates that there is both corporeal continuity and distinction between humans and other animals, as they are "both like and unlike." Stressing that the specific relationships between them have historically been altered due to changes in socioeconomic and cultural conditions, he points out that

> the 19th century, in western Europe and North America, saw the beginning of a process, today being completed by 20th century corporate capitalism, by which every tradition which has previously mediated between man and nature was broken. Before this rupture, animals constituted the first circle of what surrounded man. Perhaps that already suggests too great a distance. They were with man at the centre of his world. Such centrality was of course economic and productive. Whatever the changes in productive means and social organisation, men depended upon animals for food, work, transport, and clothing.[74]

Marx's analysis of the historical development of capitalism highlighted this transition in animal relations. For him, Descartes's depiction of animals as machines represented the status that animals were accorded in capitalist commodity production. Marx took note of the ongoing changes, such as the reduction of nonhuman animals to a source of power and the altering of their corporeal organization and very existence, imposed in order to further the accumulation of capital.

In *Capital*, Marx presented the dynamic relationship between humans and farm animals, illuminating their close proximity and interdependence. "In the earliest period of human history," he indicated, "domesticated animals, i.e. animals that have undergone modification by means of labour, that have been bred specially, play the chief part as instruments of labour along with stones, wood, bones and shells, which have also had work done to them."[75] At the same time, he specifically focused on how the historical development of capitalism, including the division of town and country that accompanied it, shaped these conditions, reducing animals simply to instruments and raw materials, as reflected in the general logic of the system. "Animals and plants which we are accustomed to consider as products of nature," Marx explained,

> may be, in their present form, not only products of, say, last year's labour, but the result of a gradual transformation continued through many generations under human control, and through the agency of human labour. As regards the instrument of labour in particular, they show traces of the labour of past ages, even to the most superficial observer, in the great majority of cases. . . . A particular product may be used as both instrument of labour and raw material in the same process. Take, for instance, the fattening of cattle, where the animal is the raw material, and at the same time an instrument for the production of manure [used to fertilize agricultural fields].[76]

Within this system of generalized commodity production, nonhuman animals often have varying relationships to capital. In the second volume of *Capital*, Marx described how capitalists assessed the lives of cows in relation to production: "Cattle as draught animals are fixed capital; when being fattened for slaughter they are raw material that eventually passes into circulation as a product, and so not fixed but circulating capital."[77] The corporeality of nonhuman animals raised, for capital, the issue of the costs (including those associated with turnover time) determined by the ecoregulatory aspects of natural reproduction. "In the case of living means of labour," explained Marx, "such as horses . . . the reproduction time is prescribed by nature itself. Their average life as means of labour is determined by natural laws. Once this period has elapsed, the wornout items must be replaced by new ones. A horse cannot be replaced bit by bit, but only by another horse."[78] While distinct in form, horses, for capital, were simply inter-changeable Cartesian machines.

The mid-nineteenth century, when Marx was writing, was a time of major transformation in human-nonhuman animal relations. Although animal power had long been in use, such as in plowing fields and transporting goods, the mechanization associated with capitalist development was radically altering animal relations. Capitalists carefully calculated whether human, nonhuman animal, or machine power could best enhance profits. In some cases in England, the costs associated with raising and caring for horses to pull barges along rivers and canals exceeded that of hiring women to carry out the same task, due to their extraordinarily low wages (and the fact that the costs of social reproduction in the household were not included in their wages), resulting in women often replacing horses as barge pullers.[79]

Capital invariably seeks to employ science and technology to speed up production in order to shorten the time associated with natural, ecoregulatory processes, such as the growth of animals, with the object of reducing turnover time and speeding up the realization of profits.[80] As Marx explained, in the context of sheep husbandry:

> It is impossible, of course, to deliver a five-year-old animal before the end of five years. But what is possible within certain limits is to prepare animals for their fate more quickly by new modes of treatment. This was precisely what [Robert] Bakewell managed to do. Previously, British sheep, just like French sheep as late as 1855, were not ready for slaughter before the fourth or fifth year. In Bakewell's system, one-year-old sheep can already be fattened, and in any case they are fully grown before the second year has elapsed. By selective breeding, Bakewell . . . reduced the bone structure of his sheep to the minimum necessary for their existence. These sheep are called the New Leicesters.[81]

Here, Marx quoted French agriculturalist Léonce de Lavergne, author of *The Rural Economy of England, Scotland, and Ireland*, who advocated further expanding meat and dairy production: "The breeder can now send three to market in the same space of time that it formerly took him to prepare one; and if they are not taller, they are broader, rounder, and have a greater development in those parts which give most flesh. Of bone, they have absolutely no greater amount than is necessary to support them, and almost all their weight is pure meat."[82]

In his critical notes on Lavergne, Marx objected to these new methods of animal production for meat and dairy, as the pursuit of endless profits led to a broad range of animal suffering and corporeal abuse—inherent in a mode of alienated speciesism in which animals were not viewed as living beings but as machines to be manipulated as such. Sheep that were bred so as to decrease bone structure—in Marx's words, "aborting bones in order to transform them to mere meat and a bulk of fat"—had a hard time supporting their own weight and standing due to their much larger, heavier bodies and weaker skeletal frames. To increase milk production for the market, calves were weaned earlier. Cattle were increasingly confined to stalls and were fed oil cakes and other high-energy-input concoctions designed to accelerate the rate of growth.[83]

Under previous agricultural practices, Marx observed, "animals remained active by staying under free air." Confined to stalls with the attendant box feeding meant that "in these prisons animals are born and remain there until they are killed off." This resulted "in serious deterioration of life force" and growth deformities in their bodies, which were regarded as mere parts, grist for the mill of capital. For Marx, all of this was "Disgusting!" It amounted to a "system of prison cells for the animals."[84]

Today, such capitalist methods for speeding up and commodifying natural reproduction also include the use of growth hormones, massive concentrated animal-feeding operations, and extensive use of antibiotics to treat ailments that arise from the conditions under which animals are raised. These approaches have only become more intensive and widespread throughout animal production for meat and dairy, as in the case of chickens, pigs, cows, sheep, and fish.[85] As environmental sociologist Ryan Gunderson stresses, the vast expansion of animals confined to industrialized production is directly linked to the ceaseless pursuit of capital accumulation.[86]

Through this analysis, Marx detailed how capitalist development created an alienated mediation between human beings and nature, in this case, nonhuman animal species. This alienated speciesism reduces animals to machines within factory farms, and animals throughout the world confront extermination due to destruction of habitat, climate change, and ocean acidification—all associated with the general workings of capitalism in the contemporary period. This rupture takes on an ironic character, Macdonald points out, as "the more their dismembered bodies intersect with ours" via commodity circulation as meat, leather, glue, etc., "the more they ultimately disappear from human life."[87] This finding, associated with alienated speciesism under capitalism, is similar to the dynamics that accompany the alienation of nature in general. As Raymond Williams indicated, the deeper the alienation from nature, the more intensive "the real interaction" with the biophysical world in regard to the resources used in commodity production and the generation of waste that pollutes ecosystems.[88]

These broad concerns regarding the operations of the capitalist system, ecological conditions, and alienated speciesism are intertwined in Marx's consideration of the metabolism of nature and society. In the 1850s and 1860s, Liebig, the leading German chemist, explained that due to the shipment of crops to distant locations British high-farming techniques were violating the law of replenishment or compensation, resulting in failure to return to the soil the nutrients that had been removed. This robbery system led to the despoliation of agricultural lands. Marx took up Liebig's analysis, including the conception of metabolic relations. He developed an even richer socioecological metabolic approach focusing on the metabolic rift, whereby an alienated social metabolism, in contradiction to the universal metabolism of nature, disrupts or ruptures natural cycles, systems, and flows.[89]

With the repeal of the Corn Laws in 1846, which ushered in free trade, Marx identified several trends within what he called the "new regime" of capitalist food production. This included a further deepening of the metabolic rift in the soil nutrient cycle, increasing the scale of the mechanized expropriation of animals, themselves treated as mere machines (or machine parts).[90] There was a drive to shift Britain toward greater meat and dairy production as part of the Norfolk rotation system (and other similar rotations), which primarily served the wealthier population. As a result, more land was converted to pasturage and for growing forage crops, such as legumes, rather than cereal and grains, while expanding the impacts of animal grazing. With more farm animals on the land, fewer workers were needed. Under this new food regime, wheat production in Britain plummeted, leading to massive imports of grain in order to feed the general population.[91] Irish lands were converted to pastures to raise pigs, cattle, and sheep, displacing much of the rural population.[92] New Leicester sheep were sent to Ireland to breed with native sheep to develop a variety that provided greater profits for capital, without any regard for the health of the animals.[93] Intensive agricultural practices expropriated the nutrients from the soil in Britain and abroad, giving rise to the increasing reliance on importing both agricultural inputs and grains. Here, the metabolic rift was expanded, robbing the nutrients of distant lands, whether it was in the form of cereal and grains for human consumption, guano to repair the degraded land, or rapeseed in the production of oil cake to feed farm animals to enrich their manure.[94]

While Lavergne celebrated the imposition of industrialized agricultural operations, intensifying animal production for meat and dairy, Marx strongly implied that a grain-based system of agriculture was a more efficient system for providing food for the population as a whole and ensuring the long-term vitality of the land.[95]

Marx's critique of alienated speciesism, associated with the degradation of humans and nonhuman animals, can be considered part of his wider ecological critique, linked to the metabolic rift.[96] The metabolic rift is not limited to external, inanimate nature, but also encompasses the expropriation of corporeal beings, where nonhuman animals are reduced to machines in a system predicated on constant expansion, which ignores and increases their suffering. Indeed, when the question of nonhuman animals arose, his analysis transcended the merely ecological framework, displaying an affinity with animals, which, for Marx, are limited, objective, "suffering beings" like humans themselves.[97]

Marx never lost his close connection to Epicurean materialism. The Epicureans taught that animal suffering and human suffering are alike for they both pertain to natural beings. In Books I and II of *De rerum natura*, the great Roman poet Lucretius presented five attacks on sacrificial practices, beginning with his description of Agamemnon's sacrifice of his daughter Iphigenia to the altar of the gods, and ending, as if to emphasize human affinity with animals, with a bereaved cow:

> For oft in front of noble shrines of gods
> A calf falls slain beside the incensed altars,
> A stream of hot blood gushing from its breast.
> The mother wandering through the leafy glens
> Bereaved seeks on the ground the cloven footprints.
> With questing eyes she seeks if anywhere
> Her lost child may be seen; she stands,
>   and fills with moaning
> The woodland glades; she comes back to the byre
> Time and again in yearning for her calf.[98]

No one could fail to recognize from such a passage that human suffering and animal suffering, as Marx suggested, are akin. Revolutionary struggle is necessary to transcend the alienation of nature associated with capitalism. Marx clearly recognized that the uprooting of alienated speciesism is part of this fight. If "fully developed humanism" is to become "naturalism," it is necessary to forge a new human-animal dialectic, one grounded in the Epicurean principle that "the world is my *friend*." Echoing Müntzer, Marx declared, "all living things must also become free."[99]

6

Capitalism and the Paradox
of Wealth

Marx concludes his radical critique in Capital *with the affirmation
that capitalist accumulation is founded on the destruction of the
bases of all wealth: human beings and their natural environment.*
—SAMIR AMIN

TODAY ORTHODOX ECONOMICS is reputedly being harnessed
to an entirely new end: saving the planet from the ecological destruction wrought by capitalist expansion.[1] It promises to accomplish
this through the further expansion of capitalism itself, cleared of its
excesses and excrescences. A growing army of self-styled "sustainable
developers" argues that there is no contradiction between the unlimited accumulation of capital—the credo of economic liberalism from
Adam Smith to the present—and the preservation of the earth. The
system can continue to expand by creating a new "sustainable capitalism," bringing the efficiency of the market to bear on nature and its
reproduction. In reality, these visions amount to little more than a
renewed strategy for profiting on planetary destruction.

Behind this tragedy-cum-farce is a distorted accounting deeply
rooted in the workings of a system that sees wealth entirely in

terms of value generated through exchange. In such a system, only commodities for sale on the market really count. External nature—water, air, living species—outside this system of exchange is viewed as a "free gift" to capital. Once such blinders have been put on, it is possible to speak, as the leading U.S. climate economist William Nordhaus, winner of the Sveriges Riksbank (Bank of Sweden) Prize in Economic Sciences in Memory of Alfred Nobel for 2018, has, of the relatively unhindered growth of the economy a century or so from now, under conditions of business as usual—despite the fact that leading climate scientists see following the identical path over the same time span as absolutely catastrophic both for human civilization and life on the planet as a whole.[2]

Such widely disparate predictions from mainstream economists and natural scientists are due to the fact that, in the normal reckoning of the capitalist system, both nature's contribution to wealth and the destruction of natural conditions are largely invisible. Insulated in their cocoon, orthodox economists either implicitly deny the existence of nature altogether or assume that it can be completely subordinated to narrow, acquisitive ends.

This fatal flaw of received economics can be traced back to its conceptual foundations. The rise of neoclassical economics in the late nineteenth and early twentieth centuries is commonly associated with the rejection of the labor theory of value of classical political economy and its replacement by notions of marginal utility/productivity. What is seldom recognized is that another critical perspective was abandoned at the same time: the distinction between wealth and value (use value and exchange value). With this, the possibility of a broader ecological and social conception of wealth was lost. These blinders of orthodox economics, shutting out the larger natural and human world, were challenged by figures inhabiting what John Maynard Keynes called the "underworlds" of economics. This included critics such as James Maitland (Earl of Lauderdale), Karl Marx, Henry George, Thorstein Veblen, and Frederick Soddy. Today, in a time of unlimited environmental destruction, such heterodox views are having a comeback.[3]

THE LAUDERDALE PARADOX

The ecological contradictions of the prevailing economic ideology are best explained in terms of what is known in the history of economics as the "Lauderdale Paradox." James Maitland, the eighth Earl of Lauderdale (1759–1839), was the author of *An Inquiry into the Nature and Origin of Public Wealth and into the Means and Causes of its Increase* (1804). In the paradox with which his name came to be associated, Lauderdale argued that there was an inverse correlation between public wealth and private riches such that an increase in the latter often served to diminish the former. "Public wealth," he wrote, "may be accurately defined,—*to consist of all that man desires, as useful or delightful to him.*" Such goods have use value and thus constitute wealth. But private riches, as opposed to wealth, required something additional, that is, had an added limitation, consisting "*of all that man desires as useful or delightful to him; which exists in a degree of scarcity.*"

Scarcity, in other words, is a necessary requirement for something to have value in exchange, and to augment private riches. But this is not the case for public wealth, which encompasses all value in use, and thus includes not only what is scarce but also what is abundant. This paradox led Lauderdale to argue that increases in scarcity in such formerly abundant but necessary elements of life as air, water, and food would, if exchange values were then attached to them, enhance individual private riches, and indeed the riches of the country—conceived of as "the sum-total of individual riches"—but only at the expense of the common wealth. For example, if one could monopolize water that had previously been freely available by placing a fee on wells, the measured riches of the nation would be increased at the expense of the growing thirst of the population.

"The common sense of mankind," Lauderdale contended, "would revolt" at any proposal to augment private riches "by creating a scarcity of any commodity generally useful and necessary to man." Nevertheless, he was aware that the bourgeois society in which he lived was already, in many ways, doing something of the very sort.

He explained that in particularly fertile periods Dutch colonialists burned "spiceries" or paid natives to "collect the young blossoms or green leaves of the nutmeg trees" to kill them off; and that in plentiful years "the tobacco-planters in Virginia," by legal enactment, burned "a certain proportion of tobacco" for every slave working their fields. Such practices were designed to increase scarcity, augmenting private riches (and the wealth of a few) by destroying what constituted public wealth—in this case, the produce of the earth. "So truly is this principle understood by those whose interest leads them to take advantage of it," Lauderdale wrote, "that nothing but the impossibility of general combination protects the public wealth against the rapacity of private avarice."[4]

From the beginning, wealth, as opposed to mere riches, was associated in classical political economy with what John Locke called "intrinsic value," and what later political economists were to call "use value."[5] Material use values had, of course, always existed, and were the basis of human existence. But commodities produced for sale on the market under capitalism also embodied something else: exchange value (value). Every commodity was thus viewed as having "a twofold aspect," consisting of use value and exchange value.[6] The Lauderdale Paradox was nothing but an expression of this twofold aspect of wealth/value, which generated the contradiction between total public wealth (the immense collection of use values) and the aggregation of private riches (the sum of exchange values).

David Ricardo, the greatest of the classical-liberal political economists, responded to Lauderdale's paradox by underscoring the importance of keeping wealth and value (use value and exchange value) conceptually distinct. In line with Lauderdale, Ricardo stressed that if water, or some other natural resource formerly freely available, acquired an exchange value due to the growth of absolute scarcity, there would be "an actual loss of wealth" reflecting the loss of natural use values—even with an increase of private riches.[7]

In contrast, Adam Smith's leading French follower, Jean-Baptiste Say, who was to be one of the precursors of neoclassical economics, responded to the Lauderdale Paradox by simply defining it away.

He argued that wealth (use value) should be subsumed under value (exchange value), effectively obliterating the former. In his *Letters to Malthus on Political Economy and Stagnation of Commerce* (1821), Say thus objected to "the definition of which Lord Lauderdale gives of *wealth*." It was absolutely essential, in Say's view, to abandon altogether the identification of wealth with use value. As he wrote:

> *Adam Smith*, immediately having observed that there are two sorts of values, one *value in use*, the other *value in exchange*, completely abandons the first, and entirely occupies himself all the way through his book with *exchangeable value* only. This is what you yourself have done, Sir [addressing Thomas Robert Malthus]; what Mr. Ricardo has done; what I have done; what we have all done: for this reason that there is no other value in political economy. . . . [Consequently] wealth consists in the value of the things we possess; confining this word *value* to the only admitted and exchangeable value.

Say did not deny that there were "things indeed which are natural wealth, very precious to man, but which are not of that kind about which political economy can be employed." But political economy was to encompass in its concept of value—which was to displace altogether the concept of wealth—nothing but exchangeable value. Natural or public wealth, as opposed to value in exchange, was to be left out of account.[8]

Nowhere in liberal political economy did the Lauderdale Paradox create more convolutions than in what Marx called the "shallow syncretism" of John Stuart Mill.[9] Mill's *Principles of Political Economy* (1848) almost seemed to collapse at the outset on this basis alone. In the "Preliminary Remarks" to his book, Mill declared (after Say) that "wealth, then, may be defined, [as] all useful or agreeable things which possess exchangeable value"—thereby essentially reducing wealth to exchange value. But Mill's characteristic eclecticism and his classical roots also led him to expose the larger irrationality of this, undermining his own argument. Thus, we find in the same section a penetrating treatment of the Lauderdale Paradox, pointing to the conflict between capital accumulation and the wealth of the commons. According to Mill:

> Things for which nothing could be obtained in exchange, however useful or necessary they may be, are not wealth in the sense in which the term is used in Political Economy. Air, for example, though the most absolute of necessaries, bears no price in the market, because it can be obtained gratuitously: to accumulate a stock of it would yield no profit or advantage to any one; and the laws of its production and distribution are the subject of a very different study from Political Economy. But though air is not wealth, mankind are much richer by obtaining it gratis, since the time and labour which would otherwise be required for supplying the most pressing of all wants, can be devoted to other purposes. It is possible to imagine circumstances in which air would be a part of wealth. If it became customary to sojourn long in places where the air does not naturally penetrate, as in diving-bells sunk in the sea, a supply of air artificially furnished would, like water conveyed into houses, bear a price: and if from any revolution in nature the atmosphere became too scanty for the consumption, or could be monopolized, air might acquire a very high marketable value. In such a case, the possession of it, beyond his own wants, would be, to its owner, wealth; and the general wealth of mankind might at first sight appear to be increased, by what would be so great a calamity to them. The error would lie in not considering, that however rich the possessor of air might become at the expense of the rest of the community, all persons else would be poorer by all that they were compelled to pay for what they had before obtained without payment.[10]

Mill signaled here, in line with Lauderdale, the possibility of a vast rift in capitalist economies between the narrow pursuit of private riches on an increasingly monopolistic basis, and the public wealth of society and the commons. Yet, despite these deep insights, Mill closed off the discussion with his "Preliminary Remarks," rejecting the Lauderdale Paradox in the end, by defining wealth simply as exchangeable value. What Say said with respect to Smith in the *Wealth of Nations*—that he entirely occupied "himself all the way through his book [after his initial definitions] with exchangeable value only"—therefore applied also to Mill in his *Principles of Political Economy*. Nature was not to be treated as wealth but as something offered "gratis," that is, as a free gift from the standpoint of capitalist value calculation.

MARX AND THE LAUDERDALE PARADOX

In opposition to Say and Mill, Marx, like Ricardo, not only held fast to the Lauderdale Paradox but also made it his own, insisting that the contradictions between use value and exchange value, wealth and value, were intrinsic to capitalist production. In *The Poverty of Philosophy*, he responded to Pierre-Joseph Proudhon's confused treatment (in *The Philosophy of Poverty*) of the opposition between use value and exchange value by pointing out that this contradiction had been explained most dramatically by Lauderdale, who had "founded his system on the inverse ratio of the two kinds of value." Indeed, Marx built his entire critique of political economy in large part around the contradiction between use value and exchange value, indicating that this was one of the key components of his argument in *Capital*. Under capitalism, he insisted, nature was rapaciously mined for the sake of exchange value: "The earth is the reservoir, from whose bowels the use-values are to be torn."[11]

This stance was closely related to Marx's attempt to look at the capitalist economy simultaneously in terms of its economic-value relations, and its material transformations of nature. Thus Marx was the first major economist to incorporate the new notions of energy and entropy, emanating from the first and second laws of thermodynamics, into his analysis of production.[12] This can be seen in his treatment of the metabolic rift—the alienated metabolism between human beings and the earth, which in this case was brought on by the shipment of food and fiber to the city, where nutrients withdrawn from the soil by plants ended up polluting the air and the water instead of being returned to the fields in the countryside. In this conception, both nature and labor were robbed, since both were deprived of conditions vital for their reproduction. As Marx argued, not "fresh air" and water but "polluted" air and water had become the mode of existence of the worker.[13]

Marx's analysis of the destruction of the wealth of nature for the sake of accumulation is most evident in his treatment of capitalist ground rent and its relation to industrial agriculture. Ricardo had rooted his agricultural rent theory in "the original and indestructible powers of the soil"; to which Marx replied, "The soil has no 'indestructible powers,'" in the sense that it could be degraded, that is, subject to conditions of ecological destruction. It is here in Marx's treatment of capitalist agriculture that the analysis of the metabolic rift and the Lauderdale Paradox are brought together within his overall critique. It is here, too, that he frequently refers to sustainability as a material requirement for any future society—the need to protect the earth for "successive generations." A condition of sustainability, he insisted, is the recognition that no one (not even an entire society or all societies put together) owns the earth—which must be preserved for future generations in accordance with the principles of good household management. For a sustainable relation between humanity and the earth to be possible under modern conditions, the metabolic relation between human beings and nature needs to be rationally regulated by the associated producers in line with their needs *and* those of future generations. This means that the vital conditions of life and the energy involved in such processes need to be conserved.[14]

For Marx, few things were more important than the abolition of the big private monopolies in land that divorced the majority of humanity from: (1) a direct relation to nature, (2) the land as a means of production, and (3) a communal relation to the earth. He delighted in quoting at length from Herbert Spencer's chapter in *Social Statics* (1851), "The Right to the Use of the Earth." There, Spencer openly declared: "Equity . . . does not permit property in land, or the rest would live on the earth by sufferance only. . . . It is impossible to discover any mode in which land can become private property. . . . A claim to the exclusive possession of the soil involves land-owning despotism." Land, Spencer insisted, properly belongs to "the great corporate body—society." Human beings were "co-heirs" to the earth.[15]

ECOLOGY AND THE LABOR THEORY OF VALUE

Ironically, green thinkers (both non-socialist and socialist) frequently charge that the labor theory of value, to which Marx adhered in his critique of capitalism, put him in direct opposition to the kind of ecologically informed value analysis that is needed today. In *Small Is Beautiful*, E. F. Schumacher observed that in modern society there is an inclination "to treat as valueless everything that we have not made ourselves. Even the great Dr. Marx fell into this devastating error when he formulated the so-called 'labour theory of value.'" Environmental sociologist Luiz Barbosa, a contributor to *Twenty Lessons in Environmental Sociology* (2009), has written that Marx "believed raw materials are given to us gratis (for free) by nature and that it is human labor that gives it value. Thus, Marx failed to notice the intrinsic value of nature." Social ecologist Matthew Humphrey gives credence to the view that "Marx's attachment to the labour theory of value in which non-human nature is perceived as valueless" can be taken as an indication of "his anthropocentric outlook."[16]

Even Marxian theorists have sometimes advanced similar misconceptions. Jean-Paul Deléage has complained that Marx "attributes no intrinsic value to natural resources" in making labor the only source of value. David Harvey, based on a similar narrowly economistic interpretation of classical historical materialism, has gone so far as to declare that "Marx could not abide social theories that depended on so-called natural conditions or forces to explain *anything* about capitalism." To be sure, Harvey states in *Marx, Capital, and the Madness of Economic Reason* that "capital rests materially on its metabolic relation with nature." Nevertheless, this observation does not lead, as in Marx, to an analysis of natural limits to capital. Rather, Harvey adopts the notion of the "free gifts of nature" in an entirely uncritical sense, insisting, in capital's own terms, that "nature . . . is a storehouse of free gifts that capital can use without paying anything"—a view more akin to that of Ricardo than Marx, since the wider ecological contradictions embedded in the narrow bourgeois conception of value are obscured.[17]

Here it is important to understand that certain conceptual categories that Marx uses in his analysis, such as nature being a "free gift . . . to capital" and the labor theory of value itself, were inventions of classical-liberal political economy that were integrated into his critique of classical political economy only insofar as they exhibited the real tendencies and contradictions of the system. Marx employed these concepts as part of a deep-seated anatomization of bourgeois society and its limited social categories, with the object of transcending it. The idea that nature was a "free gift" for exploitation was explicitly advanced by the physiocrats, and by Smith, Malthus, Ricardo, and Mill—well before Marx.[18] Moreover, it has been perpetuated in mainstream economics long after Marx. Although accepting it as a reality of an alienated bourgeois political economy, Marx was nevertheless acutely aware of the social and ecological contradictions that this entailed. Thus, he argued in *Capital* that even though the free appropriation of nature was the basis of all production (and all property), the historically specific notion of "the free gift of Nature to capital" was characteristic of the capitalist mode of production. In his *Economic Manuscript of 1861–1863*, he chided Malthus for falling back on the crude "physiocratic notion" of the environment as "a gift of nature to man," while ignoring that the *expropriation* of nature for production—and the entire value framework built upon this in capitalist society—was a fundamental flaw of bourgeois social relations.[19] For Marx, with his emphasis on maintaining the earth for future generations, capital's unceasing expropriation of the natural environment pointed to the absolute contradiction between the realm of natural wealth and the juggernaut of capital accumulation that systematically robbed it.

Nevertheless, since the treatment of nature as a "free gift" to capital was intrinsic to the workings of the capitalist economy, it continued to be included as a *basic proposition underlying neoclassical economics*. It was repeated as an axiom in the work of the great late nineteenth-century neoclassical economist Alfred Marshall, and has continued to be advanced in orthodox economic textbooks. Hence, the tenth edition of *Economics* (1987), a widely used introductory textbook by Campbell McConnell, states the following: "Land refers to all natural resources—all 'free gifts of nature'—which are useable in the production process." And further along in the same book we find: "Land has no production cost; it is a 'free and nonreproducible gift of nature.'"[20] Indeed, so crucial is this notion to neoclassical economics that it continues to live on in mainstream environmental economics. For example, Nick Hanley, Jason F. Shogren, and Ben White state in their influential *Introduction to Environmental Economics* (2001) that "natural capital comprises all [free] gifts of nature."[21]

Green critics, with only the dimmest knowledge of classical political economy (or of neoclassical economics), often focus negatively on Marx's adherence to the labor theory of value—the notion that only labor generates value. Yet it is important to remember that the labor theory of value was not confined to Marx's critique of political economy but constituted the *entire basis* of classical-liberal political economy. Misconceptions pointing to the anti-ecological nature of the labor theory of value arise due to conflation of the categories of *value* and *wealth*—since, in today's received economics, these are treated synonymously. It was none other than the Lauderdale Paradox, as we have seen, that led Say, Mill, and others to abandon the autonomous category of wealth (use value)—helping to set the stage for the neoclassical economic tradition that was to follow. In the capitalist logic, there was no question that nature was valueless (a free gift). The problem, rather, was how to jettison the concept of wealth, as distinct from value, from the core framework of economics, since it provided the basis of a critical—and what we would now call "ecological"—outlook.

Marx, as noted, strongly resisted the jettisoning of the wealth-value distinction, going so far as to criticize other socialists if they embraced the "value equals wealth" misconception. If human labor were one source of wealth, he argued—one that became the basis of value under capitalism—nature was another indispensable source of wealth. Those who, falling prey to the commodity fetishism of capitalist value analysis, saw labor as the sole source of wealth were thus attributing "supernatural creative power" to labor. "Labour," Marx pronounced at the beginning of the *Critique of the Gotha Programme*, "is *not the source* of all wealth. *Nature* is just as much the source of use values (and it is surely of such that material wealth consists!) as is labour, which itself is only the manifestation of a natural force, human labour power." In the beginning of *Capital*, he cited William Petty, the founder of classical political economy, who had said, "Labour is the father of material wealth, the earth is its mother."[22] "Man and nature," Marx insisted, were "the two original agencies" in the creation of wealth, which "continue to cooperate." Capitalism's failure to incorporate nature into its value accounting, and its tendency to confuse value with wealth, were *fundamental contradictions of the regime of capital itself.* Those "who fault Marx for not ascribing value to nature," Paul Burkett wrote, "should redirect their criticisms to capitalism itself."[23]

As with Lauderdale, though with greater force and consistency, Marx contended that capitalism was a system predicated on the accumulation of value, even at the expense of real wealth (including the social character of human labor itself). The capitalist, Marx noted, adopted as his relation to the world: "*Après moi le déluge!*"[24] Or, as he was frequently to observe, capital had a vampire-like relation to nature—representing a kind of living death maintained by sucking the blood from the world.[25]

Unworldly Economists and their Critics

Nevertheless, the whole classical conception of wealth, which had its highest development in the work of Ricardo and Marx, was to be turned upside down with the rise of neoclassical economics. This can be seen in the work of Carl Menger—one of the founders of the

Austrian school of economics and of neoclassical economics more generally. In his *Principles of Economics* (published in 1871, only four years after Marx's *Capital*), Menger attacked the Lauderdale Paradox directly (the reference to it as a "paradox" may have originated with him), arguing that it was "exceedingly impressive at first glance," but was based on false distinctions. For Menger, it was important to reject both the use value/exchange value and wealth/value distinctions; wealth was based on exchange, which was now seen as rooted in subjective utilities. Replying to both Lauderdale and Proudhon, he insisted that the deliberate production of scarcity in nature was beneficial (to capital). Standing Lauderdale on his head, he contended that it would make sense to encourage "a long continued diminution of abundantly available (non-economic) goods [such as, air, water, natural landscapes, since this] must finally make them scarce in some degree—and thus components of wealth, which is thereby increased." In the same vein, Menger claimed that mineral water could conceivably be turned eventually into an economic good due to its scarcity. What Lauderdale presented as a paradox or even a curse— the promotion of private riches through the destruction of public wealth—Menger, one of the precursors of neoliberalism in economics, saw as an end in itself.[26]

This attempt to remove the paradox of wealth from economics led to scathing indictments by Henry George, Thorstein Veblen, and Frederick Soddy, along with others within the underworld of economics. In his best-selling work *Progress and Poverty* (1879), George strongly stressed the importance of retaining a social concept of wealth:

> Many things are commonly spoken of as wealth which in taking account of collective or general wealth cannot be considered as wealth at all. Such things have an exchange value . . . insomuch as they represent as between individuals, or between sets of individuals, the power of obtaining wealth; but they are not truly wealth [from a social standpoint], inasmuch as their increase or decrease does not affect the sum of wealth. Such are bonds, mortgages,

promissory notes, bank bills, or other stipulations for the transfer of wealth. Such are slaves, whose value represents merely the
power of one class to appropriate the earnings of another class.
Such are lands, or other natural opportunities, the value of which
is but the result of the acknowledgement in favor of certain persons
of an exclusive right to their use, and which represents merely the
power thus given to the owners to demand a share of the wealth
produced by those who use them. . . . By enactment of the sovereign political power debts might be canceled, slaves emancipated,
and land resumed as the common property of the whole people,
without the aggregate wealth being diminished by the value of a
pinch of snuff, for what some would lose others would gain.[27]

Carefully examining the changing definitions of wealth in economics, George roundly condemned Say, Mill, and the nascent Austrian
school of economics for obliterating the notion of use value and defining wealth entirely in terms of exchange value. Produced wealth, he
argued, was essentially the result of "exertion impressed on matter,"
and was to be associated with producible use values. Value came from
labor. Like Marx, George drew upon the basic tenets of Greek materialism (most famously extolled by Epicurus and Lucretius), arguing
that nothing can be created merely by labor: "Nothing can come out
of nothing."[28]

Other economic dissidents also challenged the narrow orthodox economic approach to wealth. Veblen contended that the main
thrust of capitalist economics under the regime of absentee ownership was the seizure of public wealth for private benefit. Calling this
the "American plan" because it had "been worked out more consistently and more extensively" in the United States "than elsewhere,"
he referred to it, in Lauderdale-like terms, as "a settled practice of
converting all public wealth to private gain on a plan of legalised
seizure"—marked especially by "the seizure of the fertile soil and its
conversion to private gain." The same rapacious system had its forma-
tive stages in the United States in slavery and in "the debauchery and
manslaughter entailed on the Indian population of the country."[29]

Soddy, the 1921 Nobel Prize winner in chemistry, was an important forerunner of ecological economics. He was an admirer of Marx—arguing that it was a common error to think that Marx saw the source of all wealth as human labor. Marx, Soddy noted, had followed Petty and the classical tradition in seeing labor as the father of wealth, the earth as the mother.[30] The bounty of nature was part of "the general wealth" of the world. Reviving the Lauderdale Paradox, in his critique of mainstream economics, Soddy pointed out that

> the confusion enters even into the attempt of the earlier [classical] economists to define . . . "wealth," though the modern [neoclassical] economist seems to be far too wary a bird to define even that. Thus we find that wealth consists, let us say, of the enabling requisites of life, or something equally unequivocal and acceptable, but, if it is to be had in unlimited abundance, like sunshine or oxygen or water, then it is not any longer wealth in the economic sense, though without either of these requisites life would be impossible.

In this, Soddy wrote, "the economist, ignorant of the scientific laws of life, has not arrived at any conception of wealth," nor given any thought to the costs to nature and society, given the degradation of the environment.[31] Turning to Mill's contorted treatment of the Lauderdale Paradox, Soddy referred to the "curious inversions" of those who, based on making market exchange the sole criterion of value/wealth, thought that the creation of scarcity with respect to food, fuel, air, etc., made humanity richer. The result was that "the economist has effectually impaled himself upon the horns of a very awkward dilemma."[32]

Despite the strong criticisms arising from the underworld of economics, however, the dominant neoclassical tradition moved steadily away from any concept of social/public wealth, excluding the whole question of social (and natural) costs—within its main body of analysis. Thus, as ecological economist K. William Kapp explained in his landmark *Social Costs of Private Enterprise* in 1950, despite the introduction of an important analogue to the orthodox tradition with the publication of Arthur Cecil Pigou's *Economics of Welfare*, it remained true that the "analysis of social costs is carried on not within the main body of value and price theory but as a separate system of so-called welfare economics." Kapp traced the raising of the whole problem of social wealth/social costs to none other than Lauderdale, while viewing Marx as one of the most devastating critics of capitalism's robbing of the earth.[33]

THE RETURN OF THE LAUDERDALE PARADOX

Today Lauderdale's paradox is even more significant than it was when originally formulated in the early nineteenth century. Water scarcities, air pollution, world hunger, growing fuel shortages, and the warming of the earth are now dominant global realities. Moreover, attempts within the system to expand private riches by exploiting these scarcities, such as the worldwide drive to privatize water, are ever-present. Hence, leading ecological economist Herman Daly has spoken of "The Return of the Lauderdale Paradox"—this time with a vengeance.[34]

The ecological contradictions of received economics are most evident in its inability to respond to the planetary environmental crisis. This is manifested both in repeated failures to apprehend the extent of the danger facing us, and in the narrow accumulation strategies offered to solve it. The first of these can be seen in the astonishing naïveté of leading orthodox economists—even those specializing in environmental issues—arising from a distorted accounting that measures exchange values but largely excludes use values, that is, issues of nature and public wealth.

Nordhaus was quoted in *Science* magazine in 1991 as saying: "Agriculture, the part of the economy that is sensitive to climate change, accounts for just 3% of national output. That means there is no way to get a very large effect on the U.S. economy" just through the failure of agriculture. In this view, the failure of agriculture in the United States would have little impact on the economy as a whole.

Obviously, this is not a contradiction of nature but of the capitalist economy—associated with its inability to address material realities. Oxford economist Wilfred Beckerman presented the same myopic view in his book *Small Is Stupid* (1995), claiming that "even if the net output of [U.S.] agriculture fell by 50 per cent by the end of the next century this is only a 1.5 per cent cut in GNP." This view led him to conclude elsewhere that global warming under business as usual would have a "negligible" effect on world output. Likewise, Thomas Schelling, a winner of the Sveriges Riksbank Prize in Economic Sciences in Memory of Alfred Nobel, wrote in *Foreign Affairs* in 1997: "Agriculture [in the developed world] is practically the only sector of the economy affected by climate, and it contributes only a small percentage—three percent in the United States—of national income. If agricultural productivity were drastically reduced by climate change, the cost of living would rise by one or two percent, and at a time when per capita income will likely have doubled."[35]

The underlying assumption here—that agriculture is the only part of the economy that is sensitive to climate change—is obviously false. What is truly extraordinary in such views is that the blinders of these leading neoclassical economists effectively prevent even a ray of common sense from getting through. GDP measurements become everything, despite the fact that such measurements are concerned only with economic value added, and not with the entire realm of material existence. There is no understanding here of production as a system, involving nature (and humanity), outside of national income accounting. Even then, the views stated are astonishingly naïve—failing to realize that a decrease by half of agricultural production would necessarily have an extraordinary impact on the price of food. Today, with a "tsunami of hunger sweeping the world," and at least one billion people worldwide lacking secure access to food, these statements by leading mainstream environmental economists seem criminal in their ignorance. According to the Food Security International Network's *Global Report on Food Security 2019*, 113 million people in fifty-three countries were experiencing acute hunger in 2018.[36]

The same distorted accounting, pointing to "modest projected impacts" on the economy from global warming, led Nordhaus in 1993 to classify climate change as a "second-tier issue," and to suggest that "the conclusion that arises from most economic studies is to impose modest restraints, pack up our tools, and concentrate on more pressing problems." Although he acknowledged that scientists were worried about the pending environmental catastrophe associated with current trends, the views of most economists were in his opinion more "sanguine." No wonder Jason Hickel responded to news of Nordhaus's receiving the Sveriges Riksbank Prize in Economic Sciences in Memory of Alfred Nobel in 2018 with an article in *Foreign Policy* titled "The Nobel Prize for Climate Catastrophe."[37]

None of this should surprise us. Capitalism's general ideological orientation with respect to public welfare, as is well known, is one of trickle-down economics. Human labor is exploited and natural resources are expropriated with the object of generating immense riches at the top of society, which is justified by the false promise that some of this affluence will inevitably trickle down to those below. In a similar way, the ecological promises of the system could be called "trickle-down ecology." We are told that by allowing unrestrained accumulation the environment will be improved through ever-greater efficiency—a kind of secondary effect. The fact that the system's celebrated efficiency is of a very restricted, destructive kind is hardly mentioned.

A peculiarity of capitalism, brought out by the Lauderdale Paradox, is that it feeds on scarcity. Hence, nothing is more dangerous to the capitalist system than abundance. Waste and destruction are therefore rational for the system. Although it is often supposed that increasing environmental costs will restrict economic growth, the fact is that under capitalism such costs continue to be externalized on nature (and society) as a whole. This perversely provides new prospects for private profits through the selective commodification of parts of nature (public wealth).

All of this indicates that there is no real feedback mechanism from rising ecological costs to economic crisis that can be counted on to check capitalism's destruction of the biospheric conditions of civilization and life itself. By the perverse logic of the system, whole new industries and markets aimed at profiting on planetary destruction, such as the waste management industry and carbon trading, are being opened up. These new markets are justified as offering partial, ad hoc "solutions" to the problems generated nonstop by capital's laws of motion.[38]

In fact, the growth of natural scarcity is seen as a golden opportunity to further privatize the world's commons. This tragedy of the privatization of the commons only accelerates the destruction of the natural environment, while enlarging the system that weighs upon it. This is best illustrated by the rapid privatization of freshwater, which is now seen as a new mega-market for global accumulation. The drying up and contamination of freshwater diminishes public wealth, creating investment opportunities for capital, while profits made from selling increasingly scarce water are recorded as contributions to income and riches. It is not surprising, therefore, that the UN Commission on Sustainable Development proposed, at a 1998 conference in Paris, that governments should turn to "large multinational corporations" in addressing issues of water scarcity, establishing "open markets" in water rights. Gérard Mestrallet, CEO of the global water giant Suez, has openly pronounced: "Water is an efficient product. It is a product which normally would be free, and our job is to sell it. But it is a product which is absolutely necessary for life." He further remarked: "Where else can you find a business that's totally international, where the prices and volumes, unlike steel, rarely go down?" Such statements about profiting on water shortages need to be put in a context in which over two billion people now live in countries experiencing high water stress with severe water scarcity rapidly increasing.[39]

Not only water offers new opportunities for profiting on scarcity. This is also the case with respect to fuel and food. Growing fuel shortages, as world oil demand has outrun supply, has led to a global shift in agriculture from food crops to fuel crops. This has generated a boom in the agrofuel market—expedited by governments on the grounds of "national security" concerns. The result has been greater food scarcities, inducing an upward spiral in food prices and the spiking of world hunger. Speculators have seen this as an opportunity for getting richer quicker through the monopolization of land and primary commodity resources.[40]

Similar issues arise with respect to carbon-trading schemes, ostensibly aimed at promoting profits while reducing carbon emissions. Such schemes continue to be advanced despite that experiments in this respect thus far have been a failure—in reducing emissions. Here, the expansion of capital trumps actual public interest in protecting the vital conditions of life. At all times ruling-class circles actively work to prevent radical structural change in this as in other areas, since any substantial transformation in social-environmental relations would mean challenging the treadmill of capital production itself, and launching an ecological-cultural revolution.

Indeed, from the standpoint of capital accumulation, global warming and desertification are often viewed as blessings in disguise, increasing the prospects of expanding private riches. We are thus driven back to Lauderdale's question: "What opinion," he asked, "would be entertained of the understanding of a man, who, as the means of increasing the wealth of . . . a country should propose to create a scarcity of water, the abundance of which was deservedly considered one of the greatest blessings incident to the community? It is certain, however, that such a projector would, by this means, succeed in increasing the mass of individual riches."[41]

Numerous ecological critics have, of course, tried to address the contradictions associated with the devaluation of nature by designing new green accounting systems that would include losses of "natural capital."[42] Although such attempts are important in bringing out the irrationality of the system, they run into the harsh reality that the current system of national accounts *does* accurately reflect capitalist realities of the non-valuation/undervaluation of natural agents (including human labor power itself). To alter this, it is necessary to transcend the system. The dominant form of valuation, in our age of global ecological crisis, is a true reflection of capitalism's mode of social and environmental degradation—causing it to profit from the destruction of the planet.

In Marx's critique, value was conceived of as an alienated form of wealth.[43] Real wealth came from nature and labor power and was associated with the fulfillment of genuine human needs. Indeed, "it would be wrong," Marx wrote, "to say that labour which produces use-values is the *only* source of the wealth produced by it, that is of material wealth. . . . Use-value always comprises a natural element. . . . Labour is a natural condition of human existence, a condition of material interchange [metabolism] between man and nature."[44] From this standpoint, Lauderdale's Paradox was not a mere enigma of economic analysis, but rather the supreme contradiction of a system that sees nature as a mere means of accumulation.

7

The Meaning of Work in a Sustainable Socialist Society

Fie upon this quiet life. I want work.
—WILLIAM SHAKESPEARE, *HENRY IV,*
PART I, ACT II, SC. IV

THE NATURE and meaning of work, as it pertains to a future society, has deeply divided ecological, socialist, utopian, and Romantic thinkers since the Industrial Revolution.[1] Some radical theorists have seen a more just society as merely requiring the rationalization of present-day work relations, accompanied by increased leisure time and more equitable distribution. Others have focused on the need to transcend the entire system of alienated labor and make the development of creative work relations the central element of a new revolutionary society. In what appears to be an effort to circumvent this enduring conflict, current visions of sustainable prosperity, while not denying the necessity of creative work, often push it into the background, placing their emphasis instead on an enormous, unprecedented expansion of leisure hours.[2] Increased non-work time seems an unalloyed good, and is easily imaginable in the context of a no-growth society. In contrast, the very question of work is fraught with inherent difficulties, since it goes to the roots of the current socioeconomic system, its division of labor, and its class relations. Yet it remains the case that no coherent ecological mapping of a sustainable future is conceivable without addressing the issue of *Homo faber*, that is, the creative, constructive, historical role in the transformation of nature, and hence the social relation to nature, that distinguishes humanity as a species.

Within late nineteenth-century socialist-utopian literatures, it is possible to distinguish two broad tendencies regarding the future of work, represented on one side by Edward Bellamy, author of *Looking Backward*, and on the other by William Morris, author of *News from Nowhere*. Bellamy, standing for a view familiar to us today, saw enhanced mechanization, together with comprehensive technocratic organization, as the basis for increased leisure time, considered the ultimate good. In contrast, Morris, whose analysis derived from Charles Fourier, John Ruskin, and Karl Marx, emphasized the centrality of useful, enjoyable, artistic work, requiring the abolition of the capitalist division of labor. Today the mechanistic view of Bellamy more closely resembles popular conceptions of a sustainable economy than does Morris's more radical outlook. Thus, the notion of "liberation from work" as the foundation of sustainable prosperity has been strongly advanced in the writings of first-stage ecosocialist and degrowth thinkers like André Gorz and Serge Latouche.[3]

We contend here that the idea of near-total liberation from work, in its one-sidedness and incompleteness, is ultimately incompatible with a genuinely sustainable society. After first examining the hegemonic view of work in the history of Western thought, going back to the ancient Greeks, we turn to a consideration of the opposing ideas of Marx and Adam Smith. This leads to the issue of how socialist and utopian thinkers have themselves diverged on the question of work, focusing on the contrast between Bellamy and Morris. All of this points to the conclusion that the real potential for any future sustainable society rests not so much on its expansion of leisure time, but rather on its capacity to generate a new world of creative and collective work, controlled by the associated producers.

The Hegemonic Ideology of Work and Leisure

The narrative found today in every neoclassical economics textbook portrays work in purely negative terms, as a disutility or sacrifice. Sociologists and economists often present this as a transhistorical phenomenon, extending from the classical Greeks to the present. Italian cultural theorist Adriano Tilgher famously declared in 1929: "To the Greeks work was a curse and nothing else," supporting his claim with quotations from Socrates, Plato, Xenophon, Aristotle, Cicero, and other figures, together representing the aristocratic perspective in antiquity.[4]

With the rise of capitalism, work was classified as a necessary evil requiring coercion. In 1776, at the dawn of the Industrial Revolution, Adam Smith in *The Wealth of Nations* defined labor as a sacrifice, which required the expenditure of "toil and trouble . . . of our own body." The worker must "always lay down . . . his ease, his liberty, and his happiness."[5] A few years earlier, in 1770, an anonymous treatise titled an *Essay on Trade and Commerce* appeared, written by a figure (later thought to be J. Cunningham) whom Marx described as "the most fanatical representative of the eighteenth-century bourgeoisie." It advanced the proposition that to break the spirit of independence and idleness of English laborers, ideal "work-houses" should be established imprisoning the poor, turning these into "houses of terror, where they should work fourteen hours a day in such fashion that when meal time was deducted there should remain twelve hours of work full and complete." Similar views were promoted in subsequent decades by Thomas Robert Malthus, leading to the New Poor Law of 1834.[6]

Neoclassical economic ideology today treats the question of work as a trade-off between leisure and labor, downplaying its own more general designation of work as a disutility in order to present it as a personal financial choice, and not the result of coercion.[7] Yet it remains true, as German economist Steffen Rätzel observed in 2009, that at bottom, "work," in neoclassical theory, "is seen as *a bad* necessary to create income for consumption."[8]

This conception of work, which derives much of its power from the alienation that characterizes capitalist society, has of course been challenged again and again by radical thinkers. Such outlooks are neither universal nor eternal, nor is work to be regarded simply as a disutility—though the conditions of contemporary society tend to make it one, and thus necessitate coercion.[9]

Indeed, the myth that the ancient Greek thinkers in general were anti-work, representing a historical continuity with today's dominant ideology, was refuted by the Marxian classicist and philosopher of science Benjamin Farrington in his 1947 study *Head and Hand in Ancient Greece*. Farrington showed that such views, though common enough among the aristocratic factions represented by Socrates, Plato, and Aristotle, were opposed by the pre-Socratic philosophers, and contradicted by the larger historical context of Greek philosophy, science, and medicine, which had originated in traditions of hands-on craft knowledge. "The central illumination of the Milesians," the fountainhead of Greek philosophy, Farrington wrote, "was the notion that the whole of the universe works in the same way as the little bits of it that are under man's control." Thus "every human technique" developed in the work process, such as those of cooks, potters, smiths, and farmers, was evaluated not simply in terms of its practical ends, but also for what it had to say about the nature of things. In Hellenistic times, the Epicureans, and later Lucretius, carried forward this materialist view, theorizing the realm of nature based on experience derived from human craft work. All of this is evidence of the enormous respect accorded work, and artisanal labor in particular.[10]

Materialists in antiquity thus built their ideas around an intimate knowledge of work and respect for the insights it gave into the world—in sharp contrast to the idealists, who, representing the aristocratic disdain for manual labor, promoted celestial myths and anti-work ideals. This vision could be seen in a statement attributed to Socrates by Xenophon: "What are called the mechanical arts carry a social stigma and are rightly dishonored in our cities" (*Oec.* 4.2). In contrast, nothing could be further from the worldview of the Greek materialists, who saw work as the embodiment of the organic, dialectical relations between nature and society.[11]

Smith's possessive-individualist conception of work, two millennia later, drew on some of these ancient, aristocratic class prejudices, such as those attributed to Socrates, running afoul once again of the materialist standpoint. Writing in 1857–58, Marx declared in response to Smith:

> In the sweat of thy brow shalt thou labour! was Jehovah's curse on Adam. And this is labour for Smith, a curse. "Tranquility" appears as the adequate state, as identical with "freedom" and "happiness." It seems quite far from Smith's mind that the individual, "in his normal state of health, strength, activity, skill, facility," also needs a normal portion of work, and of suspension of tranquility. . . . He is right, of course, that in its historic forms as slave-labour, serf-labour, and wage-labour, labour always appears as repulsive, always as external forced labour; and not-labour, by contrast, as "freedom, and happiness." . . . [In such social formations] labour . . . has not yet created the subjective and objective conditions for itself . . . in which labour becomes attractive work, the individual's self-realization. . . . A. Smith, by the way, has only the slaves of capital in mind.[12]

Here Marx argued that Smith's idea of freedom as "not-labor," far from being an immutable truth, was the product of specific historical conditions, associated with exploited wage labor. "Labor becomes attractive work," for Marx, only under unalienated circumstances, when it is no longer a commodity. This requires new, higher forms of social production under the control of the associated producers. All of this has its roots of course in Marx's powerful early critique of alienated labor in his *Economic and Philosophical Manuscripts of 1844*.[13] For Marx, human beings were fundamentally corporeal beings. To remove humanity from its material-corporeal relations, by radically separating mental and manual labor was to guarantee human alienation.[14]

Socialist Utopianism: Bellamy and Morris

Yet if socialists could be expected to reject the hegemonic view of work relations associated with capitalism, the extent to which this translated into fundamentally different views of work relations from that of the status quo varied within socialist literature itself. Though little read today, Bellamy's *Looking Backward*, published in 1888, was the most popular book of its time after *Uncle Tom's Cabin* and *Ben-Hur*, selling millions of copies and translated into more than twenty languages. Erich Fromm noted that in 1935, "three outstanding personalities, Charles Beard, John Dewey, and Edward Weeks," each separately ranked Bellamy's novel second only to Marx's *Capital* among the most influential books of the preceding half-century.[15]

Bellamy's utopian novel appeared in a period of rapid economic expansion, industrialization, and concentration of capital in the United States. The protagonist, Julian West, wakes up in Boston in the year 2000 to discover a society entirely transformed along socialist lines.[16] The trust-building tendencies of the Gilded Age had led to the creation of one giant monopolistic firm, which was then nationalized, bringing the economy under total control by the state. The result was a highly organized, egalitarian society. All individuals were required to join the army of workers at twenty-one, spend three years working as a common laborer, and then advance to some skilled occupation, with compulsory labor ending at age forty-five. Every citizen over the course of his or her life could expect to be turned into a man or woman of leisure. In Bellamy's view, work was still conceived as a pain not a pleasure, and the point was ultimately to transcend it.

Morris, then the principal force behind the London-based Socialist League, wrote a highly critical review of Bellamy's book, focusing on its descriptions of work and leisure. He followed this in 1890 with his own socialist utopian novel, *News from Nowhere*, which presented a sharply contrasting view of work in a higher society. Morris, in E. P. Thompson's words, "was a Communist Utopian, with the full force of the transformed Romantic tradition behind him."[17] The principal influences on his understanding of the role of work in society were

Fourier, Ruskin, and Marx, all of whom had criticized, albeit from sharply distinct political perspectives, the division of labor and the distorted, alienated work relations under capitalism. From Fourier, Morris took the idea that work could be so structured as to be enjoyable.[18] From Ruskin, he adopted the idea that decorative arts and architecture of the late medieval era pointed to the different conditions in which artisans had then lived and worked, allowing them freely to channel their spontaneous thoughts, beliefs, and aesthetics into all that they made. As Thompson wrote, "Ruskin . . . was the first to declare that men's 'pleasure in their work by which they make their bread' lay at the very foundations of society, and to relate this to his whole criticism of the arts."[19] From Marx, Morris took the historical-materialist critique of the exploitation of labor that lay at the root of the cash nexus of capitalist class society.

The resulting synthesis led to Morris's famous proposition: "Art is man's expression of his joy in labor." Creative, fulfilling work, he argued, was essential to human beings, who must "either be making something or making believe to make it." Looking at the historical connection between art and labor in preindustrial times, Morris contended that "all men that have left any signs of their existence behind them have practiced art." There was always a "definite sensuous pleasure" in labor insofar as it was art, and in art insofar as it was unalienated labor; and this pleasure increased "in proportion to the freedom and individuality of the work." The primary goal of society should be the maximization of pleasure in work, in the process of fulfilling genuine human needs. It was "the lack of this pleasure in daily work" under capitalism, Morris observed, that "has made our towns and habitations sordid and hideous insults to the beauty of the earth which they disfigure, and all the accessories of life mean, trivial, ugly."[20]

Morris decried the wasted labor devoted to turning out endless amounts of useless commodities, such as "barbed wire, 100 ton guns and advertising boards for the disfigurement of the green fields along the railways and so on." He also criticized "adulterated wares" seeing these as nothing but the waste of human lives, and the accompanying pollution of the natural and social environment.[21]

Morris's examples were well chosen. "Barbed wire" and "100 ton guns" were metonyms for British imperial warfare and weapons production. (Today the United States spends over a trillion dollars a year in actual—as opposed to acknowledged—military spending.)[22] By "advertising boards" he meant the whole phenomenon of marketing. (Today more than a trillion dollars a year is spent on marketing in the United States.)[23] With his reference to "adulterated wares," he was underscoring the whole problem of adulteration of foods, or the development of additives primarily for sales and cost-cutting purposes, as well as the production of various shoddy goods, characterized by what is now called planned obsolescence. Today the penetration of the sales effort into the production process, as described in the 1920s by Thorstein Veblen in *Absentee Ownership and Business Enterprise in Modern Times* and in the 1960s by Paul Baran and Paul Sweezy in *Monopoly Capital*, affects almost all commodities. Although it is generally assumed that the production costs of commodities in today's society are socially necessary costs in some objective sense, a very large portion of the costs of commodities are in fact unnecessary from a production standpoint and are instead related to aspects of commercial product design, advertising, packaging, fashion, model changes, product obsolescence, and the like that have to do with the costs of selling rather than producing the goods.[24]

In Morris's view, the production of socially non-reproductive and harmful goods was a waste of human labor.[25] He wrote: "But think, I beseech you, of the product of England, the workshop of the world, and will you not be bewildered, as I am, at the thought of the mass of things which no sane man could desire, but which our useless toil makes—and sells?"[26]

In criticizing such production for its waste, lack of aesthetic value, and labor alienation, Morris was not attacking machine production itself, but rather insisting that production should be organized in such a way that the human being was not reduced, as Marx had said, to an "appendage of a machine." As Morris himself put it, the worker was degraded in industrial capitalist society to "not even a machine,

but an average portion of that great and almost miraculous machine
. . . the factory."[27]

In words similar to Marx's discussion of alienated labor in the 1844
Economic and Philosophic Manuscripts, Morris declared in his 1888 lecture "Art and Its Producers": "The interest of" the factory worker's "life
is divorced from the subject-matter of his labour." The proletarian's

> work has become "employment," that is, merely the opportunity
> of earning a livelihood at the will of someone else. Whatever
> interest still clings to the production of wares under this system
> has wholly left the ordinary workman, and attaches only to the
> organisers of his labour; and that interest commonly has little to
> do with the production of wares, as things to be handled, looked
> at . . . used, in short, but simply as counters in the great game of
> the world market.[28]

For Morris, Bellamy's vision was "the unmixed modern one,
unhistoric and unartistic." It presented the ideal of the "middle-class
professional," which, in the utopian Boston of *Looking Backward*,
became available to everyone after a few years of ordinary labor. "The
impression which he [Bellamy] produces is that of a huge standing
army, tightly drilled, compelled by some mysterious fate to unceasing
anxiety for the production of wares to satisfy every caprice, however
wasteful and absurd, that may cast up among them."

In sharp contrast, Morris declared that "the ideal of the future does
not point to the lessening of man's energy by the reduction of labor
to a minimum, but rather the reduction of pain in labor to a minimum, so small that it will cease to be pain." There was no barrier to
labor being creative and artistic, provided that production was not
determined by a narrow concept of productivity geared to capitalist
profits. Bellamy's utopia, with its deadening "economical semi-fatal-
ism" was concerned "unnecessarily" with finding "some incentive to
labor to replace the fear of starvation, which is at present our only
one, whereas it cannot be too often repeated that the true incentive to
useful and happy labor must be pleasure in the work itself."[29]

News from Nowhere presented Morris's own utopian vision. A man named William—called William Guest by those he meets but meant to symbolize Morris himself—awakes from a dream (though it is left intentionally ambiguous whether he is still dreaming throughout) to find himself in London in the early twenty-second century, around a century and half after a revolutionary outbreak in the 1950s that led to the creation of a communal socialist society.[30] In the utopia of Nowhere, technology is used to reduce tedious labor, but not to decenter work in general. Production is instead aimed at genuine needs and artistic production. New, less destructive forms of energy exist, and pollution has been eradicated. Workers, following the Great Change, remained tied at first to the mechanistic view of work, but gradually, "under the guise of pleasure that was not supposed to be work, work that was pleasure began to push out the mechanical toil. . . . Machines could not produce works of art, and . . . works of art were more and more called for." Art and science were shown to be "inexhaustible," as were the possibilities of human creativity through meaningful work, thereby displacing the earlier capitalist production of "a vast quantity of useless things."[31]

Today Morris's vision will no doubt strike some as a quaint and moralizing "artistic critique" of capitalism. Thinkers like Luc Boltanski and Éve Chiapello see the defeat of such a critique, represented by figures as various as Morris and Charles Baudelaire, as one of the main results of late twentieth-century post-Fordist flexibility and innovation. The "new spirit of capitalism," they argue, entails pervasive integration of artistic forms into capitalist production.

However, the weakness of Boltanski and Chiapello's analysis lies precisely in its conflation of surface appearances with the root character of the system. They thus fall prey to commodity fetishism in its newest, most fashionable forms, failing to recognize the full extent to which the "artistic critique" and the "social critique" are inextricably connected and insurmountable within the capitalist system. After the 2007–2009 crisis of global capitalism, the classical social and artistic critiques of alienation and exploitation represented by Marx and Morris seem more relevant than ever.[32]

A particular strength of Morris's vision of labor in *News from Nowhere* lies in his depiction of relative gender equality in the workplace. In a chapter titled "The Obstinate Refusers," which provides the only instance of a master craftsperson actually at work in Morris's utopian romance, that position is occupied by a woman, Mistress Philippa, a stone carver or mason. Although the foreman is male, it is Philippa who determines when and in what form the work takes place. Her daughter is also a stone carver, while a young man serves the meal. Work in the society of Nowhere is thus no longer strictly gendered (though Morris built contradictions into his analysis in this respect, depicting a world still in the process of change). [33]

Like Marx, Morris united his analysis of the possibility of creative, unalienated labor with ecological issues, recognizing that the degradation of human work relations and of nature were inseparably connected. For Marx, ownership of the land was akin to and just as irrational as the ownership of human beings, leading to the enslavement and exploitation of both. Likewise, for Morris, in capitalist society—as Clara voices it in *News from Nowhere*—people sought "to make 'nature' their slave, since they thought 'nature' was something outside them."[34] Morris argued in his day that coal production should be halved, both because of the human-wasting and health-destroying labor it required, and the massive pollution it generated. A more rational society, he argued, could allow for deep cuts in coal production while going further in fulfilling human needs, allowing for new realms of human advancement.[35]

THE CRITIQUE OF THE DIVISION OF LABOR

Marx and Morris both argued that the repulsion toward work in bourgeois society was a product of the alienated organization of labor, a view that combined the aesthetic and political-economic critiques of capitalism. From the earliest human civilizations, and even before, divisions of labor had developed between the genders, between town and country, and between mental and manual labor. Capitalism had extended and deepened this unequal division, giving it an even more alienated form by divorcing workers from the means of production and imposing a rigidly hierarchical labor regime that not only divided workers in the tasks they performed, but also fragmented the individual. This detailed division of labor was the basis of the whole class order of capital. Hence, overthrowing the regime of capital meant first and foremost transcending the estrangement of work, and creating a deeply egalitarian society based on the collective organization of labor by the associated producers.

The critique of the division of labor under capitalism was not a minor element for Morris, any more than it was for Marx. In a free translation from the French edition of Marx's *Capital*, Morris wrote: "'It is not only the labor that is divided, subdivided, and portioned out betwixt divers men: it is the man himself who is cut up, and metamorphosed into the automatic spring of an exclusive operation.' Karl Marx."[36] Morris, who complained of the "degradation of the operative into a machine," saw this as the essence of the socialist (and Romantic) critique of the capitalist labor process.[37]

These issues were brought to the fore once again in the late twentieth century in Harry Braverman's 1974 *Labor and Monopoly Capital: The Degradation of Work in the Twentieth Century*. Braverman documented how the rise of scientific management under monopoly capitalism, as exhibited in the work of Frederick Winslow Taylor's *Principles of Scientific Management*, had made the formal subsumption of labor to capital into a real material process.[38] The centralization of knowledge and control of the labor process within management allowed for an enormous extension of the detailed division of labor, and thus enhanced profits for capital. What Braverman called the general "degradation of work under monopoly capitalism" captured the material basis of the growing alienation and de-skilling of working life for the vast majority of the population.

Nevertheless, the evolution of technology and human capacities pointed toward new revolutionary possibilities that were more in tune with Marx than Smith. As Braverman wrote:

Modern technology in fact has a powerful tendency to break down ancient divisions of labor by re-unifying production processes. . . . The re-unified process in which the execution of all the steps [for example, in Smith's pin-making case] is built into the working mechanism of a single machine would seem now to render it suitable for a collective of associated producers, none of whom need spend all of their lives at any single function and all of whom can participate in the engineering, design, improvement, repair, and operation of these ever more productive machines. Such a system would entail no loss of production, and it would represent the re-unification of the craft in a body of workers far superior to the old craft workers. Workers can now become masters of the technology of their process on an engineering level and can apportion among themselves in an equitable way the various tasks connected with this form of production that has become so effortless and automatic.[39]

For Braverman, therefore, the development of technology and human knowledge and capacities, together with automation, allowed for a fuller, more creative relation to the work process in the future, breaking with the extreme detailed division of labor that characterized a capitalist system geared only to profitability. New openings existed for non-alienated work and artistry on the job, reclaiming at a higher level what had been lost with the demise of the craft worker. But this required radical social change.

A key aspect of Braverman's argument was criticism of Marxism itself, in the form it had developed in the Soviet Union, where degraded work environments similar to those of capitalism had arisen, but without the coercion of unemployment, resulting in chronic problems of productivity. Vladimir Ilyich Lenin, he pointed out, had advocated the adoption of aspects of Taylor's scientific management in Soviet industry, claiming that it combined "the refined brutality of bourgeois exploitation and a number of the greatest scientific achievements in the field." Subsequent Soviet planners disregarded the more critical elements of Lenin's argument and implemented unmodified Taylorism, in a direct mirroring of the crudest methods of capitalist labor management.

In the USSR and on the left in general, Marx's (and Morris's) critique of the capitalist labor process was thus largely forgotten, and the horizon of progress reduced to relatively minor improvements in work conditions, some degree of "workers' control," and centralized planning. "The similarity of Soviet and traditional capitalist practice," Braverman wrote, "strongly encourages the conclusion that there is no other way in which modern industry can be organized"—a conclusion, however, that went against the real potential for the development of human capacities and needs embedded in modern technology.[40] Alienation and the degradation of work were not inherent in modern work relations, but were enforced by priorities of profit and growth that had been partly replicated in the Soviet Union, undermining the original liberatory promise of Soviet society.

A World of Creative Work

The foregoing suggests that the essence of a future sustainable socialist society must be located in the labor process—in Marx's terms, the metabolism of society and nature. Visions of a post-capitalist future that pivot on the expansion of leisure time and general prosperity, without addressing the need for meaningful work, are bound to fail.

Yet today most depictions of a future sustainable society take work and production as economically and technologically determined, or as simply displaced by automation, and focus instead on maximizing leisure as society's highest aim, often coupled with basic income guarantees.[41] This can be seen in the works of theorists such as Latouche and Gorz. The former defines "degrowth," of which he is a principal proponent, as a social formation "beyond the work-based society." Dismissing left arguments for the development of a society in which work takes on a more creative role as "pro-work propaganda,"

Latouche instead argues for a society in which "leisure and play are as highly valued as work."[42]

Gorz's early ecosocialist analysis adopts a similar stance. In his 1983 *Paths to Paradise*, subtitled *On the Liberation from Work*, he returns to Aristotle's aristocratic notion that life is most rewarding outside the mundane realm of labor. Gorz envisions a vast reduction in working time—"the end of the society of work"—with employees working only a thousand hours annually over the course of twenty years of employment. Gorz's idea of the reduction of formal work, made inevitable in a future society, is in effect that of a society in which everyone is petty bourgeois—a gift of the "micro-electronic revolution" and automation.

Standard work relations, as conceived in *Paths to Paradise*, would be dominated by automation, and the resulting reduction in working hours would allow the most enjoyable, professional jobs to be shared out among more people. Yet all of this takes second place to the promise of a vast increase in free time, enabling individuals to engage in all sorts of autonomous activities, portrayed as individual leisure pursuits and home-based production and not in terms of associated labor. The normal capitalist workplace is left essentially to Taylorist scientific management, while the more complex questions surrounding automation and the degradation of work are scarcely examined. Freedom is seen as not-work in the form of pure leisure, or as home-based or informal production. The alternative socialist view, which centers on the transformation of work itself in a future society, is flatly dismissed as a dogma of "the disciples of the religion of work."[43]

Yet the kinds of total automation and robotization now projected for advanced capitalist society, which are frequently treated as representing inevitable, teleological tendencies—prompting discussions of "a world without work"—do not sit well with a conception of a steady-state economy and society, where human beings would be neither appendages to machines nor their servants.[44] Nor is today's dominant fatalism sufficiently grounded in a critique of contemporary capitalist contradictions. In today's advanced political economy, it can be argued, productivity is not too low but too high. Mere quantitative development—measured in output or GDP growth—is therefore no longer the key challenge in meeting social needs. In a more rational society based on abundance, as Robert W. McChesney and John Nichols argue in *People Get Ready*, the qualitative aspects of working conditions would be emphasized.[45] Work relations would be seen as a basis of equality and sociability, rather than inequality and asociality. Repetitive, de-skilled jobs would be replaced by forms of active employment that emphasize all-around human development. The joint stock of knowledge of society that constitutes technology would be used for the promotion of sustainable social progress, rather than for the profits and accumulation of a very few.

Not only do human beings need creative labor in their roles as individuals, they also need it in their social roles, since work is constitutive of society itself. A world in which most people are removed from work activities, as pictured in Kurt Vonnegut's futuristic novel *Player Piano*, would be little more than a dystopia.[46] The wholesale cessation of labor, as represented in many post-work schemes, could only lead to a kind of absolute alienation: the estrangement from the core of "life activity," which requires that human beings be transformative agents interacting with nature. To abolish work would constitute a break with objective existence in its most meaningful, active, and creative form—a break with human species-being itself.[47]

The failure in some visions of a sustainable prosperity to confront the full potential of freely associated human labor only serves to undermine the often courageous critiques of economic growth that characterize some of today's radical ecological visions. The unfortunate consequence is that many of the arguments for a prosperous no-growth society have more in common with Bellamy than with Morris (or Marx), since they focus almost exclusively on the expansion of leisure as not-work, while downplaying humanity's productive and creative possibilities. In truth, it is impossible to imagine a viable future that does not focus on the metamorphosis of work. For Morris, as we have seen, art and science were the two "inexhaustible" realms of human creativity that all people could participate in actively within the context of associated human labor.

In a prospective socialist society characterized by sustainable prosperity that recognizes material limits as its essential principle—in accord with Epicurus's notion that "wealth, if limits are not set for it, is great poverty"—it is crucial to envision entirely new socially and ecologically reproductive work relations.[48] The received notion that the maximization of leisure, luxury, and consumption is the primary goal of human progress, and that people will refuse to produce if not subject to coercion and driven by greed, loses much of its force in light of the deepening contradictions of our overproductive, over-consumptive society. The prevailing view goes against what we know anthropologically with respect to many pre-capitalist cultures, and falls short of a realistic conception of variable human nature, one that takes into account the historical evolution of human beings as social animals. The motivation to create and to contribute in one's life to the social reproduction of humanity as a whole, coupled with the higher norms enforced by collective labor, provide powerful stimuli for continuing free human development. The universal crisis that marks our time necessitates an epoch of uncompromising revolutionary change—one aimed at harnessing human energy for creative and socially productive work within a world of ecological sustainability and substantive equality. In the end, there is no other way in which to conceive a truly sustainable prosperity.

8

Marx's Ecology and the Left

ONE OF THE lasting contributions of the Frankfurt School of social theorists, represented especially by Max Horkheimer and Theodor Adorno's 1944 *Dialectic of Enlightenment*, was the development of a philosophical critique of the domination of nature. Critical theorists associated with the Institute for Social Research at Frankfurt were deeply influenced by the early writings of Karl Marx. Yet their critique of the Enlightenment domination of nature was eventually extended to a critique of Marx as an Enlightenment figure, especially in relation to his mature work in *Capital*. This position was expressed most notably in the work of Horkheimer and Adorno's student, Alfred Schmidt, author of *The Concept of Nature in Marx*. Due largely to Schmidt's book, the notion of Marx's anti-ecological perspective became deeply rooted in Western Marxism. Such criticisms were also closely related to questions raised regarding Frederick Engels's *Dialectics of Nature*, which was said to have improperly extended dialectical analysis beyond the human-social realm. First-stage ecosocialists such as Ted Benton and André Gorz added to these charges, contending that Marx and Engels had gone overboard in their alleged rejection of Malthusian natural limits.

So all-encompassing was the critique of the "dialectic of the Enlightenment" within the main line of the Frankfurt School, and within what came to be known as "Western Marxism" (defined largely by its rejection of the dialectics of nature associated with Engels and Soviet Marxism), that it led, ironically, to the estrangement of thinkers in this tradition not only from the later Marx, but also from natural science—and hence nature itself.[1] Consequently, when the ecological movement emerged in the 1960s and 1970s, Western Marxism, with its abstract, philosophical notion of the domination of nature, was ill-equipped to analyze the changing and increasingly perilous forms of material interaction between humanity and nature. Making matters worse, some Marxian theorists—such as Neil Smith and Noel Castree—responded by inverting the Frankfurt School critique of the domination of nature with the more affirmative notion of "the production of nature," which conceived nature and its processes as entirely subsumed within social production.[2]

Matters changed, however, with the rise in the late 1990s of a second-stage ecosocialism that returned to Marx's materialist-ecological approach, and particularly to his concept of "social metabolism," while also reincorporating elements of Engels's ecological thought. This development represented a sharp break with the earlier Frankfurt School–influenced approach to the question of Marx and nature. Surveying this history, we will examine the debates on Marxian ecology that have emerged within the left, while pointing to the possibility of a wider synthesis, rooted in Marx's concepts of the "universal metabolism of nature," the "social metabolism," and the "metabolic rift."

CRITICISMS OF MARX'S CONCEPT OF NATURE

Paul Burkett described Schmidt's *The Concept of Nature in Marx* in 1997 as "perhaps the most influential study ever written on Marx's view of nature."[3] The book appeared in Germany in 1962, the same year as Rachel Carson's *Silent Spring*, often seen as the starting point of the modern environmental movement. *The Concept of Nature in Marx* began as Schmidt's dissertation in philosophy, written between 1957 and 1960 under the supervision of Horkheimer and Adorno, and was "impregnated with the influence of 'critical theory.'"[4] It thus antedated the modern environmental movement both historically and philosophically. Yet Schmidt's work, carrying the imprimatur of the Frankfurt School, would come to shape the attitudes of many New Left theorists toward Marx in the context of the burgeoning environmental movement of the 1960s–1980s. As Marxian geographer Neil Smith put it in 1984, Schmidt's book was considered the "definitive study" of nature in Marx.[5]

The Concept of Nature in Marx was deeply affected by the broader Weberian pessimism of the Frankfurt School, which viewed the "domination of nature" as an intrinsic characteristic of modernity or "the dialectic of the Enlightenment."[6] Under Enlightenment civilization, Horkheimer and Adorno declared, "either men will tear each other to pieces or they will take all the flora and fauna of the earth with them; and if the earth is then still young enough, the whole thing will have to be started again at a much lower stage."[7] Although Schmidt brought a number of important, positive contributions to the understanding of nature in Marx, it was his more pessimistic conclusions about the mature Marx, in the spirit of Horkheimer and Adorno, that proved most influential. Rejecting the outlooks of "utopian" Marxist theorists such as Bertolt Brecht and Ernst Bloch who, based on the early Marx, sought a "reconciliation" between humanity and nature through socialism, Schmidt concluded:

> The mature Marx withdrew from the [utopian] theses expounded in his early writings. In later life he no longer wrote of a "resurrection" of the whole of nature. The new society is to benefit man alone, and there is no doubt that this is to be at the expense of external nature. Nature is to be mastered with gigantic technological aids, and the smallest possible expenditure of time and labor. It is to serve all men as the material substratum for all conceivable consumption goods.
>
> When Marx and Engels complain about the unholy plundering of nature, they are not concerned with nature itself but with considerations of economic utility. . . . The exploitation of nature will not cease in the future, but man's encroachments into

nature will be rationalized, so that their remoter consequences will remain capable of control. In this way, nature will be robbed step by step of the possibility of revenging itself on men for their victories over it.[8]

The last phrase was a reference to Engels, whose views on the need for human beings to control their social relation to nature under socialism in order to prevent ecological crises, which he referred to metaphorically as the "revenge" of nature, were interpreted by Schmidt as a case for the extreme "rationalization" and external control of nature.[9] There was no real room in Engels, any more than in Marx, Schmidt insisted, for anything but a one-sided, conqueror's approach to nature—despite Engels's criticisms of precisely this perspective. Engels was reinterpreted as representing a crude, one-sided domination of nature outlook, with the implication that such views could be foisted on Marx himself. In the end, classical historical materialism was reduced to a reified, mechanistic worldview, which advocated a narrow instrumentalism, geared to unrestrained productivism, as the only possible forward course for humanity. The mature Marx, in what became the predominant Frankfurt School interpretation, associated with Horkheimer and Adorno, thus led inexorably to the same Weberian iron cage with respect to the instrumentalist rationalization of nature as did both capitalism and Soviet Marxism.[10]

Close readers of Schmidt's work were no doubt puzzled by the contradictions in his reading of Marx. For Schmidt could not have arrived at these conclusions, in an otherwise sophisticated philosophical reading of Marx's theory of nature, without turning the early Marx against the later Marx, Marx against Engels, Marx against Brecht and Bloch, and even, as we shall see, the mature Marx against the mature Marx.[11] Brilliant as Schmidt's analysis was, it was colored by a double polemic: first, against those who sought to apply the broad anthropological, humanistic, and ecologically utopian perspectives of the early Marx to the later Marx; and second, against all those associated with a more classical historical materialism who suggested that a more sustainable path of development could be achieved under socialism.[12]

Schmidt's study was further compromised by a threefold failure to comprehend the depths of Marx's critique. First, Schmidt's deterministic notion of technology and industrialization under capitalism, and automatically carrying this over into socialism, obscured the significance in this context of Marx's historically specific critique of the capitalist value form, in which *value*, emanating from labor alone, stood in contradiction to *wealth*, derived from both nature and labor.[13] This failure to encompass the full range of Marx's critique led Schmidt (along with Horkheimer and Adorno) to a scrutiny of technology that went no deeper than Max Weber's notion of formal rationality. In contrast, for Marx the goal was not a society aimed at endless quantitative expansion of exchange value but rather the fulfillment of qualitative needs (use value). This meant that technology had to be seen in terms of humanity's changing metabolic relations with nature through production.

Second, Schmidt saw Marx's emphasis on the metabolism of nature and society as a broad philosophical "metaphor," a form of speculative metaphysics. It was not treated principally as a scientific category, related to actual material exchanges and systemic (thermodynamic) processes—though he recognized that element in Marx.[14] Third, he attributed to Marx a conception of external nature as consisting of unchanging, invariant laws—that is, a passive, dualistic, and rigidly positivist conception of nature, in which even evolutionary development within nature (outside humanity) conformed to narrowly delineated, fixed processes. Nature, outside of human nature and human society, was in this vision both passive and mechanical.

Although Schmidt briefly discussed a more dialectical concept of nature in Marx, ultimately Marx was interpreted as adhering in his mature phase to a mechanistic-positivistic scientific view.[15] "The attitude of the mature Marx," Schmidt wrote, "has in it nothing of the exuberance and unlimited optimism to be found in the idea of the future society prescribed in the Paris Manuscripts. It should rather be called skeptical. Men cannot in the last resort be emancipated from the necessities imposed by nature."[16] Hence, Marx was transformed into a forerunner of the skepticism, world-weariness, and dualistic division between natural science and social science, and between nonhuman nature and society, that characterized Schmidt's own mentors, Horkheimer and Adorno. Indeed, Adorno went so far as to declare that Marx "underwrote something as arch-bourgeois as the program of an absolute control of nature."[17]

Adhering to a neo-Kantian epistemological outlook with respect to nature and society, Horkheimer and Adorno, along with Schmidt, rejected both the Hegelian idealist philosophy of nature and the Marxian materialist dialectics of nature (associated especially with Engels), while simultaneously rejecting the early Marx's "unlimited optimism" toward the reconciliation of naturalism and humanism. The dialectic, in the Frankfurt School view, was applicable only to the reflexive realm of society and human history. Natural science, insofar as it was directed at the external, objective world apart from human beings, was depicted as inherently positivistic and separate from the human sciences. Hence, some of the most influential early Frankfurt School thinkers, with the partial exception of Herbert Marcuse, were themselves caught in the contradictions of what they called the "dialectic of Enlightenment," falling prey to a larger neo-Kantian epistemological dualism between nature and society from which there was no exit. This did not prevent them from simultaneously developing a negative philosophical critique of the Enlightenment domination of nature; but it was one that had no meaningful relation to praxis. Here their views were closest to Weber's well-known critical pessimism with respect to the Enlightenment.[18] As in Weber's tragic vision, the "iron cage" of formal rationality offered no visible escape, pointing inexorably to the disenchantment and domination of nature, against which one could only offer empty protests.

For Horkheimer, the "decay of civilization" in modern times arises from the fact that "men cannot utilize their power over nature for the rational organization of the earth"—a problem that he attributed to the formal rationalization common to both capitalism and social- ism, and endemic to the modern human relation to the environment.[19] The decay of civilization was associated with the reactionary rise of new repressive tendencies such as fascism, in which "raw nature," in "revolt against reason," represented animality, primitiveness, and crude Darwinism. "Whenever man deliberately makes nature his principle," Horkheimer wrote, "he regresses to primitive usages. . . . Animals . . . do not reason. . . . In summary, we are the heirs, for better or worse, of the Enlightenment and technological progress."[20] A vain attempt to escape this trap could only lead to a world of barbarism. It followed that Marx's notion of liberation was inevitably forced to accede to the Enlightenment vision of implacable technological progress as the determining force in history. In this sense, Horkheimer was quite distant from his Frankfurt School colleague Marcuse, who saw more room for struggle against the repressive use of technology and for the development of a non-alienated human-ecological metabolism.[21]

Schmidt recognized the abstract possibility of a more revolutionary-critical interpretation of Marx's view of nature.[22] Yet he dismissed this reading, not so much in terms of Marx's own analysis, but rather those of mid-twentieth-century critical theory, represented by Horkheimer and Adorno. "We should ask," he wrote, "whether the future society [socialism] will not be a mammoth machine, whether the prophecy of *Dialektik der Aufklärung* [*Dialectic of Enlightenment*] that 'human society will be a massive racket in nature' will not be fulfilled rather than the young Marx's dream of a humanization of nature, which would at the same time include the naturalization of man."[23] The utopian young Marx, in his view, was refuted by the realist mature Marx, who succumbed to the technocratic rationality of the Enlightenment. As a result, Marxism offered no way out of the "massive racket in nature."

Schmidt's account of Marx's concept of nature, with all of its inconsistencies and convolutions, positing one contradiction after another in Marx's own analysis, reduced historical materialism in the end to a repressive Enlightenment vision—one that reinforced and served to justify Frankfurt School skepticism, pessimism, and worldly alienation. Such views were in many ways a product of the divisions within Marxism that began in the 1930s and deepened after 1956.[24] Western Marxism, as a distinct, largely philosophical, tradition, tended to see classical Marxism—particularly Engels but also extending to Marx himself—as falling prey to positivism.

Commenting on this tendency, William Leiss, a former student of Marcuse, observed in *The Domination of Nature* that "Alfred Schmidt's excellent book . . . attempts (unsuccessfully) to present Marxism as an extreme form of Saint-Simonianism"—that is, reflecting an inherently techno-industrial relation to the conquest of nature.[25] Likewise, for Neil Smith, Schmidt depicted the socialist relation to nature as conceived by Marx as "pretty much like capitalism except worse: the domination of nature."[26] In Burkett's more critical judgment, Schmidt's analysis of *The Concept of Nature in Marx* ended up "in a quagmire of environmental despair."[27]

Despite these limitations, Schmidt, in what can be considered the most original and profound part of his work, centered his argument on Marx's now famous concept of social and ecological "metabolism." Here, he wrote, "Marx introduced a completely new understanding of man's relation to nature."[28] The metabolism category, as employed by Marx in relation to the labor process, made it possible to "speak meaningfully of a 'dialectic of nature.'" The notion of social metabolism thus pointed to what Marx himself had called the possibility of a "higher synthesis" in the human-nature relation.[29]

Nevertheless, Marx's metabolism argument was ultimately marginalized in the later parts of Schmidt's analysis.[30] Schmidt suggested that Marx's notion of metabolism as a dialectical mediation between nature and society through labor and production involved recourse to a form of metaphysical speculation—one that constituted a negative, non-historical ontology.[31] He erroneously attributed Marx's use of the metabolism concept primarily to the influence of the crudely mechanistic scientific materialist Jacob Moleschott—rather than Roland Daniels and Justus von Liebig, the two thinkers Marx drew on most directly. Schmidt saw it as both *pre-bourgeois*, in the backward-looking sense of a utopian, almost mystical attempt to resurrect a past unity, and *mechanistic*, leading him to dismiss what he previously described as a meaningful dialectic of nature.[32]

Ultimately failing to comprehend the full complexity and range of possibility opened up by Marx's concept of social metabolism—an approach that was at once philosophical, political-economic, and ecological—Schmidt rejected it as a metaphysical, metaphorical, and mechanical category, reflecting a "peculiarly unhistorical dialectic of the process of metabolism," a "rigid cyclical form of nature" that was "anterior to man."[33] Recognizing that Marx had introduced a materialist dialectic that connected nature and society, human production/reproduction and the natural-material conditions of existence, Schmidt nonetheless pulled back, wishing to avoid the question of a dialectic of nature. He thus limited the dialectic to an abstracted social realm.

This general outlook on Marx's concept of nature was carried forward and reinforced in various ways in the first-stage ecosocialism that arose in the 1970s and 1980s. Early ecosocialist thinkers, following Schmidt, criticized Marx and Marxism for allegedly downplaying natural limits to economic growth, and thus ecological constraints. They therefore eclectically promoted "the greening of Marxism" by grafting onto Marx's analysis neo-Malthusian notions of environmental constraints, together with purely ethical views of the nature-humanity interrelationship associated with deep ecology and "ecologism."[34] Although they constituted an important self-critique on the part of left theorists, these arguments generally avoided any close scrutiny of the foundations of historical materialism, particularly where issues of natural science were involved.

"The revival of Marxism in the 1960s and 1970s" took for granted, in the critical assessment of historian Eric Hobsbawm, "the nonapplicability of Marx's thought (as distinct from that of Engels, which was regarded as separable and different) to the field of the natural sciences."[35] The new Marxism of this period, as distinct from earlier periods of historical materialism, "left the natural sciences totally to one side." Marx's comprehensive analysis of the natural conditions underlying production and the capitalist economy was generally elided in studies of his work, or dismissed as uninteresting and inessential—even in early ecosocialist accounts.

The Western left concluded that an ecological outlook occupied at best only a marginal place in Marx's historical materialism, and was largely discarded in his later economic works.[36] Expressing what was then the general view within Western Marxism, Perry Anderson wrote in 1983 that "problems of the interaction of the human species with its terrestrial environment [were] essentially absent from classical Marxism."[37] This claim, however, nullified not only Engels's voluminous discussions of the relation of human beings to their natural-physical environment, but also the extensive discussions of natural-material relations and natural science—and within these, ecological concerns—by Marx himself.[38]

For an important first-stage ecosocialist like Benton, Marx had gone overboard in his critique of Thomas Robert Malthus, to the point of exhibiting a "reluctance to recognize 'nature-imposed limits' to human development" altogether. Malthus, meanwhile, was himself to be critically reappropriated in the process of the "greening of Marxism."[39] Gorz declared that socialism as a movement was "on its last legs," hobbled by its narrow productivism, inherited from classical Marxism, and by its lack of a "reflexive modernist" view of nature-society relations.[40] Likewise, Marxian economist James O'Connor, editor of the journal *Capitalism Nature Socialism*, declared that "Marx hinted at, but did not develop, the idea that there may exist a contradiction of capitalism that leads to an 'ecological' theory of crisis and social transformation."[41] Alain Lipietz, writing in *Capitalism Nature Socialism*, went even further, declaring that Marx underestimated "the irreducible character . . . of ecological constraints" and adopted "the Biblico-Christian ideology of the conquest of nature."[42]

Such first-stage ecosocialist thinkers commonly attributed the alleged ecological blind spots in Marx's political economy to intrinsic flaws in the labor theory of value. Since "all value was derived from labor power," environmental sociologist Michael Redclift wrote, "it was impossible [for Marx] to conceive of a 'natural' limit to the material productive forces of society."[43] Yet what Redclift and others failed to notice was that it was this very one-sidedness of the value form in capitalism, when seen apart from the natural form, that lay at the center of Marx's critique—associated with the contradiction between wealth (derived from natural-material use values) and value or exchange value (which left out nature altogether). In Marx's view, once it was recognized that nature—constituting, together with labor, one of the two sources of all wealth—was not included in the capitalist value calculus, but was treated as a "free gift . . . to capital," it was impossible *not* to recognize both the existence of natural limits and capital's destructive tendency to override them, in its unending drive to accumulation.[44]

First-stage ecosocialists therefore erroneously perceived Marx's critique of capitalism as, at best, neutral with respect to ecological issues and, at worst, anti-ecological—even if the early Marx had alluded to the possibility of a unity of naturalism and humanism. Yet socialism, in the view of these thinkers, remained essential, chiefly for its critique of labor exploitation. Early ecosocialist thinkers thus grafted Green concepts onto historical-materialist analysis, creating a hybrid, Centaur-like construct. In the case of Benton, perhaps the most articulate spokesperson for first-stage ecosocialism, elements of Marx's critique of political economy, such as his political hostility to "Malthusian 'natural limits' arguments"; the priority given to value theory; his neglect of ecological processes; and his alleged "Prometheanism," or extreme productivism, all "obstructed the development of historical materialism as an explanatory theory of ecological crisis." These presumed shortcomings of Marxism required an "interdisciplinary collaboration between a revised historical materialism and ecology."[45]

Yet as commendable as such a program appeared on the surface, without a thoroughgoing exploration and reconstruction of Marx's own analysis of the nature-society dialectic, the hoped-for higher synthesis could only end up as an eclectic mishmash in which the critical power of the historical-materialist tradition would be lost. More important, the criticisms of Marx within first-stage ecosocialist theory were often distorted, not only in their understanding of Marx's own ecological conceptions, but in the adoption of views (for example Malthusianism) that were antagonistic to a fully developed Marxian ecology.

THE PRODUCTION OF NATURE:
A NEW HUMAN EXEMPTIONALISM

Other left theorists took an entirely different tack, distant from both the Frankfurt School and first-stage ecosocialism. Geographer Neil Smith embraced the basic structure of Schmidt's interpretation of Marx, but sought to stand it on its head, contending that Schmidt had himself advanced a "quintessentially bourgeois conception of nature out of his reading of Marx." If Schmidt's *Concept of Nature in Marx* had argued that the mature Marx was caught in the technological determinism and extreme productivism that characterized the dialectic of Enlightenment, Smith offered a far more positive reading, depicting Marx's view as one of the "production of nature," or the constant reinvention and transformation of nature through production. As Smith's follower Noel Castree acknowledged, Smith sought to solve the problem with a one-way causality from production to nature, leading to a "hyper-constructionist" outlook. Nature was reduced to a passive concept. Smith's production of nature analysis, Castree noted, "looked more at how capitalism produces nature and less at how produced nature affects capitalism."[46] For Smith, in Castree's words, "Nature becomes internal to capitalism."[47] This kind of anthropomorphic monism subsumed nature almost completely within society, in an effort to solve the problem of "dualism," which Smith and Castree charged characterized nearly all other views of the environmental problem.[48]

Hence, in Smith's inverted Frankfurt School perspective on the domination of nature, nature as a whole was envisioned in almost Baconian terms as increasingly produced by human beings for their own ends. It was possible, he argued, to speak of "the real subsumption of nature" in its entirety within human production. The late twentieth century, he proclaimed, marked the infiltration of society into the last "remnant[s] of a recognizably external nature." Indeed, there was no longer any meaningful nature anywhere apart from human beings: "Nature is nothing if it is not social." "The production of nature," in Smith's words, was "capitalized 'all the way down.'" From this perspective, the historical production of nature represented "the unity of nature toward which capitalism drives." In this ever-increasing, capitalist-generated unity, "first nature," that is, nature at its most elemental, was "produced from within and as a part of second nature," that is, nature as transformed by society. Smith effectively dismissed any recognition of "external nature" as a dynamic, evolutionary force outside and beyond, and often interacting with, humanity itself, as "dualism," "fetishism of nature," and "nature washing." Natural science was itself to be faulted for focusing on "so-called laws of nature" outside society.[49]

"Given Marx's own treatment of nature," Smith went so far as to argue, "it may not be unreasonable to see in his vision also a certain version of the conceptual dualism of nature."[50] Marx himself was therefore partly to blame for the rise of "left apocalypticism," which Smith identified with contemporary environmentalism with its dualistic outlook.[51]

Castree followed the same line as Smith, emerging as a major proponent of the production of nature approach, though in a slightly more nuanced form. Castree stated that "Marx did not himself provide a systematic account of nature. This task was left to Alfred Schmidt."[52] The brilliance of Schmidt's analysis, for Castree, was reflected in his detection of a "fundamental flaw" in Marx. Although "Marx apparently envisioned a harmonious balance of nature and society" in his "anticipatory-utopian vision," this pointed to "a subtext of a will to power: that is, an affection for technology in the service of human well-being which could unintentionally turn into the domination of nature, and ironically (after Adorno and Hokheimer) into the domination of humans themselves."[53] Following Smith, Castree leveled the accusation of "dualism" at almost all Marxist analysts of nature-society relations, from classical Marxism to the present—hardly sparing Marx himself, whose saving grace, in Castree's view, was that he had inspired Smith's unifying conception of the "production of nature."[54] In this view, the production of nature perspective eliminated the dualism arising from the separateness of nature by subsuming nature in society. Yet most contemporary ecosocialists, Castree suggested, had failed to incorporate this advance of Smith, and had "*reintroduced* nature's putative separateness" in their treatments of Marx.[55]

Production of nature analysis, Smith and Castree declared, had gone beyond classical Marxism, in that it rejected altogether the idea of "external nature," which had infected even Engels's *Dialectics of Nature*. "As Smith correctly observes," Castree pronounced, "nature separate from society has no meaning."[56] A developed Marxian approach in this realm rejected the notions of "universal" and "external" nature, since such conceptions inevitably led to the crudities of naturalism and dualism. On this basis, Smith and Castree discarded entirely Marx's vision of a materialist, open dialectic in which human beings and society form a part of nature, and exist within it, in a complex, mediated, coevolutionary relationship.[57]

The production of nature argument was rooted in a binary conception that pitted dualism against monism. In this view, which lacked the concept of dialectical mediation in order to escape dualism, one was forced to choose between either a "monistic doctrine of universal nature" or, at the opposite extreme, a monistic doctrine of the production of nature by society—sometimes given an added nuance by reference to "co-production," and to a double or hyphenated reality.[58] The production of nature school chose the latter: a monist, hypersocial constructivism, such that nature and natural conditions were entirely subordinated to human production. This in essence is the view that environmental sociologists criticize as human exemptionalism—the anthropocentric notion that human beings are largely exempt from natural laws, or can imperialistically transform them as they wish.[59]

The logical result was Smith's critique of environmental apocalypticism, directed at the environmental movement. Writing in 2015 about the political consequences of Smith's production of nature analysis, Castree noted that "certain strands of environmental and body-politics operative outside universities are now [like Smith himself] dispensing with 'nature' as an ontological referent." Here he cited the book *Break Through*, written by leading ecological modernists Michael Shellenberger and Ted Nordhaus.[60] "In a generic sense,"

Castree declared, "this mirrors Smith's insistence that we need new terms of radical political discourse."[61]

Ironically, Castree failed to note that Shellenberger and Nordhaus's analysis represented exactly the opposite: new terms of reactionary political discourse. The Breakthrough Institute, which Shellenberger and Nordhaus head, is the principal ideological think tank in the United States dedicated to the single-minded promotion of capitalist ecological modernization. As self-designated "post-environmentalists," thinkers associated with the Breatkthrough Institute see technological innovation and market mechanisms as the solution to all environmental problems and entirely compatible with unlimited economic growth and capital accumulation. They are thus sharp critics of radical ecology and of environmentalism in general.[62]

MARX, METABOLISM, AND THE METABOLIC RIFT

To escape such one-sided views—whether idealist or mechanistic, monist or dualist—which have dominated much left analysis of the nature-society relation since Schmidt, it is necessary to turn to Marx's ecology itself, in which the materialist conception of history and the materialist conception of nature formed a dialectical unity. By excavating the ecological foundations of classical historical materialism, second-stage ecosocialist theorists since the late 1990s have moved well beyond earlier misconceptions, creating the basis for a wider ecological synthesis. Here the analysis has pivoted on the dialectical approach implicit in Marx's triadic scheme of "the universal metabolism of nature," the "social metabolism," and the metabolic rift.[63]

Although in Marx's analysis it still makes sense abstractly to differentiate nature and natural processes from the labor and production process, there is no longer any pure nature on earth untouched by human society, nor is there any pure realm of society free from the dire natural-material consequences of human actions. In the Anthropocene epoch, it is therefore all the more necessary to explore the complex, dialectical natural-social interconnections between the Earth System as a whole and capitalism as a system of alienated social metabolic reproduction *within* that Earth System. Today the drive to capital accumulation is disrupting the planetary metabolism at cumulatively higher levels, threatening irreversible, catastrophic impacts for countless species, including our own. It is in the theorization of this ecological and social dialectic, and in the development of a meaningful praxis to address it, that Marx's analysis has proven indispensable.

Second-stage ecosocialism sought to return to Marx and earthly questions. The aim was to draw on the ecological foundations of classical historical materialism to develop a more unified socioecological critique. British Marxist sociologist Peter Dickens was among those who took initial steps to open up such an analysis. In his 1992 book *Society and Nature: Towards a Green Social Theory*, he focused on Marx's early writings, such as the *Economic and Philosophic Manuscripts*, insisting that this work provides key insights into how the organization, processes, and relations of the capitalist system alienated humanity from nature. He proposed that people's understanding of nature tends to be shaped by their lived experiences within a society dominated by commodity production. Although some of the baggage of first-stage ecosocialism, such as an assumption that Marx in his mature works largely ignored natural limits and promoted an extreme productivism, still remained, Dickens's work nonetheless represented a turning point. He was critical of simply grafting deep-ecology positions onto a revised Marxism. He insisted on the need to extend Marx's method, which included both a historical-materialist and dialectical assessment of the relationship between society and nature. From a critical-realist orientation, he explained that larger emergent properties and boundaries within the biophysical world must be recognized, and that the capitalist system was "overloading these self-regulating ecosystems and stretching them to a point at which they [could] no longer cope."[64]

Second-stage ecosocialist scholarship called into question the tendency to pit the young Marx against the mature Marx, Marx against Engels, and natural science against social science. Paul Burkett explained that elemental ecological ideas ran throughout Marx's work, even though the language in which he expressed them changed. Marx had moved over the course of his studies from highly "abstract" to "more consistently historical and social-relational" concepts.[65] Burkett also pointed out that Marx and Engels were both committed to a "materialist and social-scientific approach to nature," which served as the basis for extending and developing their analysis, creating opportunities for complementary work between the social and natural sciences.[66] In other words, they insisted upon employing both a materialist conception of history and a materialist conception of nature as necessary counterparts.[67]

Their efforts to analyze the interactions and transformations in the dialectical nature-society relationship was greatly enhanced by Marx's use of metabolic analysis. Here Marx's critique of political economy merged with his assessment of ecological relations, illuminating the interpenetration of nature and society, as well as the scale and processes through which these interactions had historically developed. Marx embedded socioeconomic systems in ecology and explicitly studied the interchange of matter and energy between the larger environment and society.[68] Ecological economist Marina Fischer-Kowalski has proposed that social metabolic analysis, arising out of Marx's work, can illuminate the coupling of human and natural systems, because it "cut[s] across the 'great divide' between the natural sciences . . . and the social sciences."[69] The engagement and development of Marx's triadic scheme—metabolism of nature, social metabolism, and metabolic rift—helped solidify the second stage of ecosocialist analyses and served as the springboard for the third stage, with the result that this methodology is now widely used to address many of today's most pressing ecological challenges.

In developing his metabolic analysis, Marx drew on a long scientific and intellectual history. In the early nineteenth century, physiologists introduced the concept of metabolism to examine the biochemical processes between a cell and its surroundings, as well as the interactions and exchanges between an organism and the biophysical world. The physician and communist Roland Daniels, who was Marx's friend and comrade, extended the use of metabolism to whole complexes of organisms, foreshadowing its application in ecosystem analysis.[70] Although Daniels's work was not published for more than a century, due to his untimely death in his mid-thirties (he contracted pneumonia while in prison during the Cologne communist trials), the broad idea he represented would, through the investigations of other thinkers, become the basis for examining higher levels of organization and interdependency, including the interchange of matter and energy, between human societies and the larger environment. The German chemist Justus von Liebig helped generalize the concept of metabolism, using it to study the exchange of nutrients between Earth and humans.[71] He explained that soil required specific nutrients—such as nitrogen, phosphorus, and potassium—to produce vegetation. As plants grew, they absorbed soil nutrients. To maintain soil fertility, these nutrients had to be recycled back to the land.

Marx, who closely followed scientific debates and discoveries, incorporated the concept of metabolism into his critique of political economy, explaining that he employed the word to denote "the 'natural' process of production as the material exchange [*Stoffwechesel*] between man and nature."[72] He recognized that humans are dependent on nature and "can create nothing without" it.[73] For "the earth itself is a universal instrument . . . for it provides the worker with the ground beneath his feet and a 'field of employment' for his own particular process."[74] As a result, there is a necessary "metabolic interaction" between humans and the earth. Labor serves as "a process between man and nature, a process by which man, through his own actions, mediates, regulates and controls the metabolism between himself and nature."[75] The labor process, including exchanges with ecological systems, is influenced by the dominant economic systems and social institutions, defining what Marx saw as the social metabolism.

The complex, nuanced ecological worldview in Marx's formulation is evident in his conception of both the "universal metabolism of nature" and the social metabolism.[76] The "universal metabolism of nature" stood for the broader biophysical world.[77] Specific cycles and processes constitute and help regenerate ecological conditions. Human society exists within the earthly metabolism, continually interacting with its external natural environment in the production of goods, services, and needs. As a result, the social metabolism operates within the larger universal metabolism. Under capitalist commodity production, this relationship takes on such an alienated form that it generates ecological crises, manifesting as a "rift" in the metabolism between society and nature (or disjunctures within both the social metabolism and the wider universal metabolism). This demands the "restoration" of these necessary conditions. "The natural boundary" to human production, as Georg Lukács, following Marx, stated, "can only retreat, it can never fully disappear."[78]

Marx avoided subordinating nature to society, or vice versa, allowing him to elude "the pitfalls of both absolute idealism and mechanistic science."[79] His metabolic analysis recognizes that humans and the rest of nature are in constant interaction, resulting in reciprocal influences, consequences, and dependencies. These processes emerge within a relational, thermodynamic whole, the universal metabolism of nature.

Humans transform nature through production. However, "they do not do so just as they please; rather they do so under conditions inherited from the past (of both natural and social history), remaining dependent on the underlying dynamics of life and material existence."[80] Each mode of production generates a distinct social metabolic order that influences the interchange and interpenetration of society and ecological systems.[81] The social metabolic order of capital, for example, is expressed as a unique historical system of socioecological relations developed within a capitalist mode of social organization. Human social systems exchange with, work within, and draw on ecological systems in the process of producing and maintaining life and sociocultural conditions.

Yet within the social metabolic order of capital, this process materializes in a manner unlike other previous socioecological systems. The practical activities of life are shaped by the expansion and accumulation of capital. Marxian economist Paul Sweezy explained that in their "pursuit of profit . . . capitalists are driven to accumulate ever more capital, and this becomes both their subjective goal and the motor force of the entire economic system."[82] The compulsion to accumulate leads to continuous cycles of creative destruction (and destructive creation), as novel productive and distributive methods are developed and exploitable resources expanded to power industry and manufacture commodities. The needs of capital are imposed on nature, increasing the demands placed on ecological systems and the production of wastes.

To illustrate such social metabolic analysis, it is useful to consider how Marx, drawing on the work of chemists and agronomists, analyzed the transformations associated with capitalist agricultural production. He explained that soil "fertility is not so natural a quality as might be thought; it is closely bound up with the social relations of the time."[83] In many precapitalist societies, farm animals were directly utilized in agricultural production. They were fed grains from the farm, and their nutrient-rich manure was reincorporated into the soil as fertilizer. People who lived in the countryside primarily consumed food and fiber from nearby farms. Their waste was likewise integrated into the nutrient cycle, helping maintain soil fertility.

This particular metabolic interchange was transformed in large part by the enclosure movement, the rise of the new industrial systems, and social relations associated with capitalist development. A wider, more alienated division between town and country emerged, as food and fiber from farms were increasingly shipped to distant markets, which transferred the nutrients from one location to another. The nutrients in food were squandered, and treated as mere waste accumulated as pollution within cities and rivers.[84] Liebig, in his *Letters on Modern Agriculture*, argued that these emerging social conditions contributed to the disruption of the soil nutrient cycle. In the introduction to the 1862 edition of his *Organic Agriculture in its Application to Chemistry and Physiology* (better known as *Agricultural Chemistry*), he described the modern intensive farming practices of Britain as a system of "robbery" that exhausted the nutrients within the soil.[85] In *Capital*, Marx similarly suggested that new agricultural practices, including the application of industrial power, increased the scale of operations, transforming and intensifying the social metabolism while exacerbating the depletion of the soil nutrients.[86]

As a result, large-scale capitalist agriculture, Marx argued, progressively "disturbs the metabolic interaction between man and the earth."[87] Along with the various mechanisms used to intensify production and increase profits, it created a metabolic "rift" in the soil nutrient cycle, "robbing the soil" and "ruining the more long-lasting sources of that fertility."[88] As it violated the universal metabolism associated with the soil nutrient cycle (also conceived as a law of restitution), the rift undermined soil fertility and the conditions that supported human society. These nutrients from the consumption of food and fiber in the urban centers of the capitalist world were lost to the soil, and were turned into mere waste polluting the cities.

Reflecting on the industrialization of farming, Marx lamented that "agriculture no longer finds the natural conditions of its own production within itself, naturally, arisen, spontaneous, and ready to hand, but these exist as an independent industry separate from it—and, with this separateness the whole complex set of interconnections in which this industry exists is drawn into the sphere of the conditions of agricultural production."[89] In his discussion of "The Genesis of Capitalist Ground Rent" in volume three of *Capital*, he explained that the drive to capital accumulation "reduces the agricultural population to an ever decreasing minimum and confronts it with an ever growing industrial population crammed together in large towns; in this way it produces conditions that provoke an irreparable rift in the interdependent process of social metabolism, a metabolism prescribed by the natural laws of life itself. The result of this is a squandering of the vitality of the soil, which is carried by trade far beyond the bounds of a single country."[90]

In the nineteenth century, the rift in the soil nutrient cycle posed a significant environmental problem for European agriculture and societies. Numerous attempts were made to find affordable means of enriching the soil. Bones were ground up and spread across fields, and massive quantities of guano and nitrates were imported from Peru and Chile to Britain and other regions of the Global North to sustain agricultural production.[91] The social relations associated with this metabolic rift expanded from the local to the national and international levels, as the bounty of the countryside and distant lands was transferred to urban centers of the Global North. Just prior to the First World War, the process for producing nitrates by fixing nitrogen from the atmosphere was developed, allowing for the large-scale production of artificial nitrogen fertilizer. Nevertheless, the failure to recycle nutrients still contributes to the ongoing depletion of soil by intensive agricultural practices. As a result, the metabolic rift in the soil nutrient cycle remains a persistent problem of the modern social metabolic order.[92]

Dickens's 2004 book *Society and Nature: Changing Our Environment, Changing Ourselves* highlighted the important advances of the second stage of ecosocialism, especially the centrality of a historical-materialist conception of both nature and society, the nature-society dialectic, and metabolic analysis. He engaged a broad range of Marx's works, exploring the depth of Marx's ecology. He considered how distinct modes of production involved different demands and interactions with the larger environment, and explained—based on earlier research into "Marx's Theory of Metabolic Rift"—that "the notion of an ecological rift, one separating humanity and nature and violating the principles of ecological sustainability, continues to be helpful for understanding today's social and environmental risks."[93] Importantly, Dickens showed how to extend this analysis to contemporary environmental problems, especially those associated with cities. He proposed that "three metabolic problems" plague modern cities, namely "the provision of an adequate water supply, the effective disposal of sewage and the control of air pollution." These problems highlight how "humanity's metabolism with nature [is] not being ultimately destroyed but [is] being overloaded in the context of a particular kind of social and spatial organization."[94]

Marxist metabolic research continues to thrive. In many ways, as the late Del Weston argued in *The Political Economy of Global Warming*, the "metabolic rift is at the crux of Marx's ecological critique of capitalism, denoting the disjuncture between social systems and the rest of nature."[95] It has been employed to analyze metabolic relations and ecological rifts in contemporary agricultural, climatic, oceanic, hydraulic, and forest systems.[96] Other theorists have used the concept of the metabolic rift, and Marx's ecological materialism in general, to develop a "Marxist ecofeminism" that explores the relation between rifts in nature and in gender relations.[97]

Much of this recent scholarship examines how the social metabolism of capitalism as a global system has created specific environmental problems in the modern era by transgressing the universal metabolism of nature. The intensification of the social metabolism demands more energy and raw materials, generating an array of ecological contradictions and rifts.[98] Other analysts consider how, as capitalism confronts environmental problems or obstacles—such as a shortage or exhaustion of particular natural resources—it pursues a series of shifts and technological fixes to maintain its expansion. In this way, environmental problems are addressed by incorporating new resources into the production process, changing the location of production, or developing new technologies to increase efficiency. Yet far from mending ecological rifts, such shifts often simply create new cumulative problems, generating additional disruptions on a larger scale.[99] It is clear that the required "metabolic restoration" necessitates an ecological and social revolution to overturn the social metabolic order of capital—aimed at the creation of a higher society in which the associated producers rationally regulate the social metabolism in accord with the requirements of the universal metabolism of nature, while allowing for the fulfillment of their own human needs.[100]

MARX AND NATURE IN THE ANTHROPOCENE: TOWARD A CRITICAL SYNTHESIS

Horkheimer and Adorno wrote the *Dialectic of Enlightenment* during the Second World War while in exile in the United States. They intended it as an account of the extreme domination of nature and domination of humanity that characterized all of the warring countries, all of which were in various ways heirs of the Enlightenment. It was followed several years later by Horkheimer's *Eclipse of Reason*, which argued that through fascism in Europe and social Darwinism in the United States, the domination of nature had provoked a "revolt of nature," which was being harnessed in reactionary ways to reinforce the domination of both nature and society. For Horkheimer, "Whenever nature is exalted as a supreme principle and becomes the weapon of thought against thinking, against civilization, thought manifests a kind of hypocrisy, and so develops an uneasy conscience. . . . Indeed, the Nazi regime as a revolt of nature became a lie the moment it became conscious of itself as a revolt. The lackey of the very mechanized civilization [capitalism] that it professed to reject, it took over the inherently repressive measures of the latter."[101]

Social Darwinism emerged, Horkheimer argued, as "the main growth of the Enlightenment," and thus represented a repressive force harnessed to a naturalistic revolt against machine civilization, creating an even greater repression. The result, he wrote, was a huge Faustian tragedy. "The history of man's efforts to subjugate nature," he explained, "is also the history of man's subjection of man."[102] Yet, he insisted, there was no going back: "We are the heirs, for better or worse, of the Enlightenment and technological progress. To oppose these by regressing to more primitive stages does not alleviate the permanent crisis they have brought about. On the contrary, such expedients lead from historically reasonable to utterly barbaric forms of social domination."[103] Projecting a highly abstract, idealist philosophical argument, he concluded that "the sole way of assisting nature is to unshackle its seeming opposite, independent thought."[104]

It was in this context, as indicated above, that Schmidt wrote *The Concept of Nature in Marx*. As in Horkheimer and Adorno's work, Schmidt treated the dialectic of the Enlightenment as a form of the domination of nature, from which there was virtually no escape. Schmidt insisted that Marx, like Georg Wilhelm Friedrich Hegel, saw the labor process as the mere "outsmarting and duping of nature."[105] According to Schmidt, even when Marx pointed to nature as a "co-producer" with labor, it was in the context of the promotion of narrow human ends.[106] The needs of external nature were entirely "foreign" to Marx's whole outlook. Bloch's humane Marxian "philosophy of hope" was thus in reality a hopeless utopian quest, which turned into an empty "apocalyptic vision."[107]

Smith accepted the main formulations of Schmidt's analysis, while inverting the Frankfurt School critique, and promoting the "production of nature" as the Marxian ideal—a view that Smith acknowledged could not be found in Marx himself. Here the problem of the domination of nature simply disappeared before the unceasing expansion of the human production of nature. He thus dismissed the environmental movement's growing resistance to this unsustainable economic exploitation of nature as "left apocalypticism," condemning such "apocalypticism" even more absolutely than Schmidt had in his criticism of Bloch's so-called "apocalyptic vision." Nature, in Smith's view, was increasingly without any reality at all, outside of its production by human beings.[108]

It is here, however, that we discover, by way of contrast to the social monism of the production of nature thesis, the liberatory potential that still lingered in the work of the more adamantly socialist-humanist thinkers associated with the Frankfurt School. For in their concern with the domination of nature alongside the domination of humanity, the more critical and praxis-oriented representatives of the Frankfurt School never ceased to notice the contradictions of capitalism and the possibility of transcending contemporary reality. At the very inception of the Institute for Social Research in Frankfurt, in 1932, Erich Fromm, in his seminal paper "The Method and Function of an Analytic Social Philosophy," pointed to Marx's notion of the labor process as a metabolic relation, an integrated dialectic of nature and society.[109] Here he underscored the significance of Bukharin's 1925 book *Historical Materialism*, often dismissed for its mechanistic materialism, for its insight into this aspect of Marx's analysis.

Lukács, writing only a few years after *History and Class Consciousness* in his *Tailism* manuscript of 1925–26—though this reflected in part his break with Western Marxism—argued that a meaningful dialectics of nature in Marx was embodied in his theory of the labor process as the metabolic relation between humanity and nature. Furthermore, given that "human life is based on the metabolism with nature" meant, for Lukács, that "certain truths which we acquire in the process of carrying out this metabolism have a general validity."[110]

Marcuse, the most directly ecological of the early Frankfurt School thinkers (though this was mainly manifested in his later writings), declared: "History is also grounded in nature. And Marxist theory has the least justification to ignore the metabolism between the human being and nature, and to denounce the insistence on this natural soil of society as a regressive ideological conception."[111]

In Marcuse's more hopeful, dissenting Frankfurt School vision, rooted in Marx's *Economic and Philosophical Manuscripts*, it was possible to conceive of an ecologically based liberation movement. "What is happening," he wrote in *Counter-Revolution and Revolt*, "is the discovery (or rather rediscovery) of nature as an ally in the struggle against the exploitative societies in which the violation of nature aggravates the violation of man. The discovering of the liberating forces of nature and their vital role in the construction of a free society becomes a new force in social change."[112]

Dickens likewise drew inspiration from Marx's early writings, emphasizing in his early *Society and Nature: Towards a Green Social Theory* that a sociology of ecological liberation could be developed on the basis of the work of the young Marx. In his later book, *Society and Nature: Changing Our Environment, Changing Ourselves*, Dickens criticized Horkheimer and Adorno's "fearsome anti-Enlightenment critique" as sheer "pessimism."[113] Instead, Dickens argued for a more positive, ecological-revolutionary vision, rooted in Marx's theory of metabolic rift. "Marx's early [naturalist-humanist] background," he observed, "led him to undertake no less than an analysis of what would now be called 'environmental sustainability.' In particular, he developed the idea of a 'rift' in the metabolic relation between humanity and nature, one seen as an emergent feature of capitalist society."[114] The goal ultimately needed to be the creation of a sustainable and egalitarian society, able to "mend the 'metabolic rift' between nature and society."[115]

Still, not all on the left would agree with second-stage ecosocialists in this respect, nor with the need to focus on the question of the ecological rift or domination of nature engendered by capitalist society. According to Smith, writing in the 2007 *Socialist Register*, the Frankfurt School—referring mainly to Horkheimer, Adorno, and Schmidt—always dualistically conceived the "domination of nature" as "an inevitable condition of the human metabolism with nature." Similarly, "ecological essentialists"—his term for radical ecologists generally—"recognize a parallel attempt at domination, but they see it not as inevitable but as a destructive social choice." In sharp contrast, Smith's own "production-of-nature thesis" rejected both of these so-called dualistic views: "The domination-of-nature thesis [encompassing both perspectives] is a cul-de-sac ... the only political alternatives are an anti-social (literally) politics of nature or else resignation to a kinder, gentler domination."[116] For Smith, "The externality and universality of nature ... are not to be taken as ontological givens. The ideology of external-cum-universal nature harks back to a supposedly edenic, pre-human, or supra-human world."[117]

Indeed, Smith, in the name of combatting dualism, went so far as to dismiss the entire ecological struggle to mitigate climate change, writing: "In the end, the attempt to distinguish social [that is, anthropogenic] vis-à-vis natural contributions to climate change is not only a fool's debate but a fool's philosophy: it leaves sacrosanct the chasm between nature and society—nature in one corner, society in the other—which is precisely the shibboleth of modern Western thought that the 'production of nature' thesis sought to corrode. One does not have to be a 'global warming denier' ... to be a skeptic concerning the way that a global public is being stampeded into accepting wave upon wave of technical, economic, and social change, framed as necessary for immediate planetary survival."[118] On this basis, he condemned what he called "the apocalyptic tone of imminent environmental doom," associated with much of science and the environmental movement.[119]

By inverting the Frankfurt School's critical domination of nature thesis, and turning that into an uncritical production of nature notion (a kind of anthropomorphic social monism), Smith, Castree, and other like-minded thinkers effectively de-naturalize social theory to an extreme, imposing ecological blinders.[120] What is excluded is a more developed, dialectical perspective, pointing to the alienation of nature under capitalism.

In contrast, the enduring value of Marx's ecological materialism, incorporating such critical concepts as the universal metabolism of nature, the social metabolism, and the metabolic rift, is that it points in a coevolutionary and co-revolutionary direction, highlighting the need for a new order of social metabolic reproduction rooted in substantive equality.[121] Here social and natural necessity, natural science and social science, humanity and the earth *become one human-mediated totality*, in a wider universal struggle—pointing to a revolutionary dialectic of humanity and the earth in which the necessary outcome is a world of sustainable human development. It is this higher synthesis of the various Marxian ecological and social critiques, building on the foundations of historical materialism, that we are most in need of today.

9

Value Isn't Everything

THE RAPID ADVANCES in Marxian ecology in the last two decades have given rise to extensive debates within the left, reflecting competing conceptions of theory and practice in an age of planetary ecological and social crisis. One key area of dispute is associated with the attempt by a growing number of radical environmental thinkers to deconstruct the labor theory of value in order to bring everything in existence within a single commodity logic, replicating in many ways the attempts of liberal environmentalists to promote the notion of "natural capital," and to impute commodity prices to "ecosystem services."[1] For many in Green circles, Karl Marx and a long tradition of Marxian theorists are to be faulted for not directly incorporating the expenditure of physical work/energy by extra-human nature into the theory of value.

Indeed, for a number of contemporary left environmental thinkers, like Giorgos Kallis, Dinesh Wadiwel, and Zehra Taşdemir Yaşın, not only human beings but also nature/animals/energy produce economic value under capitalism.[2] For others adopting a more circuitous approach, like world-ecologist Jason W. Moore, the distinctive role of labor in the generation of value is formally acknowledged, but the "law of value in a capitalist society" is defined as "a law of Cheap

Nature." Labor's contribution to the production of value is viewed as epiphenomenal, largely determined by the wider appropriation of "work" or energy, in the sense of physics, carried out by the web of life as a whole.[3]

In this "new law of value," as explained in Moore's 2015 book, *Capitalism in the Web of Life*, the ultimate basis of valorization is the capitalist appropriation of the "unpaid" work of both organic and inorganic actors, focusing in particular on the Four Cheaps (labor power, energy, food, and raw materials) or what he referred to two years later, in *A History of the World in Seven Cheap Things*, written with Raj Patel, as the Seven Cheaps—adding nature, work, money, lives, and care work, while subtracting labor power and raw materials. The Four or Seven Cheaps, taken together, thus replace labor power as the real foundation of value. In this more "expansive" approach to value, the labor theory of value is relegated to a ghostlike existence, an ethereal substance, while the real basis of valorization now is the entire web of life—pointing to an *everything theory of value*. Is not the real question, Moore pointedly asks, "The Value of Everything?"[4]

To be sure, liberal environmental criticisms of Marxian value theory go back to the beginnings of contemporary Green theory. Such criticisms rest on the systematic conflation of two distinct meanings of value: intrinsic value (or the value that we attribute to things in themselves and to our relations) and commodity value. Writing in 1973 in *Small Is Beautiful*, E. F. Schumacher contended that there is a tendency in modern society "to treat as valueless everything that we have not made ourselves. Even the great Dr. Marx fell into this devastating error when he formulated the so-called 'labour theory of value.'"[5]

Charges of this kind commit the fallacy of confusing Marx's critique of capitalist commodity value with the question of intrinsic value or with wider transhistorical cultural notions of value as worth. Crucial here is the recognition that Marx was the greatest *critic* of the capitalist value form. As Moishe Postone rightly observed in *Time, Labor, and Social Domination*, Marx was concerned primarily with "the abolition of value as the social form of wealth."[6] Marx's *Capital* thus sought to explain value relations under capitalism as part of a historical process of transcending them. He distinguished between real wealth consisting of use values, representing what he called the "natural form" within production, and value/exchange value, that is, the "value form" associated with specifically capitalist production.[7] Socialism has as its specific goal overcoming the narrow value form so as to allow for the development of a rich world of needs, while rationally regulating the metabolism between humanity and nature.

It is thus the failure to perceive Marx's analysis as *critique*—far removed in that respect from liberal political economy whose concepts are designed to validate the existing order and are therefore presented as transhistorical ideals—that underlies the mistaken Green criticisms of Marxian value theory. Marx did not seek to defend or validate capitalist value relations, much less to universalize them by extending them to other realms of reality. Rather, in his perspective, the revolutionary goal was to abolish the system of commodity value altogether, and to replace it with a new system of sustainable human development controlled by the direct producers.

For Marx, the narrow pursuit of value-based accumulation, through the "robbery" of the earth itself, at the expense of "eternal natural necessity," generated a metabolic rift in the relation between human society and the larger natural world of which it was an emergent part.[8] Coupled with the related class contradictions of capitalism, these conditions pointed to the need for the expropriation of the expropriators. Hence, the great advantage of the Marxian ecological critique over the standard Green theory criticisms of capitalism is precisely that it focuses on the historical-materialist bases of contemporary ecological destruction, and points to the means of their transcendence. Rather than countering capitalism with a set of transhistorical values or ideals, its focus is on a critique of the existing mode of commodity production, accumulation, and valorization— a critique that extends to capitalism's relentless undermining of the environmental conditions of existence and of the Earth System itself. In Marx's theory, (commodity) value is *not* everything and is distinguished from real wealth (use values).[9]

But if such traditional Green criticisms of Marxian theory are easily answered, recent developments within posthumanist thought, which today are transforming the character of Green theory, have gone much further in the attempted demolition of classical historical materialism. This has occurred through the promotion of two closely connected arguments: (1) deconstruction of social labor as the basis of value, to be replaced by what is seen as a more "inclusive" physiological or energetic theory of value; and (2) subsumption of the entire web of life, in all of its aspects, under the law of value of the world commodity economy. The object of such analyses is the "destabilization of value as an 'economic' category," on which the classical Marxian critique of capitalism, with its focus on the twofold alienation of labor and nature, ultimately depends.[10] In contrast, a coherent ecological critique of capitalism requires an understanding of the dialectical contradiction between the natural form and the value form inherent in the commodity economy.

Posthumanist Ecological Critiques and Marx's Concept of Social Labor

Although Marxian economics has often been faulted by Green theorists of various kinds for not developing a physiological or energetic theory of value, and for tracing value exclusively to human labor, there is no extant economic theory—whether classical, neoclassical, neo-Ricardian, or contemporary ecological economics—that sees nature as directly productive of economic value (or value added) in the contemporary capitalist economy. With minor exceptions, all economics from the classical period to the present has perceived what nature itself provides, independent of human labor/human services, as a "free gift" to the economy—an idea that goes back to the classical theorists Adam Smith, Thomas Robert Malthus, David Ricardo, and Karl Marx, and is carried forward in contemporary neoclassical and Marxian economics. Nature, of course, provides the material basis of production and affects productivity, and rents are applied to everything from the soil to fossil fuels, and enter price determination in that way; yet commodity value in the most general sense is viewed in all schools of economics as a distinctly human product, reflecting the actual working of the capitalist economy.

For many environmental theorists, who confuse intrinsic value with economic value, to exclude animal labor or energy from a conception of value is simply anthropocentric. From a classical Marxist perspective, however, the critique of capitalist commodity production captures not only the inner logic of the accumulation process, but also the limitations and contradictions of the system, marked by the distinctions between, on the one hand, the "natural form" (use value, concrete labor, and real wealth) and the "value form" (exchange value, abstract labor, and value).[11] Both the economic and ecological contradictions of capitalism have their source in the contradictions between the valorization process and the material bases of existence inherent in capitalist commodity production. To deny the historically specific character of abstract labor as a form of social labor under capitalism is to deny the extreme character of the valorization process under capitalism and the full extent of the expropriation of nature that it entails.

Nevertheless, we are seeing today numerous attempts to conceptualize commodity value as the product not just of human labor, but of animal labor in general and, beyond that, of energy in general. Wadiwel, criticizing Marx, argues that "animal labor" should be seen as directly analogous to human labor in its role in the economy and that there is a "lack of analysis of the specific value-role of animals, not merely as commodities but as producers of value (i.e., labourers)." There is thus a need for an "animal labour theory of value" to complement or even to replace the labor theory of value. In this view, "the body and its metabolism" are "sources of surplus" that can be examined by analyzing the animal labor time of factory animals. Hence, there is a common physiological and energetic basis to value production characterizing both humans and other animals.[12]

Kallis writes in "Do Bees Produce Value?" in an exchange with Erik Swyngedouw: "The work done by nature should be integrated within the core of [the Marxian] theory of value production under capitalism, not delegated to the margins, with concepts like productivity or rent."

Like Moore, Kallis insists that value should be extended to work, in the sense of physics, where it measures the energy transferred when a force is applied to an object. "Isn't it obvious," he asks, "that the 'socially necessary labour time' for a jar of honey is not determined only by the labour of beekeepers, but also by the labour of bees?" In this view, "Value is not produced only by humans but also by ecosystems and fossil fuels." It follows that "if the bees and fossil fuels do an extraordinary amount of labour, without which . . . the total value produced [would be] several times smaller," then a value theory should be developed "that directly accounts for the work they do." An extension of the labor theory of value, he suggests, could include as "value" whatever "is produced from whoever does work (human or nonhuman, paid or unpaid)."[13]

Yaşın, drawing on Moore and on various reflections in Stephen Bunker's 1985 *Underdeveloping the Amazon*, criticizes Marx's theory of metabolic rift as dualist for externalizing ecology and not incorporating it directly in Marxian value theory. She therefore proposes a "value theory of nature," which would do exactly that. She justifies this by means of a startling misreading of Marx. Quoting Marx's statement, "It is a tautology to say that labor is the only source of exchange value, and accordingly of wealth in so far as this consists of exchange value," Yaşın oddly concludes that Marx is denying "labor is the only source of value, as is often assumed."[14] However, Marx is merely pointing to a logical tautology, nothing more. There is no question that for Marx abstract labor is the only source of commodity value in a capitalist economy, something he reiterates over and over. In contrast, real wealth, as distinct from value, is the product of *both nature and labor*.[15]

Nevertheless, Yaşın offers as a solution a *value theory of nature*— one that "internalizes nature" within the capitalist world-ecology, in line with Moore.[16] Here she draws on Bunker's criticisms of the labor theory of value and the notion that extractive resources create value independently of labor (and rent).[17] For Yaşın, this provides "a conceptual lens of nature as value-forming as well."[18] In this conception, nature is no longer outside capitalism in any sense, even in the sense of the externalization of nature by capital. In this way, the so-called epistemological rift between capitalism and nature embodied in Marx's theory of metabolic rift is dissolved.[19] According to Yaşın, "the value theory of nature" is a perspective that incorporates "ecological energy" in the conception of economic-value creation. How this actually works in economic terms is not explained.[20]

None of these ideas are new or clearly thought out. Although viewed as twenty-first-century criticisms of Marx, these same outlooks were in fact countered by him in his day, since they are, in Jean-Paul Sartre's words, little more than a "rejuvenation of . . . pre-Marxist [ideas] . . . a so-called 'going beyond' Marxism" that is "only a return to pre-Marxism."[21] This can be seen in terms of Marx's (and Frederick Engels's) responses to the physiocrats, and to thinkers in their own day such as Karl Rössler and Sergei Podolinsky. The French physiocrats, writing for a largely agricultural society, saw land as the unique source of wealth.[22] However, while correct in their emphasis on the material basis of production, they failed to recognize the social bases of capitalist valorization in labor, the analysis of which was to characterize British political economy. In Marx's terms, the physiocratic doctrine was based on a "confusion of value with material substance," that is, between use value (natural form) and exchange value (value form).[23] Nevertheless, the physiocratic way of thinking stands as a constant reminder of the importance of the natural form of the commodity, and of the contradiction between real wealth (in terms of natural-material use values) and value.

One of Marx's earliest and most gifted Russian followers was the economist Nikolai Sieber.[24] In the early 1870s, Sieber began to publish a series of articles in the journal *Znanie* (Knowledge).[25] In the first of these, he replied to a German review of Marx's *Capital* by Rössler, who had rhetorically asked why "the food in the stomach of a worker should be the source of surplus value, whereas the food eaten by a horse or an ox should not."[26] Sieber replied that Marx's *Capital* was concerned with human society and not domesticated animals and thus was directed only at the surplus value created by human beings. As Marx indicated in his notes:

The answer, which Sieber does not find, is that because in the one case the food produces human labour power (people), and in the other—not. The value of things is nothing other than the relation in which people are [socially] to each other, one which they have as the expression of expended human labour power. Mr. Rössler obviously thinks: if a horse works longer than is necessary for the production of its (labour power) horse power, then it creates value just as a worker who worked 12 hours instead of 6 hours. The same could be said of any machine.[27]

Here, Marx points to the basis of value in social labor, adding that in capitalist value accounting, animals are viewed as machines and their contribution to production treated in exactly the same way.

If Sieber did not grasp the essential point at first, he did subsequently, perhaps as a result of correspondence with Marx. In 1877, Yu G. Zhukovskii, a follower of Ricardo, criticized Marx for arguing that only human labor created surplus value. Zhukovskii argued, as explained by James D. White, that "anything which bore fruit, be it a tree, livestock or the earth, all were capable of providing exchange value. For Zhukovskii one of the main sources of value was Nature."[28] In response to Zhukovskii, Sieber said that a good Ricardian ought to be able to grasp that human labor was the sole source of value, which reflected the division of labor and the fragmentation of society. In the following year, the classical-liberal political-economist Boris Chicherin presented essentially the same argument as Zhukovskii.[29] Here, Sieber's response was unequivocal, cutting into the commodity fetishism basic to the classical-liberal view:

But to people it *appears* as though things exchange themselves one for another, that things themselves have exchange value, etc., and that the labour embodied in the thing given is reflected in the thing received. Here lies the whole groundlessness of the refutations of Mr. Chicherin, and before him of Zhukovskii, that neither the one nor the other could understand, or wanted to understand . . . that Marx presents to the reader the whole doctrine of value and its forms not on his own behalf, but as the peculiar way people at a given stage of social development necessarily understand their mutual relations based on the social division of labour. In fact, every exchange value, every reflection or expression of it, etc. represents nothing but a myth, while what exists is only socially-divided labour, which by the force of the unity of human nature, seeks for itself unification and finds it in the strange and monstrous form of commodities and money.[30]

There is no transhistorical rationality to the capitalist valorization process, nor should this be attributed to it. Rather, it is based on a "strange and monstrous" alienation of labor, along with the alienation and externalization of nature itself. Here it is important to understand that, in Marx's theory, *concrete labor*, that is, physiological labor—labor directly involved in the production/transformation of natural-material use values, the labor of individual human beings relying on brain, blood, and muscles—is in dialectical opposition to that *abstract labor* upon which capitalist valorization is based.[31]

Concrete labor is defined by Marx as "a condition of existence . . . an eternal natural necessity which mediates the metabolism between man and nature, and therefore of human life itself."[32] Abstract labor, in contrast, is a specifically capitalist social construct in which labor is homogeneous and removed from all its concrete, physical aspects, including the metabolism of human labor itself. Value is then a kind of "'reified' . . . labor" reflecting social equalizations of an abstractly "homogeneous human labor."[33] Marx argued that it is abstract labor in this sense, reflecting a definite social relation between human beings, that is the basis of value, not concrete, physiological labor. For this reason, "not an atom of matter enters into the objectivity of commodities as values."[34] As Isaak Rubin noted in his celebrated *Essays on Marx's Theory of Value*: "The expenditure of physiological energy as such is not abstract labor and does not create value."[35] For Marx, then, value, as opposed to use value, is not some universal, physical quality inherent in production throughout history. Rather, it is the crystallization of capitalist relations of production and accumulation.

To refer to an animal, physiological, or energy theory of value is to miss the point of the specifically reified character of value in capitalist society, the source of its increasingly distorted "creative destruction" of the world at large.

Even in Marx's day, attempts were made to transform the labor theory of value into a general energy theory of value. However, such attempts inevitably failed to comprehend the specific, social basis of abstract labor and of value under capitalism, seeing this as a mere physical process. The notion of an energy theory of value was raised by one of Marx's early followers, Sergei Podolinsky, often considered the leading nineteenth-century precursor of contemporary ecological economics.[36] Podolinsky attempted to integrate thermodynamics into the analysis of the economy and raised the question of the transformation of the labor theory of value into an energetic theory of value. Marx studied Podolinsky's work closely, taking extensive notes on the latter's work, and commenting on it in letters to Podolinsky that have been lost. However, it was Engels who provided a detailed assessment of Podolinsky's analysis in two letters to Marx.[37] Engels praised Podolinsky's argument for its integration of thermodynamics with the theory of production, but criticized Podolinsky for his crude calculations of energy transfers from agricultural labor, which excluded such factors as the energy contained in the fertilizer and the coal used in production. Engels also noted Podolinsky's failure to comprehend the enormous complexities of calculating all the quantitative and qualitative inputs of energy entering both into the human metabolism in the process of human labor and the reproduction of labor power. There is little doubt that Marx and Engels would have strongly rejected Podolinsky's notion of human beings as Sadi Carnot's "perfect thermodynamic machine."[38]

Engels elsewhere criticized attempts to calculate the energy going into even the simplest products in order to generate an energy theory of value, emphasizing that such calculations were virtually impossible given the nature of joint production.[39] Beyond this, of course, proponents of an energy theory of value failed to understand, as Marx stressed, that economic value was a social relation specific to capitalist society, rooted in class and the division of labor—not a universal, physical reality. Nicholas Georgescu-Roegen, the founder of modern twentieth-century ecological economics, sided with Engels against Podolinsky, insisting on the irrationality of an energy theory of value, which could not begin to comprehend the social basis of value in a capitalist economy.[40] All existing comprehensive conceptions of economic valuation, though differing amongst themselves, necessarily focus on the social basis of economic value. For critical ecological economists, the contradictions of the narrow capitalist value form create ecological (as well as economic) rifts that are inherent in the nature of the system. Indeed, for Georgescu-Roegen it was this that led to the ecological destructiveness of the prevailing economic order, and the creation of massive environmental problems resulting from its distorted conception of growth.[41]

An idealistic approach to value that looks for transhistorical bases of economic valuation, even if these are based on physical properties, fails to comprehend the integrative, dialectical levels that constitute emergent reality. The economic relations of society can no more be explained by energetics than they can be explained by "selfish genes."[42] Both are forms of reductionism that neglect the distinctive nature of historical reality. Attempts to generate a more harmonious view of reality by incorporating all of nature into the system of economic valuation fail to perceive that the existing system of production is not a harmonious, but rather an alienated, one.

EXPANSIVE VALUE THEORY AND THE DECENTERING OF LABOR VALUE

The most ambitious attempt to deconstruct the labor theory of value from a posthumanist left-ecological standpoint is to be found in the work of Moore, particularly in his *Capitalism in the Web of Life*. Moore's analysis influenced Kallis, Wadiwel, and Yaşın in their criticisms of Marxian value theory and in their calls for a more general physiological or energy theory of value.[43]

Moore takes as a central epistemological basis of his work the elimination of "Cartesian dualisms," which he perceives everywhere, including in the distinction between society and nature.[44] The goal is a social-monist analysis—or what he calls a "monist and relational view"—in which everything in the web of life consists of "bundles of human and extra-human natures."[45] The object here is to dissolve, in the manner of Bruno Latour, all objective distinctions.[46] Accompanying this approach is a conflating of various meanings of concepts. Recognizing that there are two classic meanings of value, viewed as intrinsic worth and economic (commodity) value, Moore proposes to meld them together into a single, monist analysis. Opposed to the views of "Marxists," who "since Marx have defended . . . the law of value as an economic process," he proposes to unite within one single framework both economic value and the broad analysis of "those objects and relations that capitalist civilization deems valuable."[47]

This conflation of Marx's value critique with the notion of value as a broad, normative cultural pattern, characteristic of civilizations in general, is accomplished in Moore's analysis via a metamorphosis of Marx's historical notion of the law of value into a transhistorical category. Marx and all subsequent Marxian economists have viewed the law of value as standing for the laws of motion of capitalism, the system's equilibrating characteristics based on the process of equal exchange, and the distribution of class-based income forms.[48] As the U.S. Marxian economist Paul Baran succinctly explained, in Marx

the law of value [can be seen] as a set of propositions describing the characteristic features of the economic and social organization of a particular epoch of history called capitalism. This organization is characterized by the prevalence of the principle of quid pro quo in economic (and not only economic) relations among members of society; by the production (and distribution) of goods and services as commodities; by their production and distribution on the part of the independent producers with the help of hired labor for an anonymous market with the view to making profit.[49]

In contrast to Marx's notion of the law of value, as depicted here, for Moore, "all civilizations have laws of value—broadly patterned priorities for what is valuable and what is not."[50] Although "law of value" is often employed in Moore's work in ways that suggest its affinity to the Marxian critique, in his world-ecology theory it metamorphosizes into a suprahistorical category—one of such vagueness that it embraces not only all activity of civilizations, but also the work/energy of the entire Earth System over hundreds of millions of years insofar as it impacts human production.

Related to this, Moore systematically conflates the concept of work as in physics, where it is identified with the expenditure of energy, with the labor of human beings within society. In this way, he develops a universal concept of appropriated "unpaid work," encompassing everything from a lump of coal to household labor. Both the lump of coal and a woman engaged in social reproduction in the household are said to have their work appropriated without pay.[51] Indeed, most work in the world, we are told, is unpaid. This, of course, follows logically—quite apart from the issue of unpaid subsistence work and household labor—from a framework in which a waterfall, a living tree, and the ocean tides, indeed nearly all of what we call organic and inorganic existence insofar as it bears upon production, are to be regarded as "unpaid."[52] It is the appropriation of such unpaid material existence that Moore sees as the main basis of the capitalist system, the source of its dynamism, and which is summed up by the law of value. This is operationalized in his notion of Cheap Nature. In his original conception of the Four Cheaps, labor power is seen as just one "cheap" alongside others—in a single flat ontology that also encompasses food, energy, and raw materials. In his later conception of Seven Cheaps, with Patel, labor power disappears altogether to be subsumed under the more general category of "work," which encompasses all energetic flows and all potential energy from whatever source, organic or inorganic—the activity of the universe.[53]

Similarly, in the name of combatting dualism, Moore strives to conflate nature and society, subsuming the former within the latter. Any concept of nature as a larger environment of which human beings are only a part, and which is therefore partly external to them, is downgraded, as is natural science itself. In its place we are given conflated Latourian conceptions of "bundles of human and extra-human natures," and such capacious categories as the web of life, world-ecology, *oikeios* (a classical Greek word associated with Theophrastus, meaning a plant's suitable place or location, appropriated by Moore as a way of avoiding such terms as nature and ecology), and the "Capitalocene."[54] On top of this, there are constant references to hyphenated couplets such as capitalism-in-nature/nature-in-capitalism.[55] In all of this, the goal is to subsume nature within capitalist society—or at the very least to reduce everything to bundles, webs, and imbroglios.[56] Such views rely, in Latourian fashion, on a "flat ontology" of human and nonhuman actors where everything is seen as existing on a single plane, and constantly intermixed and conflated—mere networks or webs without clear demarcations—as opposed to a dialectical critical realism that emphasizes complexity, mediation, and integrated levels, in a changing, evolving universe.[57]

Just as there cannot be any opposition of society or capitalism to nature—as this is alleged to be a dualistic perspective—so there cannot be, in Moore's general conflationist method, any ecological crisis distinguished from economic crisis.[58] The ecological problem can only be seen through the lens of the accumulation of capital, not outside of it. It is to be viewed in terms of market criteria and not in terms of the effects on ecosystems and the climate, much less the struggle for sustainable human development. Marx's concept of the metabolic rift addressing the contradictions between capitalism and nature is rejected as rooted in a "dualistic" (not dialectical) understanding.

Proceeding on the basis of such questionable logical and methodological principles, Moore's world-ecology takes as its main object "a certain destabilization of value as an 'economic category.'"[59] This is accomplished by seeing value as the product of work in the sense of physics—that is, as energy. In his new, expansive law of value, as he frequently explains, "Value does not *work* unless most work is not valued."[60] This, however, is a truism insofar as "most work" here refers to the work/energy of the entire Earth System and indeed the universe as a whole—the ancient solar energy embodied in fossil fuels, the work of a river, the growth of ecosystems—all of which are to be regarded as "unpaid" work or potential work. Given that work in terms of physics encompasses the entire physical realm, it is obvious that it is of greater quantitative significance than the mere exercise of labor power (however measured). Labor's energy is dwarfed by fossil fuel energy. "Coal and oil," Moore tells us, "are dramatic examples of this process of appropriating unpaid work," constituting the real, hidden foundation of the law of value.[61]

But what is it exactly that is *unpaid* in relation to coal and oil? In economics, the "free gift" that coal and oil provide is the result of ancient sunlight, going back millions of years, which formed coal, oil, and natural gas as low-entropy energy sources. It is this that gives fossil fuels their use value. At the base of the value edifice, for Moore, is the "*accumulated* unpaid work" that occurs "in the form of fossil fuels produced through the earth's biogeological processes" over hundreds of millions of years.[62]

In Marxian political economy, the pricing of natural resources is determined by monopoly rents. Such resources, which represent crucial use values for production, capable of enhancing labor productivity, acquire (but do not create) value via rents based on scarcity that are deductions from the surplus value generated in the economy.[63] At the same time, the extraction, refining, distribution, transport, and storage of these resources in the commodity economy involve value added from the employment of human labor. Yet, none of this is considered in Moore's analysis. The entire theory of rent is excluded. Marx's complex distinction between natural-material use value and exchange value/value is replaced with one singular law of value. The work of a barrel of oil or a waterfall or a turnip or a cow is "unpaid," which then is presented as the hidden ecological source of value, lying behind labor power itself.

"For good reason," Moore writes, "[Jason] Hribal asks, 'Are animals part of the working class?'"—given all the unpaid work they perform.[64] "The capital relation," Moore goes on to tell us, "transforms the work/energy of *all* natures into . . . value." Or, as we learn at another point, the law of value is all about "the transforming [of] nature's *work* into the bourgeoisie's *value*."[65] In Moore's Green arithmetic, unpaid work in the form of the earth's biogeochemical processes plus unpaid subsistence labor constitute the greater part of what underlies the law of value while the exploitation of labor power within production dwindles into insignificance in comparison.

It would be wrong, though, to attribute all of this simply to post-humanist ecology. Rather, Moore's decentering of the Marxian labor theory of value and his notion that nature's work should be treated as the hidden source of value grows largely out of various tendencies in liberal environmental thought. A key basis for his analysis is Richard White's historical treatment of the Columbia River, *The Organic Machine*. White arranges his history rather spaciously around what he says are "qualities that humans and the Columbia River share: energy and work"—though, in contrast to Moore, White points out that there are "huge differences between human work and the work of nature." Still, White, in an analogy that guides his analysis, writes: "Like us, rivers work. They absorb and emit energy, they rearrange the world."[66]

Of greater importance is Moore's strong adherence to the notion of unpaid ecosystem services, as developed by liberal neoclassical economists, notably Robert Costanza. Costanza is famous for trying to promote an energy theory of economic value within a liberal neoclassical economic perspective, in effect, a cost of production theory ultimately rooted in solar energy. This led Paul Burkett, in his *Marxism and Ecological Economics*, to refer to the extreme "reductionism," as well as historical irrationality, of Costanza's approach.[67] Costanza's attempt to promote a notion of nature as economic value resulted, in the 1990s, in a major split in the journal *Ecological Economics*, of which he was the chief editor. The more radical theorists, associated with the great, pioneering systems-ecologist Howard Odum, argued, in effect, for an approach that distinguished between use value/real wealth and exchange value/value, that is, between the natural form and the value form, along lines similar to Marx (utilizing Odum's notion of "*emergy*" or embodied energy as a natural-material or use-value category counterposed to economic value). Odum later sought to synthesize his systems ecology with Marxian theory in this regard, and developed a theory of unequal ecological exchange on this basis.[68]

Odum's radical ecological approach ran directly against the liberal tendencies of Costanza (Odum's former student). This led to a growing conflict between the radical ecological economists and natural scientists associated with Odum, on the one hand, and the liberal neoclassical-oriented theorists around Costanza, on the other. Alf Hornborg, a cultural anthropologist with connections to Marxian theory, played a key polemical role as a critic of Odum's approach within the journal, attacking both Odum and Marx and siding with Costanza.[69] In the end, Odum and his radical associates on the editorial board were virtually banned from the publication.[70]

Moore subsequently incorporated Costanza-like ecosystem-services and energy-value approaches into his analysis.[71] His work thus took the form of a Marxified version of the mainstream ecosystem-services argument, associated with Costanza's estimates of the tens of trillions of dollars that ecosystems provide unpaid each year to the world economy—calculated on the basis of the imputation of commodity values to natural processes.[72] Rather than addressing the ecological contradictions of the capitalist system, and the inherent opposition between natural-material use values and exchange value, as did radical and Marxian ecological economists, Costanza and his team of liberal ecological economists wrote of the need to embrace the notion of natural capital. Solutions to environmental contradictions were seen as requiring the internalization of nature within the commodity economy. The ecological problem was thus reduced to the presumption that everything in nature, insofar as it could be seen as aiding the economy (directly or indirectly), had value and needed to be given a price—a view underpinned by the concept of natural capital.[73]

Moore's main concrete innovation in *Capitalism and the Web of Life* and other works was to seek to turn Costanza's perspective on its head, arguing that capitalism throughout its history is rooted in the fact that extra-human work (as well as much human work) is appropriated without pay. Nevertheless, from a classical-Marxian perspective, the severe weaknesses of an analysis that largely rejects the labor theory of value—along with the distinctions between use value, exchange value, and rent theory—while idealistically seeking to expand the notion of value production to all work/energy in nature, are all too apparent.

THE NATURAL FORM AND THE VALUE FORM

The substance of value in a capitalist economy is, in Marx's conception, abstract labor. The *value form* (or exchange value) is thus to be distinguished from the *natural form* (or use value). The *natural form* stands for the "tangible, sensible form of existence," involving natural-material and technical properties and constituting real wealth. The *value form* of the commodity is its "social form," which points to the general concept of *value* as a crystallization of abstract labor.[74] It is the opposition between the natural form and the value form, inherent to capitalist production, that generates the economic and ecological contradictions associated with capitalist development. By the very fact that capitalism is a system of accumulation, the value form comes to dominate completely over the natural form in commodity production. "As useful activity directed to the appropriation of natural factors, in one form or another," Marx writes, "labour is a natural condition of human existence, a condition of material interchange [metabolism] between man and nature." However, every commodity obtains its exchange value, its value form, precisely "through the alienation of its use-value," often leading to the destruction of the metabolism between human beings and nature.[75] Out of this arises Marx's general conception of the metabolic rift, or the "irreparable rift in the interdependent process of social metabolism, a metabolism prescribed by the natural laws of life itself."[76]

The logic of capitalism, associated with the law of value, is a formally rational one, which is at the same time substantively irrational, with the irrational aspects gradually taking on ever greater importance.

Indeed, capitalism is based at the outset, via "so-called primitive accumulation," on the externalization of natural properties. Such organic properties, though incorporated in production as use values and representing the natural form of the commodity, are alienated in their value form and excluded from value, based on abstract human labor.[77] Natural properties, including human-natural properties, that is, human corporeal existence, are thus approached one-sidedly only insofar as they facilitate the production of value. A further level of externalization occurs through the imposition of many of the costs of production on nature (including human corporeal existence, which is outside the circuit of value) *as externalities*, with the negative effects falling not only on the environment, but also on human beings. The result is that capitalism promotes the creative destruction of life itself, extending eventually to the entire Earth System.

Ahistorical, idealistic attempts to envision the internalization and integration of social and environmental costs within the market system, or to see nature as the true source of value, only play down the social (including class and other forms of oppression) and eco-logical contradictions of the capitalist system. The goal of that system is the accumulation of capital. To put a price on a forest, so that its work/energy is no longer "unpaid," that is, to commodify it—to turn it into so many millions of board feet of standing timber—is no more likely to save the forest than the lack of a price. This is because the real issue is not the so-called tragedy of the commons, but the system of capital accumulation.[78] Songbirds are dying off because their habitats are being destroyed by the historical expansion of the system—not simply because they are considered "valueless" from the standpoint of the market. Whales are killed to be sold directly as a market com-modity, while they are also being annihilated as a side effect of the expansion of the system through the destruction of their ecosystems. All of this suggests that sustainable human development requires not the incorporation of nature into the system of value, but the abolition of commodity value itself.

Any form of analysis that seeks to eliminate the deep-seated dialectical contradictions between the natural form and the value form, between the capitalist economy and the larger socioecological metabolism in order to imagine a more harmonious integration, is inherently caught in a narrow, monistic view—one that fails to comprehend the complex, interdependent dialectics of nature and humanity in an attempt to reduce all the levels of existence to a "singular metabolism."[79] Such a false harmony can only be, in Marx's words, "the *flat*, stilted product of a thin, drawn, antithetical reflection" that seeks to redraw "boundaries" rather than to eliminate the system that—through its externalization and alienation—has generated these rifts in material existence.[80] What is called for today is not a radical r*evaluation* of nature, but a revolutionary ecological and social transformation—a new realm of *freedom as necessity*, directed at the rational regulation of the metabolism of nature and society by the associated producers.[81] Here is Rhodes, jump here![82]

10

The Planetary Emergency, 2020–2050

CAPITALISM TODAY is caught in a seemingly *endless crisis*, with economic stagnation and upheaval circling the globe.[1] While the world has been fixated on the economic problem, global environmental conditions have been rapidly worsening, confronting humanity with its *ultimate crisis*: one of long-term survival. The common source of both of these crises resides in the process of capital accumulation. Likewise, the common solution is to be sought in a "revolutionary reconstitution of society at large," going beyond the regime of capital.[2]

It is still possible for humanity to avert what economist Robert Heilbroner once called "ecological Armageddon."[3] The means for the creation of a just and sustainable world currently exist, and are to be found lying hidden in the growing gap between what could be achieved with the resources already available to us, and what the prevailing social order allows us to accomplish. It is this latent potential for a quite different human metabolism with nature that offers the master key to a workable ecological "exit strategy."

THE APPROACHING ECOLOGICAL PRECIPICE

Science today tells us that at most we have a generation in which to carry out a radical transformation in our economic relations, and our relations with the earth, if we want to avoid a "point of no return," after which vast changes in the earth's climate will likely be beyond our ability to prevent and will be irreversible.[4] At that point it will be impossible to stop the ice sheets in Antarctica and Greenland from continuing to melt, and the sea level from rising by as much as "tens of meters."[5] Nor will we be able to prevent the Arctic sea ice from vanishing completely in the summer months, or carbon dioxide and methane from being massively released by the decay of organic matter currently trapped beneath the permafrost—both of which represent positive feedback for dangerously accelerating climate change.

Extreme weather events are already becoming more frequent and destructive. A research article in the *Proceedings of the National Academy of Sciences* in 2012 indicated that the record-breaking heat wave that hit the Moscow area with disastrous effect in 2010 was made five times more likely, in the decade ending in that year, as compared with earlier decades, due to the warming trend. This meant "an approximate 80% probability" that it "would not have occurred without climate warming." Other instances of extreme weather, such as the deadly European heat wave in 2003 and the serious drought in Oklahoma and Texas in 2011, have been shown to be significantly impacted by earth warming. Hurricane Sandy, which devastated much of New York and New Jersey at the end of October 2012, was undoubtedly amplified to a considerable extent by climate change. In the past few years, meteorological research has determined that the likelihood of an event such as the 2017 heat wave in the Euro-Mediterranean region has increased by three times when compared to the 1950s; while the likelihood of a severe drought on the Northern Great Plains such as occurred in 2017 was found to have increased by 1.5 times compared to only decades before.

According to the American Meteorological Association, climate scientists projected as early as the 1990s that global warming "would at some point become sufficiently strong to push an extreme event beyond the bounds of natural variability." Since 2016, climate change impacts have escalated to the extent that scientists have documented various extreme-weather events that "could not have happened without the warming of the climate through human-induced climate change." For example, the record sea temperatures in the Tasman Sea between New Zealand and Australia in 2017 would have been "impossible," a recent study determined, aside from climate change.

"The climate danger threshold" or the point of irreversible climate change is usually thought of as a 2°C (3.6°F) increase in global average temperature, which has been described as equivalent at the planetary level to the "cutting down of the last palm tree" on Easter Island. Reaching this threshold could put the Earth System on a pathway to a Hothouse Earth, or irreversible pathway driven by biogeochemical feedbacks. An increase of 2°C in global average temperature coincides roughly with cumulative carbon emissions of around one trillion metric tons. Based on current emissions trends it is predicted by climate scientists at the University of Oxford that we will hit the one trillion metric ton mark in a decade and a half. We could avoid emitting the trillionth metric ton at present if we were to reduce global anthropogenic carbon emissions beginning immediately by an annual rate of more than 3 percent a year.[6]

To be sure, climate science is unable to pinpoint precisely how much warming will push us past the planetary tipping point.[7] But all the recent indications are that if we want to avoid planetary disaster we need to stay at all costs *below* a 2°C increase in global average temperature, and preferably below 1.5°C. As a result, most of the governments in the world as part of the 2015 Paris Climate Accord signed on to staying below 2°C, and if possible below a 1.5°C increase. Compared to the issue of staying below 2°C, all the discussions of what the climate will be like if the world warms to 3°C, 4°C, or all the way to 6°C, are relatively meaningless.[8] Well before such catastrophic temperatures are attained, we will likely have already reached the limits of our ability to control the climate change process, and we will then be left with the task of adapting to apocalyptic ecological conditions, spinning out of control. In the words of James Hansen, the world's leading climatologist, we are facing a "planetary emergency"—since if we approach 2°C "we will have started a process that is out of humanity's control."[9]

Keeping global temperature increases below 2°C is correlated with the United Nations Intergovernmental Panel on Climate Change (IPCC) target of avoiding at all costs carbon concentration in the atmosphere of 450 parts per million (ppm). However, long-term climate stability, according to the scientific consensus, requires a carbon concentration of no more than 350 ppm, essentially equal to the mid-twentieth century level—as compared to the current level of about 415 ppm. A carbon concentration of 350 ppm is still in reach if net carbon emissions globally are reduced by 45 percent below 2010 levels by 2030 and to zero by 2050. (Zero net emissions by 2050 are necessary to stay below 1.5°C and by 2070 to stay below 2°C.) But this would still require negative emissions of around 150 billion metric tons, essentially sucking carbon out of the atmosphere, through either improved agricultural and forestry practices (Agriculture, Forestry and Other Land Use—AFOLU), or, more questionably, Bioenergy and Carbon Capture and Sequestration (BECCS) and/or Direct Air Carbon Capture and Sequestration (DACCS) technologies. All IPCC scenarios for stabilizing the climate now require the removal of 100 billion to one trillion metric tons of carbon from the atmosphere by means of Carbon Dioxide Removal (CDR) through some combination of AFOLU, BECCS, or DACCS. In its 2018 report, the IPCC, for the first time, considered low-energy/sustainable development approaches that would allow for a more rapid decrease in carbon emissions with afforestation as the only CDR option considered.[10]

In its 2014 (Fifth Assessment, AR5) report, most mitigation scenarios considered by the IPCC had included BECCS. In the intervening years, however, there have been strong criticisms of this approach, as indicated in the IPCC's 2018 *Global Warming of 1.5° C* report.[11] According to an article in *Earth's Future* by Lena R. Boysen of the Max

Planck Institute of Meteorology and others, implementing BECCS on the scales imagined would "require utilizing a major fraction of the global land surface (natural or agricultural areas), with intolerably large environmental and social costs." Failing to attain zero net carbon emissions by 2050 would undoubtedly force today's younger generations to experiment with various geoengineering technologies, involving purposeful intervention in the Earth System, including solar radiation management, with potentially even more catastrophic consequences to world populations, compounding the overall problem of climate change.[12]

Many people thought that the Great Financial Crisis would result in a sharp curtailment of carbon emissions, helping to limit global warming. Carbon emissions dipped by 1.4 percent in 2009, but this brief decline was more than offset by a record 5.9 percent growth of carbon emissions in 2010, even as the world economy as a whole continued to stagnate. This rapid increase was attributed primarily to the increasing fossil fuel intensity of the world economy, and to the continued expansion of emerging economies, notably China.[13] Although there were frequent claims that global carbon emissions were flattening after 2015, this has now been shown to be an illusion with global carbon emissions increasing by 1.6 percent in 2017, and by 2.7 percent in 2018, reaching an all-time high. U.S. carbon emissions, meanwhile, rose by 3.4 percent in 2018. Both the absolute decoupling of economic growth and carbon emissions and the flattening out of carbon emissions globally after 2015—two panaceas raised in the last few years—have proved to be false. The decline in global carbon intensity (carbon emissions per GDP) of the global economy in 2017 was 2.6 percent. This was not enough to meet even the inadequate commitments of nations in the Paris Accords to a 3 percent per year reduction in carbon intensity. In contrast, the rate of reduction in carbon intensity necessary to stay below 2°C, given economic growth, is estimated to be 6.4 percent per annum.[14]

In an influential article published in *Nature Climate Change*, "Asymmetric Effects of Economic Decline on CO_2 Emissions," Richard York used data from over 150 countries between 1960 and

2008 to demonstrate that carbon dioxide emissions do not decline in the same proportion in an economic downturn as they increase in an economic upturn. Thus, for each 1 percent in the growth of GDP per capita, carbon emissions grew by 0.733 percent, whereas for each 1 percent drop in GDP, carbon emissions fell by only 0.430 percent. These asymmetric effects can be attributed to built-in infrastructural conditions—factories, transportation networks, and homes—meaning that these structures do not disappear during recessions and continue to influence fossil fuel consumption. It follows of necessity that a boom-and-bust economic system cannot reduce carbon emissions; that can only be achieved by an economy that reduces such emissions on a steady basis along with changes in the infrastructure of production and society in general.[15]

Indeed, there is reason to believe that there is a strong pull on capitalism in its current monopoly-finance phase to seek out more fossil fuel–intensive forms of production the more deeply it falls into the stagnation trap, resulting in repeated attempts to restart the growth engine by, in effect, giving it more gas. The notion that a stagnant-prone capitalist growth economy—what Herman Daly calls a "failed growth economy"—would in the long run be even more intensively destructive of the environment as a whole was advanced as early as 1976 by the pioneering Marxist environmental sociologist Charles H. Anderson. As Anderson put it, "As the threat of stagnation mounts, so does the need for throughput in order to maintain tolerable growth rates."[16]

The hope of many that peak crude oil production and the end of cheap oil would serve to limit carbon emissions has proven false. It is clear that in the age of enhanced worldwide coal production, fracking, and tar-sands oil there is no shortage of carbon with which to heat up the planet. Today's known stocks of oil, coal, and gas reserves are at least five times the planet's remaining carbon budget, amounting to 2.8 gigatons in carbon potential, and the signs are that the capitalist system intends to burn it all.[17] As Bill McKibben observed in relation to these fossil fuel reserves: "Yes, this coal and oil is still technically in the soil. But it's already economically aboveground."[18] Corporations and governments count these carbon resources as financial assets, which means they are intended for exploitation. Not too long ago, environmentalists were worried about the world running out of fossil fuels (especially crude oil); now this has been inverted by climate change concerns.

Nor is this all. As bad as the climate crisis is, it is important to understand that it is *only a part of the larger global ecological crisis*—since climate change is merely one among a number of dangerous "anthropogenic rifts" in planetary boundaries that have come to define the Anthropocene.[19] Ocean acidification, destruction of the ozone layer, loss of biological diversity, the disruption of the nitrogen and phosphorus cycles, growing freshwater shortages, land-cover change, and chemical pollution all represent global ecological transformations/crises. Already we have crossed the planetary boundaries (designated by scientists based on departure from Holocene conditions) not only in relation to climate change, but also with respect to species extinction and the nitrogen cycle. Extinction is occurring at about a thousand times the "background rate," a phenomenon known as the "sixth extinction," which refers back to the five previous periods of mass extinctions in earth history—the most recent of which, 65 million years ago, resulted in the demise of the dinosaurs. Nitrogen pollution now constitutes a major cause of dead zones in oceans. Other developing planetary rifts, such as ocean acidification—known as the "evil twin" of climate change since it is also caused by carbon emissions—and chronic loss of freshwater supplies, which is driving the global privatization of water, are of growing concern. All of this raises basic questions of survival: the ultimate crisis confronting humanity.[20]

The scale and speed of the ecological challenge, manifested not only in climate change but also in numerous other planetary rifts, constitutes irrefutable evidence that the root cause of the environmental problem lies in our socioeconomic system, particularly in the dynamic of capital accumulation.

The Ultimate Crisis

Faced with such intractable problems, the response of the dominant interests has always been that technology, supplemented by market magic and population control, can solve all problems, allowing for unending capital accumulation and economic growth without undue ecological effects by means of an absolute decoupling of growth from environmental throughput. Thus, when asked about the problems posed by fossil fuels (including tar sands oil, shale oil and gas, and coal), President Obama responded: "All of us are going to have to work together in an effective way to figure out how we balance the imperative of economic growth with very real concerns about the effect we're having on our planet. And ultimately, I think this can be solved with technology."[21] Even some versions of the proposed Green New Deal—though not the most radical and comprehensive versions—try to reduce the climate problem to a mere technological question, setting aside wider social and ecological questions.[22]

Yet, the dream that technology alone, considered in some abstract sense, can solve the environmental problem, allowing for unending economic growth without undue ecological effects through an absolute decoupling of one from the other, is quickly fading.[23] Not only are technological solutions limited by the laws of physics, namely the second law of thermodynamics, which tells us that it is not possible to convert one form of energy to another with 100 percent efficiency, but they are also subject to the laws of capitalism itself.[24] Technological change under the present system routinely brings about *relative* efficiency gains in energy use, reducing the energy and raw material input per unit of output. Yet, this seldom results in *absolute* decreases in environmental throughput at the aggregate level; rather, the tendency is toward the ever-greater aggregate use of energy and materials. This is captured by the well-known Jevons Paradox, named after the nineteenth-century economist William Stanley Jevons, who pointed out that gains in energy efficiency almost invariably increase the absolute amount of energy used, since such efficiency feeds economic expansion. Jevons highlighted how each new steam engine from James Watt's famous engine on was more efficient in its use of coal than the one before, yet the introduction of each improved steam engine nonetheless resulted in a greater absolute use of coal.[25]

In reality the Jevons Paradox as originally conceived is merely a restrictive application of the efficiency paradox of capitalism in general. Gains in labor productivity, for example, do not generally lead to fewer overall working hours in the economy, since the object of all such gains is to promote further accumulation. New areas of labor expansion are therefore generated. As Karl Marx remarked, the lessening of toil is "by no means the aim of the application of machinery under capitalism. . . . The machine is a means for producing surplus-value" and enhancing capital accumulation without end.[26]

Marx captured the expansive nature and logic of capitalism as a system in what he called "the general formula of capital," or M-C-M'. In a simple commodity economy, money exists merely as an intermediary to facilitate exchange between distinct commodities associated with definite use values, or C-M-C. The exchange begins with one use value and ends with another, with the consumption of the final commodity constituting the end of the process. Capitalism, however, takes the form of M-C-M', with money (M) being exchanged for labor and material means of production with which to produce a new commodity (C), to be exchanged for more money (M'), which realizes the original value plus added value, that is, surplus value or profit (M + Δ m). Here the process does not logically end with the receipt of M'. Rather the profit is reinvested so that it leads in the next phase to M-C-M'', and then to M-C-M''', in an unending sequence only interrupted by periodic economic crises. Capital in this conception is nothing but self-expanding value, and is indistinguishable from the drive to accumulate on an ever-increasing scale: "Accumulate, accumulate! That is Moses and the prophets!"[27]

This ceaseless drive for the amassing of greater and greater wealth, requiring more and more throughput of energy and resources, as well as reserves of labor, generating more waste, constitutes "the absolute general law of environmental degradation under capitalism."[28] Today the scale of the human economy has become so large that its everyday activities, such as carbon dioxide emissions and freshwater use, now threaten the fundamental biogeochemical processes of the planet.

Ecological analysis points irrefutably to the fact that we are up against the earth's limits. Not only is continued exponential economic growth no longer possible for any length of time, it is also necessary to *reduce* the ecological footprint of the world economy. And since there is no such thing as an absolute decoupling of the economic growth from the throughput of energy and materials taken as a whole, this means that exponential economic growth, particularly in the rich countries, must cease, while economies must be aimed at the rational satisfaction of human needs.[29] As an immediate objective, the world economy must wean itself entirely from fossil fuels as an energy source—well before the one trillion metric ton of carbon is emitted into the atmosphere.[30]

Monopoly Capital and Economic/Ecological Waste

In order to understand why the ecological problem is so intractable for capitalism, and what this tells us about the necessary exit from our present planetary emergency, it is useful to look at a passage by *Monthly Review* editors Harry Magdoff and Paul M. Sweezy, written more than four decades ago, but well worth examining at length today:

Take . . . the deep-seated faith that increasing production and productivity are the sovereign panacea for all the ills of capitalism. . . . It is clear that this myth has been severely shaken as we have become aware of growing shortages of raw materials and energy sources and of the increasingly severe impact of multifarious forms of pollution on the health and well-being of whole populations. Instead of a universal panacea, it turns out that growth is itself a cause of disease. But how is one to stop growth and yet keep capitalist enterprise afloat? In the absence of growth, for example, industries that produce machinery and other means of production would wither, since they would be confined to making only replacement equipment. Declining capital goods industries in turn would result in reduced employment and thus declining consumer demand, which in turn would end up in shutdowns of factories manufacturing consumer goods.

But this is only one side of the picture. Suppose we forget about trying to control growth and instead focus on abating the effects of growth by reducing pollution and arranging for a more rational use of raw materials and energy. Such an approach, it is clear, would entail a high degree of social planning: nothing less than a wholesale redirection of the economy involving, among other things, changes in population distribution, methods of transportation, and plant locations—none of which can be subjected to real social planning without violating the rights of private property in land, factories, stocks and bonds, etc.

From whichever side the problem is approached—controlling growth or restructuring existing production, transportation, and residential patterns—we come up against antagonisms and conflicts of interest that capitalists and those charged with protecting capitalist society cannot, in the very nature of the case, face up to. In the final analysis, what stands in the way of any effective action is the contradiction between the social potential of present-day technology and the antisocial results of private ownership of the means of production.[31]

Despite the fact that environmental problems are immeasurably worse than in 1974, when the above was written, this analysis has lost none of its relevance. Today it is even more evident that the economic growth of the existing system, rather than being "a universal panacea," is "a cause of disease." Thus, it is even more the case that "what is essential for success is a reversal, not a mere slowing down, of the underlying trends of the last few centuries."[32] Nevertheless, where capitalism is concerned, mere quantitative expansion is a requirement for the existence of the system itself. "Capitalism," as Murray Bookchin observed, "can no more be 'persuaded' to limit growth than a human being can be 'persuaded' to stop breathing. Attempts to 'green' capitalism, to make it 'ecological,' are doomed by the very nature of the system *as* a system of endless growth."[33]

Matters are no better on the other side of the picture, as portrayed by Magdoff and Sweezy. Capitalism's inability to engage in social and economic planning is reflected in decades of failed environmental policy. Although there have been some relatively minor environmental improvements, all attempts at comprehensive planning and action of the kind needed to avert what the scientific community is pointing to as a sure path of destruction have been systematically repulsed by the system. Instead technological change is invoked as a *deus ex machina*, supposedly allowing us to proceed along the current path of production, distribution, and consumption. There is no doubt that the social-technological potential already exists to address our most chronic environmental problems and to improve human existence—if we were to use present human capacities and natural resources in a rational and planned way. Yet, this existing potential is simply discarded: as all such rational solutions necessarily cross swords with the "antisocial [and anti-ecological] results of private ownership of the means of production."

Capitalism in its monopoly stage is a system with such a high level of labor productivity that it is constantly prone to overaccumulation of capital and stagnation due to market saturation and scarcity of profitable outlets for productive investment. In order to continue to exist and reap monopolistic profit margins under these conditions it has mutated into an economy of built-in waste: both economic and ecological. Ours is a society characterized by (1) a gargantuan and ever-expanding sales effort penetrating into the structure of production itself; (2) planned obsolescence, including planned psychological obsolescence; (3) production of luxury goods for an opulent minority; (4) prodigious military and penal-state spending; and (5) the growth of a whole speculative superstructure in the form of finance, insurance, and real estate markets. It is a characteristic of such a system that much of the vast economic surplus of modern society shows up as economic waste built into production itself. All of this uses up enormous amounts of energy and resources and contributes to the ecological end-waste dumped on the planet. It also maximizes the toxicity of production, since plastics and other petrochemical-based goods are more toxic as well as cheaper economically.[34] It is for this reason that leading systems ecologist Howard T. Odum, in a paper on Marx, insisted that the key to addressing our environmental problem necessarily involves eliminating built-in "luxury and waste," including the enormous social overhead costs of an irrational, class-exploitative society.[35]

Among the early theorists of monopoly capitalism at the beginning of the twentieth century, it was the iconoclastic U.S. economist and sociologist Thorstein Veblen who most powerfully argued that a system dominated by giant corporations, prone to overproduction and overcapacity associated with its monopolistic pricing policy, was inherently characterized by the proliferation of economic waste.[36] The result was the undermining of the use value structure of production, leading to a squandering of natural resources and human labor, a growing gap between the actual and potential production, and a failure to fulfill genuine social needs. Under monopoly capitalism, characterized by what economists call "monopolistic competition," "The producers," Veblen wrote,

> have been giving continually more attention to the salability of their product, so that much of what appears on the books as production-cost should properly be charged to the production of saleable appearances. The distinction between workmanship and salesmanship has progressively blurred in this way, until it will doubtless hold true now that the shop-cost of many articles produced for the market is mainly chargeable to the production of saleable appearances . . . .
>
> It is presumably safe to say that the containers account for one-half the shop-cost of what are properly called "package goods," and for something approaching one-half of the price paid by the consumer. In certain lines, doubtless, as, e.g., in cosmetics and household remedies, this proportion is exceeded by a very substantial margin.[37]

Veblen's argument on the proliferation of economic waste in the world of the giant corporation had an enormous influence on political-economic critics in the United States and elsewhere for much of the twentieth century, including figures such as Scott Nearing, K. William Kapp, Vance Packard, Joan Robinson, and John Kenneth Galbraith.[38]

However, it was the Marxian political-economists Paul A. Baran and Sweezy, in their work *Monopoly Capital*, who were to take Veblen's insight the furthest. The sales effort that characterized monopoly capitalism, they argued, went far beyond mere advertising and sales promotion. Rather what had emerged was "a condition in which the sales and production efforts interpenetrate to such an extent as to become virtually indistinguishable," signaling "a profound change in what constitutes socially necessary costs of production as well as in the nature of the social product itself." Baran and Sweezy referred to this phenomenon in their correspondence as "the interpenetration effect." They illustrated this by referring to an influential economic study that had been carried out in regard to changes in car models. Estimating the direct yearly costs of car model changes in the 1950s, most of which were related simply to appearance or to the "horse-power race," the study's authors demonstrated that such costs were "staggeringly high," amounting to over 25 percent of the total costs of the cars sold. And none of this included the related costs attributable to waste that were expended over the life of the vehicles, such as planned obsolescence, higher repair costs, and increased gasoline consumption. Nor did it question the enormous monopolistic profits of automobile manufacturing corporations or the huge dealers' mark-ups, running at 30 to 40 percent.[39]

The theory of monopoly capital thus suggests that the economic waste of capitalist society is not only found on the surface of society, as evident in military spending, advertising, speculation, and the like, but rather extends into production in ways that are rarely analyzed even by radical social and environmental critics of the system. It is generally assumed today that any good produced is manufactured under optimum conditions and is aimed at the satisfaction of consumer sovereignty. But nothing could be further from the truth in either case. Much of the production in today's U.S. economy constitutes economic waste in Veblen's sense of "expenditure" that "does not serve human life or human well-being as a whole" and belongs to the category of unproductive labor.[40] As Baran and Sweezy put it: "The designer of a new model of a consumer durable good, the engineer retooling the factory for the production of that model, the blue-collar worker affixing chrome to the automobile or compounding a new 'edition' of a toothpaste, the printer manufacturing a fancy new wrapper for an old soap, and the construction worker helping to build a new corporate 'crystal palace' are all members of the huge sales army which is supported by a considerable part of society's output."[41]

It follows that a great deal of the labor in modern production is unproductive, both in the sense of not contributing to but rather being paid out of society's economic surplus, and in the sense of carrying out functions necessary to capitalism but not to a rationally ordered society. This also represents the destruction of the rational use-value structure of the capitalist economy, since production is no longer dominated by *social use values*, C, but increasingly by *specifically capitalist use values*, C^K, having as their sole purpose the promotion of exchange value. The problem of M-C-M' is then transformed by the introduction of such specifically capitalist use values into one of M-C^K-M'. The quantitative advancement of exchange value, and hence economic growth as measured in our society, can no longer be assumed to constitute an advancement of human welfare in aggregate, but more likely constitutes the opposite, becoming the chief source of today's ultimate crisis.[42]

In his 1960 book *The Waste Makers*, Packard quoted leading industrial designer Brooks Stevens who said, "Our whole economy is based on planned obsolescence." Nevertheless, Stevens, in line with defenders of the corporate system more generally, denied that this constituted a system of "organized waste," on the questionable grounds that it contributed positively to economic growth.[43]

Taking all of this into consideration, it is clear that we live in a world not of increasing real wealth but rather of "illth," to use John Ruskin's memorable term.[44] In their pioneering Index of Sustainable Economic Welfare in *For the Common Good* (1994), Herman Daly and John Cobb provided an analysis of total economic welfare, incorporating ecological costs in addition to traditional income data, demonstrating that per capita sustainable economic welfare was in decline, beginning in the 1980s, even while GDP was on the rise.[45] But this attempt at a more accurate reckoning of changes in material welfare—since it did not scrutinize the actual production process itself—only scratched the surface of the irrationalities built into the laws of motion of contemporary monopoly-finance capital and its increasingly destructive relation to the environment.[46]

Today the evermore wasteful nature of capitalist production, viewed from a qualitative or use-value perspective, is starkly evident. The packaging industry, much of which is devoted to marketing wares, is the third largest industry in the world after food and energy.[47] It has been estimated that packaging costs an average of 10 to 40 percent of non-food produce items purchased. The packaging of cosmetics sometimes costs three times as much to produce as the actual contents.[48] Around 300 million tons of plastic are produced globally each year. Only two-thirds of this is enough, according to the *Guardian*, "to cover the 48 contiguous states of the U.S. in plastic food wrapping." Advertising for some products, such as soap or beer, is 10–12 percent of the retail cost per unit sold, while with some toys advertising is 15 percent of the retail cost.[49] The sales promotion budgets of corporations meanwhile have historically exceeded that of their advertising budgets.[50] Hundreds of billions of dollars are spent on marketing services in the United States alone.[51]

There is no obvious way of estimating the full cost of the economic and ecological waste built into the irrational structure of production under such a system; nevertheless, it is clear that it is evident everywhere. Much, if not most, of the final price of goods is related to costs associated mainly with the *realization* of capitalist profits through the enhancement of sales; and it encourages waste within production since the design of products is subordinated to sales needs. It follows that social and ecological planning geared directly to the production of necessary use values and not the artificial promotion of exchange value could promote genuine human needs at a sharply reduced ecological cost. This is even more the case if we recognize the possibility of social planning of essential consumption, food, housing, health services, education, urban structure, transportation, etc.

Mainstream environmental critics often attribute the increasingly wasteful and destructive forms of consumption that blight our society to the failings of the ordinary consumer under the assumption of "consumer sovereignty," one of the principal tenets of orthodox economics. But with the sales effort governing the production of the commodities themselves, consumer sovereignty is a mere illusion. Individuals in monopoly-capitalist society are subject to relentless marketing propaganda nearly every moment of their waking lives. Indeed, as Galbraith argued through his famous "dependence effect," the structure of consumption is largely dependent on the structure of production, and not the other way around.[52]

Marketing commodities in ways that exploit the alienation of human beings in monopoly-capitalist society is now a fine art. As early as 1933, sociologist Robert S. Lynd observed in a monograph titled "The People as Consumers," written for the President's Research Committee on Social Trends, that "advertising, branding, and style" changes were designed to take full advantage of the social insecurity and alienation brought on by changing economic conditions. Corporations looked on "job insecurity, monotony, loneliness, failure to marry, and other situations of tension" as opportunities for elevating "more and more commodities to the class of personality buffers. At each exposed point the alert merchandiser is ready with a panacea."[53] The symbolic need that commodities thus attain in our society is crucial to what Juliet Schor has called "the materiality paradox," that is, the selling of material goods to satisfy needs that cannot be met by material commodities.[54] Ironically, it is this inability to obtain genuine satisfaction from these commodities that ensures capital a permanent market. Marketing plays on these social vulnerabilities, creating an endless series of new wants, enhancing the overall wastefulness of the system.

Monopoly capitalism demands an ever-faster circulation of commodities in order to increase sales. Durability is the enemy of the system. Maximum profits are thus generated by a throwaway culture. The economic life of cell phones in the United States is only a couple of years due to both planned and psychological obsolescence, with the result that 140 million cell phones reached what the Environmental Protection Agency refers to as their "end of life" (EOL) in 2007. Some 250 million computers and peripherals reached their EOL in the same year.[55] Steve Jobs urged customers to buy an iPod every year to keep up with the latest technology.[56] More than 150 billion single-use beverage containers are purchased in the United States every year, while 300 million take-out cups are bought and discarded *each day*. Since the 1960s, one-time-use containers have risen from 6 percent of packaged soft drinks to 99 percent by 2012. As of 2015, some 6.5 billion metric tons of plastic waste has been generated in total, around 9 percent of which has been recycled, 12 percent has been incinerated, and 79 percent has accumulated in the environment generally or in landfills. In 2014 plastic recycling in the United States was less than a third the level of Europe and a little more than a third that of China. The more than 100 billion pieces of mostly unwanted junk mail delivered to homes and businesses in the United States each year add 50 million tons of greenhouse gases annually. In an economy designed to maximize overall waste, products are systematically made so as to no longer be repairable. Consumers are therefore compelled to discard them and return to the market and buy them again.[57]

Similarly, waste in the food system is encouraged by the whole structure of production, distribution, and consumption. According to the Food and Agricultural Organization of the United Nations, around half of all fruit and vegetable and seafood products, and 60 percent of all root and tuber crops in the United States and Oceania are lost or wasted, primarily in the service sector and at the consumer level. Meanwhile, actual food waste (discarding food that could be eaten) in sub-Saharan Africa and South and Southeast Asia is only about 6 to 10 percent of that of North America and Europe.[58]

The macro-inefficiency of the system, the lack of anything resembling social and economic planning, and the prodigious mountains of waste, are omnipresent realities wherever we turn—though, like the proverbial fish in the water, we are often unable to see it. The structure of cities organized around a "car-first" transportation system, the proliferation of strip malls, urban traffic congestion, the casino economy, the litigious society, the war economy, the penal state, and the lavish, conspicuous consumption of the 1 percent—all point to a world of extreme excess, accompanied by tremendous social deprivation and environmental degradation. It is estimated that the average U.S. licensed driver age sixteen or older spends around 300 hours a year behind the wheel. In the 1980s, U.S. drivers drove an average of about 10,000 miles a year; today it is around 13,000. Americans drove 3.2 trillion miles on U.S. roads in 2016. For each million cars in the United States, asphalt paving equaling nearly 200,000 football fields is required.[59]

A number of studies have shown that the economic surplus in the United States—much of which finds its statistical trace in economic waste associated with advertising, military spending, and other forms of socially unproductive output—constitutes more than 50 percent of GDP.[60] To this should be added the unnecessary costs associated with "the interpenetration effect." None of this, moreover, considers the actual harm inflicted on human beings and the environment—so-called "negative externalities." Indeed, capitalism, as Kapp once argued, is "an economy of unpaid costs."[61]

What all of this means is that most of the economy is directed at anything but the needs of the vast majority of the human beings who work and generate output. "For all its stinginess," Marx wrote, "capitalist production is thoroughly wasteful with human material, just as . . . [it is] very wasteful of material resources, so that it loses for society what it gains for the individual capitalist."[62] The result under today's monopoly-finance capital is that by any rational standards the material progress at present is becoming more negative all the time. As Barry Commoner and Anderson both pointed out as early as the 1970s, we are overshooting nature's capacity to sustain our economic activities and thereby generating an enormous "ecological debt" that must eventually be paid merely for our continued survival.[63]

Odum, who spent the last two decades of his life perfecting a devastating ecological critique of neoclassical economics in which he repeatedly emphasized the overlap between his views and Marx, provided perhaps the clearest and most comprehensive general analysis in his day of what needs to be done in the face of the planetary crisis. He argued that it was possible to find a social resolution to conditions of climax accumulation represented by ecological overshoot by altering the structure of production and consumption on a global scale, as well as reorienting the economic system to real wealth in terms of use values. This meant recognizing that "a principal waste in our society is using fuels in nonproductive activity. We drive more cars than necessary, drive them too often, and drive cars with too much horsepower. We use cars for commuting because cities are not organized with alternative transportation. Because higher costs of energy do cause people to eliminate some stupid wastes, higher fuel taxes may be needed in the United States for these wasteful uses."

Crucial to the development of sustainable economic conditions, Odum insisted, was the elimination of unequal ecological exchange. He demonstrated that in the late 1990s the United States was gaining 2.5 times more real wealth in natural-material use values (measured in terms of embodied energy) than it exported, mainly to the disadvantage of underdeveloped countries. Needed social change also required "controlling global capitalism's inherent tendency for short-term exploitation of resources," which could undermine the national/international "resource basis . . . causing collapse." Capitalist growth was "identified," in his conception, "as a large-scale analog of weed overgrowth." Globally, "the exclusive dominance of large-scale capitalism" should be "replaced with an emphasis on cooperation with the environment and among nations."[64]

In order to transcend what he called a "cancerous capitalism" that overdrafted resources and energy, Odum insisted that it would be essential to eliminate the economic and ecological "waste and luxury" that did not support jobs, real productivity, and real wealth. Hence, he suggested that it would be essential, among other things, to:

1) Change industry from a focus on construction (that is, net investment) to maintenance (replacement investment);
2) Place an upper limit on individual incomes;
3) Reduce unearned income from interest and dividends;
4) Downsize by reducing upper-level salaries rather than discharging employees;
5) Provide public work programs for the unemployed;
6) Decentralize organizational hierarchy;
7) Limit the power of private cars;
8) Eliminate plastic discard packaging;
9) Prioritize ecological net production over consumption;
10) Promote an optimal economy through high-diversity, efficient cooperation;
11) Share information without profit;
12) Promote equity between nations in ecological exchange; and
13) Use agricultural varieties that need less input.

Odum was clear that this transition required a break with "imperial capitalism."[65] "Socialistic ideals about distribution," he observed, "are more consistent with [a] steady state than growth," whereas for capitalism it was exactly the opposite.[66]

THE GLOBAL SOUTH AND THE ULTIMATE CRISIS

Ecological footprint analysis tells us that the world is in overshoot, currently using resources at a rate that would be sustainable for almost two Earths. The main source of this environmental overdraft is to be found in the excesses of the rich countries, which are now, however, being duplicated to a considerable extent throughout the globe. Indeed, if the whole world population were to have the ecological footprint per capita of the United States, four Earths would be needed.[67] The very size of the ecological footprint of a rich economy such as the United States is an indication of its heavy reliance on unequal ecological exchange, extracting resources from the rest of the globe, particularly underdeveloped countries, in order to enhance its own growth and power.

Odum was able to demonstrate concretely that while the United States received more than twice as much embodied energy from trade as it exported, Ecuador was exporting five times the embodied energy that it received. Trade between the two was thus enormously disadvantageous to Ecuador in real wealth terms, while providing a massive ecological benefit to the U.S. economy.[68] To a large extent the current wealth of the rich countries has been based on a historic system of ecological robbery.

It follows that the downsizing of ecological footprints to get the world back in accord with environmental limits must necessarily fall disproportionately on the rich capitalist countries. The only just and sustainable solution is one of contraction and convergence, whereby global per capita carbon emissions and ecological footprints are equalized, along with the elimination of imperialist rent (including both economic and ecological unequal exchange).[69] Moreover, carbon emissions are cumulative. The United States and Britain have each generated carbon emissions per capita since the Industrial Revolution that are ten times the global mean, with a corresponding responsibility for its mitigation.[70]

The Global South is in many ways more immediately imperiled than the North by climate change and by the other planetary rifts. It is here too that an international peasant movement, La Vía Campesina, has emerged, and with it hopes of the development of an environmental proletariat.[71] Meanwhile the propaganda machine of the rich capitalist countries portrays emerging economies—notably China, where carbon emissions now exceed those of the United States but where per capita emissions are far lower—as constituting the single greatest threat to the environment. Understanding the relation of the Global South to the ultimate crisis is therefore crucial.

Comparison of the economy-ecology nexus of underdeveloped countries with that of developed monopoly-capitalist economies only serves to highlight the waste-ridden character of the latter. High levels of energy and carbon (fossil fuel) intensity have characterized the major industrial countries in the post–Second World War era.[72] This high-energy intensity was made possible by the imperial system of ecological (and economic) unequal exchange. Stripped of their vast imperial-ecological and fossil fuel subsidies, the rich economies would be readily perceived as the inefficient systems they are.[73]

Simon Kuznets, often viewed as the foremost figure in the development of national income accounting in the United States, pointed to some of the crucial contradictions in comparing the GDPs of developed and underdeveloped economies. In a 1949 article "National Income and Industrial Structure," Kuznets argued that the rich capitalist countries were grossly overvalued in national income terms in comparison with less industrialized and less commercialized economic formations, because all purchases that passed through the market—even costs that were mere "offsets" for the inefficiency and destructiveness of concentrated industrial-capitalist production— were seen as enhancing national income and economic growth.[74] Yet, it was well known (with specific reference to China) that "preindustrial" or underdeveloped economies were able to produce a higher nutritional content at lower cost; were more efficient "in respect to distance" in the bringing together of producers with consumers, and in not requiring the packaging and processing of produce to avoid spoliation; and were able to provide security to individuals over their life cycle through the organization of "family and community life" (which in the rich economies requires insurance).[75]

Kuznets argued that much of what was counted as income and economic growth in modern industrial society, such as "extra transportation and handling," could be "nettified" (or netted out) as mere offsets to the inefficiencies and destructiveness of concentrated industrial and urban life. Here Kuznets included unnecessary dependence on the automobile; much of the cost of housing; the enormous amounts spent on distribution, transportation, and communication; expenditures on banks, employment agencies, brokerage houses, etc. A great deal of what was counted as GDP and as economic growth therefore consisted of nothing more than "libations of oil on the machinery of industrial society." In highly industrialized economies, "production, in the narrow sense of converting hides into shoes," Kuznets observed, "accounts for merely a small part of the values of finished goods, whereas" in the underdeveloped economies "it accounts for practically all of it. The transportation and distribution activities in an industrial society can thus be clearly seen as offsets to the [real material] disadvantages of large-scale, machine manufacturing."

For Kuznets, then, many of the additional costs incurred by advanced industrial societies were intermediate offsets to negative features associated with those societies, adding nothing essential to final use values. However, from a social-planning or socialist perspective, as in Baran and Sweezy's analysis, the criticism went even deeper, since the bulk of these artificial social costs could be classified not just as offsets to urban-industrial life, but as products of the exploitative, profit-centered, and monopolistic character of the capitalist economy, and thus socially irrational in that sense as well.[76]

Ironically, Kuznets is today often associated with what is known as the Environmental Kuznets Curve, or an inverted U-shaped curve standing for the hypothesis that environmental conditions initially worsen with industrialization and income growth, and then eventually improve at higher levels of industrialization and income, reversing the negative environmental effects. Kuznets had presented a similar hypothesis with respect to the effect of economic development on inequality. He did not, however, extend this argument to the quite different realm of the environment. Rather his name was simply stamped on the hypothetical Environmental Kuznets Curve by later economic analysts. Not only has the Environmental Kuznets Curve been shown to be false when environmental effects as a whole are considered, but Kuznets's own discussion of economic formations and their ecological aspects actually constitutes one of the most powerful theoretical counters to the Environmental Kuznets Curve postulate.[77]

Indeed, it is impossible today to make a reasonable case for the environmental benefits of the system of capital accumulation. In today's increasingly globalized monopoly-finance capital, the ecological, social, and economic irrationalities of the organization of production are visible on a planetary scale. This is particularly the case with agribusiness, given its heavy, almost exclusive, dependence on intensive carbon inputs at every stage of the production process (including fertilizer production); its destruction of subsistence farming; its vast food processing, packaging, and supermarket chains; and its global distributional and transportation networks that maximize food miles. According to the *New York Times*: "Cod caught off Norway is shipped to China to be turned into filets, then shipped back to Norway for sale." This is due primarily to the global labor arbitrage, which takes advantage of low unit labor costs in China and other poor countries. For China, unit labor costs in 2014 were only about 45 percent of the U.S. level, leading multinational corporations to carry out production in the Global South due to its cheap labor, while shipping these goods to the Global North for final consumption. The global labor arbitrage explains why it is that "half of Europe's peas are grown and packaged in Kenya." One study looked at a typical Swedish breakfast of bread, butter, cheese, apple, coffee, cream, orange juice, and sugar, and concluded that the food had traveled the equivalent of 24,901 miles, the circumference of the planet—much of this because of differential wage costs between the Global North and South. The average food item in U.S. consumption now travels over 1,500 miles from field to table. Food miles associated with consumption in the United Kingdom amounted to the equivalent of "33 billion vehicle-kilometers in 2002."[78]

Again and again agribusiness has been shown to be less efficient in producing *food per acre* (as opposed to food per unit labor cost) than intensive, small organic farming, which is also less damaging to the environment and is far superior in providing a livelihood for people and whole communities on the land.[79] Hence, La Vía Campesina claims that in order to provide food security, livelihoods, jobs, and human health, as well as to protect the environment, global food production has to be in the hands of small-scale sustainable farmers, as opposed to large, monopolistic agribusiness corporations and supermarket chains. "The moral of the tale," Marx observed in the 1860s, "is that the capitalist system runs counter to a rational agriculture, or that a rational agriculture is incompatible with the capitalist system . . . and needs either small farmers working for themselves or the control of the associated producers."[80]

The world revolt of small-scale farmers increasingly places ecology at the forefront, as groups of rural workers organize to fight the logic of capital in order to establish social control over ecological-material relationships and forge more meaningful, less alienated, and more sustainable conditions for life. According to environmental sociologists Mindi Schneider and Philip McMichael in the *Journal of Peasant Studies*, "Marx's concept of the 'metabolic rift' . . . in the context of an international peasant mobilization embracing the science of ecology . . . has become the focal point of attempts to restore forms of agriculture that are environmentally and socially sustainable."[81]

Odum insisted that increasing constraints on fossil fuel use would spell the end of today's petrofarming system: "The high yields from industrial agriculture generated a very cruel illusion because the citizens, the teachers, and the leaders did not understand the energetics involved. . . . A whole generation of citizens thought that higher efficiencies in using the energy of the sun had arrived. This was a sad hoax, for people of the developed world no longer eat potatoes made from solar energy. . . . People are really eating potatoes made partly of oil."[82]

Without the subsidy provided by fossil fuels, today's agribusiness system would simply collapse. As a result, it will be necessary to return to more ecologically efficient forms of traditional agriculture combined with modern know-how. In this way, the knowledge system will in many ways be inverted. Rather than agribusiness corporations providing technical directions to traditional peasant farmers, small peasant farmers will provide much of the inspiration for the most appropriate agricultural practice, rooted in thousands of years of cumulative knowledge of soil cultivation, supplemented by the advancements associated with modern agroecology. "Policies about population and development appropriate to low-energy restoration," Odum wrote, "may be like those formerly found in low-energy cultures like the Yanomamo Indians of Venezuela."[83]

The notion that the areas of the Global South, including China and India, can easily incorporate the billions of people now engaged in small-scale agriculture into their overcrowded urban centers is the product of a development ideology according to which the rich countries of Western Europe are said to have rapidly absorbed their own rural populations within their emerging, industrialized cities. In reality there were huge waves of emigration of Europeans to the colonies taking the pressure off the cities. (In the United States, which was a receiving ground for much of this European emigration, urbanization occurred much more gradually. By 1900, nearly 80 percent of the British population lived in cities, while 40 percent of the U.S. population did. It took until 1960 before 70 percent of the U.S. population resided in cities, and until 2000 before it reached 80 percent.)

Such an industrialization-urbanization pattern, relying on mass emigration, is clearly not feasible in today's Global South, which does not have the outlet for mass emigration on the scale now needed. Indeed, in the age of Donald Trump, walls against migrants are rapidly being built in the United States and Europe. Nor do developing countries today have the favorable economic conditions—expansion into a whole "new" continent (albeit leading to the genocidal conquest of the original inhabitants)—under which the United States emerged as a world industrial power. What is happening instead in many countries is the huge growth of urban slums as people migrate from the countryside into cities that contain insufficient employment opportunities. Around one-third of the world's city dwellers now live in slums.[84]

In response to these realities, governing agricultural development, urbanization, and the movement of peoples, a New Rural Reconstruction Movement has emerged in China—associated in particular with the pioneering ecological thinking of Wen Tiejun—that rejects large-scale farming-agribusiness systems as a viable pattern of development in today's circumstances. Instead agriculture is to be rooted in the village system of collective land rights (the product of the Chinese Revolution) and the utilization of traditional knowledge of some 240 million small household farmers, further informed by contemporary ecological science. This transformation of food production and socioecological relationships also involves expanding rural education, medical services, and infrastructure. This strategy is "committed to the Three Ps (the People's Principles): people's livelihood, people's solidarity, and people's cultural diversity."[85]

THE SOCIETY OF SUSTAINABLE HUMAN DEVELOPMENT

"Labour," Marx insisted, "is first of all, a process between man and nature, a process by which man, through his own actions, mediates, regulates and controls the metabolism between himself and nature."[86] It is this central metabolic relation between human beings and the natural environment that is now being called into question by capitalism on a planetary scale generating constant and ever-growing metabolic rifts.[87] Even as global monopoly-finance capital falls prey to an endless stagnation crisis due to its own internal contradictions, it is also crossing all ecological boundaries in its drive for endless accumulation, thus activating its external contradictions on the broadest, most planetary scale.[88]

Economic growth under capitalism is inseparable from an increase, to quote Daly, in "the metabolic flow of useful matter and energy from environmental sources, through the economic subsystem (production and consumption), and back to environmental sinks as waste." The key to a sustainable society is thus the rational regulation of this "metabolic flow relative to natural cycles that regenerate the economy's resource depletion and absorb its waste emissions, as well as providing countless other natural services."[89] Recognizing these material constraints, and the fact that production was ultimately nothing but the relation between human beings and nature, Marx defined socialism as a society in which "socialized man, the associated producers, govern the human metabolism with nature in a rational way . . . accomplishing it with the least expenditure of energy and in conditions most worthy and appropriate for their human nature."[90]

We are a long way from the rational, social regulation of the human metabolism with nature envisioned by Marx in the nineteenth century. Today the rift in this metabolism is threatening the entire planet as a place of habitation for humanity and countless other species. The gravity of the problem that faces us in addressing both the current planetary emergency and the inordinately destructive social metabolism of capital should not be downplayed. In order to avoid catastrophic climate change, it will be necessary, science tells us, to find a way to keep the fossil fuels in the ground. We need to stay well below a trillion metric tons of carbon emissions if we are to have a reasonable chance of avoiding irreversible and catastrophic climate change. Rapidly cutting fossil fuel consumption, however, means removing the energy subsidy on which today's system of global monopoly-finance capitalism critically relies, calling the whole system into question.[91] At the same time, it will be necessary to reverse the other planetary rifts, such as species extinction, the rupture of the nitrogen and phosphorus cycles, ocean acidification, the depletion or overuse of freshwater, the elimination of natural vegetative ground cover, and the degradation of the soil—in order to not close off the future. Here too we are forced to confront the nature of our social system.

The really inconvenient truth is that there is no possible way to accomplish any, much less all, of these things other than by breaking with the underlying logic of the accumulation of capital, $M\text{-}C\text{-}M'$—and today's even deadlier $M\text{-}C^K\text{-}M'$. What is required both for long-term human survival and for the creation of a new condition of "plenitude" is a smaller ecological footprint for the global economy, coupled with a system of comprehensive social, technological, and economic planning—one that is of, by, and for the people.[92] It means abandonment of the myth of absolute economic growth as the panacea for all of society's ills, and the shift to a sustainable, steady-state economy rooted in sustainable human development rather than the accumulation of capital.[93]

Nevertheless, the grim reality is that climate change and other planetary rifts demand urgent action within a timeline of a generation or less, leaving virtually no options other than revolutionary social change. In its 2018 report, the IPCC declared that what was required by 2050 were "system transitions" that were "unprecedented in terms of scale." Will Steffen and a team of Earth System scientists, writing for the *Proceedings of the National Academy of Sciences* in 2018, declared that to avoid a pathway to Hothouse Earth—in which the planet would heat up uncontrollably beyond a certain threshold (likely represented by a 2°C increase in global average temperature), as nonlinear feedbacks came into play—fundamental transformations in "the present dominant socioeconomic system" are required. As Minqi Li cautioned in *The Rise of China and the Demise of the Capitalist World Economy*, barring a very rapid shift away from capitalism, the system will inevitably lead us into global catastrophe, even omnicide. And if this were to occur, even if socialism triumphs in the second half of the century, "the task for future socialist governments will no longer be about preventing catastrophes but trying to survive them as they are taking place." All that can be said with certainty is that the sooner the world reverses the logic of capitalism in a global movement toward socialism, the greater the chance for human survival.[94]

"It is impossible to think of anything at all concerning the elementary conditions of social metabolic reproduction," István Mészáros wrote, "which is not lethally threatened by the way in which capital relates to them—the only way in which it can" as a mere means to accumulation. Indeed, as early as 1971, at the opening of the modern environmental era, Mészáros declared:

A basic contradiction of the capitalist system of control is that it cannot separate "advance" from *destruction*, nor "progress" from *waste*—however catastrophic the results. The more it unlocks the powers of productivity, the more it must unleash the powers of destruction; and the more it extends the volume of production, the more it must bury everything under mountains of suffocating waste. The concept of *economy* is radically incompatible with the "economy" of capital production, which, of necessity, adds insult to injury by first using up with rapacious wastefulness the *limited resources* of our planet, and then further aggravates the outcome by *polluting and poisoning* the human environment with its mass-produced waste and effluence.[95]

Ironically, it is in the very waste and destructiveness of what Odum called the "cancerous capitalism" of today that we are able to discover the *potential* for a more rational, just, and sustainable society. Baran and Sweezy, looking at the explosive growth of finance, already visible in their time, together with "advertising, product differentiation, artificial obsolescence, model changes, and the other devices of the sales effort," observed: "The prodigious volume of resources absorbed in all these activities does in fact constitute necessary costs of capitalist production. What should be crystal clear is that an economic system in which *such* costs are socially necessary has long ceased to be a socially necessary economic system."[96]

11

The Long Ecological Revolution

ASIDE FROM the stipulation that nature follows certain laws, no idea was more central to the scientific revolution of the seventeenth century, and to the subsequent development of what came to be known as modern science, than that of the conquest, mastery, and domination of nature. Up until the rise of the ecological movement in the late twentieth century, the conquest of nature was a universal trope, often equated with progress under capitalism (and sometimes socialism). To be sure, the notion, as utilized in science, was a complex one. As Francis Bacon, the idea's leading early proponent, put it, "nature is only overcome by obeying her." Only by following nature's laws, therefore, was it possible to conquer her.[1]

After the great Romantic poets, the strongest opponents of the idea of the conquest of nature during the Industrial Revolution were Karl Marx and Frederick Engels, the founders of classical historical materialism. Commenting on Bacon's maxim, Marx observed that in capitalism the discovery of nature's "autonomous laws appears merely as a ruse so as to subjugate it under human needs," particularly the needs of accumulation. Yet despite its clever "ruse," capital can never fully transcend nature's material limits, which continually reassert themselves, with the result that "production moves in contradictions which are constantly overcome but just as constantly posited." Its treatment of natural limits as mere barriers to be overcome, not as actual boundaries, gives capital its enormously dynamic character. But that same refusal to recognize natural limits also means that capital tends to cross critical thresholds of environmental sustainability, causing needless and sometimes irrevocable destruction.[2] Marx pointed in *Capital* to such "rifts" in the socioecological metabolism of humanity and nature engendered by capital accumulation, and to the need to restore that metabolism through a more sustainable relation to the earth, maintaining and even improving the planet for successive human generations as *"boni patres familias"* (good heads of the household).[3]

In his *Dialectics of Nature*, written in the 1870s, Engels turned the Baconian ruse on its head in order to emphasize ecological limits:

> Let us not, however, flatter ourselves overmuch on account of our human victories over nature. For each such victory nature takes its revenge on us. Each victory, it is true, in the first place brings about the results we expected, but in the second and third places it has quite different, unforeseen effects which only too often cancel out the first. . . . Thus at every step we are reminded that we by no means rule over nature like a conqueror over a foreign people, like someone standing outside nature—but that we, with flesh, blood, and brain, belong to nature, and exist in its midst, and that all our mastery of it consists in the fact that we have the advantage over all other creatures of being able to learn its laws and apply them correctly.[4]

Although key parts of Marx and Engels's ecological critique remained long unknown, their analysis was to have a deep influence on later socialist theorists. Still, much of actually existing socialism, particularly in the Soviet Union from the late 1930s through the mid-1950s, succumbed to the same extreme modernizing vision of the conquest of nature that characterized capitalist societies. A decisive challenge to the notion of the domination of nature had to await the rise of the ecological movement in the latter half of the twentieth century, particularly following the publication of Rachel Carson's *Silent Spring* in 1962. The new ecological criticism of the environmental destruction brought on by modern science and technology and by unbridled industrialism—associated with a simplistic notion of human progress focusing on economic expansion alone—led to an alternative emphasis on sustainability, coevolution, and interconnection, of which ecology was emblematic. Science was said to have been misused, insofar as it had aided in the violation of nature's own laws, ultimately threatening human survival itself. Through the development of the concept of the biosphere and the rise of the Earth System perspective (in which Soviet ecology played a crucial role), science increasingly came to be integrated with a more holistic, dialectical view, one that took on new radical dimensions that challenged the logic of the subordination of the earth and humanity to profit.[5]

Recent years have brought these issues renewed relevance, with the climate crisis and the introduction of the Anthropocene as a scientific classification of the changed human relation to the planet. The Anthropocene is commonly defined within science as a new geological epoch succeeding the Holocene epoch of the last 12,000 years; a changeover marked by an "anthropogenic rift" in the Earth System since the Second World War.[6] After centuries of scientific understanding founded on the conquest of nature, we have now, indisputably, reached a qualitatively new and dangerous stage, marked by the advent of nuclear weapons and climate change, which the Marxist historian E. P. Thompson dubbed "Exterminism, the Last Stage of Civilization."[7]

From an ecological perspective, the Anthropocene—which stands not just for the climate crisis, but also rifts in planetary boundaries generally—marks the need for a more creative, constructive, and coevolutionary relation to the earth. In ecosocialist theory, this demands the reconstitution of society at large on a more egalitarian and sustainable basis. A long and continuing ecological revolution is needed, one that will necessarily occur in stages, over decades and centuries. But given the threat to the earth as a place of human habitation—marked by climate change, ocean acidification, spe-cies extinction, loss of freshwater, deforestation, toxic pollution, and more—this transformation requires immediate reversals in the regime of accumulation. This means opposing the logic of capital, whenever and wherever it seeks to promote the "creative destruc-tion" of the planet. Such a reconstitution of society at large cannot be merely technological, but must transform the human metabolic relation with nature through production, and hence the whole realm of social metabolic reproduction.[8]

No revolutionary movement exists in a vacuum; it is invariably con-fronted with counterrevolutionary doctrines designed to defend the status quo. In our era, ecological Marxism, or ecosocialism, the most comprehensive challenge to the structural crisis of our times, is being countered by capitalist ecomodernism—the outgrowth of an earlier ideology of modernism, which from the first opposed the notion that economic growth faced natural limits. If ecosocialism insists that a rev-olution to restore a sustainable human relation to the earth requires a frontal assault on the system of capital accumulation, and that this can only be accomplished by more egalitarian social relations and more consciously coevolutionary relations to the earth, ecomodernism promises precisely the opposite.[9] Ecological contradictions, accord-ing to this ideology, can be surmounted by means of technological fixes and continued rapid growth in production, with no fundamental changes to the structure of our economy or society.[10] The prevailing liberal approach to ecological problems, including climate change, has long put capital accumulation before people and the planet. It is main-tained that through new technologies, demographic shifts (such as population control), and the mechanisms of the global "free market," the existing system can successfully address the immense ecological challenges before us. In short, the solution to the ecological crises pro-duced by capitalist accumulation is still more capitalist accumulation. All the while, we have been rapidly nearing the "climate cliff" (that is, the breaking of the carbon budget) represented by the trillionth metric ton of carbon released into the atmosphere, now less than a decade and a half away if current trends continue.[11]

In these dire circumstances, it is dispiriting but not altogether surprising that some self-styled socialists have jumped on the ecomodernist bandwagon, arguing against most ecologists and ecosocialists that what is required to address climate change and environmental problems as a whole is simply technological change, coupled with progressive redistribution of resources. Here again, the Earth System crisis is said not to demand fundamental changes in social relations and in the human metabolism with nature. Rather it is to be approached in instrumentalist terms as a formidable barrier to be overcome by means of extreme technology.

The best current example of this tendency on the left in the United States is the Summer 2017 issue of *Jacobin*, titled *Earth, Wind, and Fire*. According to the authors featured in the weightier second half of this special issue and their related works, the solution to climate change and other ecological problems is primarily one of innovation in the development and application of new technologies and does not require a critique of the process of capital accumulation or economic growth. Activist groups such as Greenpeace and most ecosocialists come under attack for their "catastrophism" or apocalypticism, their direct action, and their emphasis on the need for qualitative changes in the human relation to the environment.[12] Indeed, most of the issue, packed with colorful charts and graphics, espouses a techno-optimism in which ecological crises can be solved through a combination of non-carbon energy (including nuclear power), geoengineering, and the construction of a globe-spanning negative-emissions energy infrastructure.

If this stance is "socialist," it is only in the supposedly progressive, ecomodernist sense of combining state-directed technocratic planning and market regulation with proposals for more equitable income distribution. In this vision, ecological necessities are once again subordinated to notions of economic and technological development that are treated as inexorable. Nature is not a living system to be defended, but a foe to be conquered. As if to punctuate this position, the *Jacobin* issue includes as an epigraph a quotation from Leon Trotsky, taken from his *Literature and Revolution* (1924):

Faith merely promises to move mountains; but technology, which takes nothing "on faith," is actually able to cut down mountains and move them. Up to now this was done for industrial purposes (mines) or for railways (tunnels); in the future this will be done on an immeasurably larger scale, according to a general industrial and artistic plan. Man will occupy himself with re-registering mountains and rivers, and will earnestly and repeatedly make improvements in nature. In the end, he will have rebuilt the earth, if not in his own image, at least according to his own taste. We have not the slightest fear that this taste will be bad.[13]

Trotsky was hardly alone in promoting such reckless productivism in the early 1920s, and can be at least partly excused as an individual of his time. To repeat the same error nearly a century later, however, when we face the destabilization of the world's ecosystems and human civilization, is to capitulate to the forces of destruction. The current attempt to claim the conquest of nature and ecomodernization as a "socialist" project is dangerous enough that it warrants a thorough critique. Otherwise, we risk turning back the clock on the vital political and theoretical advances made by the ecological left over the last half-century.

THE NEW PROMETHEAN SOCIALISM

The first half of *Jacobin*'s playfully titled *Earth, Wind, and Fire* issue is fairly uncontroversial from a left standpoint, cataloguing capitalism's environmental depredations and calling for radical change. However, editorial board member Connor Kilpatrick sets the tone for the issue's second part when he suggests that Donald Trump and capitalist entrepreneurs appeal to a broad public by promising a future of economic growth and new technology, while the ecological movement offers only "a politics of fearmongering and austerity."[14] The second half makes the implications of Kilpatrick's criticism explicit, developing over the course of several articles a thoroughly ecomodernist, techno-utopian vision that is ultimately incompatible with the goals and methods of the grassroots ecological movement.

The penultimate article in the issue, Leigh Phillips and Michal Rozworski's "Planning the Good Anthropocene," along with Phillips's prior work, captures the essence of this putatively progressive eco-modernist perspective. Phillips is the author of the 2015 book *Austerity Ecology and the Collapse-Porn Addicts*, and Rozworski is a Toronto-based union researcher and commentator, who frequently writes for *Jacobin*.[15] In his book, Phillips directs polemical attacks on such varied left thinkers, living and dead, as Theodor Adorno, Ian Angus, David Harvey, Max Horkheimer, Derrick Jensen, Naomi Klein, Annie Leonard, Herbert Marcuse, Bill McKibben, Lewis Mumford, Juliet Schor, Richard York, and ourselves. He also challenges the concept of planetary boundaries of leading Earth System scientists. At the same time, Phillips gives his ecomodernist seal of approval to Erle Ellis, Roger Pielke Jr., and the Breakthrough Institute (where both are senior fellows); Alex Williams and Nick Srnicek, authors of the *Accelerate Manifesto*; and Slavoj Žižek (for his dismissal of the notion of Mother Earth).

One chapter in Phillips's book, criticizing Greenpeace's Leonard, is titled "In Defense of Stuff"; another, attacking the work of ourselves and others associated with *Monthly Review*, is called "There Is No 'Metabolic Rift.'" Phillips dismisses the idea that Marx advanced ecological values, despite mountains of evidence to the contrary, and accuses the entire ecological left of "doom-mongering" and "catastrophism." Klein is said to promote an "eco-austerity" that is ultimately no different from the neoliberal version. Phillips flatly rejects the notion that there are limits to economic growth, asserting that "you *can* actually have infinite growth on a finite world," by making more with less. According to some estimates, he informs us, "the planet can sustain up to 282 billion people . . . by using *all* the land."[16]

For Phillips, bigger is beautiful: "The socialist must defend economic growth, productivism, Prometheanism." The former Soviet Union, for example, is faulted not for its extreme productivism, but for its lack of democratic planning and insufficient concern for human welfare. He presents a sweepingly anthropocentric definition of nature: "We are nature, and all that we do to nature is natural." It follows that "our skyscrapers are not separate from nature; they *are* nature." (By the very same logic, one might add, so are our nuclear weapons.) Human progress means transgressing all purported natural limits. Viewed in these terms, "Energy is freedom. Growth is freedom." Other species have value only insofar as they provide utilitarian benefits to society. Thus "we should care when species go extinct, not because of their intrinsic worth . . . but because the loss of species means a decline in the effectiveness of the services that living systems provide to humans."[17]

Overall, the New Left of the 1960s and its successors are faulted for rejecting the "Promethean ambition" of evermore production— "*more* stuff." Likewise, Phillips sees the Brazilian Landless Workers Movement as out of step with social needs, precisely because it attempts to reconnect workers to the land. What is required is "a high-energy planet, not modesty, humility and simple living." Ecomodernism would concentrate the land and rely on large-scale agricultural production.[18]

So enamored is Phillips of nuclear power as the solution to climate change that he says that "a substantial, global reversal of neoliberalism and an embrace of a strong, *democratic* public-sector ethos" is climatically advantageous mainly because it will allow us to deploy "what is absolutely the strongest weapon we have in our arsenal against global warming"—namely nuclear power. No mention of Fukushima here.[19]

Phillips and Rozworski bring this same perspective to their contribution to *Jacobin*'s special issue—and were no doubt enlisted for that precise purpose. They tout nuclear power as a viable alternative to fossil fuels, as part of a broader ecomodernist fantasy in which economic growth has no limits and humanity rules as the "collective sovereign of Earth." Although they endorse some form of state planning, they raise no direct objection to the commodification of nature, labor, and society under capitalism, and seem unconcerned by the ways that existing structures of production and consumption distort and exploit human needs. Instead, the future lies entirely with the new machines that can provide humanity with evermore goods, while commanding on an ever-increasing scale "the biogeochemical processes we must understand, track, and master" in order to "coordinate ecosystems." The goal is self-consciously one of Promethean control of nature through science and technology. It is hardly surprising therefore that Phillips's outlook, as first articulated in *Austerity Ecology and the Collapse-Porn Addicts*, has been lauded by the premier corporate-funded ecomodernist think tank, the Breakthrough Institute, or that the title phrase of the Phillips and Rozworski piece, "The Good Anthropocene," is lifted directly from Breakthrough Institute's *An Ecomodernist Manifesto*.[20]

In another bold appropriation, Peter Frase, author of the 2016 book *Four Futures: Life After Capitalism*, titles his contribution to the issue "By Any Means Necessary," a phrase made famous by Malcolm X, but here denoting planetary-wide interventions in nature. *Four Futures* shows Frase to be enamored with the idea of the Promethean mastery over the earth. The "grand future" he depicts in what purports to be a realistic ecosocialist scenario (albeit drawing on science-fiction) consists of "terraforming our own planet, reconstructing it into something that can continue to support us and at least some of the other living creatures that currently exist—in other words making an entirely new nature." Like Phillips and Rozworski, Frase has no interest in reducing our impact on nature or treading lightly on the earth; rather, we must "manage and care for nature" in order to better serve our own interests. Following the conservative philosopher of science and Breakthrough Institute senior fellow Bruno Latour, Frase insists that in the face of the global ecological crisis we need to be engaged in "Loving Our [Frankenstein] Monsters." That is, we must learn to identify with the technological-industrial world we have created (or are in the process of creating), with its planned markets, smart parking meters, RoboBees, and new potentialities for geoengineering the planet—all viewed as perfectly compatible with "socialist ecology."[21]

In "By Any Means Necessary," Frase focuses on climate change. Chiding the ecological movement for its "green moralizing," he calls on the left to embrace wholeheartedly attempts to geoengineer the planet. He praises Oliver Morton's 2015 book *The Planet Remade*, which proposes to inject sulfur aerosols into the atmosphere to block the sun's rays (though scientists have pointed out that the added calamitous effects of this are likely to be far worse than global warming alone).[22] Frase himself makes a case for "cloud brightening," by which clouds can be made to reflect more sunlight away from the earth. "We have to recognize," he writes, "that we are, and have been for a long time, the manipulators and managers of nature." If the left fails to embrace planetary geoengineering, "the bourgeoisie will simply carry out their work without us." In Frase's view, socialists have no choice but to climb onto the geoengineering bandwagon, even if this means going against the ecological movement. Still, "the purpose of raising the prospect of geoengineering in a left context," he says, is "not as a substitute for decarbonization, but as part of a larger portrait of ecosocialism."

There is no danger, Frase assures us, to be found in geoengineering technology itself, only in how it is managed (a sophism akin to "Guns don't kill people, people do"). Defending himself in advance against "the charge of hubris and Prometheanism," he states, no doubt with an eye on Engels, that "the socialist project does not aim at *controlling* nature. Nature is never under our control, and there are always unintended consequences." But missing from his analysis is any notion that social relations must change in order to effect qualitative shifts in the human metabolism with nature. For Frase, the object seems to be keeping the whole juggernaut going as much as possible, with neither social nor ecological relations seriously addressed in what amounts to a technological tinkerer's solution. The only alternative to such an extreme ecomodernist strategy, we are led to believe, is a "hair shirt" austerity, a term that he uses in common with Phillips to ridicule the ecological movement.[23]

Daniel Aldana Cohen's article "The Last Stimulus" promotes a form of Green Keynesianism. Against those on the left who argue for the need to develop a steady-state economy—a system no longer governed by the drive for unsustainable and destructive economic growth—Cohen insists that we should take seriously the hype surrounding green capitalism:

> Global political and financial leaders now want to invest a trillion dollars a year in clean energy alone. The budget for climate adaption policies will be comparably huge. . . . Business as "usual" is changing fast. . . . Thanks to political pressure, millions of workers' retirement funds are already investing in a happy old age in a stable climate. Globally, trillions of dollars in workers' retirement savings are up for grabs. . . . Regional and national governments all over the world are setting up green banks, financial institutions to help shape the booming investment in the energy transition. . . . This past year, employment in the solar sector expanded seventeen times faster than in the economy as a whole.

From this, Cohen derives his thesis that "so far, green capitalists are the ones shaping the future. They get it. We could too." While not an advocate of unbridled Prometheanism like Phillips and Frase, he nevertheless sees the solution largely in the fairly conventional terms of state management of technology, the market, and urban development.[24]

Christian Parenti, a *Nation* columnist and author of *Tropic of Chaos: Climate Change and the New Geography of Violence* (2012), is the best-known of the *Earth, Wind, and Fire* contributors. The foreboding title of his article, "If We Fail," refers to the worst-case scenario of unmitigated climate change, namely the Venus Syndrome. As described by climatologist James Hansen and recounted by Parenti, the earth would end up "a lifeless rock swathed in boiling-hot, toxic, water vapors." Parenti seizes on this apocalyptic image to urge the left to accept drastic technological solutions, which fortunately, he says, are well within reach. Citing an experiment in Iceland, he advocates the building of carbon capture and sequestration (CCS) plants that would strip carbon from the atmosphere and sequester it by depositing it in basalt rock. This CCS-in-basalt approach, he claims, offers a "fairly simple," readymade solution to the climate problem. The only difficulty he sees is that such a CCS scheme must be sponsored by the state rather than private enterprise, since it offers few opportunities for profit. And this is where progressives with their support of affirmative government have an essential role to play. The "good news" is that "a radical climate solution, counterintuitively perhaps, requires that we use *more*, not less, energy. But energy, in the form of solar energy, is the one economic input that is truly infinite."

Parenti does not, however, address the immense obstacles to the building of CCS plants on the scale and with the speed he imagines. As the energy analyst Vaclav Smil has pointed out: "In order to sequester just a fifth of current CO_2 emissions we would have to create an entirely new worldwide absorption-gathering-compression-transportation-storage industry whose annual throughput would have to be about 70 percent larger than the annual volume now handled by the global crude oil industry, whose immense infrastructure of wells, pipelines, compressor stations and storage took generations to build." CCS technology requires unimaginable quantities of water: as much as 130 billion tons every year, or about half the annual flow of the Columbia River, would be needed to capture and sequester carbon dioxide equal to the annual emissions of the United States alone. And the problems only start there, since the larger technological, economic, and ecological obstacles to such massive attempts at negative-emissions technologies are gargantuan, raising unimaginable difficulties.

Although not discussed by Parenti, similar problems of scale arise with respect to the most favored carbon dioxide removal approach among scientists, since it is theoretically capable of providing negative emissions, namely, Bio-energy with Carbon Capture and Sequestration (BECCS). Implementation of such schemes on a global scale would, however, require a very large portion of the land area and water currently used by world agriculture, imposing intolerable environmental and social costs. More rational schemes propose improved agriculture and forestry, rooted in agroecology, for which Cuba is currently the most developed model.

If Phillips in his analysis argues that *all is nature*—that everything in society, from farms to factories to skyscrapers, is "natural"—Parenti suggests the opposite: *all is society*, to the point that the natural world can scarcely be said to exist at all. It is easy from this standpoint to argue, as he does, in favor of meat factories and fish farms as partial solutions to our ecological problems, while the consequences for ecosystems and the animals themselves are rendered invisible. "Our mission as a species," he writes, "is not to retreat from, or to preserve, something called 'nature,' but rather to become fully conscious environmental makers. Extreme technology under public ownership will be central to a socialist project of civilizational rescue, or civilization will not last." In both these views (all is nature and all is society), employed in this way, the object is identical: to wish away ecological contradictions and seek the total conquest of the environment, effectively maintaining, rather than fundamentally transforming, existing social and economic structures.[25]

In a short article, "We Gave Greenpeace a Chance," cultural critic Angela Nagle takes that organization and the broader ecological movement to task. She rejects what she calls Greenpeace's "diminutive direct action" and the "'deep green' primitivism" often associated with the radical environmental movement. Instead she opts once again for hyper-technological solutions to environmental problems, including the global expansion of nuclear energy plants, declaring that "human interference in the natural world is now the only way to save it." With respect to Trump's claim that global warming is a myth concocted by China "to make US manufacturing noncompetitive," Nagle quips that on first hearing this her "only sense of shock . . . was that someone was actually talking about manufacturing again." Like Phillips, Rozworski, Frase, and Parenti, she urges the left to abandon its "aversion to ambitious technologies and Promethean modernity" and to love our monsters.[26]

Other articles in the issue launch similarly one-sided attacks on the Sierra Club (Branko Marcetic, "People Make the World Go Round") and food cooperatives (Jonah Walters, "Beware Your Local Food Cooperative"). In the latter article, we are led to believe that some of the more radical food cooperatives in the 1970s were simply the product of "Maoist true believers" and "self-styled guerrillas, schooled in the messianic Marxism-Leninism of the late New Left" and "following the model of the Black Panther Party"—in a series of pejoratives designed to throw scorn on these experiments.[27]

What is remarkable about the contributions to *Jacobin*'s special issue on the environment and related works by its writers and editors is how removed they are from genuine socialism—if this involves a revolution in social and ecological relations, aimed at the creation of a world of substantive equality and environmental sustainability. What we get instead is a mechanistic, techno-utopian "solution" to the climate problem that ignores the social relations of science and technology, along with human needs and the wider environment. Unlike ecological Marxism and radical ecology generally, this vision of a state-directed, technocratic, redistributive market economy, reinforced by planetary geoengineering, does not fundamentally challenge the commodity system. The ecological crisis brought on by capitalism is used here to justify the setting aside of all genuine ecological values. The issue's contributors instead endorse a "Good Anthropocene," or a renewed conquest of nature, as a means of perpetuating the basic contours of present-day commodity society, including, most disastrously, its imperative for unlimited exponential growth. Socialism, conceived in these terms, becomes nearly indistinguishable from capitalism—not a movement to replace generalized commodity society, but homologous with the fundamental structure of capitalist modernity. At best, this represents a foreshortening of the socialist vision for the sake of success in the liberal political arena. But the cost of such a compromise with the status quo is the loss of any conception of an alternative future.

The Long Ecological Revolution

How then are we to see the necessary ecological and social revolution of our time? In the nineteenth century, Engels emphasized the imperative for society to develop in accord with nature as the only genuine scientific view: "Freedom does not consist in any dreamt-of independence from natural laws, but in the knowledge of these laws, and the possibility this gives of systematically making them work towards definite ends. This holds good in relation both to the laws of external nature and to those which govern the bodily and mental existence of men themselves—two classes of laws which we can separate from each other at most only in thought but not in reality."[28] Moreover, there was no way to shortchange natural necessity. Engels argued that the Baconian ruse of the conquest of nature—obeying nature's laws for the sole purpose of promoting capital accumulation—would ultimately prove disastrous, since it ignored the larger consequences in the pursuit of short-term gain. In contrast, the object of "scientific socialism" was not a vain attempt to conquer nature, but rather the advancement of human freedom in accord with the conditions imposed by the material world.[29]

Today, the growing awareness of such problems, and of the inescapable human connection to the natural world as a whole, has led scientists to explore more sustainable forms of development, as in agroecology, biomimicry, and systems of ecological resilience. "The overarching goal of an ecological society," Fred Magdoff and Chris Williams write in their book *Creating an Ecological Society*, "is to maintain the long-term health of the biosphere while equitably providing for human needs."[30] This is not an impossible task, but it does require the development of science at a higher level—one not simply concerned with mechanical manipulation of the earth and its inhabitants for private gain, but founded on the understanding and concern for the complex collectivities that constitute living systems and human life itself. This requires ecological planning, but that in turn is only possible if social relations also change, reconceiving freedom in terms of needs deeper and wider than those of individual self-interest in a commodity economy.

What this means is that we should not be stampeded by the climate crisis—however catastrophic its likely consequences—into embracing the very same attitudes toward the human relation to the natural world that generated the current unprecedented threats to human civilization. To do so is to seal our fate. We cannot escape the long-term ecological consequences of capitalist development through the Faustian bargain of building more and more nuclear power plants around the globe, or by recklessly injecting sulfur particles into the atmosphere—all for the purpose of infinitely expanding commodity production and capital accumulation. Beyond their technical and economic infeasibility, such plans must be opposed because of the immense, unforeseen repercussions that would inevitably result. To argue, for example, for CCS (or BECCS) technology as the primary solution to the climate crisis is to argue for devoting an immense share of resources to such plants, rivaling in scale the world's entire existing energy infrastructure, with all sorts of added ecological and social costs and consequences.[31]

There are better and faster ways of addressing the climate crisis through revolutions in social relations themselves. Moreover, any purportedly socialist approach to environmental problems that focuses only on climate change, ignoring or even rejecting the idea of other planetary boundaries, and sees the solution as purely technological, represents a failure of nerve. It constitutes a refusal to embrace a new, wider realm of freedom, to meet the challenge that historical reality now imposes on us.[32] Humanity cannot continue to develop in the twenty-first century without embracing more collective and sustainable forms of production and consumption in line with biospheric realities.

Here it is important to recognize that today's monopoly-finance capitalism is a system built on waste. The larger part of production is squandered on negative (or specifically capitalist) use values, in such forms as military spending, marketing expenditures, and the inefficiencies, including planned obsolescence, built into every product. The consumption of evermore meaningless and destructive "goods" is offered as a substitute for all those things that people truly want and need.[33] Indeed, as Marxist economist Paul A. Baran wrote, "People steeped in the culture of monopoly capitalism do not want what they need and do not need what they want."[34] Beyond the mere physical necessities of food, shelter, clothing, clean water, clean air, and so on, these needs include love, family, community, meaningful work, education, cultural life, access to the natural environment, and the free and equal development of every person. The capitalist order drastically limits or perverts all of this, creating artificial shortages in essential goods in order to generate a driving desire for non-essentials, all for the purpose of greater profitability and polarization of income and wealth. The United States alone currently spends more than a trillion dollars a year both on the military and on marketing—the latter aimed at inducing people to buy things that they would not otherwise be disposed to purchase.[35]

There is no doubt that the current planetary ecological crisis requires technological change and innovation. Improvements in solar and wind power and other alternatives to fossil fuels are an important part of the ecological equation. It is not true, however, that all the technologies needed to address the planetary emergency are new, or that technological development alone is the answer. The wonders of smart machines notwithstanding, there is no solution to the global ecological crisis as a whole compatible with capitalist social relations. Any ecological defenses erected in the present must be based on opposition to the logic of capital accumulation. Nor can intervention by the state, acting as a kind of social capitalist, do the trick. Rather, a long ecological revolution adequate to the world's needs would mean altering the human-social metabolism with nature, countering the alienation of both nature and human labor under capitalism. Above all we must be concerned with maintaining ecological conditions for future generations—the very definition of sustainability.

From this standpoint, a multitude of things can be done now, if humanity mobilizes itself to create an ecological society.[36] Given the vast waste inherent in the regime of monopoly-finance capital, which has penetrated into the very structure of production, it is possible to implement forms of revolutionary conservation that both expand the realm of human freedom and allow for rapid readjustment to the necessity imposed by the Earth System crisis. It is far more efficient and feasible to cut carbon emissions drastically than it would be to construct a globe-spanning CCS infrastructure, which would rival or

THE ROBBERY OF NATURE

exceed in size the current world energy infrastructure. It would be far more rational to carry out a rapid, revolutionary phase-out of carbon emissions than to risk imposing new threats to the diversity of life and human civilization through attempts to geoengineer the entire planet.

Ecological Marxism offers an opening-up of human freedom and creativity in manifold ways, calling upon humanity as a whole to rebuild its world on ecological foundations in line with the earth itself. Promises of a global technological fix—which becomes more nonsensical if one looks beyond climate change to the numerous planetary boundaries threatened by the capitalist "conquest of nature"—can only lead to elite politics and elite management. It is the ultimate hubris, the final call for the human domination of nature as a means of class domination. Such Promethean views are designed to avoid the reality of the contemporary social and ecological crisis—namely, that revolutionary changes in the existing relations of production are unavoidable. Modernizing the forces of production is not enough; more important is establishing the conditions for sustainable human development. Much can be learned from indigenous and traditional forms of working the land: because human society under capitalism has become alienated from the earth, it follows that less alienated societies offer vital insight into the practice of a more sustainable existence.

Critics on both left and right might reply that it is "too late" for an ecological revolution. The answer to this is, as Magdoff and Williams eloquently state:

> Too late for what? To struggle for a better world means taking the world as it is and working to transform it. Although the ecological and political conditions and trends are in many respects quite desperate, we are not condemned to continue degrading the environment or our social conditions. . . . A certain amount of global warming will continue regardless of what we do with all of its negative side effects. . . . However, we can stop the slide to an even more degraded Earth, poorer in species and in the health of remaining species. We can use the vast amount of available human and material resources to reorient the economy

to benefit all people. An ecological society will allow us to do all the things that are currently off the table, that capitalism has repeatedly shown itself unable to achieve: providing all people with the ability to develop their full potential.[37]

But to achieve these things, we will need to break with "business as usual," that is, with the current logic of capital, and introduce an entirely different logic, aimed at the creation of a fundamentally different social metabolic system of reproduction. To overcome centuries of alienation of nature and human labor, including the treatment of the global environment and most people—divided by class, gender, race, and ethnicity—as mere objects of conquest, expropriation, and exploitation, will require nothing less than a long ecological revolution, one that will necessarily entail victories and defeats and ever-renewed striving, occurring over centuries. It is a revolutionary struggle, though, that must commence now with a worldwide movement toward ecosocialism, one capable from its inception of setting limits on capital. This revolt will inevitably find its main impetus in an environmental proletariat, formed by the convergence of economic and ecological crises and the collective resistance of working communities and cultures—a new reality already emerging, particularly in the Global South. It will necessarily be a battle fought disproportionately by the young, given the enormous burden being put on today's youth, but the struggle must be waged by us all.[38]

In the long ecological revolution before us, the world will necessarily proceed from one earthly struggle to another. If the advent of the Anthropocene tells us anything, it is that humanity, through a single-minded pursuit of economic gain benefitting a relative few, is capable of producing a fatal rift in the biogeochemical cycles of the planet. It is time therefore to find another path: one of sustainable human development. This constitutes the entire meaning of revolution in our time.

Notes

Preface

1. Epigraph: Karl Marx and Frederick Engels, *Collected Works* (New York: International Publishers, 1975), vol. 5, 28. Translation according to Joseph Fracchia, "Organisms and Objectifications," *Monthly Review* 68/10 (March 2017): 7.
2. Karl Marx, *Capital*, vol. 3 (London: Penguin, 1981), 949.
3. Marx, *Capital*, vol. 3, 949; Marx and Engels, *Collected Works*, vol. 30, 54-66. For an explanation of how Marx's concepts are intertwined, creating a coherent ecological vision, see John Bellamy Foster and Brett Clark, "Marxism and the Dialectics of Ecology," *Monthly Review* 68/5 (October 2016): 1-6.
4. Karl Marx, *Early Writings* (London: Penguin, 1974), 260–61; Karl Marx, "The Value-Form," *Capital and Class* 2/1 (1978): 134.
5. Karl Marx, *Capital*, vol. 3, 754.
6. Karl Marx, *Capital*, vol. 1 (London: Penguin, 1976), 638.
7. Marx and Engels, *Collected Works*, vol. 37, 592, 732–33; Marx, *Capital*, vol. 3, 734, 878–79.
8. Marx and Engels, *Collected Works*, vol. 4, 330.
9. Marx, *Early Writings*, 239; John Bellamy Foster, *Marx's Ecology* (New York; Monthly Review Press, 2000), 74.
10. Marx, *Early Writings*, 254.

Introduction

This introduction is adapted and revised for this book from John Bellamy Foster and Brett Clark, "The Robbery of Nature: Capitalism and the Metabolic Rift," *Monthly Review* 70/3 (July–August 2018): 1–20.

1. Karl Marx, *Capital*, vol. 1 (London: Penguin, 1976), 637–38. On how Marx saw the exploitation process as revealing the expropriation of the surplus labor of the worker within production, which was concealed by equal exchange relations within circulation, see *Capital*, vol. 1, 728–29; Karl Marx and Frederick Engels, *Collected Works* (New York: International Publishers, 1975), vol. 33, 301; vol. 34, 134; Karl Marx, *Texts on Method* (Oxford: Blackwell, 1975), 186–87.

2. Karl Marx, *Capital*, vol. 3 (London: Penguin, 1981), 949–50. In his recent biography of Marx, Sven-Eric Liedman writes that "in his treatment, Engels made rearrangements in the text and moved the expression 'irreparable break' to a later context, where the reader gets the impression that it is the transition from small-scale to large-scale agriculture that creates the growing gap." This is incorrect, however. Engels moved not only this passage but the whole section (some two pages of discussion) on the transition from small-scale to large-scale agriculture to the end to form a conclusion, preserving intact Marx's argument—and thus not creating any false impression, as Liedman contends. Sven-Eric Liedman, *A World to Win* (London; Verso, 2018), 479; Karl Marx, *Economic Manuscript of 1864–1865* (Boston: Brill, 2016), 797–98, 882–83.

3. See Justus von Liebig, "1862 Preface to *Agricultural Chemistry*," *Monthly Review* 70/3 (July–August 2018): 146–50; William H. Brock, *Justus von Liebig* (Cambridge: Cambridge University Press, 1997), 177–78.

4. On Marx's corporeal materialism, see Joseph Fracchia, "Organisms and Objectifications: A Historical-Materialist Inquiry into the 'Human and Animal,'" *Monthly Review* 68/10 (March 2017): 1–16; John Fox, *Marx, the Body, and Human Nature* (London: Palgrave Macmillan, 2015).

5. Justus von Liebig, *Letters on Modern Agriculture* (London: Walton and Maberly, 1859), 175–77; Liebig, *The Natural Laws of Husbandry* (New York: Appleton, 1863), 177–78. The quoted sentence from *Letters on Modern Industry* was Liebig's restatement of a proposition by the practical farmer Albrecht Brecht: "A farmer can afford to sell and permanently alienate only that portion of the produce of his farm which has been supplied by the atmosphere—a field from which nothing is abstracted can only increase, not decrease in productive power."

6. Liebig *Letters on Modern Agriculture*, 179, 254–55; Liebig, *The Natural Laws of Husbandry*, 233; Kohei Saito, *Karl Marx's Ecosocialism* (New York: Monthly Review Press, 2017), 154.

7. Saito, *Karl Marx's Ecosocialism*, 68–70; John Bellamy Foster, *Marx's Ecology* (New York: Monthly Review Press, 2000), 159–61.

8. Liebig, *Letters on Modern Agriculture*, 175–77, 220, 230; Justus von

Liebig, Introduction to *Agricultural Chemistry*, 7th ed. (1862), trans. Lady Gilbert, archives, Rothamsted Research, Hertfordshire, UK (hereafter Liebig, *Einleitung*; page numbers refer to Gilbert translation), 72, 80–85. Although Liedman claims that "most" of Liebig's readers saw him as simply a proponent of industrial progress through the use of fertilizers, and only a "minority" interpreted him otherwise, this is too simple a depiction of the intellectual climate of the time. It is true that Liebig's most severe indictment of British high farming, in his introduction to the 1862 edition of *Agricultural Chemistry*, was never published in English, being considered too incendiary. But especially after the publication of his *Letters on Modern Agriculture*, Liebig's criticism of the wasting of soil nutrients and its relation to the sewage in the towns was widely debated, for example in the London *Times*. His analysis was taken up by many leading thinkers of the time, extending to political economy in the works of Henry Carey in the United States and Wilhelm Roscher in Germany. The importance of his critical analysis in the era's debates over the political economy of agriculture can hardly be overstated, and was not, as Liedman suggests, a particular obsession on Marx's part. See Liedman, *A World to Win*, 478–79; Foster, *Marx's Ecology*, 147–63; Saito, *Karl Marx's Ecosocialism*, 75–78, 183–86, 221–26.

9.   F. M. L. Thompson, "The Second Agricultural Revolution, 1815–1880," *Economic History Review* 21/1 (1968): 62–77.

10.   Karl Marx, *Dispatches for the New York Tribune* (London: Penguin, 2007), 169. See also chapter 4 in this book.

11.   See chapter 4.

12.   On Liebig and the sewage controversy, see Ian Angus, "Cesspools, Sewage, and Social Murder: Ecological Crisis and Metabolic Rift in Nineteenth-Century London," *Monthly Review* 70/3 (July–August 2018): 33–69.

13.   Liebig, *Letters on Modern Agriculture*, 137–38, 147, 161; *Cultivator: Journal for the Farm and Garden* 8, third series (1860): 22; David Ricardo, *Principles of Political Economy and Taxation* (Cambridge: Cambridge University Press, 1951), 67.

14.   Liebig, *Letters on Modern Agriculture*, 28; Fred Magdoff and Harold van Es, *Building Soils for Better Crops* (Burlington, VT: Sustainable Agricultural Publications, 2000), 149; John Bellamy Foster and Paul Burkett, *Marx and the Earth* (Chicago: Haymarket, 2016), 29. It is worth emphasizing, following Magdoff and Es, that the vitality of the soil is best seen in terms of the *soil organic matter* in all its numerous aspects, including a diversity of microorganisms such as bacteria, viruses, fungi, protozoa, and of plant roots, insects, and earthworms,

while constituting the home of larger animals as well. The living portion represents 15 percent of the overall soil organic matter. Soil organic matter also includes organic material at various levels of decomposition. Although the nutrient cycle is at the center of soil metabolism, of which Liebig was the leading nineteenth-century analyst, it would be a mistake to reduce the vitality of the soil simply to the question of nutrients or soil chemistry alone. Magdoff and Es, *Building Soils*, 9–10.

15. Liebig, *The Natural Laws of Husbandry*, 180, 210. Although known as Liebig's Law of the Minimum, it was first advanced by Liebig's contemporary, the German soil scientist Philipp Carl Sprengel. See R. R. van der Ploeg, W. Böhm, and M. B. Kirkham, "On the Origin of the Theory of Mineral Nutrition of Plants and the Law of the Minimum," *Soil Science Society of America Journal* 63 (1999): 1055–62.

16. Foster, *Marx's Ecology*, 149–63; Saito, *Karl Marx's Ecosocialism*.

17. Gregory T. Cushman, *Guano and the Opening of the Pacific World* (Cambridge: University of Cambridge Press, 2013), 45, 170–73.

18. Liebig, *Einleitung*, 76–78; Liebig, *Letters on Modern Agriculture*, 219–22, 269–70; *Census of England and Wales for the Year 1861*, vol. 3, *General Report*, 5. Liebig's figures for the import of guano greatly exceed those presented in a table by Thompson in his classic article. Nevertheless, Liebig's data is in line with the numbers presented in the work of more recent historians who have examined official records. See C. Alexander G. de Secada, "Arms, Guano, and Shipping," *Business History Review* 59/4 (1985): 597–621; Brett Clark and John Bellamy Foster, "Guano," in *Ecology and Power*, ed. Alf Hornborg, Brett Clark, and Kenneth Hermele (London: Routledge, 2012), 75; Thompson, "The Second Agricultural Revolution," 75.

19. Liebig, *Einleitung*, 79–81.

20. Ibid., 79, 94; Liebig, *Letters of Modern Industry*, 183, 188; Saito, *Karl Marx's Ecosocialism*, 202.

21. Liebig, *Einleitung*, 85; Brock, *Justus von Liebig*, 178.

22. Liebig, *Einleitung*, 96, 101.

23. Liebig, *The Natural Law of Husbandry*, 233.

24. See Foster, *Marx's Ecology*, 39–65.

25. Karl Marx, *Early Writings* (London: Penguin, 1974), 318–19, 323–28, 348–50, 359–60, 389–91.

26. Saito, *Karl Marx's Ecosocialism*, 72–78; Roland Daniels, *Mikrokosmos* (Frankfurt am Main: Lang, 1988).

27. Karl Marx, *Grundrisse* (London: Penguin, 1973), 158; Karl Marx, *A Contribution to a Critique of Political Economy* (Moscow: Progress Publishers, 1970), 51–52.

28. Marx, *Contribution to a Critique of Political Economy*, 86; *Capital*, vol. 1, 133.

29. Marx, *Grundrisse*, 271, 489; Marx and Engels, *Collected Works*, vol. 30, 54–66; John Bellamy Foster, "Marx and the Rift in the Universal Metabolism of Nature," *Monthly Review* 65/7 (2013): 1–19.

30. See Fred Magdoff and Chris Williams, *Creating an Ecological Society* (New York: Monthly Review Press, 2017), 76, 217.

31. Marx contended that Liebig used the word *labor* in a quite "different sense from that adopted by political economy," thereby confusing his analysis. For Liebig's approach to labor, which he conflated with the "labor" of organisms in general, see Justus von Liebig, *Familiar Letters on Chemistry* (London: Taylor, Walton, and Maberly, 1851), 468–69.

32. Marx, *Grundrisse*, 360–61; Marx, *Texts on Method*, 190–91; Georg Wilhelm Friedrich Hegel, *Science of Logic* (New York: Humanity, 1969), 450–56; Saito, *Karl Marx's Ecosocialism*, 75–76.

33. Marx, *Capital*, vol. 1, 290.

34. Marx, *Grundrisse*, 527.

35. Mette Ejrnæs, Karl Gunnar Persson, and Søren Rich, "Feeding the British," *Economic History Review* 61/S1 (2008): 140–71; Marx, *Dispatches for the New York Tribune*, 169; chapter 4 in this book.

36. Marx, *Capital*, vol. 1, 638–39.

37. Ibid., 638.

38. Marx, *Economic Manuscript of 1864–65*, 882.

39. Marx, *Capital*, vol. 3, 754.

40. Karl Marx, *Theories of Surplus Value*, part 2 (Moscow: Progress Publishers, 1968), 24.

41. Marx and Engels, *Collected Works*, vol. 46, 62.

42. Karl Marx and Frederick Engels, *Ireland and the Irish Question* (Moscow: Progress Publishers, 1971), 120–42; Karl Marx, *On the First International* (New York: McGraw Hill, 1973), 90; Marx, *Capital*, vol. 1, 860. Eamonn Slater has brilliantly shown that Marx's argument on the robbery of the soil and the resulting metabolic rift had its counterpart in Ireland, where cultivators were actively prevented from replenishing the soil. See Slater, "Marx on the Colonization of Irish Soil," Social Science Institute, Maynooth University, MUSSI Working Paper Series 3 (January 2018): 4, 10.

43. Karl Marx, "Drafts of a Reply to Vera Zasulich," in *Late Marx and the Russian Road, ed.* Teodor Shanin (New York: Monthly Review Press, 1983), 121; Marx and Engels, *Collected Works*, vol. 46, 63–64.

44. Marx, *Capital*, vol. 3, 949.

45. Paul Burkett, "Marx's Vision of Sustainable Human Development," *Monthly Review* 57/5 (2005): 34–62; John Bellamy Foster, *The Ecological*

Revolution (New York: Monthly Review Press 2008); John Bellamy Foster, Brett Clark, and Richard York, *The Ecological Rift* (New York: Monthly Review Press, 2010); Fred Magdoff, "Ecological Civilization," *Monthly Review* 62/8 (2011): 1–25.

46. Foster, *Marx's Ecology*, 36, 225.

47. Karl Marx, *The Poverty of Philosophy* (New York: International Publishers, 1963), 110, 228; Lucretius, *On the Nature of the Universe*, trans. Ronald Melville (Oxford: Oxford University Press), 93 (III: 869).

48. Lucretius, *The Scheme of Epicurus* (*De rerum natura*), trans. Thomas Charles Baring (London: Kegan Paul, Trench, 1884), 21 (I: 450–52). Other translations from Lucretius convey the same idea in slightly different and less colorful language. W. E. Leonard's translation reads: "A property is that which not at all / Can be disjoined and severed from anything / Without a final dissolution"; trans. Melville: "A property is something that cannot be separated / Or removed from a thing without destroying it"; trans. Cyril Bailey: "That is a property which can in no way case be sundered or separated without the fatal disunion of the thing." Lucretius, *On the Nature of Things*, trans. W. E. Leonard (New York: Dutton, 1921), 18; Lucretius, *On the Nature of the Universe*, trans. Melville, 16; Lucretius, *Lucretius on the Nature of Things*, trans. Cyril Bailey (Oxford: Oxford University Press, 1910), 41–42.

49. Ariel Salleh, "From Metabolic Rift to 'Metabolic Value,'" *Organization & Environment* 23/2 (2010): 205–19; Ariel Salleh, ed., *Eco-Sufficiency and Global Justice* (London: Pluto, 2009).

50. Howard Waitzkin, *The Second Sickness* (Boston: Rowman and Littlefield, 2000).

51. Norman Wentworth DeWitt, *Epicurus and His Philosophy* (Minneapolis: University of Minnesota Press, 1954), 133.

52. Karl Marx, *Early Writings* (New York: McGraw Hill, 1964), 207; Foster, "Marx and the Rift in the Universal Metabolism of Nature"; Fracchia, "Organisms and Objectifications."

53. Joseph Fracchia, "Beyond the Human–Nature Debate: Human Corporeal Organisation as the 'First Fact' of Historical Materialism," *Historical Materialism* 13/1 (2005): 43.

54. Marx, *Capital*, vol. 1, 875.

55. Ibid., 891–95.

56. Ibid., 748.

57. Ibid., 915. Also see Roxanne Dunbar-Ortiz, *An Indigenous Peoples' History of the United States* (Boston: Beacon, 2014); and chapter 1 in this book.

58. Edward E. Baptist, *The Half Has Never Been Told* (New York: Basic

Books, 2016); Sven Beckert, *Empire of Cotton* (New York: Vintage, 2014).

59. Watt Stewart, *Chinese Bondage in Peru: A History of the Chinese Coolie in Peru: 1849–1874* (Westport, CT: Greenwood, 1951), 96–98; see also Brett Clark, Daniel Auerbach, and Karen Xuan Zhang, "The Du Bois Nexus: Intersectionality, Political Economy, and Environmental Injustice in the Peruvian Guano Trade in the 1800s," *Environmental Sociology* 4/1 (2018): 54–66.

60. Marx, *Capital*, vol. 3, 182.

61. Ibid., 365.

62. Marx and Engels, *Collected Works*, vol. 2, 7–9.

63. John Green, *A Revolutionary Life* (London: Artery, 2008), 70; Steven Marcus, *Engels, Manchester, and the Working Class* (New York: W. W. Norton, 1985), 98–99; Roy Whitfield, "The Double Life of Friedrich Engels," *Manchester Region History Review* (Spring–Summer 1988): 13–19; Charles Dickens, *The Old Curiosity Shop* (New York: Dutton, 1908), 327.

64. Marx and Engels, *Collected Works*, vol. 4, 447–48.

65. See Waitzkin, *The Second Sickness*, 67–70; Brett Clark and John Bellamy Foster, "The Environmental Conditions of the Working Class: An Introduction to Selections from Frederick Engels's *The Condition of the Working Class in England in 1844*," *Organization & Environment* 19/3 (2006): 375–88.

66. Marx and Engels, *Collected Works*, vol. 4, 448–54, 498–99.

67. Ibid., 492–94.

68. Ibid., 495–96.

69. Ibid., 531–35.

70. Ibid., 450.

71. Marx, *Capital*, vol. 1, 552–53.

72. Marx, *Capital*, vol. 3, 181–85.

73. Ibid., 185.

74. Marx, *Capital*, vol. 1, 809–11.

75. Anthony Wohl, *Endangered Lives* (Cambridge, MA: Harvard University Press, 1983), 50–52.

76. Marx, *Capital*, vol. 1, 811.

77. Ibid., 718.

78. Marx and Engels, *Collected Works*, vol. 4, 399–400.

79. Marx, *Capital*, vol. 1, 359–61.

80. Wohl, *Endangered Lives*, 52–53.

81. Marx, "A Workers' Inquiry," available at http://marxists.org; Asad Haider and Salar Mohandesi, "Workers' Inquiry: A Genealogy,"

Viewpoint 3, September 27, 2013, http:// https://www.viewpointmag. com/2013/09/27/workers-inquiry-a-genealogy/.
82. Fracchia, "Beyond the Human-Nature Debate," 50.
83. Ibid., 57.
84. Marx, *Capital*, vol. 1, 342.
85. Lucretius, *On the Nature of Things*, trans. Leonard, 45 (II: 15-20).
86. Salleh, ed., *Eco-Sufficiency and Global Justice*, 24–25, 306. For Salleh, metabolic value constitutes a larger category of socioecological value, extending beyond use value.
87. Marx, *Grundrisse*, 489.
88. Marx, *Early Writings*, 61, 328, 389; István Mészáros, *Marx's Theory of Alienation* (London: Merlin, 1970), 82, 100–101, 163–65; Marx and Engels, *Collected Works*, vol. 3, 7.
89. Marx and Engels, *Collected Works*, vol. 1, 64; translation according to Mészáros, *Marx's Theory of Alienation*, 351.
90. Marx, *Capital*, vol. 3, 959.
91. Liedman, *A World to Win*, 479–80.
92. Marx and Engels, *Collected Works,* vol. 5, 141–42.

1. The Expropriation of Nature
This chapter is adapted and revised for this book from John Bellamy Foster and Brett Clark, "The Expropriation of Nature," *Monthly Review* 69/10 (March 2018): 1–27.

1. Karl Marx and Frederick Engels, *Collected Works* (New York: International Publishers, 1975), vol. 28, 429. Translation as "age of dissolution" from Karl Marx, *Pre-Capitalist Economic Formations*, ed. E. J. Hobsbawm (New York: International Publishers, 1964), 109.
2. *Spoliation* is the action or condition of being robbed and despoiled. It was commonly applied in the nineteenth century in Justus von Liebig's writings as well as in English translations from Marx's *Capital* to refer to the spoliation of the earth or soil. The concept is still widely employed in the sense of environmental spoliation. Thus, Max Ajl states, "The history of capitalism has been a history of environmental spoliation." Likewise, Amiya Kumar Bagchi observes that "environmental spoliation" occurred "before the advent of capitalism," though the latter was to give it a more global and relentlessly systematic character. Ajl quoted in Belen Fernandez, "The Earth Versus Capitalism," *Al Jazeera*, April 22, 2017, http://aljazeera.com; Amiya Kumar Bagchi, *Perilous Passage: Mankind and the Global Ascendancy of Capital* (New York: Rowman and Littlefield, 2005), 8.

3. David Harvey, *Marx, Capital, and the Madness of Economic Reason* (Oxford: Oxford University Press, 2018), 89–93.

4. The focus on expropriation in this article is paralleled by Nancy Fraser, who, building on social reproduction theory, has related this to the expropriation of nature and Marx's theory of metabolic rift. See our discussion of Fraser's work in this respect in chapter 3 of this book, as well as Michael C. Dawson, "Hidden in Plain Sight: A Note on Legitimation Crises and the Racial Order," *Critical Historical Studies* 3/1 (2016): 143–61.

5. Marx and Engels, *Collected Works*, vol. 28, 428, 433–34; vol. 29, 210, 674; vol. 33, 301; Karl Marx, *Grundrisse* (London: Penguin, 1973), 674; Karl Marx, *Capital*, vol. 1 (London: Penguin, 1976), 374, 729; Marx, *Capital*, vol. 3 (London: Penguin, 1981), 958; Karl Renner, *The Institutions of Private Law and Their Social Functions* (London: Routledge and Kegan Paul, 1949), 205. In all of his economic manuscripts from the *Grundrisse* up through the *Economic Manuscript of 1861–63* (including his *Theories of Surplus Value*), Marx uses the phrase *appropriation without exchange* to refer to expropriation. Thereafter, in *Capital*, he substitutes *appropriation without an equivalent*. The two phrases are identical in meaning, since in Marx's analysis, exchange is the exchange of equivalents. In what follows, we have chosen in this book to use the two phrases interchangeably.

6. Marx, *Capital*, vol. 1, 873. Marx referred to "so-called primary [mistranslated as 'primitive'] accumulation," which was a category of classical political economy. However, he indicated his skepticism toward the term and generally employed the term "expropriation" (representing "the secret of primary accumulation") to explain the origins of capitalism through the dissolution of previous property forms and the separation of the workers from the natural conditions of production (the land). Moreover, so-called primary accumulation was not simply a historical precondition of capitalism, but a historical condition in all of its phases, since the boundaries of the capitalist system were constantly in flux. It took the form of expropriation of previous property forms (or non-commodity property) and thus was not, as Maurice Dobb noted, a form of accumulation, but rather *the expropriation of titles to property* and of the elemental means of production themselves. See Marx, *Capital*, vol. 1, 871, 873, 931–32; Maurice Dobb, *Studies in the Development of Capitalism* (New York: International Publishers, 1947), 178-79. See also Renner, *The Institutions of Private Law*, 90.

7. Marx and Engels, *Collected Works*, vol. 28, 431; Marx, *Capital*, vol. 1, 915. Expropriation, as in the expropriation of land, as Karl Renner

noted in his classic work on the Marxian theory of private law, should not be confused with mere *dispossession*, that is, the physical removal of the connection to real property, although the latter is normally involved as well. Rather, expropriation is not simply a physical act but a *legal* one, even if what is given formal legal justification is actually robbery—for example, the claiming of the commons by the lords or the discovery doctrine in the Americas—because it establishes the title to the expropriated commodity now and into the future, and to continuing appropriation and accumulation on that basis. Renner, *The Institutions of Private Law*, 208; Michael Tigar, *Law and the Rise of Capitalism* (New York: Monthly Review Press, 2000), 308–10. For Marx, possession (like appropriation) establishes a juridical claim to property, but should not be confused with ownership or the title to property (in the bourgeois sense), which constitutes a stronger juridical claim. Expropriation or appropriation without exchange, insofar as it relates to ownership of property normally relates to the latter. Paul Phillips, *Marx and Engels on Law and Laws* (Oxford: Robertson, 1980), 172–73.

8. Karl Marx, *The Eighteenth Brumaire of Louis Bonaparte* (New York: International Publishers, 1963), 128. Translation slightly amended.

9. Marx did not address the burning of witches in his analysis, though the connection of this to the development of capitalism has been well documented in such work as Silvia Federici, *Caliban and the Witch* (Brooklyn, NY: Autonomedia, 2014). On literal wife selling, see especially E. P. Thompson, *Customs in Common* (New York: New Press, 1991), 404–66. Marx, while not exploring the selling of women as chattel slaves, did refer extensively to the husband "selling" his wife and children to work in industry and a kind of enslavement in this context, made possible by the fact that the latter were "exploited by the head of the family." Marx, *Capital*, vol. 1, 1083; Lise Vogel, *Marxism and the Oppression of Women* (Chicago: Haymarket, 2013), 64–65.

10. Marx and Engels, *Collected Works*, vol. 29, 298; vol. 30, 54–66; vol. 37, 732–33.

11. Marx, *Capital*, vol. 1, 926; Karl Polanyi, *The Great Transformation* (Boston: Beacon, 2001), 188.

12. Sven Beckert, *Empire of Cotton* (New York: Vintage, 2014), xv–xvi.

13. Robin Blackburn, *The Making of New World Slavery* (London: Verso, 1997), 542.

14. Marx, *Capital*, vol. 1, 928.

15. Paul A. Baran and Paul M. Sweezy, *Monopoly Capital* (New York: Monthly Review Press, 1966), 336–38.

16. Hegel referred to "the absolute right of appropriation which man has over all 'things,' without which existence is impossible. Property in its most general sense is nothing but the right of such appropriation." See G. W. F. Hegel, *The Philosophy of Right* (Oxford: Oxford University Press, 1952), 41–45.

17. Marx and Engels, *Collected Works*, vol. 28, 25. Translation here follows Karl Marx, *Grundrisse* (London: Penguin, 1973), 87–88.

18. Marx, *Capital*, vol. 1, 169–72; Stephen Hymer, "Robinson Crusoe and the Secret of Primitive Accumulation," *Monthly Review* 23/4 (September 1971): 11–36. Say quoted in Pierre-Joseph Proudhon, *What Is Property?* (Cambridge: Cambridge University Press, 1993), 70. On Locke's "political theory of appropriation" see C. B. Macpherson, *The Political Theory of Possessive Individualism* (Oxford: Oxford University Press, 1962), 194–262.

19. Marx and Engels, *Collected Works*, vol. 37, 732–33; Marx, *Capital*, vol. 3, 878–79; Paul Burkett, "Nature's 'Free Gifts' and the Ecological Significance of Value," *Capital and Class* 68 (1999): 89–110. World-system ecological theorist Jason W. Moore mistakenly argues that Marx "deployed the term [appropriation] more or less interchangeably with the exploitation of wage labor." As we have seen, nothing could be more opposed to Marx's actual argument, which insisted that property in all of its forms in all societies is appropriation (*Aneignung*), and that no production whatsoever could exist apart from appropriation. In bourgeois society, however, there arises specific socioeconomic laws of capitalist appropriation. Hence, it is not *appropriation* as such, which simply refers to property in general, but capitalist appropriation without exchange, or *expropriation* (*Enteignung*), that is crucial in analyzing the system's external boundaries. See Jason W. Moore, *Capitalism in the Web of Life* (London: Verso, 2015), 17; Moore, "Endless Accumulation, Endless (Unpaid) Work?," *Occupied Times*, April 29, 2015, https://theoccupiedtimes.org.

20. Proudhon, *What Is Property?*, 13–16; Marx and Engels, *Collected Works*, vol. 1, 220; vol. 28, 412–13. Marx's argument with respect to Proudhon only concerns the theft of property, not the question, later to be writ large in Marx's analysis of the robbery of the earth itself.

21. Marx and Engels, *Collected Works*, vol. 28, 428, 433–38; vol. 29, 210, 674; vol. 30, 134, 301.

22. See G. E. M. de Ste. Croix, *Class Struggle in the Ancient Greek World* (London: Duckworth, 1981), 49–55.

23. Marx, *Capital*, vol. 1, 267; Franklin, "Positions to be Examined, Concerning National Economy," in Benjamin Franklin, *Works*, vol. 2 (Boston: Charles Tappan, 1844), 376. Marx quotes Franklin in a

shortened form, without ellipses, perhaps for effect. The full statement is: "There seems to be but three ways for a nation to acquire wealth. The first is by *war*, as the Romans did, in plundering their conquered neighbors. The second by *commerce*, which is generally *cheating*. The third by *agriculture*, the only honest way." Franklin's short essay emphasizes that cheating is possible because of the number of intermediaries.

24. Marx, *Capital*, vol. 1, 591.

25. Marx, *Capital*, vol. 1, 728–29; Marx and Engels, *Collected Works*, vol. 28, 433–34; vol. 33, 301; vol. 34, 134. Marx explained that "the contract by which he [a worker] sold his labour-power to the capitalist proved in black and white, so to speak, that he was free to dispose of himself. But when the transaction was concluded, it was discovered that he was no 'free agent,' that the period of time for which he is free to sell his labour-power is the period of time for which he is forced to sell it, that in fact the vampire [capitalist] will not let go 'while there remains a single muscle, sinew or drop of blood to be exploited.'" See Marx, *Capital*, vol. 1, 415-16. On the significance of the vampire image in Marx, see Paul Burkett, *Marx and Nature* (Chicago: Haymarket, 2014), 138, 283; Mark Neocleous, "The Political Economy of the Dead: Marx's Vampires," *History of Political Thought* 24/4 (2003): 668–84.

26. Marx and Engels, *Collected Works*, vol. 33, 301; vol. 34, 134; Renner, *The Institutions of Private Law*, 205.

27. James Steuart, *An Inquiry into the Principles of Political Oeconomy* (London: Millar and Cadell, 1767), 181–83, 361–63, 395; Marx and Engels, *Collected Works*, vol. 33, 14; Karl Marx, *Theories of Surplus Value*, part 1 (Moscow: Progress Publishers, 1963), 41–43; Mark Obrinsky, *Profit Theory and Capitalism* (Philadelphia: University of Pennsylvania Press, 1983), 12. Naturally, no economy for Marx can be based simply on profit upon expropriation, because it has to first produce. See Marx, *Capital*, vol. 1, 175. It is clear that Steuart's distinction between value relations and profit upon expropriation was fundamental to Marx, leading the latter to commence his *Theories of Surplus Value* with Steuart as the most important transitional figure between mercantilist political economy and the more developed political economy represented by Adam Smith a decade later. Basing his analysis on Marx's theory of profit upon expropriation, Kozo Uno defined mercantilism as an economic formation relying on "expropriatory gain." See Kozo Uno, *The Types of Economic Policies Under Capitalism* (Boston: Brill, 1971), 37, 68.

28. Marx and Engels, *Collected Works*, vol. 28, 433–34; vol. 29, 163–64; 297–98; vol. 30, 351, 385–86; vol. 32, 253; vol. 33, 13–14, 35, 67, 241,

351; vol. 34, 134; Karl Marx, *Capital*, vol. 3 (London: Penguin, 1981), 327, 388–89, 448. See also Georg Lukács, *The Young Hegel* (Cambridge, MA: MIT Press, 1975), 175–76; Costas Lapavitsas, *Profiting Without Producing* (London: Verso, 2013), 141–47.

29.   Marx, *Capital*, vol. 1, 777, 930.

30.   Marx, *Capital*, vol. 1, 267, 342–43, 638, 733–34, 745, 917; Marx, *Capital*, vol. 3, 448, 745; Marx and Engels, *Collected Works*, vol. 32, 253, 405; vol. 33, 17; Marx, *Grundrisse*, 853; Paul A. Baran and Paul. M. Sweezy, "Some Theoretical Implications," *Monthly Review* 64/3 (July–August 2012): 59; Karl Marx, *Capital*, vol. 2 (London: Penguin, 1976), 559–60. For "spoliation," see Marx and Engels, *Collected Works*, vol. 35, 242; vol. 37, 613. Marx in this passage literally refers to the "sucking out" of the elemental properties of the soil (*diebrutale Aussaugung des Bodens*). In another place where Marx, according to the English translations, employs "spoliation" (or "despoiling") in relation to the exploitation/ expropriation of labor power, he is actually referring directly to robbery (*Beraubung*). Comments and translation here were provided by Joseph Fracchia. See Marx and Engels, *Collected Works*, vol. 35, 242; Marx, *Capital*, vol. 1, 343. David Harvey uses the phrase "accumulation by dispossession" to get at the phenomenon of expropriation. But in Marx's own terms, this would be better rendered "profit upon expropriation." More recently, Jason W. Moore, varying on Harvey, has coined the notion of "accumulation by appropriation"—a phrase that is nonsensical from Marx's standpoint, given that property in its most general sense (encompassing all of its specific forms) is nothing but appropriation. See Marx and Engels, *Collected Works*, vol. 28, 25; David Harvey, *The New Imperialism* (Oxford: Oxford University Press, 2013), 137–82; Moore, "Endless Accumulation, Endless (Unpaid) Work?"

31.   In referring to the category of profit by deduction, that is, the reduction of wages below the value of labor power, Marx insisted that "despite the important part which this method plays in practice, we are excluded from considering it here by our assumption that all commodities, including labour-power, are bought and sold at their full value," that is, under conditions of the exchange of equivalents. See Marx, *Capital*, vol. 1, 431.

32.   Karl Polanyi, *Primitive, Archaic and Modern Economies* (Boston: Beacon, 1968), 88. Although the concept of unequal exchange is often used in Marxian theory—see Arghiri Emmanuel, *Unequal Exchange* (New York: Monthly Review Press, 1972)—such a concept was outside of Marx's framework, in which exchange always meant exchange of equivalents, and in which "without exchange" and "without equivalent" were treated as synonymous.

33. Karl Marx, *Dispatches from the New York Tribune* (London: Penguin, 2007), 126. Marx writes that "trade everywhere mediates exchange and exchange value, a mediation which we can call trade." See Marx and Engels, *Collected Works*, vol. 28, 433.

34. Polanyi, *Primitive, Archaic and Modern Economies*, 89–93 106–7, 149–56; Paresh Chattopadhyay, *Marx's Associated Mode of Production* (London: Palgrave Macmillan, 2016). In Polanyi's terms, reciprocity is a form of "appropriational movements" that lacks the strict quantifiable equivalence of exchange, since directed at use value rather than exchange value, and thus addressing incommensurables. See also Juan Martinez-Alier, *The Environmentalism of the Poor* (Northampton, MA: Elgar, 2002), 216–17; and Stefano B. Longo, Rebecca Clausen, and Brett Clark, *The Tragedy of the Commodity* (New Brunswick, NJ: Rutgers University Press, 2015). Similar issues are raised by István Mészáros in his analysis of "the nature of exchange under communal social relations." See István Mészáros, *Beyond Capital* (New York: Monthly Review Press, 1995), 758–70.

35. "Expropriate," "Expropriation," *The Compact Edition of the Oxford English Dictionary* (Oxford: Oxford University Press, 1971), 935; Renner, *The Institutions of Private Law*, 204–8. Joseph Schumpeter saw *spoliation* as so much the essence of the concept of *expropriation* (in Marx's notion of primary accumulation) that he substituted the former term for the latter. Joseph A. Schumpeter, *Capitalism, Socialism and Democracy* (New York: Harper and Row, 1942), 17.

36. Marx, *Pre-Capitalist Economic Formations*, 109.

37. Marx, *Grundrisse*, 489; see also Marx and Engels, *Collected Works*, vol. 28, 413.

38. It is common for commentators on Marx's notion of primary accumulation to refer to its atheoretical character. However, this misconception is usually based on the scrutiny of Marx's section on "So-Called Primitive [Primary] Accumulation" in *Capital*, vol. 1, missing altogether Marx's broader theoretical discussion in the *Grundrisse*. For a developed interpretation of Marx's treatment of primary accumulation in the *Grundrisse*, which avoided this error, see Roman Rosdolsky, *The Making of Marx's Capital* (London: Pluto, 1977), 268–81. According to Schumpeter, writing on Marx's theory, "Primitive [primary] accumulation...continues throughout the capitalist era." See Schumpeter, *Capitalism, Socialism and Democracy*, 18.

39. See John Bellamy Foster, "Marx and the Rift in the Universal Metabolism of Nature," *Monthly Review* 65/7 (December 2013): 1–19; chap. 8 in this book.

40. Marx and Engels, *Collected Works*, vol. 28, 251, 425–38 (translation

in Marx, *Pre-Capitalist Economic Formations*, 86–118). In Marx's dialectic, the metabolic rift, or the main ecological contradiction engendered by capitalism, is a product of the "alienated mediation" of the social metabolism of humanity and nature, arising ultimately from the alienation of land and labor. See Karl Marx, *Early Writings* (London: Penguin, 1974), 261; John Bellamy Foster and Brett Clark, "Marxism and the Dialectics of Ecology," *Monthly Review* 68/5 (October 2016): 1–5; Louis Krader, "Introduction," in Karl Marx, *Ethnological Notebooks* (Assen: Van Gorcum, 1972), 47, 55.

41.   Marx and Engels, *Collected Works*, vol. 28, 425–38 (translation in Marx, *Pre-Capitalist Economic Formations*, 86–118); Marx, *Capital*, vol. 1, 914. For Marx, "the conditions of production . . . in their simplest form are the natural elements themselves." See Marx and Engels, *Collected Works*, vol. 31, 241. Our discussion here does not attempt to address the historical and theoretical complexities of the debate on the transition from feudalism to capitalism. Nevertheless, it should be noted that the key to this debate lies in the distinction, first introduced by Paul Sweezy, and adhered to by later thinkers such as Robert Brenner and Ellen Meiksins Wood, between the "dissolution" in the mercantilist age of feudal relations of production and the actual formation also in the mercantilist stage of a self-propelling capitalist form of appropriation and accumulation, only to be fully realized at the time of the Industrial Revolution. See Ellen Meiksins Wood, *The Origin of Capitalism* (London: Verso, 1999), 30–35.

42.   Polanyi, *The Great Transformation*, 77–78.

43.   Ibid., 187.

44.   The "natural economy" stands for those modes of production outside the exchange relation altogether. Hence, in this context Marx refers to "appropriation without circulation" of commodities. Here force often plays a more direct role, as in a slave economy. Yet natural economy can also be seen as related to subsistence production. See Marx, *Capital*, vol. 2 (London: Penguin, 1978), 555; *Capital*, vol. 3, 922. For a brief treatment of the concept of natural economy in the work of Marx and Rosa Luxemburg, see Scott Cook, *Understanding Commodity Economies* (New York: Rowman and Littlefield, 2004), 114, 130–31, 151.

45.   William H. Brock, *Justus von Liebig* (Cambridge: Cambridge University Press, 1997), 177–78; Max Weber, following Liebig, Marx, and others, used *Raubbau* to refer to "land-robbing agriculture." Max Weber, "German-Agriculture and Forestry," *Kölner Zeitschrift für Soziologie und Sozialpsychologie* 57/1 (1907–1908): 143, 147; Weber, *General Economic History* (Mineola, NY: Dover, 2003), 82–83. See also John

Bellamy Foster and Hannah Holleman, "Weber and the Environment," *American Journal of Sociology* 117/6 (2012): 1650–55.

46. Justus von Liebig, *Letters on Modern Agriculture*, (London: Walton and Maberly, 1859), 175–78, 183, 220; Liebig, *Familiar Letters on Chemistry* (Philadelphia: Peterson, 1852), 44. The *Familiar Letters* was published as part of *Complete Works on Chemistry*, comprising a number of separate works printed under a single cover. See also John Bellamy Foster, *Marx's Ecology* (New York: Monthly Review Press, 2000), 147–54.

47. Marx, *Capital*, vol. 1, 637–38; Marx, *Capital*, vol. 3, 756, 948–49; Marx and Engels, *Collected Works*, vol. 34, 200; vol. 37, 592, 613; Kohei Saito, *Karl Marx's Ecosocialism: Capital, Nature, and the Unfinished Critique of Political Economy* (New York: Monthly Review Press), 197.

48. Charles Lyell, *Principles of Geology*, ed. James A. Secord (London: Penguin, 1997), 276–77. Marx and Engels (as well as Charles Darwin) would clearly have deplored Lyell's views in this respect. See John Bellamy Foster, "Capitalism and the Accumulation of Catastrophe," *Monthly Review* 63/7 (December 2011): 1–17.

49. John Locke, *Two Treatises of Government* (Cambridge: Cambridge University Press, 1988), 297–301; Barbara Arneil, *John Locke and America: The Defense of English Colonialism* (Oxford: Oxford University Press, 1996), 168–200; Peter Olsen, "John Locke's Liberty Was for Whites Only," *New York Times*, December 25, 1984; Neal Wood, *John Locke and Agrarian Capitalism* (Berkeley: University of California Press, 1984), 61; E. P. Thompson, *Customs in Common* (New York: New Press, 1991), 164–65; William Cronon, *Changes in the Land* (New York: Hill and Wang, 1983), 57–63, 78–80. For Locke, common land based on customary rights as in England was to be accorded some property rights, since it had been improved by labor, but the land in the Americas was common land in the altogether different sense of non-property, and thus open to absolute expropriation. Marx clearly had Locke's political theory of appropriation in mind when he pointed out that "ideologically and juridically the ideology of property founded on labor is transferred without much more ado to property founded on the *expropriation of the immediate producers*." See Marx, *Capital*, vol. 1, 1084; Macpherson, *The Political Theory of Possessive Individualism*, 203–20; Allan Greer, *Property and Dispossession: Natives, Empires and Land in Early Modern America* (Cambridge: Cambridge University Press, 2018), 245–47, 269–70.

50. Marx, *Capital*, vol. 1, 133, 733–34.

51. Moishe Postone observes that "although productivist critiques of capitalism have focused only on the possible barriers to economic

growth inherent in capital accumulation, it is clear that Marx criticized both the accelerating boundlessness of 'growth' under capitalism as well as its crisis-ridden character. Indeed, he demonstrates that these two characteristics should be analyzed as intrinsically connected." Postone, *Time, Labor, and Social Domination* (Cambridge: Cambridge University Press, 1993), 312–13.

52.   John Bellamy Foster, Brett Clark, and Richard York, *The Ecological Rift* (New York: Monthly Review Press, 2010), 284–87. On production as only changing the *form* of what nature provides, see Marx, *Capital*, vol. 1, 133–34; Elmar Altvater, *The Future of the Market* (London: Verso, 1993), 189–92; K. K. Valtukh, *Marx's Theory of Commodity and Surplus Value* (Moscow: Progress Publishers, 1987), 17–19.

53.   Marx and Engels, *Collected Works*, vol. 28, 336–37 (translation according to Marx, *Grundrisse*, 409–10); Marx and Engels, *Collected Works*, vol. 30, 54–56; Francis Bacon, *Novum Organum* (Chicago: Open Court, 1994), 29, 43.

54.   Marx, *Capital*, vol. 3, 178, 182.

55.   Nancy Fraser, "Roepke Lecture in Economic Geography—From Exploitation to Expropriation: Historic Geographies of Racialized Capitalism," *Economic Geography* 94/1 (2018): 10; Michael C. Dawson, "Hidden in Plain Sight"; Peter Linebaugh, *Stop, Thief! The Commons, Enclosures, and Resistance* (Oakland, CA: PM, 2014), 73.

56.   Dawson, "Hidden in Plain Sight," 149: Marx, *Capital*, vol. 1, 914–36.

57.   Karl Marx and Frederick Engels, *On Colonialism* (Moscow: Foreign Languages Publishing house, n.d.), 252. See also Eric Williams, *Capitalism and Slavery* (Chapel Hill: University of North Carolina Press, 1994).

58.   Wilfred H. Schoff, ed., *The Periplus of the Erythraean Sea: Travel and Trade in the Indian Ocean by a Merchant of the First Century* (London: Longmans, Green, 1912), sec. 6, 24; Beckert, *Empire of Cotton*, 32–39.

59.   Basil Davidson, *The African Slave Trade* (Boston: Little, Brown, 1980), 164.

60.   Beckert, *Empire of Cotton*, 35-47.

61.   Clive Ponting, *The Green History of the World* (New York: St. Martin's, 1991), 207; Blackburn, *The Making of New World Slavery*, 483; E. J. Hobsbawm, *Industry and Empire* (London: Penguin, 1969), 58.

62.   James S. Olsen, *Encyclopedia of the Industrial Revolution in America* (Santa Barbara, CA: Greenwood, 2001), xv; Beckert, *Empire of Cotton*, 51; Hobsbawm, *Industry and Empire*, 49, 57–58, 149.

63.   Marx, *Capital*, vol. 1, 925.

64.   Williams, *Capitalism and Slavery*, 105.

65.   Marx and Engels, *Collected Works*, vol. 28, 35.

66. Roxanne Dunbar-Ortiz, *An Indigenous Peoples' History of the United States* (Boston: Beacon, 2014); Michael Tigar, *Law and the Rise of Capitalism*.

67. Marx, *Capital*, vol. 1, 917–18.

68. Tigar, *Law and the Rise of Capitalism*, 308–9.

69. W. E. B. Du Bois, *The Souls of Black Folk* (New York: Modern Library, 2003), 115; see also Brett Clark and John Bellamy Foster, "Land, the Color Line, and the Quest of the Golden Fleece: An Introduction to W. E. B. Du Bois's *The Souls of Black Folk* and *The Quest of the Silver Fleece* (Selections)," *Organization & Environment* 16/4 (2003): 459–69.

70. Beckert, *Empire of Cotton*, 40; Sven Beckert, "Slavery and Capitalism," *Chronicle of Higher Education*, December 12, 2014; Edward E. Baptist, *The Half Has Never Been Told: Slavery and the Making of American Capitalism* (New York: Basic Books, 2016); Williams, *Capitalism and Slavery*.

71. Marx, *Capital*, vol. 1, 377.

72. John Elliott Cairnes, *The Slave Power* (London: Parker, Son, and Bourn,1862), 110–11; Marx, *Capital*, vol. 1, 377.

73. The slave trade continued to deposit slaves illegally in the southern United States up to 1860. See Vanessa Romo, "Reporter May Have Discovered *Clotilda*, the Last American Slave Ship," National Public Radio, January 25, 2018.

74. Cairnes, *The Slave Power*, 54–57; Marx, *Capital*, 1014.

75. Julia Ott, "Slaves: The Capital that Made Capitalism," Public Seminar, April 9, 2014, http://publicseminar.org; Baptist, *The Half Has Never Been Told*. See also Herbert Gutman, *Slavery and the Numbers Game* (Urbana: University of Illinois Press, 1975).

76. Marx, *Capital*, vol. 1, 303–4; Frederick Law Olmsted, *A Journey in the Seaboard Slave States in the Years 1853–54* (New York: Putnam, 1904), vol. 1, 50–51; Cairnes, *The Slave Power*, 53–56; Eugene D. Genovese, *The Political Economy of Slavery* (New York: Vintage, 1967), 89; Hal Draper, *The Marx-Engels Glossary* (New York: Schocken, 1986), 157. Marx also read and referenced Henry Carey's *The Slave Trade* (1853), which Carey sent to Marx since he had quoted the latter extensively in the book on enclosures in Scotland. In *The Slave Trade*, Carey argued that there was a dialectic between slave production and exhaustion of the soil. Nevertheless, Marx ultimately found the work of Cairnes and Olmsted more fruitful in this respect. See Henry Carey, *The Slave Trade* (Philadelphia: Hart, 1853), 103–06; Marx, *Capital*, vol. 1, 892.

77. Genovese, *The Political Economy of Slavery*, 85-88. Genovese wrote: "The essence of soil exhaustion is not the total exhaustion of the land, nor merely 'the progressive reduction of crop yields from cultivated lands,' for the reduction may be arrested at a level high enough to meet

local needs. An acceptable general theory of the social effects of soil exhaustion must be sufficiently flexible to account for the requirements of different historical epochs. The rise of capitalism requires a theory that includes the inability of the soil to recover sufficient productivity to maintain a competitive position. The main problem lies in the reaction of social institutions, rather than in the natural deterioration of the soil. The Old South, specifically, had to compete in economic development with the exploding capitalist power of the North, but its basic institution, slavery, rendered futile its attempts to fight the advance of soil exhaustion and economic decline."

78.   Beckert, *Empire of Cotton*, 328.
79.   Marx and Engels, *Collected Works*, vol. 37, 613; Marx, *Capital*, vol. 1, 756. On the exportation of the soil, see Marx's comments on Ireland in Marx, *Capital*, vol. 1, 860; Olmsted, *A Journey in the Seaboard Slave States*, vol. 1, 304.
80.   Beckert, *Empire of Cotton*, 67–73; Bagchi, *Perilous Passage*; Paul Baran, *The Political Economy of Growth* (New York: Monthly Review Press, 1957).
81.   Marx and Engels, *Collected Works*, vol. 46, 63–64; also see Prabhat Patnaik, "Marx on Imperialism," *Peoples Democracy* 41/52 (December 24, 2017), http://peoplesdemocracy.in.
82.   F. M. L. Thompson, "The Second Agricultural Revolution," *Economic History Review* 21/1 (1968): 62–77.
83.   See chapter 4 in this book.
84.   Olmsted, *A Journey in the Seaboard Slave States*, vol. 1, 46–47. Genovese explains that some plantations owners in the South purchased Peruvian guano, especially between 1840 and 1850. It was found to be particularly effective in enriching exhausted soils in Maryland and Virginia. But the fertilizer required proper care when applying, plus it was expensive, so many plantation owners did not use this resource. The American Guano Company imported second-rate guano, but even this inferior fertilizer was too expensive, considering the amount of guano that would have been necessary to enrich the lands of large plantations. Thus, owners did not invest in fertilizers, exacerbating the spoliation of the land. Following the Civil War, massive quantities of fertilizers on these lands were required to increase the productivity of the soil. See Genovese, *The Political Economy of Slavery*, 85–95.
85.   Liebig, *Letters on Modern Agriculture*; Liebig, *Familiar Letters*.
86.   Marx, *Capital*, vol. 3, 949; Foster, *Marx's Ecology*; Saito, *Karl Marx's Ecosocialism*.
87.   Quoted in Erland Mårald, "Everything Circulates," *Environment and History* 8 (2002): 74.

88. Marx, *Capital*, vol. 1, 860.
89. George W. Peck, *Melbourne and the Chincha Islands* (New York: Charles Scribner, 1854); Jimmy M. Skaggs, *The Great Guano Rush* (New York: St. Martin's, 1994).
90. W. M. Mathew, *The House of Gibbs and the Peruvian Guano Monopoly* (London: Royal Historical Society, 1981); W. M. Mathew, "Foreign Contractors and the Peruvian Government at the Outset of the Guano Trade," *Hispanic American Historical Review* 52/4 (1972): 598–620; W. M. Mathew, "A Primitive Export Sector," *Journal of Latin American Studies* 9/1 (1977): 35–57; Skaggs, *The Great Guano Rush*.
91. Heraclio Bonilla, "Peru and Bolivia," in *Spanish America after Independence c. 1820–c. 1870,* ed. Leslie Bethell (Cambridge: Cambridge University Press, 1987), 239–82; Shane Hunt, "Growth and Guano in Nineteenth-Century Peru," Discussion Paper no. 34 for the Research Program in Economic Development, Princeton University, unpublished, 1973.
92. Gregory T. Cushman, *Guano and the Opening of the Pacific World* (Cambridge: Cambridge University Press, 2013), 59–60; Mathew, *The House of Gibbs*, 122; C. Alexander G. de Secada, "Arms, Guano, and Shipping," *Business History Review* 59/4 (1985): 597–621; Genovese, *The Political Economy of Slavery*, 92–94.
93. Marx, *Capital*, vol. 1, 348.
94. Marx, *On Colonialism*, 115; Immigration Research Center, "Coolie Trade in the 19th Century," University of Minnesota, http://cla.umn.edu; Gaiutra Bahadur, quoted in Lakshmi Gandhi, "A History of Indentured Labor Gives 'Coolie' Its Sting," National Public Radio, November 25, 2013; Katharine Comar, "The History of Contract Labor in the Hawaiian Islands," *American Economic Association* 4/3 (1903): 1–61; Karl Marx, *The Poverty of Philosophy* (New York: International Publishers, 1963), 112; Marx and Engels, *On Colonialism*, 123; Gaiutra Bahadur, *Coolie Woman* (Chicago: University of Chicago Press, 2014); Dawson, "Hidden in Plain Sight," 150; Arnold J. Meagher, *The Coolie Trade: The Traffic in Chinese Laborers to Latin America 1847–1874* (San Bernardino, CA: Xlibris, 2008); Moon-Ho Jung, *Coolies and Cane* (Baltimore: Johns Hopkins University Press, 2006).
95. Michael J. Gonzales, "Chinese Plantation Workers and Social Conflict in Peru in the Late Nineteenth Century," *Journal of Latin American Studies* 21 (1955): 385–424; Peter Blanchard, "The 'Transitional Man' in Nineteenth–Century Latin America," *Bulletin of Latin American Research* 15/2 (1996): 157–76; Stephen M. Gorman, "The State, Elite, and Export in Nineteenth-Century Peru," *Journal of Interamerican Studies and World Affairs* 21/3 (1979): 395–418; Evelyn Hu-DeHart, "Coolies,

Shopkeepers, Pioneers," *Amerasia Journal* 15/2 (1989): 91–116; Evelyn Hu-DeHart, "Huagong and Huashang," *Amerasia Journal* 28/2 (2002): 64–90; Cushman, *Guano and the Opening of the Pacific World*, 55; Brett Clark, Daniel Auerbach, and Karen Xuan Zhang, "The Du Bois Nexus: Intersectionality, Political Economy, and Environmental Injustice in the Peruvian Guano Trade in the 1800s," *Environmental Sociology* 4/1 (2018): 54–66.

96. Lawrence A. Clayton, "Chinese Indentured Labor in Peru," *History Today* 30/6 (1980): 19–23; "Chincha Islands," *Friends' Intelligencer*, February 11, 1854; A. J. Duffield, *Peru in the Guano Age* (London: Bentley and Son, 1877); Cushman, *Guano and the Opening of the Pacific World*; Brett Clark and John Bellamy Foster, "Ecological Imperialism and the Global Metabolic Rift," *International Journal of Comparative Sociology* 50/3–4 (2009): 311–34. More recently, with the rise of organic agriculture and the partial recovery of guano deposits in Peru, this fertilizer has found a new global market. The labor process, as far as the use of picks and shovels to fill sacks with guano, is similar to what it was in the nineteenth century. See Simon Romero, "Peru Guards Its Guano as Demand Soars Again," *New York Times*, May 30, 2008.

97. Alanson Nash, "Peruvian Guano," *Plough, the Loom and the Anvil*, August 1857.

98. Peck, *Melbourne and the Chincha Islands*, 207.

99. "Chinese Coolie Trade," *Christian Review*, April 1862; see also Basil Lubbock, *Coolie Ships and Oil Sailers* (Glasgow: Brown, Son and Ferguson, 1955), 35; Charles Wingfield, *The China Coolie Traffic from Macao to Peru and Cuba* (London: British and Foreign Anti-Slavery Society, 1873).

100. "Chincha Islands," *Nautical Magazine and Naval Chronicle*, April 1856; see also "Guano Trade," *New York Observer and Chronicle*, July 24, 1856; "Chinese Coolie Trade," 1862; "Chincha Islands," *Friends' Intelligencer*, February 11, 1854.

101. Nancy Fraser, "Behind Marx's Hidden Abode," *New Left Review* 86 (March–April 2014): 55–72; Robert Cushman Murphy, *Bird Islands of Peru* (New York: G. P. Putnam's Sons, 1925).

102. Joachim Radkau, *Nature and Power* (Cambridge: Cambridge University Press, 2008), 191.

103. Marx, *Capital*, vol. 3, 369.

104. Ibid., 910–11.

105. William Blake, *Complete Poetry and Prose* (New York: Anchor, 1988), 45–51; Kevin Hutchings, *Romantic Ecologies and Colonial Cultures in the British-Atlantic World, 1770–1850* (Montreal: McGill-Queens University Press, 2009), 70–91; John Gabriel Stedman, *Narrative*

of a Five Years Expedition Against the Revolted Negroes of Surinam (Baltimore: Johns Hopkins University Press, 1988).

106. Nancy Fraser, "Expropriation and Exploitation in Racialized Capitalism: A Reply to Michael Dawson," *Critical Historical Studies* 3/1 (2016): 176–78.

107. Riccardo Bellofiore, "Between Schumpeter and Keynes: The Heterodoxy of Paul Marlor Sweezy and the Orthodoxy of Paul Mattick," *Continental Thought and Theory* 1/4 (2017), 107–8.

108. Harvey, *The Madness of Economic Reason*, 89–93.

2. The Rift of Éire

1. Philip Campanile and Michael Watts, "Nature and Ecology," *The Bloomsbury Companion to Marx*, ed. Jeff Diamanti, Andrew Pendakis, and Imre Szeman (London: Bloomsbury, 2019), 358; Alan Rudy, "Marx's Ecology and Rift Analysis," *Capitalism Nature Socialism* 12 (June 2001): 61.

2. Stephen Howe, "Historiography," in *Ireland and Empire*, ed. Kevin Kenny (Oxford: Oxford University Press, 2004), 246.

3. Key works include Eamonn Slater and Terrence McDonough, "Marx on Nineteenth-Century Colonial Ireland," *Irish Historical Studies* 36/142 (November 2008): 153–72; Eamonn Slater and Eoin Flaherty, "Marx on Primitive Communism," *Irish Journal of Anthropology* 12/2 (2009): 5–34; Eoin Flaherty, "Geographies of Communality, Colonialism, and Capitalism," *Historical Geography* 41 (2013): 39–79; Eamonn Slater, "Marx on Colonial Ireland," *History of Political Thought*, 39/4 (Winter 2018): 719–48; Slater, "Marx on the Colonization of Irish Soil," MUSSI Working Paper Series 3 (January 2018); Slater, "Engels on Ireland's Dialectics of Nature," *Capitalism Nature Socialism* 29/4 (2018): 31–50.

4. Anthony Coughlan, "Ireland's Marxist Historians," in *Interpreting Irish History*, ed. Ciaran Brady (Dublin: Irish Academic Press, 1994), 291.

5. Slater and McDonough, "Marx on Nineteenth-Century Colonial Ireland," 154; Hal Draper, ed., *The Marx-Engels Chronicle* (New York: Schocken Books, 1985), 138.

6. Karl Marx and Frederick Engels, *Ireland and Irish Question* (New York: International Publishers, 1972), 120–48; Slater and McDonough, "Marx on Nineteenth-Century Colonial Ireland," 158–59.

7. Slater, "Marx on the Colonization of Irish Soil," 40.

8. Marx and Engels, *Ireland and the Irish Question*, 131–35, 210. Marx in his outline for his December 1867 talk does not include a title/subtitle to designate the 1801–46 period, but it is clear from his description that the "Period of Rack-Renting," which we employ here, is appropriate. In relation to the new conditions in the 1846–66

period, Marx refers to "The Clearing of the Estate of Ireland" which conforms to what he and Engels, along with their contemporaries, referred to as "extermination," encompassing both of its classical meanings as exclusion and annihilation, in the case of the cottiers. Indeed, Engels refers to 1846–70 as "The Period of Extermination," which we have followed here, based on the entry for "extermination," *Compact Edition of the Oxford English Dictionary* (Oxford: Oxford University Press, 1971), 938. Marx utilized the term "extermination" in this sense in 1858 in an article for the *New York Tribune*. See Marx and Engels, *Ireland and the Irish Question*, 90.

9.   Marx and Engels, *Ireland and the Irish Question*, 127, 140; Dean M. Braa, "The Great Potato Famine and the Transformation of the Irish Peasant Society," *Science and Society* 61/2 (1997): 193–215.

10. Isaac Butt, *The Irish People and the Irish Land* (Dublin: John Falconer, 1867), 94–95.

11. Marx and Engels, *Ireland and the Irish Question*, 61, 132.

12. Helen Litton, *The Irish Famine* (Dublin: Wolfhound Press, 1994), 9.

13. Slater, "Marx on the Colonization of Irish Soil," 13–15.

14. Litton, *Irish Famine*, 9–10; Ross, *Ireland*, 206–7; Slater and McDonough, "Marx on Nineteenth Century Colonial Ireland," 36.

15. Marx and Engels, *Ireland and the Irish Question*, 77.

16. Ibid., 132–3.

17. Ibid., 59–60, 123–24.

18. Ibid., 109.

19. Slater, "Marx on the Colonization of Irish Soil," 20.

20. Marx and Engels, *Ireland and the Irish Question*, 133.

21. Cormac Ó Gráda, "Irish Agricultural History," *Agricultural History Review* 38/2 (1990): 165–73.

22. Léonce de Lavergne, *The Rural Economy of England, Scotland, and Ireland* (London: Blackwell, 1855), 343.

23. Slater, "Marx on the Colonization of Irish Soil," 21.

24. Ibid., 21–22.

25. Ibid., 21–23; Jonathan Bell and Mervyn Watson, *Irish Farming, Implements and Techniques, 1750–1900* (Edinburgh: John Donald, 1986), 57–58.

26. Karl Marx, *Capital*, vol. 3 (London: Penguin, 1981), 790.

27. Slater, "Marx on the Colonization of Irish Soil," 24.

28. T. Walsh, P. F. Ryan, and J. Kilroy, "A Half Century of Fertiliser and Lime Use in Ireland," *Dublin: Journal of the Statistical and Social Inquiry Society of Ireland* (1956/1957): 104–36; Slater, "Marx on the

Colonization of Irish Soil," 22–24; George Hill, *Facts from Gweedore* (Belfast: Institute of Irish Studies, 1971).

29.   Slater, "Marx on the Colonization of Irish Soil," 23–25.

30.   Lavergne, *The Rural Economy of England, Scotland, and Ireland*, 353–54.

31.   James S. Donnelly, *The Great Irish Potato Famine* (Phoenix Mill, Gloucestershire: Sutton Publishing, 2001), 1

32.   Marx and Engels, *Ireland and the Irish Question*, 133.

33.   Lavergne, *The Rural Economy of England, Scotland, and Ireland*, 355.

34.   Marx, *Capital*, vol. 3, 763.

35.   Donnelly, *The Great Irish Potato Famine*; Christine Kinealy, *The Great Calamity* (Dublin: Gill and McMillan, 1994); Davis Ross, *Ireland: History of a Nation* (New Lanark, Scotland: Geddes and Grosset, 2006), 223–28; Cecil Woodham-Smith, *The Great Hunger* (London: Hamish Hamilton, 1962); Litton, *The Irish Famine*.

36.   Jean Beagle Ristaino and Donald H. Pfister, "'What a Painfully Interesting Subject': Charles Darwin's Studies of Potato Late Blight," *Bioscience* 66/12 (December 2016): 1035–45; Sarah Maria Schmidt, "Anton de Bary—The Father of Plant Pathology," *Microbes Eat My Food*, January 27, 2015, https://microbeseatmyfood.wordpress.com/2015/01/27/anton-de-bary-the-father-of-plant-pathology/.

37.   Karl Marx and Frederick Engels, *Collected Works*, vol. 21 (New York: International Publishers, 1975), 327.

38.   Marx and Engels, *Ireland and the Irish Question*, 147.

39.   Marx and Engels, *Ireland and the Irish Question*, 141. Lavergne also referred to the "short-sighted and hungry exhaustion of the productive powers of the soil" in Ireland. See Lavergne, *The Rural Economy of England, Scotland, and Ireland*, 356. Based on contemporary ecological knowledge, we can amplify Marx's analysis by underscoring that by growing one variety the narrow genetic base of the crop meant that there was no resistance to the disease anywhere in the country. Inadequate rotations also contributed to disease prevalence. The disease infects plants by airborne spores and raindrop splash causing soil with spores to get on the leaves. This is still a difficult problem for organic growers of both potatoes and tomatoes, but using blight-resistant varieties, good rotations, and mulching the soil surface with straw helps considerably. (We would like to thank Fred Magdoff for emphasizing these points.)

40.   Marx and Engels, *Ireland and the Irish Question*, 134.

41.   Ibid., 147.

42.   Ibid., 76, 134.

43.   Ibid., 138.

44. Ibid., 135–36. The value of output per "standard man days" in crop production dropped by around 17 percent between 1851 and 1861. Michael Turner, *After the Famine* (Cambridge: Cambridge University Press, 1996), 191.

45. Marx and Engels, *Ireland and the Irish Question*, 122.

46. Justus von Liebig, *Letters on Modern Agriculture* (London: Walton and Maberly, 1859), 175–70, 220, 230; Karl Marx, *Dispatches for the New York Tribune* (London: Penguin, 2007); Marx and Engels, *Ireland and the Irish Question*, 126, 133–34, 147–48.

47. Marx and Engels, *Ireland and the Irish Question*, 122, 136.

48. Ibid., 136; Karl Marx, *Capital*, vol. 1 (London: Penguin, 1976), 860.

49. Marx and Engels, *Ireland and the Irish Question*, 123, 126.

50. Ibid., 138.

51. Marx, *Capital*, vol. 1, 870.

52. Marx and Engels, *Ireland and the Irish Question*, 188, 191.

53. Ibid., 90.

54. Ibid., 190, 210: Butt, *The Irish People and the Irish Land*, 172; Lavergne, *The Rural Economy of England, Scotland, and Ireland*, 367; "Extermination," *Oxford English Dictionary*, 938.

55. Marx and Engels, *Ireland and the Irish Question*, 123, 126, 137–38, 142.

56. Marx viewed Fenianism as reflecting a "socialist tendency (in a negative sense directed against the appropriation of the soil)." See Marx and Engels, *Ireland and the Irish Question*, 147.

57. We owe our understanding of these longer-term developments to correspondence with Eamonn Slater.

58. Marx, *Capital*, vol. 1, 860.

59. Marx and Engels, *Ireland and the Irish Question*, 141.

60. Jonathan Swift, "Maxims Controlled in Ireland," in *Swift's Irish Writings* (London: Palgrave Macmillan, 2010), 118; Thomas Prior, "Extracts from Thomas Prior, *A List of the Absentees of Ireland*," in *The Great Irish Famine: A History in Documents*, ed. Karen Sonnelitter (Peterborough, ONT: Broadview Press, 2018), 32: Marx and Engels, *Collected Works*, vol. 21, 222.

61. John Leslie Foster, *An Essay on the Principle of Commercial Exchanges* (London: J. Hatchard Bookseller to Her Majesty, 1804), 22–44. There were similarities between the "drain" of surplus from colonial Ireland as depicted here and the British drain of surplus from India. See Utsa Patnaik, "Revisiting the 'Drain,' or Transfers from India to Britain in the Context of Global Diffusion of Capitalism," in *Agrarian and Other Histories*, ed. Shubhra Chakrabarti and Utsa Patnaik (New Delhi; Tulika Books, 2017), 277–317.

62. Foster, *An Essay on the Principle of Commercial Exchanges*, 27.

63. Marx and Engels, *Ireland and the Irish Question*, 133.
64. Ibid., 142.

3. Women, Nature, and Capitalism in the Industrial Revolution
This chapter is adapted and revised for this book from John Bellamy Foster and Brett Clark, "Women, Nature, and Capital in the Industrial Revolution," *Monthly Review* 69/8 (January 2018): 1–24.

1. See especially Silvia Federici, *Revolution at Point Zero* (Oakland, CA: PM, 2012); Federici, "Notes on Gender in Marx's Capital," *Continental Thought and Theory* 1/4 (2017): 19–37; Susan Ferguson and David McNally, "Capital, Labour-Power and Gender or Relations: Introduction to the Historical Materialism Edition," in Lise Vogel, *Marxism and the Oppression of Women* (Chicago: Haymarket, 2013), xvii–xl; Shahrzad Mojab, ed., *Marxism and Feminism* (London: Zed, 2015), especially the essays by Frigga Haug and Judith Whitehead; Tithi Bhattacharya, ed., *Social Reproduction Theory* (London: Pluto, 2017), including essays by Ferguson, Nancy Fraser, McNally, and Vogel; Heather A. Brown, *Marx on Gender and the Family* (Chicago: Haymarket, 2012); Paresh Chattopadhyay, "Women's Labor Under Capitalism and Marx," *Bulletin of Concerned Asian Scholars* 31/4 (1999): 67–75; Leopoldina Fortunati, *The Arcane of Reproduction* (Brooklyn, NY: Autonomedia, 1995); Maria Mies, *Patriarchy and Accumulation on a World Scale* (London: Zed, 2014); Johanna Brenner, *Women and the Politics of Class* (New York: Monthly Review Press, 2000); Ariel Salleh, "Ecological Debt, Embodied Debt" and "From Eco-Sufficiency to Global Justice," in *Eco-Sufficiency and Global Justice*, ed. Salleh (London: Pluto, 2009). See also Eli Zaretsky, *Capitalism, the Family, and Personal Life* (New York: Harper and Row, 1976).
2. The very term "reproductive labor" raises complex questions within Marxian theory. Marx, following classical political economy, often distinguished work in general and social labor in general, both of which were seen as directed at the production of use values, from wage labor (and more specifically value-generating productive labor) under capitalist commodity production, which has the promotion of exchange value and capital accumulation as its alienated object. (See Karl Marx, *Capital*, vol. 1 (London: Penguin, 1976), 998–99. Here Engels added a useful note to *Capital*, vol. 1 (left out of the Penguin edition), in which he stated: "The English language has two different expressions for these two different aspects of labour: in the Simple Labour process, the process of producing Use Values, it is *Work*; in the process of creation of Value, it is *Labour*, taking the term in its strictly

economic sense." See Karl Marx and Frederick Engels, *Collected Works* (New York: International Publishers, 1975), vol. 35, 196. Work in its general meaning, for Marx, transcends the capitalist system entirely, as does the concept of social labor—that is, labor in general, distinct from its historical specific form in capitalist production—both of which are related to the production of use values and the primary mediation of human needs. When Marx discusses "family labor" or reproductive labor in the household, he has in mind a certain kind of social labor, referred to here as "reproductive labor," which, insofar as it is family labor, is unpaid and external to the valorization process of capital (see Marx, *Capital*, vol. 1, 517–18). Most of *Capital* is devoted not to the analysis of social labor in its many aspects and historical forms, but rather to the analysis of labor exploitation in the context of capitalist commodity production. Such value-generating wage labor under capitalism, then, needs to always be understood as a specific historical form distinct from work (in general) and social labor (including family labor), which transcend the narrow confines of capitalist valorization and are external to it. Nevertheless, with the further development of the capitalist system, as we shall see, even the social labor involved in the reproduction of the family increasingly becomes appended to the needs of commodity production as a whole.

3.   The concept of the "dissolution of the family" was fundamental to Marx and Engels's work from the beginning. See Marx and Engels, *Collected Works*, vol. 5, 180. The idea of "the dissolution of the family" in ethical terms, related to education, was first introduced by Georg Wilhelm Friedrich Hegel. But this concept was to be given an entirely different meaning, as the following analysis will show, in the development of Marx and Engels's materialist analysis. See G. W. F. Hegel, *The Philosophy of Right* (Oxford: Oxford University Press, 1952), 117–19.

4.   Engels, *The Condition of the Working Class in England* (Oxford: Oxford University Press, 2009).

5.   The concept of expropriation, which Marx used as his central category in Part 8 of *Capital*, vol. 1, on "So-Called Primitive Accumulation," clearly had a wider significance in relation to enclosures, imperial conquest, enslavement, the expropriation of reproductive labor, the destruction of super-exploited labor, and the rifts created by the plundering of the earth itself—all forms of robbery that were external to capital's pure value logic based on equal exchange. For a number of years, we have been developing an approach employing the concept of expropriation to refer to Marx's critique in this way. See, for example, John Bellamy Foster, Brett Clark, and Richard York, *The Ecological Rift* (New York: Monthly Review Press, 2010), 62, 435; John Bellamy Foster,

Foreword, in István Mészáros, *The Necessity of Social Control* (New York: Monthly Review Press, 2015), 10–14. Fraser has independently developed the same analytical approach—proceeding, however, from social reproduction theory rather than metabolic rift analysis. See esp. Nancy Fraser, "Expropriation and Exploitation in Racialized Capitalism," *Critical Historical Studies* 3/1 (2016): 163–78.

6. Marx and Engels, *Collected Works*, vol. 37, 732–33.

7. Federici, "Notes on Gender in Marx's Capital," 21. It should be noted that in this article we are primarily concerned with what Federici called "the woman's question" in the time that Marx was writing, in the early to mid–nineteenth century, and the implications of this for our own time, which necessarily requires a brief look at subsequent developments, primarily in the advanced capitalist countries, from the late nineteenth century to the present day. We do not address here the question of reproductive labor in earlier periods of capitalism, such as the era of primary accumulation (the mercantilist stage of capitalism). The most important work on gender and the family in the period of primary accumulation is undoubtedly Silvia Federici, *Caliban and the Witch* (Brooklyn, NY: Autonomedia, 2004).

8. Maxine Berg, "What Difference Did Women's Work Make to the Industrial Revolution?," *History Workshop* 35 (1993): 34; Melanie Reynolds, *Infant Mortality and Working-Class Childcare* (London: Macmillan, 2016), 77.

9. Berg, "What Difference Did Women's Work Make," 29; Maxine Berg, "Women's Work and the Industrial Revolution," *ReFresh* 12 (1991): 3.

10. Joyce Burnette, "Women Workers in the British Industrial Revolution," Economic History Association, http://eh.net, November 12, 2017; Sally Alexander, *Becoming a Woman* (New York: New York University Press, 1995), 7. Some earlier studies, such as the work of Louise Tilly and Joan Scott, insisted that married women were "only a small proportion of all female factory operatives" and that, "at its height, in the 1870s" only "about one-third of the British textile industry's women employees were married or widowed." However, the 1870s were not the height of female employment in the Industrial Revolution but considerably beyond it, and the inclusion of large numbers of children among the total of "female workers" distorts the overall results. More recent research, going beyond the limits of the census data, has emphasized that large numbers of married and widowed women were employed at all levels of the industrial labor force—working as factory operatives and other operatives. In some localities, more than two-thirds of married and widowed women were in the labor force. See Louise A. Tilly and Joan W. Scott, *Women, Work and Family* (New York: Holt, Rinehart

and Winston, 1978), 124; Berg, "What Difference Did Women's Work Make?," 37–39.

11. Burnette, "Women Workers in the British Industrial Revolution."

12. In their otherwise insightful introduction to Lise Vogel's *Marxism and the Oppression of Women*, Ferguson and McNally mistakenly state that "female participation rates in paid employment stabilized at around 25 percent across the nineteenth century." Their sole source for this is an article written by Jane Humphries in the *Cambridge Journal of Economics* in 1977, where Humphries provides the same number and cites as her source Geoffrey Best's 1972 book, *Mid-Victorian Britain*, where the same number is provided. Best indicates that his source is an article by Charles Booth in the *Journal of the Royal Statistical Society* in 1886. Booth's figures, drawn from census data, are now seen in the historical research of the last few decades to be vastly understated in precisely this respect, reflecting an undercounting of women employed during the Industrial Revolution. This is significant to the present argument since Humphries claimed that Marx was wrong about the threatened dissolution of the working-class family associated with the high labor participation of all family members—arguing instead that around three-quarters of all women in Britain throughout the nineteenth century (here including all classes and rural as well as urban regions) were outside the paid labor force—a conclusion that today's historians have shown to be incorrect, particularly in its implications with regard to working-class women. See Ferguson and McNally, "Capital, Labour–Power, and Gender-Relations," in Vogel, *Marxism and the Oppression of Women*, xxx–xxxi; Jane Humphries, "Class Struggle and the Persistence of the Working-Class Family," *Cambridge Journal of Economics* 1/3 (1977): 251; Geoffrey Best, *Mid-Victorian Britain* (New York: Schocken, 1972), 100; Alexander, *Becoming a Woman*, 7–9; Edward Higgs and Amanda Wilkinson, "Women Occupations and Work in Victorian Census Revisited," *History Workshop* 81 (2016): 17–38.

13. Berg, "Women's Work and the Industrial Revolution," 3.

14. Marx, *Capital*, vol. 1, 517.

15. John Stuart Mill, "Employment of Children in Manufactories," *Examiner*, January 29, 1832, 67–68; Karl Marx, *On the First International* (New York: McGraw-Hill, 1973), 93. Under the influence of his wife, Harriet Taylor, Mill later reversed his view that women should be excluded from employment in manufacturing industry and emphasized their right to competition in the labor market. See John Stuart Mill, *Three Essays* (Oxford: Oxford University, 1975), 458.

16. In our explanation, we have elaborated slightly on Marx's method of factoring various groups out of the numbers in order to focus on the

proletarian sectors, based on examination of the 1861 census to which he was referring. In using the census data here, Marx was primarily concerned with two things: the gender construction of the proletarian workforce and the high numbers of domestic servants. The key to his method seems to have been to focus on three of the six "classes" of occupations/conditions in the census: the Agricultural, Industrial, and Domestic classes, excluding altogether the Professional, Commercial, and Indefinite and Non-productive classes, as stipulated in the census. Mining was a subcategory of Industrial. Mining, like agriculture, was a largely rural activity, separated from the urban proletariat. Marx made the point, based on the 1861 census, that the number of domestic servants (most of whom were female) exceeded that of textile workers (largely female) and employees in mining put together (*Census of England and Wales for the Year 1861, Population Tables*, vol. 2 [London: Her Majesty's Stationery Office, 1863], Table 18, xl; Marx, *Capital*, vol. 1, 575). See also B. R. Mitchell, *Abstract of British Historical Statistics* (Cambridge: Cambridge University Press, 1962), 60–61.

17. Not all the figures that Marx provides precisely match the data in the published 1861 census, though the results are extremely close, and the differences are so slight as to have no real bearing on his conclusions. For example, Marx's figures for male domestic servants (by which he clearly meant adult males) come out to 11.4 percent of domestic servants, while the census, as published in 1863, reports 12.5 percent. The one area where there seems a notable difference is in the designation of ages differentiating children from adults. In Marx's data, the cut-off in the textile industry is age thirteen, while in the 1861 census as published in 1863 the data is divided into those above and below twenty years of age. All of this suggests that Marx may have been using a slightly different, perhaps preliminary, or summary version of the census—or that the census was revised (*Census of England and Wales*, Table 18, xl).

18. Marx, *Capital*, vol. 1, 574–75; "Occupations: Census Returns for 1851, 1861 and 1871," Victorian Web, http://victorianweb.org; Brown, *Marx on Gender and the Family*, 77. The Victorian censuses did not record employment and unemployment as a situation, which inevitably distorted the data.

19. Marx, *Capital*, vol. 1, 575; Deborah Valenze, *The First Industrial Woman* (Oxford: Oxford University Press, 1995), 171–80.

20. Marx, *Capital*, vol. 1, 796–97.

21. Ibid., 364–66, 595–99.

22. Karl Marx, *Wage-Labour and Capital/Value, Price and Profit* (New York: International Publishers, 1935), 46–47.

23. Margaret Hewitt, *Wives and Mothers in Victorian Industry* (London: Rockliff, 1958), 22.

24. Rev. J. Elder Cumming, "On the Neglect of Infants in Large Towns," *Transactions of the National Association for the Promotion of Social Science* (1874): 723–24; Hewitt, *Wives and Mothers in Victorian Industry*, 29, 99.

25. Hewitt, *Wives and Mothers in Victorian Industry*, 106–10.

26. Marx, *Capital*, vol. 1, 520–22.

27. Hewitt, *Wives and Mothers in Victorian Industry*, 102, 136–37, 141; Reynolds, *Infant Mortality and Working-Class Child Care, 1850–1899*, 2–3, 74, 146.

28. Anthony S. Wohl, *Endangered Lives* (Cambridge, MA: Harvard University Press, 1983): 50–52. See also chapter 4 in this book.

29. Ivy Pinchbeck, *Women Workers and the Industrial Revolution, 1750–1850* (London: Cass, 1969), 310; Bridget Hill, *Women, Work, and Sexual Politics in Eighteenth-Century England* (London: Blackwell, 1989), 105–15. On epidemics and the social epidemiology of the Industrial Revolution, see Howard Waitzkin, *The Second Sickness* (New York: Free Press, 1983).

30. Caroline Davidson, *A Woman's Work Is Never Done* (London: Chatto and Windus, 1982), 184.

31. Marx, *Capital*, vol. 1, 620–21; Ferguson and McNally, xxix–xxx; Brown, *Marx on Gender and the Family*, 95–96; Chattopadhyay, "Women's Labor Under Capitalism and Marx," 69, 74; Fortunati, *The Arcane of Reproduction*, 91, 170–71. On Owenism and the struggles of working-class women, see Barbara Taylor, *Eve and the New Jerusalem* (New York: Pantheon, 1983). The destruction of the working-class family was already a central thesis adopted in 1845 in Frederick Engels, *The Condition of the Working Class in England*, 140.

32. Marx and Engels, *Collected Works*, vol. 24, 340. Translation quoted in Vogel, *Marxism and the Oppression of Women*, 75.

33. Federici, *Revolution at Point Zero*, 94; Federici, "Notes on Gender in Marx's *Capital*," 27. See also Zaretsky, *Capitalism, the Family, and Personal Life*.

34. Marx, *Capital*, vol. 1, 517–18.

35. Ibid., 621.

36. Sara Horrell and Jane Humphries, "Women's Labour Force Participation and the Transition to the Male Breadwinner Family," *Economic History Review* 48/1 (1995): 93; Berg, "Women's Work and the Industrial Revolution," 4.

37. Federici, *Caliban and the Witch*, 98–99.

38. Marx, *Capital*, vol. 1, 599; Brown, *Marx on Gender and the Family*, 90.

39. Frederick Engels, *The Origin of the Family, Private Property, and the State* (Moscow: Progress Publishers, 1948), 74. Emphasis added.

40. Paul M. Sweezy, *The Theory of Capitalist Development* (New York: Monthly Review, 1970), 11–20.

41. Marx, *On the First International*, 10; Michael A. Lebowitz, *Beyond Capital* (New York: St. Martin's, 1992).

42. For example, Marx writes: "Since certain family functions, such as nursing and suckling children, cannot be entirely suppressed, the mothers who have been confiscated by capital must try substitutes of some sort. Domestic work, such as sewing and mending, must be replaced by the purchase of ready-made articles. Hence the diminished expenditure of labour in the house is accompanied by an increase expenditure of money outside." See Marx, *Capital*, vol. 1, 518. See also Federici, "Notes on Gender in Marx's *Capital*," 26–27; Ferguson and McNally, "Capital, Labour-Power and Gender-Relations," xxvii–xxviii. Such statements in Marx's analysis were almost invariably included in footnotes or in talks to workers, like *Wage Labour and Capital*. This has led to the criticism that he gave them little importance. However, in Marx's dialectical critique such points logically were meant to be addressed later, along with the concrete determination of wages themselves—which is never fully addressed in his analysis. His practice therefore was always to place such points in endnotes, as a way of raising more concrete questions to be dealt with later. See Kenneth Lapides, *Marx's Wage Theory in Historical Perspective* (Tucson, AZ: Wheatmark, 2008), 210–35.

43. Karl Marx, *Grundrisse* (London: Penguin, 1973), 334–35, 409–10.

44. Karl Marx, *Early Writings* (London: Penguin, 1975), 261, 409–10.

45. Marx, *Capital*, vol. 1, 599.

46. Ibid., 871. In referring to the concept of primary or prior accumulation, Marx was explicit that this category was taken chiefly from Adam Smith. Marx indicated reservations about the concept, which from his standpoint was neither simply "previous" nor "accumulation." He therefore referred to it as "*so-called* primitive [primary] accumulation" (italics added). His solution was to focus on expropriation as the key to boundary conditions of capitalism—not only in relation to its origins but implicitly in all of its stages, including "modern colonialism." See Marx, *Capital*, vol. 1, 775, 873, 939. On the importance of conceiving Marx's analysis as "primary accumulation" rather than "primitive accumulation," and its applicability to all stages of capitalism, see Harry Magdoff, "Primitive Accumulation and Imperialism," *Monthly Review* 65/5 (October 2013): 13–25. On the origins of the concept in classical political economy, see Michael Perelman, *The Invention of Capitalism*

(Durham: Duke University Press, 2000). For the relation of primary accumulation to the restructuring of gender and traditional patriarchal family relations with the rise of capitalism, see Federici, *Caliban and the Witch*. On the connection between expropriation and the "background 'conditions of possibility' for exploitation," see Nancy Fraser, "Behind Marx's Hidden Abode: For an Expanded Conception of Capitalism," *New Left Review* 86 (2014): 55–72.

47.   The concept of "conditions of production" and its role in Marx's analysis, addressing such aspects as the external environment and the conditions of reproduction in the household, was brought to the fore by James O'Connor in his pioneering work in ecological Marxism. See James O'Connor, *Natural Causes* (New York: Guilford Press, 1998), 144–57.

48.   Jason W. Moore uses the term "appropriation" to refer to the human extraction of the "unpaid work" of nature —which he calls "the web of life." In Marx's analysis, however, the "free appropriation" of nature and natural processes—as well as the social appropriation of reproductive labor—could not be materially transcended, any more than it would be possible to materially transcend the condition of human beings as objective beings, having their object—their means of existence— outside themselves. It is only the *alienated mediation* of the human relation to the web of life, that is, *expropriation* of nature/natural processes, subsistence labor, reproductive labor—all that lies outside the value circuit of capital—that is subject to transcendence through revolutionary struggle in history. The only answer to the regime of capital, for Marx, is to expropriate the expropriators, as the first step in the creation of a new order of what István Mészáros calls "social metabolic reproduction." See Jason W. Moore, *Capitalism in the Web of Life* (London: Verso, 2015), 17, 29, 54, 70, 101–02, 146–47; Marx, *Early Writings*, 389–90; Marx, *Grundrisse*, 87–88; Marx, *Capital*, vol. 1, 929; István Mészáros, *Beyond Capital* (New York: Monthly Review Press, 1995), 39–71.

49.   On the theory of metabolic rift and the dialectic of barriers and boundaries (which Marx took from Hegel), see Kohei Saito, *Karl Marx's Ecosocialism* (New York: Monthly Review, 2017); Foster, Clark, and York, *The Ecological Rift*, 73, 284–86. On Marx's later work on the ethnology of the family, see Brown, *Marx on Gender and the Family*, 176–209.

50.   Mészáros, *Beyond Capital*, 142–253.

51.   Rosa Luxemburg, *The Accumulation of Capital* (New York: Monthly Review Press, 1951).

52.   Marx and Engels, *Collected Works*, vol. 37, 732–33. See also Paul

Burkett, "Nature's 'Free Gifts' and the Ecological Significance of Value," *Capital and Class* 23 (1999): 89–110. The mistaken view that Marx erred in not attributing commodity value to women's unpaid labor in the household in capitalist conditions still frequently appears in the literature. What is not understood in such criticisms, as Paresh Chattopadhyay notes, is that "in his formulation of wage determination Marx was not offering any prescriptive formula, far less his own desideratum in this regard. He was only rigorously showing how wage determination arose from the reality of capitalism itself." Chattopadhyay, "Women's Labor Under Capitalism and Marx," 73. For recent examples of the continuing confusion in this regard see Rohini Hensman, "Revisiting the Domestic Labour Debate: An Indian Perspective," *Historical Materialism* 19/3 (2011): 7–8; Peter Custers, *Capital Accumulation and Women's Labour in Asian Economies* (New York: Monthly Review Press, 2012), 46–47, 88; Fortunati, *The Arcane of Reproduction*, 8–11, 69–98, 157.

53. Marilyn Waring, *Counting for Nothing* (Toronto: University of Toronto Press, 2009), 204.

54. Karl Marx and Frederick Engels, *Selected Correspondence* (Moscow: Progress Publishers, 1975), 180; Marx, *Capital*, vol. 1, 132, 134.

55. In *The German Ideology*, Marx and Engels refer to "the latent slavery in the family." See Marx and Engels, *Collected Works*, vol. 5, 46. In referring to slavery in this context, Marx and Engels clearly had in mind not chattel slavery, but ancient slavery, and the common designation of women in the patriarchal (particularly aristocratic) family as occupying the status of slaves, in the sense of the disposal over their labor power by others. For a detailed analysis of this and its implications with respect to Marx's analysis, see G. M. E. de Ste. Croix, *The Class Struggle in the Ancient Greek World* (London: Duckworth, 1981), 98–111.

56. The notion of capitalism as a robbery system in relation to the soil was introduced by Justus von Liebig and taken over by Marx. See John Bellamy Foster, *Marx's Ecology* (New York: Monthly Review Press, 2000), 147–63.

57. Eleanor Marx-Aveling and Edward Aveling, *Thoughts on Women and Society* (New York: International Publishers, 1987), 17.

58. Marx, *Capital*, vol. 1, 517–18; Chattopadhyay, "Women's Labor Under Capitalism and Marx," 69–70.

59. Chattopadhyay, "Women's Labor Under Capitalism," 68, 71–72. Marx quotation from Chattopadhyay's translation.

60. Paresh Chattopadhyay, *Marx's Associated Mode of Production* (London: Palgrave Macmillan, 2016), 87; "Women's Labor Under Capitalism," 72.

61. Fraser, "Behind Marx's Hidden Abode," 62.

NOTES TO PAGES 94–98

62. Frederick Engels, *The Housing Question* (Moscow: Progress Publishers, 1979), 14–15; Marx and Engels, *Selected Correspondence*, 358–59. In Marx and Engels's analysis this increase in surplus value through the cheapening of variable capital by means of substitution of subsistence/household labor was known as "profits by deduction." See John Bellamy Foster, "A Missing Chapter of *Monopoly Capital*," *Monthly Review* 64/3 (July–August 2012): 13–15.

63. Nancy Fraser, "Crisis of Care? On the Social-Reproductive Contradictions of Contemporary Capitalism," in Bhattacharya, *Social Reproduction Theory*, 23.

64. Fraser, "Behind Marx's Hidden Abode," 60, 63, 70.

65. Marx, *Early Writings*, 261.

66. Mészáros, *Beyond Capital*, 137.

67. Fraser, "Behind Marx's Hidden Abode," 60.

68. Fraser, "Crisis of Care?," 26.

69. Ibid., 21, 24–25; Martha Gimenez, "Capitalism and the Oppression of Women: Marx Revisited," *Science and Society* 69/1 (2005): 11–32.

70. Fraser, "Crisis of Care?," 26.

71. Ibid., 24, 26–29.

72. Mészáros, *Beyond Capital*, 203.

73. Fraser, "Crisis of Care?," 27–29.

74. The notion of the shift from the formal to the real subsumption of reproductive labor follows Marx's famous distinction with respect to productive (commodity) labor in "The Results of the Immediate Process of Production." See Marx, *Capital*, vol. 1., 101–9, 138. See also Salar Mohandesi and Emma Teitelman, "Without Reserves," in Bhattacharya, *Social Reproduction Theory*, 60–62.

75. Mies, *Patriarchy and Accumulation on a World Scale*, 74–81; Fraser, "Crisis of Care?," 28; Harry Magdoff, *The Age of Imperialism* (New York: Monthly Review Press, 1969); Magdoff, *Imperialism* (New York: Monthly Review Press, 1978); John Bellamy Foster and Hannah Holleman, "The Theory of Unequal Ecological Exchange: A Marx-Odum Dialectic," *Journal of Peasant Studies* 41/2 (2014): 199–233.

76. Fraser, "Crisis of Care?," 29–31.

77. Paul A. Baran and Paul M. Sweezy, *Monopoly Capital* (New York: Monthly Review Press, 1966).

78. Ibid.; Michael Dawson, *The Consumer Trap* (Urbana: University of Illinois Press, 2003).

79. Harry Braverman, *Labor and Monopoly Capital* (New York: Monthly Review Press, 1998), 188–91; Susan Strasser, *Never Done* (New York: Pantheon, 1982), 242–312.

80. Batya Weinbaum and Amy Bridges, "The Other Side of the Paycheck: Monopoly Capital and the Structure of Consumption," *Monthly Review* 28/3 (1976): 96.

81. Fraser, "Behind Marx's Hidden Abode," 61.

82. Mohandesi and Teitelman, "Without Reserves," 60–62.

83. Fraser, "Crisis of Care?," 30–31.

84. Immanuel Wallerstein, *Historical Capitalism* (London: Verso, 1983), 39; see also Wilma Dunaway, ed., *Gendered Commodity* (Stanford, CA: Stanford University Press, 2013); Joan Smith and Immanuel Wallerstein, eds., *Creating and Transforming Households* (Cambridge: Cambridge University Press, 1992); Mies, *Patriarchy and Accumulation on a World Scale*, 112–44.

85. Fraser, "Crisis of Care?," 32–34.

86. Pat Armstrong and Hugh Armstrong, *The Double Ghetto* (Toronto: McClelland and Stewart, 1978).

87. Johanna Brenner points out that this racial and class division is firmly entrenched within the United States. She explains that "the most well-explored instance of race/gender intersectionality has been the different locations of white women and women of color in the work of social reproduction. Historically and today, whether in the private household (domestic servant and her employer) or in the public sphere (hotel maids/nurses' aides/kitchen workers and professional/supervisors/administrative support staff) women of color do the most menial and dirty work." Brenner, *Women and the Politics of Class*, 295. On the care gap, see Nancy Folbre, *The Invisible Heart* (New York: New Press, 2001).

88. Fraser, "Crisis of Care?," 33–35.

89. Foster, Clark, and York, *The Ecological Rift*, 207–11; John Bellamy Foster, "The Age of Planetary Crisis," *Review of Radical Political Economics* 29/4 (1997): 124–34.

90. Fraser, "Behind Marx's Hidden Abode," 63; John Bellamy Foster, "Marx's Theory of Metabolic Rift," *American Journal of Sociology* 105/2 (1999): 366–405.

91. Mészáros, *Beyond Capital*, 142–253; Foster, Clark, and York, *The Ecological Rift*, 401–22.

92. Salleh, "Ecological Debt, Embodied Debt" and "From Eco–Sufficiency to Global Justice," 1–40, 291–312.

93. Marx, *Capital*, vol. 1, 552–53.

94. Fraser, "Crisis of Care?," 36.

95. All these conditions of socialism were in fact stipulated by Marx. See Marx, *Capital*, vol. 3 (London: Penguin, 1981), 754, 911, 948–49. See also chapter 7 in this book.

4. Marx as a Food Theorist

This chapter is adapted and revised for this book from John Bellamy Foster, "Marx as a Food Theorist," *Monthly Review* 68/7 (December 2016): 1–22.

1. Epigraph: Karl Marx, *Grundrisse* (London: Penguin, 1973), 92.
2. See, for example, Fred Magdoff, John Bellamy Foster, and Frederick Buttel, eds., *Hungry for Profit* (New York: Monthly Review Press, 2000); Fred Magdoff and Brian Tokar, eds., *Agriculture and Food in Crisis* (New York: Monthly Review Press, 2010); Michael Carolan, *The Sociology of Food and Agriculture* (New York: Routledge, 2012). On food regime theory, see Philip McMichael, "A Food Regime Genealogy," *Journal of Peasant Studies* 36/1 (2009): 139–69; Robert Albritton, *Let Them Eat Junk* (London: Pluto Press, 2009).
3. Stephen Mennell, Anne Murcott, and Anneke H. van Otterloo, eds., *The Sociology of Food* (Thousand Oaks, CA: Sage, 1992), 1–2. See also William Alex McIntosh, *Sociologies of Food and Nutrition* (New York: Plenum, 1996), 1; Jane Dixon, *The Changing Chicken* (Sydney: University of South Wales Press, 2002), 14.
4. F. M. L. Thompson, "The Second Agricultural Revolution," *Economic History Review*, 21/1 (April 1968): 62–77. Thompson dates the First Agricultural Revolution to the late seventeenth century, the high point of which was to be the Norfolk four-course crop rotation, and sees the Second Agricultural Revolution as occurring mainly in the mid-nineteenth. See also B. A. Holderness, "The Origins of High Farming," in Holderness and Michael Turner, eds., *Land, Labour and Agriculture, 1700–1920* (London: Hambledon, 1991), 149–64.
5. Karl Marx and Frederick Engels, *Collected Works* (New York: International Publishers, 1975), vol. 5, 41–42; Joseph Fracchia, "Beyond the Human Nature Debate: Human Corporeal Organisation as the 'First Fact' of Historical Materialism," *Historical Materialism* 13/1 (2005): 33–61.
6. Karl Marx, *Capital*, vol. 3 (London: Penguin, 1981), 770.
7. In his 1848 speech "On the Question of Free Trade," Marx mocked those free traders and political economists who wanted to reduce the whole complex food question simply to the need for "cheap food." Karl Marx, *The Poverty of Philosophy* (New York: International Publishers, 1963), 206–7.
8. Anthony S. Wohl, *Endangered Lives* (Cambridge, MA: Harvard University Press, 1983), 50–52.
9. Karl Marx, *Capital*, vol. 1 (London: Penguin, 1976), 809–11.
10. Marx, *Capital*, vol. 1, 834–35; Marx, *On the First International* (New York: McGraw-Hill, 1973), 5–7.

11. Howard Waitzkin, *The Second Sickness* (New York: Free Press, 1983), 67; Marx and Engels, *Collected Works*, vol. 5, 399–400.
12. "Adulteration," Oxford English Dictionary, compact ed. (Oxford: Oxford University Press, 1971), vol. 1, 33.
13. Marx and Engels, *Collected Works*, vol. 4, 370.
14. It is significant that Marx followed the issue of food adulteration so closely that he continued to update these sections through the final French edition of *Capital* in 1875, as can be seen by his reference to the 1874 parliamentary report on food adulteration. Marx, *Capital*, vol. 1, 750; Marx and Engels, *Collected Works*, vol. 19, 253.
15. Mary P. English, *Victorian Values* (Bristol, UK: Biopress, 1990), 65, 102, 121; Wohl, *Endangered Lives*, 52–54.
16. Arthur Hill Hassall, *Adulterations Detected; Or, Plain Instructions for the Discovery of Frauds in Food and Medicine* (London: Longman, Brown, Green, Longmans and Roberts, 1857), 20; *Report on the Microscopical Examination of Different Waters (Principally Those Used in the Metropolis) During the Cholera Epidemic of 1854*, Appendix 8, "Report of the Committee for Scientific Inquiries in Relation to the Cholera-Epidemic of 1854" (London: Her Majesty's Stationery Office, 1855), 384–521; Edwin Lankester, *A Guide to the Food Collection in the South Kensington Museum* (London: Her Majesty's Stationery Office, 1860), 100–102; Royal Society of Chemistry, "The Fight Against Food Adulteration," http://rsc.org.
17. Hassall, *Adulterations Detected*, 1–8.
18. Tremenheere quoted in Marx, *Capital*, vol. 1, 278.
19. Marx and Engels, *Collected Works*, vol. 19, 254.
20. E. P. Thompson, "The Moral Economy of the English Crowd in the Eighteenth Century," *Past and Present* 50 (1971): 80–81.
21. Marx, *Capital*, vol. 1, 359–61.
22. Marx and Engels, *Collected Works*, vol. 19, 252–55. Marx's research on bread consumption in history led him to examine why the Romans appeared to eat far more wheat than the average inhabitant of France in his own time. He explained this was in part a result of the imperfections and adulterations that characterized modern milling and baking. Marx, *Grundrisse*, 834–35.
23. Marx, *Capital*, vol. 1, 359, 750; Marx and Engels, *Collected Works*, vol. 19, 254.
24. Wohl, *Endangered Lives*, 52–53.
25. Simon quoted in Marx, *Capital*, vol. 1, 811; Simon, *Public Health Reports*, vol. 2, 96–97.
26. World Hunger Education Service, "Hunger in America: 2016 United States Hunger and Poverty Facts," http://worldhunger.org.

27. Fred Magdoff and John Bellamy Foster, *What Every Environmentalist Needs to Know About Capitalism* (New York: Monthly Review Press, 2011), 23–24.

28. Harriet Friedmann, "International Regimes of Food and Agricultures Since 1870," in *Peasants and Peasant Societies*, ed. Teodor Shanin (Oxford: Blackwell, 1987), 258–76; Harriet Friedmann and Phillip McMichael, "Agriculture and the State System," *Sociologia Ruralis* 29/2 (1989): 93–117.

29. McMichael, "A Food Regime Genealogy," 140.

30. Hugh Campbell, "Breaking New Ground in Food Regime Theory," *Agriculture and Human Values* 26 (2009): 309–19.

31. Colin A. M. Duncan, *The Centrality of Agriculture* (Montreal: McGill–Queens University Press, 1996), 51, 69–71. The view of English agriculture in the third quarter of the nineteenth century constituting a "golden age" was quite common among economic historians in the 1960s. See, for example, E. J. Hobsbawm, *Industry and Empire* (London: Penguin, 1969), 106, 199. It was largely dispelled, however, by the 1980s.

32. See Thompson, "The Second Agricultural Revolution"; E. J. T. Collins, "Did Mid–Victorian Agriculture Fail?: Output, Productivity and Technological Change in Nineteenth Century Farming," *ReFRESH* 21 (1995): 5–8; "Rural and Agricultural Change," in Collins, ed., *The Agrarian History of England And Wales, Part VII (1850–1914)* (Cambridge, UK: Cambridge University Press, 2000), 72–78; E. J. Jones, "The Changing Basis of English Agricultural Prosperity, 1853–1873," *Agricultural History Review* 10 (1962): 1–19; B. A. Holderness, "The Origins of High Farming," in Holderness and Turner, *Land, Labour and Agriculture, 1700*–1920, 151. In Holderness's words, "high farming remained high-risk farming," and failed "in stiffening the backbone of British cereal production in the long term." Holderness, "The Origins of High Farming," 151.

33. Duncan, *The Centrality of Agriculture*, 9–10, 54, 64–69, 72, 90, 94. Duncan's book relied on the work of the Japanese Marxist Kozo Uno, who claimed that England had developed not only the basis of a purely capitalist society, but also an agriculture uniquely suited to its needs as a self–regulating system. Kozo Uno, *Principles of Political Economy* (Atlantic Highlands, NJ: Humanities, 1980), 106–7.

34. Harriet Friedmann, "What on Earth Is the Modern World System?," *Journal of World–System Research* 11/2 (2000): 489–91. In addition to Duncan, Friedman relies on the work of the British geographer T. P. Bayliss–Smith, who in the early 1980s studied the "pre-industrial" system of agriculture in Wiltshire, England, in the 1820s, before the

advent of high farming. However, since the issue in question is the state of agriculture in the third quarter of the nineteenth century, and not the first, Bayliss-Smith's analysis has no direct relevance. Guano imports, for example, did not begin until the 1840s, while bone imports totaled only 1,400 tons in 1821–24, as opposed to 68,340 tons in 1854–58. These developments were crucial, as F. M. L. Thompson contends, in breaking the earlier "closed-circuit system of agriculture." Indeed, the massive imports of natural fertilizers, far exceeding the growth of agricultural productivity, can be seen as a manifestation of growing ecological disruption of natural cycles—the primary concern of Marx's metabolic rift analysis. T. P. Bayliss-Smith, *The Ecology of Agricultural Systems* (Cambridge: Cambridge University Press, 1982), 37–55; Thompson, "The Second Agricultural Revolution," 75; Brett Clark and John Bellamy Foster, "Guano: The Global Metabolic Rift and the Fertilizer Trade," in *Ecology and Power*, ed. Alf Hornborg, Brett Clark, and Kenneth Hermele (London: Routledge, 2012), 74–75.

35. Mindi Schneider and Philip McMichael, "Deepening, and Repairing, the Metabolic Rift," *Journal of Peasant Studies* 37/3 (2010): 465, 469–74. The rigid separation of industry from agriculture is central to Duncan's whole work, captured by his phrase "the centrality of agriculture." In this view, Marx was wrong to focus on the industrial disruption of agriculture; rather, agriculture in mid-nineteenth-century England should be viewed as largely independent of industry. This division allows Schneider and McMichael to argue, ostensibly following Friedmann, that English agriculture at the time was ecologically sustainable but "socially unsustainable"—a view most ecological Marxists would find absurd. See Schneider and McMichael, "Deepening, and Repairing, the Metabolic Rift," 474. Marx, in contrast, to such views argued as early as 1859 that "agriculture to an increasing extent becomes just a branch of industry and is completely dominated by capital." Karl Marx, *A Contribution to a Critique of Political Economy* (Moscow: Progress Publishers, 1970), 213.

36. Mark Overton, "Agricultural Revolution in England 1500–1850," BBC, February 17, 2011.

37. Jones, "The Changing Basis of English Agricultural Prosperity," 104; Collins, "Rural and Agricultural Change," 93–95. Marx was aware of Mechi, since most of Walter Good's 1866 *Political, Agricultural, and Commercial Fallacies*, which Marx read and cited, was critical of Mechi and his high-farming ideas. Walter Good, *Political, Economic, and Commercial Fallacies* (London: Edward Stanford, 1866).

38. Mette Erjnaes, Karl Gunnar Persson, and Søren Rich, "Feeding the British," *Economic History Review* 61/1 (2008): 147.

39. Thompson, "The Second Agricultural Revolution," 68–74; Erjnaes, Persson, and Rich, "Feeding the British," 146.

40. Erjnaes, Persson, and Rich, "Feeding the British," 146.

41. Ibid., 146–47. See also Karl Marx, *Dispatches for the New York Tribune* (London: Penguin, 2007), 169; Karl Marx and Frederick Engels, *Ireland and the Irish Question* (Moscow: Progress Publishers, 1971), 126, 133–34, 147–484. Marx wrote of the "new regime" of food production in English for the *New York Tribune* in 1855. He also discussed the new regime in relation to Ireland, arguing that the potato blight of 1845–46 had hastened the repeal of the Corn Laws, and hence the advent of the new "regime after 1846" in England, Scotland, and Ireland. It is clear that in connecting the abolition of the Corn Laws and excessive pasturage to the decrease in food production, namely the grain harvest, Marx was referring to the general shift in British agriculture toward an increasingly meat-based system of production, coupled with the overall industrialization of agriculture, which was soon to emerge as a major theme. This is verified by Marx's letter to Ferdinand Lassalle, written a few days before the *Tribune* piece, in which he made similar observations linking the Corn Laws' repeal to the decrease in cereal production, increased pasturage in Scotland and Ireland, and the rising imports of wheat. Marx and Engels, *Collected Works*, vol. 39, 511–14.

42. Karl Marx, *Theories of Surplus Value*, part 2 (Moscow: Progress Publishers, 1968), 159; *Capital*, vol. 1, 348; David R. Montgomery, *Dirt: The Erosion of Civilizations* (Berkeley: University of California Press, 2012), 184–85.

43. Marx, *On the First International*, 90; *Capital*, vol. 1, 860.

44. Marx, *Capital*, vol. 1, 831–33.

45. Léonce de Lavergne, *The Rural Economy of England, Scotland, and Ireland* (London: Blackwell, 1855), 13–25, 34–51, 184–87, 196; "High Farming in Norfolk," *The Economist*, May 11, 1851, 511. Bakewell's experiments in sheep breeding were also described by Charles Darwin, *The Origin of Species* (Cambridge, MA: Harvard University Press, 1964; facsimile of first edition), 36.

46. Lavergne, *The Rural Economy*, 19, 196.

47. Karl Marx, *Capital*, vol. 2 (London: Penguin, 1978), 313–15; Lavergne, *The Rural Economy*, 184–87.

48. "High Farming in Norfolk," *The Economist*, 511.

49. Karl Marx, Marx-Engels Archives, Sign. B. 106, 336, quoted in Kohei Saito, "Why Ecosocialism Needs Marx," *Monthly Review* 68/6 (November 2016): 62. See also Holderness, "The Origins of High Farming," 160–61.

50. Today broiler chickens—"meat birds" or "broilers"—reach a market

weight of five pounds in five weeks, in contrast to the ten weeks required to reach four-pound market weight forty years ago. This is only achieved by using chickens specially bred for rapid weight gain and large breasts, crammed by the thousand into massive windowless sheds and fed a high-energy feed laced with antibiotics. The poultry "farmer" of our contemporary system has been converted into a laborer for large, vertically integrated "protein" corporations. See "Modern Meat Chicken Industry," Penn State Extension, http://extension.psu.edu. For a metabolic rift analysis of contemporary livestock agribusiness, see Ryan Gunderson, "The Metabolic Rift of Livestock Agribusiness," *Organization and Environment* 24/4 (2011): 404–22; Richard Lewontin, "The Maturing of Capitalist Agriculture: Farmer as Proletarian," in Magdoff, Foster, and Buttel, eds., *Hungry for Profit*, 93–106.

51. Marx and Engels, *Ireland and the Irish Question*, 121–22. Marx argued that British colonial agriculture, whether in relation to Ireland or India, simply made matters worse. "The English...in the East Indies . . . only managed to spoil indigenous agriculture and to swell the number and intensity of famines." Karl Marx, "Letter to Vera Zasulich," third draft, in Teodor Shanin, ed., *Late Marx and the Russian Road* (New York: Monthly Review Press, 1983), 121.

52. Marx and Engels, *Collected Works*, vol. 39, 512; Marx, *Dispatches for the New York Tribune*, 113–19.

53. Marx, *Capital*, vol. 1, 870.

54. Collins, "Did Mid-Victorian Agriculture Fail?"; Collins, "Rural and Agricultural Change," 72–78.

55. Collins, "Did Mid-Victorian Agriculture Fail?"

56. E. J. T. Collins, "Food Supplies and Food Policy," in Collins, ed., *The Agrarian History of England and Wales*, 34; Marx, *Dispatches for the New York Tribune*, 166–69. Collins observes: "High-farming prosperity owed far more to high prices than to higher output or improvements in biotechnical efficiency." Collins, "Rural and Agricultural Change," 127.

57. Marx, *Capital*, vol. 1, 908; *Capital*, vol. 3, 904, 909.

58. See John Bellamy Foster, "Marx's Theory of Metabolic Rift," *American Journal of Sociology* 105/2 (1999): 366–405.

59. Daniel Tanuro, "A Plea for the Ecological Reconstruction of Marxism," presentation at the Historical Materialism conference, London, November 10, 2012, http://europe-solidaire.org.

60. Lavergne, *The Rural Economy*, 51; Marx, *Capital*, vol. 3, 768–69.

61. The argument here relies on John Bellamy Foster and Paul Burkett, *Marx and the Earth* (Chicago: Haymarket, 2016), 27–30, where we received help from Fred Magdoff.

62. Duncan, *The Centrality of Agriculture*, 188. Oddly, Duncan in this passage

describes high farming with the aid of guano as "superproductive," despite all empirical evidence to the contrary. Ostensibly to bolster his criticisms of Marx, he also quotes historian F. M. L. Thompson as calling English farming in the early nineteenth century a "self-renewing" extractive industry. But Duncan overlooks the larger point Thompson was making in the very same sentence: that English farming in the "golden age" was organized on a "manufacturing" or industrial basis, and was not self-sufficient, but rather required massive infusions of bones, guano, and oil cake from abroad. This was, Thompson wrote, "the essence of the Second Agricultural Revolution"—as Marx had suggested more than a century earlier. See Thompson, "The Second Agricultural Revolution," 64.

63. Justus von Liebig, *Letters on Modern Agriculture* (London: Walton and Maberty, 1859), 175–78, 183, 220; Marx, *The Poverty of Philosophy*, 162; John Bellamy Foster, *Marx's Ecology* (New York: Monthly Review Press, 2000), 149–63. Marx described soil depletion as a slow process, especially when offset by the robbing of nutrients from other countries. He generally reserved the term soil "exhaustion" for extreme cases like those of the slavery-based South in the United States. See Marx, *Capital*, vol. 3, 756.

64. Doncaster Agricultural Association quoted in Thompson, "The Second Agricultural Revolution," 69.

65. Thompson, "The Second Agricultural Revolution," 73–74; Good, *Political, Agricultural, and Commercial Fallacies*, 368.

66. Schneider and McMichael, "Deepening, and Repairing, the Metabolic Rift," 472.

67. See Nathan Rosenberg, *Perspectives on Technology* (Cambridge: Cambridge University Press, 1976), 136; Marx, *Capital*, vol. 3, 894. On the intensity of inputs in high farming, see Holderness, "The Origins of High Farming," 150–51.

68. Duncan, *The Centrality of Agriculture*, 65, 69, 72. Duncan argues that Marx was "misled" in his critique of English high farming by "bourgeois radicals."

69. Carolan, *The Sociology of Food and Agriculture*, 249–50.

70. Marx, *Capital*, vol. 1, 638.

5. Marx and Alienated Speciesism

This chapter is adapted and revised for this book from John Bellamy Foster and Brett Clark, "Marx and Alienated Speciesism," *Monthly Review* 70/7 (December 2018): 1–20.

1. Ted Benton, "Humanism = Speciesism: Marx on Humans and Animals,"

Radical Philosophy 50 (1988): 4, 6, 8, 11–12; Ted Benton, *Natural Relations: Ecology, Animal Rights and Social Justice* (London/New York: Verso, 1993), 32–35.

2. Renzo Llorente, "Reflections on the Prospects for a Non-Speciesist Marxism," in *Critical Theory and Animal Liberation*, ed. John Sanbonmatsu (Lanham, MD: Rowman and Littlefield, 2011), 126–27. Llorente, while arguing that Marx himself was speciesist, denies that speciesism is inherent to Marxism.

3. John Sanbonmatsu, *The Postmodern Prince* (New York: Monthly Review Press, 2004), 215–18; Sanbonmatsu, Introduction to *Critical Theory and Animal Liberation*, 17–19.

4. Katherine Perlo, "Marxism and the Underdog," *Society and Animals* 10/3 (2002): 304; David Sztybel, "Marxism and Animal Rights," *Environmental Ethics* 2/2 (1997): 170–71.

5. Richard D. Ryder, "Speciesism," in *Encyclopedia of Animal Rights and Animal Welfare*, ed. Marc Bekoff (Westport, CT: Greenwood Press, 1998), 320.

6. For a criticism of this, see Bradley J. Macdonald, "Marx and the Human/Animal Dialectic," in *Political Theory and the Animal/Human Relationship*, ed. Judith Grant and Vincent G. Jungkuz (Albany: State University of New York Press, 2011), 36.

7. Benton, *Natural Relations*, 42.

8. Benton, "Humanism = Speciesism," 1; Karl Marx, *Early Writings* (London: Penguin, 1974), 348.

9. Marx, *Early Writings*, 239.

10. Some critics do highlight, out of context, Marx and Engels's criticisms of the Society for the Preservation of Animals as evidence of their lack of sympathy for animals. For a powerful rejoinder, see Ryan Gunderson, "Marx's Comments on Animal Welfare," *Rethinking Marxism* 23/4 (2011): 543–48.

11. Macdonald, "Marx and the Human/Animal Dialectic," 41–42. Macdonald distinguishes between what he calls the "dialectical dualism"—reflecting processes of "objectification" or "externalization"— inherent to the human relation to nature and the "alienated speciesism" characteristic of capitalism. Alienated speciesism, in these terms, is just the other side of alienated species-being. On the concepts of objectification and externalization (and the distinction between these and Marx's alienation), see Georg Lukács, *History and Class Consciousness* (London: Merlin Press, 1971), xxxvi; Lukács, *The Young Hegel* (Cambridge, MA: MIT Press, 1975), 537–67.

12. See Marx and Engels, *Collected Works* (New York: International Publishers, 1975), vol. 1, 25–107, 403–509; Epicurus, *The Epicurus*

Reader (Indianapolis, IN: Hackett Publishing, 1994); Lucretius, *On the Nature of the Universe* (Oxford: Oxford University Press, 1997). On Marx and Epicurus, see John Bellamy Foster, *Marx's Ecology* (New York: Monthly Review Press, 2000), 21–65.

13. On Lucretius and the human-animal relation, see Alma Massaro, "The Living in Lucretius' *De rerum natura*: Animals' *ataraxia* and Humans' Distress," *Relations* 2/2 (2014), http://ledonline.it/Relations. On Epicurus's proto-evolutionary views, see John Bellamy Foster, Brett Clark, and Richard York, *Critique of Intelligent Design* (New York: Monthly Review Press, 2008), 49–64.

14. For Lucretius on environmental destruction, see Lucretius, *On the Nature of the Universe* (Oxford: Oxford University Press, 1999), Book VI; Jack Lindsay, *Blast Power and Ballistics: Concepts of Force and Energy in the Ancient World* (London: Frederick Muller, 1974), 379–81; H. S. Commager Jr., "Lucretius's Interpretation of the Plague," *Harvard Studies in Classical Philology* 62 (1957): 105–18.

15. Karl Marx and Frederick Engels, *Collected Works*, vol. 5, 141.

16. Marx and Engels, *Collected Works*, vol. 1, 453.

17. Benton, *Natural Relations*, 35.

18. Sztybel, "Marxism and Animal Rights," 171.

19. Marx and Engels, *Collected Works*, vol. 1, 75, 448, 452–53.

20. Plutarch, *Moralia*, vol. 14, Loeb Classical Library (Cambridge, MA: Harvard University Press, 1967), 129–47, (pp. 1104–1106).

21. Marx and Engels, *Collected Works*, vol. 1, 74. On the Epicurean attack on religion and his opposition to Plato, see Benjamin Farrington, *The Faith of Epicurus* (London: Weidenfeld and Nicolson, 1967).

22. Marx and Engels, *Collected Works*, vol. 1, 74–76.

23. Marx, *Early Writings*, 389–90.

24. Sztybel, "Marxism and Animal Rights," 173–74.

25. Epicurus, *The Epicurus Reader*, 32; Frederick Engels to Friedrich Adolph Sorge, March 15, 1883, in *Karl Marx Remembered*, ed. Philip S. Foner (San Francisco: Synthesis Publications, 1983), 28. See also Foster, *Marx's Ecology*, 77–78.

26. Joseph Fracchia, "Organisms and Objectifications: A Historical-Materialist Inquiry into the 'Human and Animal,'" *Monthly Review* 68/10 (March 2017): 1–3.

27. Marx, *Early Writings*, 239; Thomas Müntzer, *Collected Works* (Edinburgh: T and T Clark, 1988), 335.

28. Benton, "Humanism = Speciesism," 8, 12; *Natural Relations*, 33, 37.

29. René Descartes, *Discourse on Method* (Chicago: Open Court, 1899), 59–63.

30. Alice Kuzniar, "A Higher Language: Novalis on Communion with

Animals," *German Quarterly* 76/4 (2003): 426–42; Robert Ausch, *An Advanced Guide to Psychological Thinking* (Lanham, MD: Lexington Books, 2015), 90.

31. Julian Jaynes and William Woodward, "In the Shadow of Enlightenment, II: Reimarus and his Theory of Drives," *Journal of the History of Behavioral Sciences* 10/2 (1974): 144–59; John H. Zammito, *The Gestation of German Biology* (Chicago: University of Chicago Press, 2018), 134–49; Zammito, "Herder Between Reimarus and Tetens: The Problem of an Animal-Human Boundary," in *Herder: Philosophy and Anthropology*, ed. Anik Waldow and Nigel DeSouza (Oxford: Oxford University Press, 2017), 127–46; Günter Zöller, *Fichte's Transcendental Philosophy* (Cambridge: Cambridge University Press, 1998), 63; James Muldoon, *Hegel's Philosophy of Drives* (Aurora, CA: Noesis Press, 2014); G. W. F. Hegel, *The Philosophy of Nature* (Oxford: Oxford University Press, 2004), 406–9.

32. Dorothea E. von Mücke, *The Practices of the Enlightenment* (New York: Columbia University Press, 2015), 33–38; Zammito, *The Gestation of German Biology*, 138–39; Kurt Danziger, "The Unknown Wundt: Drive, Apperception, and Volition," in *Wilhelm Wundt in History*, ed. Robert W. Rieber and David K. Robinson (New York: Kluwer Academic/ Plenum Publishers, 2001), 101–2; Muldoon, *Hegel's Philosophy of Drives*, 107–11.

33. Reimarus quoted in Zammito, *The Gestation of German Biology*, 139.

34. Zammito, *The Gestation of German Biology*, 139–40.

35. Marx and Engels, *Collected Works*, vol. 1, 19.

36. Zammito, *The Gestation of German Biology*, 141–42; Mücke, *The Practices of the Enlightenment*, 35.

37. Immanuel Kant, *On History* (New York: Bobbs-Merrill), 55–56; Mücke, *The Practices of the Enlightenment*, 36–38.

38. Johann Gottfried von Herder, *Philosophical Writings* (Cambridge: Cambridge University Press, 2002), 78–81; Zammito, "Herder Between Reimarus and Tetens."

39. Ausch, *An Advanced Guide to Psychological Thinking*, 91.

40. Marx, *Early Writings*, 329; Karl Marx, *Capital*, vol. 1 (London: Penguin, 1976), 284. In addition to Reimarus, Marx may have been influenced in the writing of this passage by Darwin's section on the "Cell-Making Instinct of the Hive-Bee," in the *Origin of Species*, a work he had studied closely. See Charles Darwin, *On the Origin of Species* (Cambridge, MA: Harvard University Press, 1964; facsimile of the first edition), 224–35.

41. Marx, *Early Writings*, 389–90; Christopher Dowrick, "The Roots of Consciousness," *History of Political Thought* 5/3 (Winter 1984): 472, 476.

42. See Arend Th. Van Leeuwen, *Critique of Earth* (New York: Charles Scribner's Sons, 1974), 53–54; Giorgio Agamben, *The Man Without Content* (Stanford, CA: Stanford University Press, 1999), 84.

43. *Gattungswesen* is variously translated as "generic essence," "species being," and "generic being." In developing his concept of species (or generic) being (*Gattungswesen*), Marx was drawing not only on Feuerbach but on Hegel's earlier notion of the "generic essence" (*Gattungswesen*) of humanity, associated with the universal consciousness promoted by the state. In Marx's own analysis, this "universal generic essence" constituted the higher-order consciousness or self-consciousness distinguishing human species being. As self-conscious actors, human beings transformed nature and the world through their labor, and hence their own social relations and themselves. See G. W. F. Hegel, *The Philosophy of Right* (Oxford: Oxford University Press, 1952), 200–201, 372; Karl Marx, *Early Writings*, 192, 328–29; Charles Taylor, *Hegel* (Cambridge: Cambridge University Press, 1975), 549; Taylor, *Hegel and Modern Society* (Cambridge: Cambridge University Press, 1979), 143; George Márkus, *Marxism and Anthropology* (Assen, Netherlands: Van Gorcum, 1978), 3–15; Paul Heyer, *Nature, Human Nature, and Society* (Westport, CT: Greenwood Press, 1982), 13, 73–96; István Mészáros, *Marx's Theory of Alienation* (London: Pluto Press, 1972), 14.

44. Ludwig Feuerbach, *The Fiery Brook* (New York: Anchor Books, 1972), 97–99; Zöller, *Fichte's Transcendental Philosophy*, 63; Marx W. Wartofsky, *Feuerbach* (Cambridge: Cambridge University Press, 1977), 5–6, 206–8.

45. Márkus, *Marxism and Anthropology*, 4–5; Boris Henning, "Self-Knowledge, Estrangement, and Social Metabolism," *Monthly Review* 70/10 (March 2019): 44.

46. Shlomo Avineri, *The Social and Political Thought of Karl Marx* (Cambridge: Cambridge University Press, 1971), 65–95.

47. Marx, *Early Writings*, 327; Benton, "Humanism = Speciesism," 5–9; Llorente, "Reflections on the Prospects for a Non-Speciesist Marxism," 126–27; Sanbonmatsu, Introduction to *Critical Theory and Animal Liberation*, 17–19.

48. Mészáros, *Marx's Theory of Alienation*, 173–80.

49. Macdonald, "Marx and the Human/Animal Dialectic," 41.

50. Marx and Engels, *Collected Works*, vol. 5, 58–59. The critical line of argument based on the essence of the fish was first introduced by Engels in his notes on "Feuerbach" in preparation for the writing of the *German Ideology*. Marx and Engels, *Collected Works*, vol. 5, 13.

51. Marx and Engels, *Collected Works*, vol. 4, 125–26. Marx preferred Bacon's physics to that of Descartes, seeing matter in motion in the

former's conceptualization as taking the form of a drive (*Trieb*) rather than a mere mechanism as in the latter's. See Leeuwen, *Critique of Earth*, 15–20; Marx and Engels, *Collected Works*, vol. 4, 127–30.

52. Marx, *Capital*, vol. 1, 512. Descartes had himself explicitly referred to the automata or moving parts as these were employed in human industry in the "manufacturing" (handicraft) period, which he then applied to the description of animals. See Descartes, *Discourse on Method*, 59–60. In capitalist valuation, as Marx remarks, animals are treated as machines—which he saw as reflecting the contradiction between nature and commodity value. See James D. White, "Nikolai Sieber and Karl Marx," *Research in Political Economy* 19 (2001): 6.

53. Benton, "Humanism = Speciesism," 16.

54. Marx, *Early Writings*, 239.

55. Ibid., 327.

56. Charles Lyell, *Principles of Geology* (London: Penguin, 1997), 276–77.

57. Marx and Engels, *Collected Works*, vol. 25, 459.

58. See Foster, *Marx's Ecology*, 120, 180–82; and Foster, Clark, and York, *Critique of Intelligent Design*.

59. Marx, *Early Writings*, 356.

60. Karl Marx, *Grundrisse* (London: Penguin, 1973), 105.

61. Gunnar Broberg, "*Homo sapiens*: Linnaeus's Classification of Man," in *Linnaeus: The Man and His Work*, ed. Sten Lindroth, Gunnar Eriksson, and Gunnar Broberg (Berkeley: University of California Press, 1983), 156–79.

62. Marx and Engels, *Collected Works*, vol. 42, 322.

63. Karl Marx and Frederick Engels, *Marx-Engels-Gesamtausgabe* IV, 26 (Berlin: Akademie Verlag, 2011), 214–19; Joseph Beete Jukes, *The Student's Manual of Geology* (Edinburgh: Adam and Charles Black, 1872).

64. Karl Marx and Frederick Engels, *Selected Correspondence* (Moscow: Progress Publishers, 1975), 102; Foster, *Marx's Ecology*, 166.

65. Marx and Engels, *Collected Works*, vol. 41, 232.

66. Fracchia, "Organisms and Objectifications," 3.

67. Marx and Engels, *Collected Works*, vol. 25, 452–59; Stephen Jay Gould, *An Urchin in the Storm* (New York: W. W. Norton, 1987), 111.

68. For contemporary discussions of the complex evolutionary dynamics between gene, organism, and environment, see Richard Lewontin, *The Triple Helix* (Cambridge, MA: Harvard University Press, 2000); Richard Levins and Richard Lewontin, *The Dialectical Biologist* (Cambridge, MA: Harvard University Press, 1985); Richard Lewontin and Richard Levins, *Biology Under the Influence* (New York: Monthly Review Press, 2007).

69. Marx and Engels, *Collected Works*, vol. 25, 460.

70. Ibid., 503.

71. Karl Marx, *Texts on Method* (Oxford: Blackwell, 1975), 190–91; Marian Comyn, "My Recollections of Karl Marx," *The Nineteenth Century and After*, vol. 91, available at http://marxists.org.

72. Charles Darwin, *The Descent of Man* (1871; repr. Princeton: Princeton University Press, 1981), 105, 136–37. Darwin's reference to "social habits" here referred specifically to inheritance of acquired characteristics—an idea usually associated with Jean-Baptiste Lamarck, but which Darwin had, by this time, introduced as a supplementary principle to natural selection—as in the form of certain habitual social behaviors. Darwin suggested, as a possible example of this, that children of laborers were said to inherit larger hands than the children of gentry due to the passing on of acquired characteristics resulting from "social habits" of use and disuse. See Darwin, *The Descent of Man*, 117–18, 157, 160–61; Helen P. Liepman, "The Six Editions of the 'Origin of Species,'" *Acta Biotheoretica* 30 (1981): 199–214. Engels was influenced by Darwin's views in this regard and, in a similar way, referred to the inheritance of acquired characteristics in relation to hands. See Marx and Engels, *Collected Works*, vol. 25, 453–54. Nevertheless, one could also read here Darwin's reference to the social—though this was clearly not his primary meaning—as standing for the more general notion of human beings as social animals, emphasized by Marx and Engels, resulting in cumulative social development and the enhancement of practical intelligence, passed on through education, and reflected in the cultural capacity to manipulate the world through exosomatic instruments. From the start, *Homo sapiens*, as Engels above all understood in the nineteenth century, were products of a complex process of what is now called gene-culture coevolution, which explains the origin of human corporeal organization, particularly the development of the human brain. See Gould, *An Urchin in the Storm*, 111. The whole issue of the inheritance of acquired characteristics, it should be added, is attracting renewed interest in biology due to the development of epigenetics. See Peter Ward, *Lamarck's Revenge* (New York: Bloomsbury Publishing, 2018); Eva Jablonka and Mario J. Lamb, *Epigenetic Inheritance and Evolution* (Oxford: Oxford University Press, 1995).

73. John Berger, *About Looking* (London: Vintage International, 1991), 4.

74. Berger, *About Looking*, 3–4.

75. Marx, *Capital*, vol. 1, 285–86.

76. Ibid.

77. Marx, *Capital*, vol. 2 (London: Penguin, 1978), 241.
78. Ibid., 250; Paul Burkett, *Marx and Nature* (Chicago: Haymarket Books, 2014), 43–47; Daniel Auerbach and Brett Clark, "Metabolic Rifts, Temporal Imperatives, and Geographical Shifts: Logging in the Adirondack Forest in the 1800s," *International Critical Thought* 8/3 (2018): 468–86.
79. Marx, *Capital*, vol. 1, 517.
80. Burkett, *Marx and Nature*, 41–47.
81. Marx, *Capital*, vol. 2, 314–15.
82. Ibid., 315; Léonce de Lavergne, *The Rural Economy of England, Scotland, and Ireland* (London: Blackwell, 1855), 13–25, 34–51, 184–87, 196.
83. Karl Marx, Marx-Engels Archives, International Institute of Social History, Sign. B., 106, 336, quoted in Kohei Saito, "Why Ecosocialism Needs Marx," *Monthly Review* 68/6 (November 2016): 62; chapter 4 in this book.
84. Marx, Marx-Engels Archives, International Institute of Social History, Sign. B., 106, 336, quoted in Saito, "Why Ecosocialism Needs Marx," 62 (translation altered slightly); chapter 4 in this book.
85. For useful discussions of these issues, see William D. Heffernan, "Concentration of Ownership and Control in Agriculture," in *Hungry for Profit*, ed. Fred Magdoff, John Bellamy Foster, and Frederick H. Buttel (New York: Monthly Review Press, 2000), 61–75; Tony Weis, *The Global Food Economy* (New York: Zed Books, 2007); Tony Weis, *The Ecological Hoofprint* (New York: Zed Books, 2013); Stefano B. Longo, Rebecca Clausen, and Brett Clark, *The Tragedy of the Commodity* (New Brunswick, NJ: Rutgers University Press, 2015); Stefano B. Longo, Rebecca Clausen, and Brett Clark, "Capitalism and the Commodification of Salmon: From Wild Fish to a Genetically Modified Species," *Monthly Review* 66/7 (2014): 35–55.
86. Ryan Gunderson, "From Cattle to Capital: Exchange Value, Animal Commodification and Barbarism," *Critical Sociology* 39/2 (2011): 259–75; see also David Naguib Pellow, *Total Liberation* (Minneapolis: University of Minnesota Press, 2014).
87. Macdonald, "Marx and the Human/Animal Dialectic," 41.
88. Raymond Williams, *Problems in Materialism and Culture* (London: Verso, 1980), 83.
89. John Bellamy Foster, "Marx and the Rift in the Universal Metabolism of Nature," *Monthly Review* 65/7 (2013): 1–19.
90. Chapter 4 in this book; John Bellamy Foster and Paul Burkett, *Marx and the Earth* (Leiden: Brill, 2016), 29–31.
91. Mette Erjnaes, Karl Gunnar Persson, and Søren Rich, "Feeding the British," *Economic History Review* 61/1 (2008): 147.

92. Karl Marx and Frederick Engels, *Ireland and the Irish Question* (Moscow: Progress Publishers, 1971), 121–22.

93. Kohei Saito, *Karl Marx's Ecosocialism* (New York: Monthly Review Press, 2017), 209.

94. Chapter 4 in this book.

95. Ibid.; Marx, *Capital*, vol. 1, 637–38; Marx, *Capital*, vol. 2, 313–15; Karl Marx, *Capital*, vol. 3 (London: Penguin, 1981), 916, 949–50.

96. Macdonald, "Marx and the Human/Animal Dialectic," 42; John Bellamy Foster, Brett Clark, and Richard York, *The Ecological Rift* (New York: Monthly Review Press, 2010).

97. Marx, *Early Writings*, 389–90.

98. Lucretius, *On the Nature of the Universe* (Oxford: Oxford University Press, 1997), 46 (II: 350–65). Compare Lucretius's description of the sacrifice of Iphigenia by Agamemnon on the altar of the gods— Lucretius, *On the Nature of the Universe*, 5–6 (I: 80–101). See Massaro, "The Living in Lucretius' *De rerum natura*," 45–58.

99. Marx and Engels, *Collected Works*, vol. 5, 141; Marx, *Early Writings*, 239, 348.

6. Capitalism and the Paradox of Wealth

This chapter was extensively revised, updated, and adapted for this book from John Bellamy Foster and Brett Clark, "The Paradox of Wealth: Capitalism and Environmental Destruction," *Monthly Review* 61/6 (December 2009): 1–18, and from "The Paradox of Wealth" in John Bellamy Foster, Brett Clark, and Richard York, *The Ecological Rift* (New York: Monthly Review Press, 2010): 53–72.

1. Epigraph: Samir Amin, *Modern Imperialism, Monopoly Finance Capital, and Marx's Law of Value* (New York: Monthly Review Press, 2018), 85.

2. See the discussion of Nordhaus's stance on climate change in Richard York, Brett Clark, and John Bellamy Foster, "Capitalism in Wonderland," *Monthly Review* 61/1 (May 2009), 4–5; Jason Hickel, "The Nobel Prize for Climate Catastrophe," *Foreign Policy*, December 6, 2018, http://www.foreignpolicy.com. On the ideological character of the Sveriges Riksbank Prize (the Nobel Prize) in Economics, see Avner Offer and Gabriel Söderberg, *The Nobel Factor* (Princeton: Princeton University Press, 2016).

3. John Maynard Keynes, *The General Theory of Employment, Interest and Money* (London: Macmillan, 1973), 32.

4. James Maitland, Earl of Lauderdale, *An Inquiry into the Nature and Origin of Public Wealth and into the Means and Causes of Its Increase* (Edinburgh: Archibald Constable and Co., 1819), 37–59; Maitland,

Lauderdale's Notes on Adam Smith, ed. Chuhei Sugiyama (New York: Routledge, 1996), 140–41. Lauderdale was closest to Malthus in classical political economy, but generally rejected classical value theory, emphasizing the three factors of production (land, labor, and capital). Marx, who took Ricardo as his measure of bourgeois political economy, therefore had little genuine interest in Lauderdale as a theorist, apart from the latter's sense of the contradiction between use value and exchange value. Still, Lauderdale's devastating critique of the pursuit of private riches at the expense of public wealth earns him a position as one of the great dissident voices in the history of economics.

5.   Robert Brown, *The Nature of Social Laws* (Cambridge: Cambridge University Press, 1984), 63–64.

6.   Karl Marx, *A Contribution to the Critique of Political Economy* (Moscow: Progress Publishers, 1970), 27. In this chapter, for simplicity's sake, we do not explicitly address Marx's distinction between *exchange value* and its basis in *value* (abstract labor), treating them as basically synonymous within the limits of our discussion.

7.   David Ricardo, *On the Principles of Political Economy and Taxation,* vol. 1: *Works and Correspondence of David Ricardo* (Cambridge: Cambridge University Press, 1951), 276–87; George E. Foy, "Public Wealth and Private Riches," *Journal of Interdisciplinary Economics* 3 (1989): 3–10.

8.   Jean-Baptiste Say, *Letters to Thomas Robert Malthus on Political Economy and Stagnation of Commerce* (London: G. Harding's Bookshop, Ltd., 1936), 68–75.

9.   Karl Marx, *Capital*, vol. 1 (London: Penguin, 1976), 98.

10.   John Stuart Mill, *Principles of Political Economy with Some of their Applications to Social Philosophy* (New York: Longmans, Green, and Co., 1904), 4, 6. Mill appears to break out of these limits only briefly in his book, in his famous discussion of the stationary state. See Mill, *Principles of Political Economy*, 452–55.

11.   Karl Marx, *The Poverty of Philosophy* (New York: International Publishers, 1964), 35–36; Marx, *Theories of Surplus Value*, part 2 (Moscow: Progress Publishers, 1968), 245; Marx to Engels, August 24, 1867, in Karl Marx and Frederick Engels, *Selected Correspondence* (Moscow: Progress Publishers, 1975), 180–81.

12.   See John Bellamy Foster and Paul Burkett, *Marx and the Earth* (Chicago: Haymarket, 2016), 89–164.

13.   Karl Marx, *Early Writings* (New York: Vintage, 1974), 359–60.

14.   Karl Marx, *Capital*, vol. 3 (London: Penguin, 1981), 911, 959; Marx, *Theories of Surplus Value*, part 2, 245. For a discussion of the metabolic rift, see John Bellamy Foster, *The Ecological Revolution* (New York: Monthly Review Press, 2009), 161–200.

15. Karl Marx, *Dispatches for the New York Tribune* (London: Penguin, 2007), 128–29; Herbert Spencer, *Social Statics* (New York; D. Appleton and Co., 1865), 13–44. Herbert Spencer was to recant these views beginning in 1892, which led Henry George to polemicize against him in *A Perplexed Philosopher* (New York: Charles L. Webster & Co., 1892). See also George R. Geiger, *The Philosophy of Henry George* (New York: Macmillan, 1933), 285–335.

16. E. F. Schumacher, *Small Is Beautiful* (New York: Harper and Row, 1973), 15; Luiz C. Barbosa, "Theories in Environmental Sociology," in *Twenty Lessons in Environmental Sociology*, ed. Kenneth A. Gould and Tammy Lewis (Oxford: Oxford University Press, 2009), 28; Mathew Humphrey, *Preservation Versus the People?* (Oxford: Oxford University Press, 2002), 131–41.

17. Jean-Paul Deléage, "Eco-Marxist Critique of Political Economy," in *Is Capitalism Sustainable?*, ed. Martin O'Connor (New York: Guilford, 1994), 48; David Harvey, "Commentary" in Utsa Patnaik and Prabhat Patnaik, *A Theory of Imperialism* (New York: Columbia University Press, 2017), 162, emphasis added to the quote; David Harvey, *Marx, Capital, and the Madness of Economic Reason* (Oxford: Oxford University Press, 2018), 94.

18. Thomas Robert Malthus, *Pamphlets* (New York: Augustus M. Kelley, 1970), 185; Ricardo, *Principles of Political Economy*, 76, 287; Paul Burkett, "Nature's 'Free Gifts' and the Ecological Significance of Value," *Capital and Class* 68 (1999): 89–110; Burkett, *Marxism and Ecological Economics* (Chicago: Haymarket, 2006), 25–27, 31, 36.

19. Marx and Engels, *Collected Works* (New York: International Publishers, 1975), vol. 37, 732–33; vol. 34, 74, 156–59.

20. Campbell McConnell, *Economics* (New York: McGraw Hill, 1987), 20, 672; Alfred Marshall, *Principles of Economics* (London: Macmillan, 1895), chap. 2.

21. Nick Hanley, Jason F. Shogren, and Ben White, *Introduction to Environmental Economics* (Oxford: Oxford University Press, 2001), 135.

22. Karl Marx, *Critique of the Gotha Programme* (New York: International Publishers, 1938), 3; Marx, *Capital*, vol. 1, 134.

23. Paul Burkett, *Marx and Nature* (New York: St. Martin's Press, 1999), 99.

24. Karl Marx, *Critique of the Gotha Programme*, 3; Marx, *Capital*, vol. 1, 133–34, 381, 751–52; Burkett, *Marx and Nature*, 99.

25. On Marx's use of the vampire metaphor, see Mark Neocleous, "The Political Economy of the Dead: Marx's Vampires," *History of Political Thought* 24/4 (Winter 2003): 668–84.

26. Carl Menger, *Principles of Political Economy* (Auburn, AL: Ludwig von Mises Institute, 2007), 110–11. For related views see Eugen

Böhm–Bawerk, *Capital and Interest* (South Holland, IL.: Libertarian Press, 1959), 127–34.

27. Henry George, *Progress and Poverty* (New York: Modern Library, no copyright, published 1879), 39–40.

28. Henry George, *Complete Works* (New York: Doubleday, 1904), vol. 6, 121–28, 158, 212–25, 242, 272–76, 292; George, *A Perplexed Philosopher*, 51–61; Marx, *Capital*, vol. 1, 323.

29. Thorstein Veblen, *Absentee Ownership* (New York: Augustus M. Kelley, 1923), 168–70.

30. Frederick Soddy, *Wealth, Virtual Wealth, and Debt* (London: Allen and Unwin, 1933), 73–74.

31. Frederick Soddy, *Cartesian Economics* (London: Hendersons, 1922), 15–16; Soddy, *Matter and Energy* (New York: Henry Holt and Co., 1912), 34–36.

32. Soddy, *Wealth, Virtual Wealth, and Debt*, 63–64.

33. K. William Kapp, *The Social Costs of Private Enterprise* (New York: Schocken, 1971), 8, 29, 34–36, 231.

34. Herman E. Daly, "The Return of the Lauderdale Paradox," *Ecological Economics* 25 (1998): 21–23; Daly, *Ecological Economics and Sustainable Development* (Cheltenham, UK: Edward Elgar, 2007), 105–06; Herman E. Daly and John B. Cobb Jr., *For the Common Good* (Boston: Beacon Press, 1994), 147–48.

35. Nordhaus quoted in Leslie Roberts, "Academy Panel Split on Greenhouse Adaptation," *Science* 253 (September 13, 1991): 106; Wilfred Beckerman, *Small Is Stupid* (London: Duckworth, 1995), 91; Beckerman, "The Environment as a Commodity," *Nature* 357 (June 4, 1992): 371–72; Thomas C. Shelling, "The Cost of Combating Global Warming," *Foreign Affairs* (November–December 1997): 8–9; Daly, *Ecological Economics and Sustainable Development*, 188–90.

36. Fred Magdoff and Brian Tokar, "Agriculture and Food in Crisis," *Monthly Review* 61/3 (July–August 2009), 1–3; Food Security Information Network, *Global Report on Food Crises 2019* (2019), 1, http://www.fsincop.net.

37. William D. Nordhaus, "Reflections on the Economics of Climate Change," *Journal of Economic Perspectives* 7/4 (Fall 1993): 22–23: Hickel, "The Nobel Prize for Climate Catastrophe." On the role that discounting played in Nordhaus's systematic downplaying of the economic effects of climate change, see John Bellamy Foster, Brett Clark, and Richard York, *The Ecological Rift* (New York: Monthly Review Press, 2010), 95–98.

38. The argument that such a feedback mechanism exists is known in Marxist ecological analysis as the "second contradiction of capitalism."

See James O'Connor, *Natural Causes* (New York: Guilford Press, 1998). For a critique see Foster, *The Ecological Revolution*, 201–12.

39.   Maude Barlow and Tony Clarke, *Blue Gold* (New York: New Press, 2002), 88, 93, 105; United Nations, "Water Scarcity," http://www.unwater.org/water–facts/scarcity/.

40.   Fred Magdoff, "World Food Crisis," *Monthly Review* 60/1 (May 2008): 1–15.

41.   Lauderdale, *Inquiry into the Nature and Origin of Public Wealth*, 41–42.

42.   On green accounting, see Andrew John Brennan, "Theoretical Foundations of Sustainable Economic Welfare Indicators," *Ecological Economics* 67 (2008): 1–19; Daly and Cobb, *For the Common Good*, 443–507.

43.   Burkett, *Marx and Nature*, 82–84.

44.   Marx, *A Contribution to a Critique of Political Economy*, 36; Marx, *Capital*, vol. 1, 638.

7. The Meaning of Work in a Sustainable Socialist Society

This chapter was first published online as John Bellamy Foster, "The Meaning of Work in a Sustainable Society: A Marxian View," Centre for the Understanding of Sustainable Prosperity, University of Surrey, UK, March 2017, and appeared in revised form in *Monthly Review* 69/4 (September 2017): 1–14. It has been adapted and revised for this book.

1.   This essay is dedicated to Harry Magdoff, and was inspired by his article "The Meaning of Work," *Monthly Review* 34/5 (October 1982): 1–15.

2.   For an important book on ecological-economic sustainability that nevertheless devotes only a small portion of its analysis to the subject of work, see Tim Jackson, *Prosperity Without Growth* (London: Earthscan, 2011).

3.   See André Gorz, *Paths to Paradise* (London: Pluto, 1985); Serge Latouche, *Farewell to Growth* (Cambridge, UK: Polity, 2009). First-stage ecosocialist thinkers like Gorz tried to combine Green analysis and socialist theory, with the former often preempting the latter. In contrast, second-stage ecosocialists or ecological Marxists have sought to build on the ecological foundations of classical historical materialism. On this distinction, see John Bellamy Foster and Paul Burkett, *Marx and the Earth* (Boston: Brill, 2016), 1–11.

4.   Adriano Tilgher, *Homo Faber* (Chicago: Regnery, 1958), 3–10; Aristotle, *The Politics* (Oxford: Oxford University Press, 1958).

5.   Adam Smith, *The Wealth of Nations* (New York: Modern Library, 1937), 30–33.

6.   Anonymous author quoted in Paul Lafargue, "The Right to Be Lazy"

(1883), chap. 2, available at http://marxists.org; Karl Marx, *Capital*, vol. 1 (London: Penguin, 1976), 685, 789, 897.

7. David A. Spencer, *The Political Economy of Work* (London: Routledge, 2009), 70.

8. Steffen Rätzel, "Revisiting the Neoclassical Theory of Labor Supply—Disutility of Labor, Working Hours, and Happiness," Otto von Guericke University Magdeburg, Faculty of Economics and Management, Paper No. 5, 2, http://uni-magdeburg.de. Emphasis added.

9. Rätzel, in the study cited above, demonstrates that even under current conditions, work is not simply a disutility but a basis for human happiness. It seems obvious that this would be even more the case in non-alienated work environments.

10. Benjamin Farrington, *Head and Hand in Ancient Greece* (London: Watts, 1947), 1–9, 28–29. See also Ellen Meiksins Wood, *Peasant-Citizen and Slave* (London: Verso, 1998), 134–45.

11. See Foster and Burkett, *Marx and the Earth*, 65. The views of Greek society on work were deeply affected by the existence of slavery. However, this had a greater impact on the aristocracy, which was heavily dependent on slave labor, than the *demos*, with its bases in free citizens, consisting mainly of artisans and peasants. These class distinctions within the *polis* were reflected in the divisions between idealist and materialist views. See Elllen Meiksins Wood and Neal Wood, *Class Ideology and Ancient Political Theory* (Oxford: Oxford University Press, 1978).

12. Karl Marx, *Grundrisse* (London: Penguin, 1973), 611–12. Marx was here referring to the same passage from Smith quoted above.

13. Karl Marx, *Early Writings* (London: Penguin, 1974), 322–34.

14. Joseph Fracchia, "Organisms and Objectifications: A Historical-Materialist Inquiry Into the 'Human and Animal.'" *Monthly Review* 68/10 (March 2017): 1–16.

15. Erich Fromm, "Introduction," in Edward Bellamy, *Looking Backward* (New York: New American Library, 1960), v. The first volume of *Capital* was only translated into English in 1886 and thus was treated as a work of the previous half–century.

16. Bellamy, *Looking Backward*; Magdoff, "The Meaning of Work," 1–2.

17. E. P. Thompson, *William Morris, Romantic to Revolutionary* (New York: Pantheon, 1976), 792. For an excellent study of Morris's conception of work, see Phil Katz, *Thinking Hands: The Power of Labour in William Morris* (London: Heatherington, 2005).

18. William Morris, *News from Nowhere* (Oxford: Oxford University Press), 79; William Morris and Ernest Belfort Bax, *Socialism: Its Growth and Outcome* (London: Sonnenschein, 1893), 215; Jonathan Beecher, *Charles Fourier* (Berkeley: University of California Press, 1986), 274–96.

19. Thompson, *William Morris*, 35–37; John Ruskin, *The Stones of Venice*, vol. 2 (New York: Collier, 1900), 163–65.

20. William Morris, *Collected Works* (New York: Longmans, Green, 1910), vol. 23, 173; Morris, *News from Nowhere and Selected Writings and Designs* (London: Penguin, 1962), 140–43; Morris, *Signs of Change* (London: Longmans, Green, 1896), 119.

21. May Morris, ed., *William Morris: Artist, Writer, Socialist*, vol. 2 (Cambridge: Cambridge University Press, 1936), 478–79; William Morris, *Signs of Change*, 17.

22. Mark Strauss, "Ten Inventions that Inadvertently Transformed Warfare," *Smithsonian*, September 18, 2010, http://smithsonianmag.com; John Bellamy Foster, Hannah Holleman, and Robert W. McChesney, "The U.S. Imperial Triangle and Military Spending," *Monthly Review* 60/5 (October 2008): 1–19; Brian Wang, "US Defense Spending Will Surge Past $1 Trillion a Year and Get Surprising Little," *Next Big Future*, September 28, 2018, www.nextbigfuture.com.

23. Fred Magdoff and John Bellamy Foster, *What Every Environmentalist Needs to Know About Capitalism* (New York: Monthly Review Press, 2011), 46–53.

24. On Marx's analysis of food adulteration in nineteenth-century England, which undoubtedly influenced Morris, see chapter 4 in this book. For a discussion regarding the penetration of the sales effort into production, see Thorstein Veblen, *Absentee Ownership and Business Enterprise in Modern Times* (New York: Augustus M. Kelley, 1923), 24–325; Paul A. Baran and Paul M. Sweezy, *Monopoly Capital* (New York: Monthly Review Press, 1966), 112–41; chapter 10 in this book.

25. The critique of economic and ecological waste and its theorization in terms of the social reproduction have long been central to Marxian political economy, including concepts of specifically capitalist use value and negative use value. See for example Baran and Sweezy, *Monopoly Capital*; Michael Kidron, *Capitalism and Theory* (London: Pluto, 1974); John Bellamy Foster, "The Ecology of Marxian Political Economy" *Monthly Review* 63/4 (September 2011): 1–16. These analyses frame waste not in ethical but rather in economic and ecological terms, as criteria of social reproduction. A nuclear weapon, for example, is a dead end, with no direct contribution to social reproduction.

26. Morris, *Signs of Change*, 148–49.

27. Marx, *Capital*, vol. 1, 799; William Morris, "Art and Its Producers," in *Art and Its Producers and the Arts and Crafts To-day* (London: Longmans, 1901), 9–10.

28. Morris, "Art and Its Producers," 9–10. The suspension points, meant to indicate a pause, are Morris's own.

29. William Morris, *Political Writings* (Bristol: Thoemmes 1994), 419–25.

30. The dates provided in the text leave matters somewhat uncertain. Morris changed some of the dates in the serialized version in *Commonweal*, pushing events further into the future. For example, the bridge, mentioned in chapter 2, is said to have been built in 1971 in the *Commonweal* version, though in the book it dates to 2003. Following here the dates in the 1891 edition, the Great Change occurs during the early 1950s. The civil war begins in 1952, and appears to be over by the time of the "clearing of houses" in 1955. William Guest is informed early in the text that the bridge built in 2003 was "not very old" by historical standards. Hammond later refers to the new epoch as having lasted for around 150 years, which would presumably place it in the early 2100s. A more oblique reference to "two hundred years ago" would seem to refer to the time since the end of the nineteenth or the beginning of the twentieth century. Morris, *News from Nowhere*, 8, 14, 46, 69, 94, 184.

31. Ibid., 40, 78–85, 140, 153–55.

32. Luc Boltanski and Éve Chiapello, *The New Spirit of Capitalism* (London: Verso, 2005), 38, 466–67, 535–36. On the historical contradictions of Fordist and post-Fordist thought, see John Bellamy Foster, "The Fetish of Fordism," *Monthly Review* 39/10 (March 1988), 1–13.

33. Morris, *News from Nowhere*, 148–51. Morris's feminist intent here is evident in the name Philippa, a clear tribute to his contemporary Philippa Fawcett, an extremely gifted mathematician and advocate for women's equality, whom Morris much admired. William Morris, *We Met Morris: Interviews with William Morris, 1895–96* (Reading, UK: Spire, 2005), 93–95. As a complex mimetic work of art, Morris's utopian romance depicts a society that has undergone a great change and is still changing—a mimesis that reflects not only on the prehistory of capitalism but also the past, present, and future potential of Nowhere. This is clearest in Morris's treatment of gender.

34. Morris, *News from Nowhere*, 154; Marx, *Capital*, vol. 3 (London: Penguin, 1981), 911.

35. See Morris, *News from Nowhere*, 59; John Bruce Glasier, *William Morris and the Early Days of the Socialist Movement* (London: Longmans, Green, 1921), 76, 81–82.

36. Thompson, *William Morris*, 37–38; Marx, *Capital*, vol. 1, 481.

37. Ruskin, *The Stones of Venice*, vol. 2, 163; Thompson, *William Morris*, 37–38.

38. Harry Braverman, *Labor and Monopoly Capital* (New York: Monthly Review Press, 1998), 320.

39. Ibid., 320.

40. Ibid., 8–11. Beginning in the 1930s, human relations psychology was introduced into management, ostensibly to make labor more pleasurable and less alienating, though this did not involve a fundamental shift away from the objective degradation of work itself. Braverman addresses this in a chapter titled "The Habituation of the Worker to the Capitalist Mode of Production."

41. Many progressive visions of the future substitute a kind of technological determinism for human agency. See for example the arguments in Paul Mason, *Postcapitalism* (London: Penguin, 2015).

42. Latouche, *Farewell to Growth*, 81–88.

43. Gorz, *Paths to Paradise*, 29–40, 53, 67, 117; Herbert Applebaum, *The Concept of Work* (Albany: State University of New York Press, 1992), 561–65. It might be argued that Gorz's analysis of work in his later, *Capitalism, Socialism, Ecology* is more nuanced. But in his later work, Gorz adopts the notion that the classical conception of work is one of "pain, annoyance and fatigue," and that the notion of work as part of the creative process was a nineteenth-century invention of the workers' movement. He states: "The ideology of work, which argues that 'work is life' and demands that it be taken seriously and treated as a vocation, and the attendant utopia of a society ruled by the associated producers [Marx's conception], play right into the hands of the employers, consolidate capitalist relations of production and domination, and legitimate the privileges of a work elite." See Gorz, *Capitalism, Socialism, Ecology* (London: Verso, 1994), 53, 56.

44. Derek Thompson, "A World Without Work," *Atlantic*, July–August 2015.

45. Robert W. McChesney and John Nichols, *People Get Ready* (New York: Nation Books, 2016), 96–114.

46. Kurt Vonnegut Jr., *Player Piano* (New York: Simon and Schuster, 1952).

47. Marx, *Early Writings*, 327–29.

48. Brad Inwood and L. P. Gerson, eds., *The Epicurus Reader* (Indianapolis: Hackett, 1994), 37.

8. Marx's Ecology and the Left

This chapter is adapted and revised for this book from John Bellamy Foster and Brett Clark, "Marx's Ecology and the Left," *Monthly Review* 69/2 (June 2016): 1–25, which was an extensively revised version of their earlier "Marx's Universal Metabolism of Nature and the Frankfurt School," a chapter in *Changing Our Environment, Changing Ourselves*, ed. James Ormrod (London: Palgrave Macmillan, 2016), 101–35 (a *festschrift* for Peter Dickens).

1. Russell Jacoby, "Western Marxism," in *A Dictionary of Marxist Thought*,

ed. Tom Bottomore (Oxford: Blackwell, 1983); Fredric Jameson, *Valences of the Dialectic* (London: Verso, 2009), 6–7; John Bellamy Foster, Brett Clark, and Richard York, *The Ecological Rift* (New York: Monthly Review Press, 2010), 215–25.

2. Noel Castree, "Marxism and the Production of Nature," *Capital and Class* 72 (2000): 5–36; Neil Smith, *Uneven Development* (Athens: University of Georgia Press, 2008).

3. Paul Burkett, "Nature in Marx Reconsidered," *Organization & Environment* 10/2 (1997): 164.

4. Alfred Schmidt, *The Concept of Nature in Marx* (London: New Left Books, 1970), 9.

5. Smith, *Uneven Development*, 31–32.

6. Max Horkheimer and Theodor W. Adorno, *The Dialectic of Enlightenment* (New York: Continuum, 1972).

7. Ibid., 224.

8. Schmidt, *The Concept of Nature in Marx*, 154–55. The idea of a "reconciliation" of nature and humanity was a constant theme of the Frankfurt School. In practice, however, it took the form of negative criticisms of various ways of reconciling nature with humanity and society. See Martin Jay, *The Dialectical Imagination* (New York: Little, Brown, 1973), 267–73.

9. Frederick Engels, "Dialectics of Nature," in Karl Marx and Frederick Engels, *Collected Works* (New York: International Publishers, 1975), vol. 25, 460–64; Schmidt, *The Concept of Nature in Marx*, 155–56, 160.

10. References here to the Frankfurt School's critique of the "dialectic of the Enlightenment" (and of Marx and nature) relate primarily to Schmidt, as well as to Horkheimer and Adorno. It excludes most notably—unless otherwise indicated—Herbert Marcuse, who, though reflecting some of the same tendencies, was to respond affirmatively and dialectically to the growth of environmentalism in the 1970s.

11. On Schmidt's criticisms of Bloch and Brecht, see Schmidt, *The Concept of Nature in Marx*, 124–28, 154–63. See also Bertolt Brecht, *Tales from the Calendar* (London: Methuen, 1966); Ernst Bloch, *The Principle of Hope*, vol. 1 (Cambridge, MA: MIT Press, 1986).

12. The first of the two polemical attacks was directly referred to by Schmidt. The second was not noted by Schmidt himself and was simply a product of his strict adherence to Western Marxism's criticism of dialectical materialism. Schmidt, *The Concept of Nature in Marx*, 9.

13. Schmidt recognizes the philosophical significance of Marx's view of nature as the ultimate source of all wealth, without realizing its importance to Marx's political-economic and ecological critique. Schmidt, *The Concept of Nature in Marx*, 77–78. On Marx's value theory

and ecological critique, see Foster, Clark, and York, *The Ecological Rift*, 53–64.

14. Schmidt, *The Concept of Nature in Marx*, 76, 80, 88–90.

15. Ibid., 15, 59, 63–64, 90, 98, 139, 157, 162.

16. Ibid., 139.

17. Theodor W. Adorno, *Negative Dialectics* (New York: Continuum, 1973), 244.

18. John Bellamy Foster and Hannah Holleman, "Weber and the Environment," *American Journal of Sociology* 117/6 (2012): 1660–62.

19. Horkheimer quoted in William Leiss, *The Domination of Nature* (Boston: Beacon, 1974), 154.

20. Max Horkheimer, *The Eclipse of Reason* (New York: Continuum, 1974), 123–27.

21. See Herbert Marcuse, *Counterrevolution and Revolt* (Boston: Beacon, 1972), 59–78; Marcuse, *The Aesthetic Dimension* (Boston: Beacon, 1978), 16.

22. Schmidt, *The Concept of Nature in Marx*, 154.

23. Ibid., 156; see also Jay, *The Dialectical Imagination*, 259, 347.

24. "Western Marxism" arose as a specific tradition in the West, defined in part by its rejection of the dialectics of nature. See Jacoby, "Western Marxism," 523–26.

25. Leiss, *Domination of Nature*, 217.

26. Smith, *Uneven Development*, 44.

27. Burkett, "Nature in Marx Reconsidered," 173.

28. Schmidt, *The Concept of Nature in Marx*, 78–79.

29. Karl Marx, *Capital*, vol. 1 (New York: Vintage, 1976), 637.

30. Schmidt, *The Concept of Nature in Marx*, 11.

31. Ibid., 88.

32. Marx took his wider ecological notion of metabolism initially from the work of his friend the physician Roland Daniels, who may have been the first to point toward a larger ecosystemic perspective. See Roland Daniels, *Mikrokosmos* (New York: Peter Lang, 1988), 49. (Kohei Saito first brought this to our attention in personal correspondence. We are also grateful to Joseph Fracchia for his translations from the German in this regard.) Later Justus von Liebig's analysis of the soil problem, in which he incorporated the metabolism concept, proved decisive for Marx. See the discussion in John Bellamy Foster, *Marx's Ecology* (New York: Monthly Review Press, 2000), 147–54; Kohei Saito, "The Emergence of Marx's Critique of Modern Agriculture: Ecological Insights from His Excerpt Notebooks," *Monthly Review* 66/5 (October 2014): 25–46. Despite Schmidt's claim that Marx took his analysis of metabolism from Jacob Moleschott, there is no evidence of this, though

considerable evidence suggests Marx's reliance on other thinkers. See Schmidt, *The Concept of Nature in Marx*, 86–88.

33. Schmidt, *The Concept of Nature in Marx*, 11, 76, 90, 176. Reiner Grundmann considered Marx's metabolism argument the strongest of the three approaches to ecological questions, the first being "capitalist production as a cause of ecological problems," and the second the alienation of nature. Yet Grundmann, like Schmidt, interpreted Marx's metabolism argument in simple instrumentalist-mechanistic terms, thereby losing sight of its complexity and missing the importance of Marx's theory of ecological crisis. See Reiner Grundmann, *Marxism and Ecology* (Oxford: Oxford University Press, 1991), 90–98, 121–22.

34. See Ted Benton, ed., *The Greening of Marxism* (New York: Guilford, 1996); Mark J. Smith, *Ecologism* (Minneapolis: University of Minnesota Press, 1998), 71–73.

35. Eric J. Hobsbawm, Preface, in *J.D. Bernal*, ed. Brenda Swann and Francis Aprahamian (London: Verso, 1999), xix.

36. On the appropriation problem, see John Bellamy Foster, "Marx's Theory of Metabolic Rift," *American Journal of Sociology* 105/2 (1999): 391–96.

37. Perry Anderson, *In the Tracks of Historical Materialism* (London: Verso, 1983), 83.

38. Russell Jacoby sees the split that occurred in Marxism in terms of their distinct appropriations of Hegel. "Soviet Marxism," he wrote, "was regularly sustained by a scientific Hegel, and European Marxism was regularly sustained by a historical Hegel." See Jacoby, *The Dialectic of Defeat* (Cambridge: Cambridge University Press, 1981), 57–58.

39. Ted Benton, "Marxism and Natural Limits," *New Left Review* 178 (1989): 55, 60, 64.

40. André Gorz, *Capitalism, Socialism, Ecology* (London: Verso, 1994), vii–9, 29, 100; Gorz, *Ecology as Politics* (London: Pluto, 1983).

41. James O'Connor, *Natural Causes* (New York: Guilford Press, 1998), 160.

42. Alain Lipietz, "Political Ecology and the Future of Marxism," *Capitalism Nature Socialism* 11/1 (2000): 74–75.

43. Michael Redclift, *Development and the Environmental Crisis* (New York: Methuen, 1984), 7.

44. Karl Marx, *Capital*, vol. 3 (New York: International Publishers, 1967), 745; see also Paul Burkett, "Nature's 'Free Gifts' and the Ecological Significance of Value," *Capital and Class* 23 (1999): 89–110; Burkett, "Nature in Marx Reconsidered," 173–74.

45. Ted Benton, "Introduction to Part Two," in Benton, ed., *The Greening of Marxism*, 103–10.

46. Castree, "Marxism and the Production of Nature," 27–28.
47. Ibid., 28; Noel Castree, "Marxism, Capitalism, and the Production of Nature," in *Social Nature*, ed. Noel Castree and Bruce Braun (Malden, MA: Blackwell, 2001), 204–5.
48. Castree points to these contradictions in Smith's analysis, while nonetheless arguing that Smith's approach to the production of nature is basically the one on which Marxian theorists should build—though in a more nuanced way.
49. Smith, *Uneven Development*, 31, 44–47, 78–91, 244–47; Neil Smith, "Nature as an Accumulation Strategy," *Socialist Register 2007* (New York: Monthly Review Press, 2006), 23–28.
50. Smith, *Uneven Development*, 31.
51. Ibid., 247.
52. Noel Castree, "The Nature of Produced Nature: Materiality and Knowledge Construction in Marxism," *Antipode* 27/1 (1995): 16–18.
53. Ibid., 17.
54. Castree, "Marxism and the Production of Nature," 9–10, 21.
55. Ibid., 8. It should be noted that since Smith and Castree had already faulted Marx for being dualistic, what ecosocialists were actually being charged with was not a misinterpretation of Marx but a failure to conform to Smith's own monistic production of nature thesis. Contrary to such views, our own assessment is that neither Marx nor his major followers were dualistic. Rather, what Smith and Castree in their mechanistic-monistic worldviews mistook for dualism was really a dialectical analysis of the interpenetration of opposites.
56. Castree, "Marxism and the Production of Nature," 17.
57. Ibid., 13–15; Castree, "The Nature of Produced Nature," 20–21, 24. Castree refers abstractly here to the "materiality of nature" but denies its "externality" or "universality," which he characterizes as "essentialist."
58. Castree, "Marxism and the Production of Nature," 17; Jason W. Moore, *Capitalism in the Web of Life* (London: Verso, 2015), 46, 80–86.
59. See William R. Catton Jr. and Riley E. Dunlap, "Environmental Sociology: A New Paradigm," *American Sociologist* 13 (1978): 41–49; John Bellamy Foster, "The Planetary Rift and the New Human Exemptionalism," *Organization & Environment* 25/3 (2012): 1–27.
60. Noel Castree, "Capitalism and the Marxist Critique of Political Ecology," in *The Routledge Handbook of Political Ecology*, ed. Tom Perreault, Gavin Bridge, and James McCarthy (London: Routledge, 2015), 291; Michael Shellenberger and Ted Nordhaus, *Break Through* (New York: Houghton Mifflin, 2007).
61. Castree, "Capitalism and the Marxist Critique of Political Ecology," 291.

62. In his more recent work, Castree relies heavily on the analysis of the French philosopher and sociologist of science Bruno Latour, a senior fellow of the Breakthrough Institute.

63. Karl Marx and Frederick Engels, *Collected Works*, vol. 30, 54–66; Karl Marx, *Capital*, vol. 3 (London: Penguin, 1991), 949.

64. Peter Dickens, *Society and Nature: Towards a Green Social Theory* (Philadelphia: Temple University Press, 1992), 80; see also 76–81, 175–95, for the broader discussions noted above.

65. Paul Burkett, *Marx and Nature* (New York: St. Martin's Press, 1999), 8–9.

66. Ibid., 9.

67. Foster, *Marx's Ecology*.

68. Ibid.; Foster, Clark, and York, *The Ecological Rift*.

69. Marina Fischer-Kowalski, "Society's Metabolism: The Intellectual History of Material Flow Analysis, Part I, 1860–1970," *Journal of Industrial Ecology* 2/1 (1998): 62.

70. Saito, "The Emergence of Marx's Critique of Modern Agriculture."

71. Justus von Liebig, *Letters on Modern Agriculture* (London: Walton and Maberly, 1859), 175–83, 220; Saito, "The Emergence of Marx's Critique of Modern Agriculture"; Foster, *Marx's Ecology*, 160–62.

72. Karl Marx, *Texts on Method* (Oxford: Blackwell, 1975), 209; see also Karl Marx and Frederick Engels, *Collected Works*, vol. 24, 553.

73. Karl Marx, *Economic and Philosophic Manuscripts of 1844* (New York: International Publishers, 1964), 109.

74. Marx, *Capital*, vol. 1, 286–87.

75. Ibid., 283.

76. John Bellamy Foster, "Marx and the Rift in the Universal Metabolism of Nature," *Monthly Review* 65/7 (December 2013): 8.

77. Marx and Engels, *Collected Works*, vol. 30, 54–66.

78. Georg Lukács, *Labour* (London: Merlin Press, 1980), 34.

79. Foster, "Marx and the Rift in the Universal Metabolism of Nature," 8.

80. Ibid., 8.

81. Foster, *Marx's Ecology*; Foster, Clark, and York, *The Ecological Rift*; István Mészáros, *Beyond Capital* (New York: Monthly Review Press, 1995).

82. Paul Sweezy, "Capitalism and the Environment," *Monthly Review* 56/5 (October 2004): 86–93.

83. Karl Marx, *The Poverty of Philosophy* (New York: International Publishers, 1971), 162–63.

84. Foster, *Marx's Ecology*; Erland Mårald, "Everything Circulates," *Environment and History* 8 (2002): 65–84; Marx, *Capital*, vol. 1.

85. Liebig, *Letters on Modern Agriculture*, 175–83, 220; Foster, *Marx's Ecology*, 149–54.
86. Marx, *Capital*, vol. 1, 637–39.
87. Ibid., 637–38.
88. Ibid.; Marx, *Capital*, vol. 3, 949.
89. Karl Marx, *Grundrisse* (New York: Penguin, 1993), 527.
90. Karl Marx, *Capital*, vol. 3 (New York: Penguin, 1991), 949.
91. Brett Clark and John Bellamy Foster, "Ecological Imperialism and the Global Metabolic Rift: Unequal Exchange and the Guano/Nitrates Trade," *International Journal of Comparative Sociology* 50/3–4 (2009): 311–34.
92. Fred Magdoff, "Ecological Civilization," *Monthly Review* 62/8 (January 2011): 1–25; Philip Mancus, "Nitrogen Fertilizer Dependency and Its Contradictions: A Theoretical Exploration of Social-Ecological Metabolism," *Rural Sociology* 72/2 (2007): 269–88.
93. Peter Dickens, *Society and Nature: Changing Our Environment, Changing Ourselves* (Cambridge: Polity, 2004), 81; John Bellamy Foster, "Marx's Theory of Metabolic Rift," *American Journal of Sociology* 105/2 (1999): 366–405.
94. Dickens, *Society and Nature: Changing Our Environment*, 84–85.
95. Del Weston, *The Political Economy of Global Warming* (New York: Routledge, 2014), 66.
96. Kelly Austin and Brett Clark, "Tearing Down Mountains: Using Spatial and Metabolic Analysis to Investigate the Socio-Ecological Contradictions of Coal Extraction in Appalachia," *Critical Sociology* 38/3 (2012): 437–57; Brett Clark and Richard York, "Carbon Metabolism: Global Capitalism, Climate Change, and the Biospheric Rift," *Theory and Society* 34/4 (2005): 391–428; Rebecca Clausen and Brett Clark, "The Metabolic Rift and Marine Ecology: An Analysis of the Oceanic Crisis within Capitalist Production," *Organization & Environment* 18/4 (2005): 422–44; Matthew T. Clement, "A Basic Accounting of Variation in Municipal Solid-Waste Generation at the County Level in Texas, 2006: Groundwork for Applying Metabolic-Rift Theory to Waste Generation," *Rural Sociology* 74/3 (2009): 412–29; Ryan Gunderson, "The Metabolic Rifts of Livestock Agribusiness," *Organization & Environment* 24/4 (2001): 404–22; Stefano B. Longo, "Mediterranean Rift: Socio-Ecological Transformations in the Sicilian Bluefin Tuna Fishery," *Critical Sociology* 38/3 (2012): 417–36; Stefano B. Longo, Rebecca Clausen, and Brett Clark, *The Tragedy of the Commodity* (New Brunswick: Rutgers University Press, 2015); Daniel Auerbach and Brett Clark, "Metabolic Rifts, Temporal Imperatives, and Geographical Shifts: Logging in the Adirondack Forest in the 1800s,"

International Critical Thought 8/3 (2018): 468-486; Fred Magdoff, "Ecological Civilization"; Mancus, "Nitrogen Fertilizer."

97. Pamela Odih, *Watersheds in Marxist Ecofeminism* (Newcastle upon Tyne, UK: Cambridge Scholars, 2014); Ariel Salleh, "From Eco-Sufficiency to Global Justice" in Salleh, *Eco-Sufficiency and Global Justice* (London: Pluto, 2009), 291-312.

98. Paul Burkett, *Marxism and Ecological Economics* (Leiden: Brill, 2006); Foster, Clark, and York, *The Ecological Rift*.

99. Brett Clark and Richard York, "Rifts and Shifts," *Monthly Review* 60/6 (November 2008): 13-24; Longo, Clausen, and Clark, *The Tragedy of the Commodity*; Weston, *The Political Economy of Global Warming*; Richard York and Brett Clark, "Critical Materialism: Science, Technology, and Environmental Sustainability," *Sociological Inquiry* 80/3 (2010): 475-99; Richard York and Brett Clark, "Nothing New Under the Sun? The Old False Promise of New Technology," *Review: A Journal of the Fernand Braudel Center* 33/2-3 (2010): 203-24.

100. For an excellent elaboration of Marx's concept of "metabolic restoration," see Weston, *The Political Economy of Global Warming*, 168-78. See also Rebecca Clausen, "Healing the Rift," *Monthly Review* 59/1 (May 2007): 40-52; Rebecca Clausen, Brett Clark, and Stefano B Longo, "Metabolic Rifts and Restoration: Agricultural Crises and the Potential of Cuba's Organic, Socialist Approach to Food Production," *World Review of Political Economy* 6/1 (2015): 4-32; Fred Magdoff and John Bellamy Foster, *What Every Environmentalist Needs to Know About Capitalism* (New York: Monthly Review Press, 2010).

101. Horkheimer, *Eclipse of Reason*, 123.

102. Ibid., 105.

103. Ibid., 127.

104. Ibid., 127. On the question of what Horkheimer meant by the Nazi "revolt of nature," see Franz Josef Brüggemeier, Marc Cioc, and Thomas Zeller, eds., *How Green Were the Nazis?* (Athens: Ohio University Press, 2005).

105. Schmidt, *The Concept of Nature in Marx*, 157.

106. Ibid., 162.

107. Ibid., 162.

108. Smith, *Uneven Development*, 247.

109. Erich Fromm, *The Crisis of Psychoanalysis* (Greenwich, CT: Fawcett, 1970), 153-54. See also Nikolai Bukharin, *Historical Materialism* (New York: International Publishers, 1925).

110. Georg Lukács, *A Defence of "History and Class Consciousness": Tailism and the Dialectic* (London: Verso, 2003), 96, 106, 113-14, 130-31; Georg Lukács, *History and Class Consciousness* (London: Merlin, 1968), xvii;

Georg Lukács, *Conversations with Lukács* (Cambridge, MA: MIT Press, 1974), 43.

111. Herbert Marcuse, *The Aesthetic Dimension* (Boston: Beacon, 1978), 16.
112. Marcuse, *Counter-Revolution*, 59–60.
113. Dickens, *Society and Nature: Changing Our Environment*, 10.
114. Ibid., 80.
115. Ibid., 144.
116. Smith, "Nature as an Accumulation Strategy," 24–25.
117. Ibid., 23.
118. Smith, *Uneven Development*, 244.
119. Smith, "Nature as an Accumulation Strategy," 27–29; Smith, *Uneven Development*, 247.
120. See Moore, *Capitalism in the Web of Life*, 85–86. Moore presents a social "monist and relational" view, rooted in a metaphorical concept of "singular metabolism," and defined in terms of "bundled" society-nature relations, in which he equates capitalism and "world ecology," rejecting Marx's own theory of metabolic rift.
121. On coevolution, see Richard B. Norgaard, *Development Betrayed* (London: Routledge, 1994). On co-revolution, see David Harvey, *The Enigma of Capital* (Oxford: Oxford University Press, 2010), 228–31. On a new order of social metabolic reproduction, see Mészáros, *Beyond Capital*, 170–77.

9. Value Isn't Everything

This chapter is adapted and revised for this book from John Bellamy Foster and Paul Burkett, "Value Isn't Everything," *Monthly Review* 70/6 (November 2018): 1-17, a slightly revised version of an article with the same title published in *International Socialism* (Autumn 2018).

1. Jason W. Moore, "The Value of Everything? Work, Capital, and Historical Nature in the Capitalist World-Ecology," *Review* 37/3–4 (2014): 245, 261, 280. On natural capital, see Paul Hawken, Amory Lovins, and L. Hunter Lovins, *Natural Capitalism: Creating the Next Industrial Revolution* (Boston: Little, Brown, 1999). For a critique see John Bellamy Foster, *Ecology Against Capitalism* (New York: Monthly Review Press, 2002), 26–43. On ecosystem services, see Jason W. Moore, *Capitalism in the Web of Life* (Brooklyn: Verso, 2015), 64; Moore, "The Value of Everything?" 261; Robert Costanza et al., "The Value of the World's Ecosystem Services and Natural Capital," *Nature* 387 (1997): 253–60; Robert Costanza et al., "Changes in the Global Value of Ecosystem Services," *Global Environmental Change* 26 (2014): 152–58.

2. Zehra Taşdemir Yaşın, "The Adventure of Capital with Nature: From the Metabolic Rift to the Value Theory of Nature," *Journal of Peasant Studies* 44/2 (2017): 377–401; Giorgos Kallis and Erik Swyngedouw, "Do Bees Produce Value? A Conversation Between an Ecological Economist and a Marxist Geographer," *Capitalism Nature Socialism* 29/3 (2018): 36–50; Dinesh Wadiwel, "Chicken Harvesting Machine: Animal Labor, Resistance, and the Time of Production," *South Atlantic Quarterly* 117/3 (2018): 527–49; Dinesh Wadiwel, "On the Labour of Animals," Progress in Political Economy blog, August 28, 2018, http://ppesydney.net. For an older argument on this topic, see Stephen Bunker, *Underdeveloping the Amazon: Extraction, Unequal Exchange, and the Failure of the Modern State* (Champaign: University of Illinois Press, 1985).

3. Moore, "The Value of Everything?," 250, 280. For a criticism of Moore's views in this respect, see Jean Parker, "Ecology and Value Theory," *International Socialism* 153 (2017).

4. Moore, *Capitalism in the Web of Life*, 70; Moore, "The Value of Everything?" 245, 267; Jason W. Moore, "Value in the Web of Life, or, Why World History Matters to Geography," *Dialogues in Human Geography* 7/3 (2017), 327–28; Jason W. Moore and Raj Patel, *A History of the World in Seven Cheap Things: A Guide to Capitalism, Nature, and the Future of the Planet* (Oakland: University of California Press, 2017).

5. Ernst F. Schumacher, *Small Is Beautiful: A Study of Economics as if People Mattered* (London: Blond & Briggs,1973), 15.

6. Moishe Postone, *Time, Labor, and Social Domination: A Reinterpretation of Marx's Critical Theory* (Cambridge: Cambridge University Press, 1993), 27.

7. Karl Marx, "The Value-Form," *Capital & Class* no. 4 (1978): 134.

8. Karl Marx, *Capital*, vol. 1, (London: Penguin, 1976), 133.

9. Karl Marx, *Critique of the Gotha Programme*, 1875, available at http:// marxists.org.

10. Jason W. Moore, "The Capitalocene, Part II: Abstract Social Nature and the Limits to Capital," Research Gate (June 2014): 29, http:// researchgate.net.

11. Marx, "The Value-Form," 134; Karl Marx, *A Contribution to the Critique of Political Economy*, 1859, available at http:// marxists.org; Isaak Illich Rubin, *Essays on Marx's Theory of Value*, (1928; repr. Detroit: Black and Red, 1972), 131–58.

12. Wadiwel, "Chicken Harvesting Machine"; Wadiwel, "On the Labour of Animals."

13. Kallis, in Kallis and Swyngedouw, "Do Bees Produce Value?" 36, 39, 44, 47, 49. Kallis was influenced by Moore in developing his argument

that fossil fuels and energy in general create value. See Giorgos Kallis, "Socialism Without Growth," *Capitalism Nature Socialism* 30/2 (2019): 189–206.

14. Yaşın, "The Adventure of Capital with Nature," 378, 394; Marx, *A Contribution to the Critique of Political Economy*, 36.
15. Marx, *A Contribution to the Critique of Political Economy*, 35–36.
16. Yaşın, "The Adventure of Capital with Nature," 378, 389.
17. Ibid., 389–92; Bunker, *Underdeveloping the Amazon*, 20–47.
18. Yaşın, "The Adventure of Capital with Nature," 387, 392.
19. Ibid., 378.
20. Ibid., 397–398.
21. Jean-Paul Sartre, *Search for a Method* (New York: Knopf, 1963), 7.
22. Paul Burkett, *Marxism and Ecological Economics: Toward a Red and Green Political Economy* (Leiden: Brill, 2006), 23–37.
23. Karl Marx, *Theories of Surplus Value*, part 1, (1863; repr. Moscow: Progress, 1969), 60.
24. The following discussion of Sieber draws on John Bellamy Foster and Paul Burkett, *Marx and the Earth: An Anti-Critique* (Leiden: Brill, 2016), 107–10.
25. On Sieber's Marxian economics and his critique of Ricardian theory, see Nikolai Sieber, "Marx's Theory of Value and Money," 1871, repr. *Research in Political Economy* 19 (2001).
26. Karl Rössler, quoted in James D. White, "Nikolai Sieber and Karl Marx," *Research in Political Economy* 19 (2001), 5–6.
27. Karl Marx, "Iz chernovoi tetradi K. Marks," *Letopisi Marksizma* 4 (1927): 61, quoted in White, "Nikolai Sieber and Karl Marx," 6.
28. White, "Nikolai Sieber and Karl Marx," 6–7.
29. Boris N. Chicherin, *Liberty, Equality, and the Market* (New Haven: Yale University Press, 1998), 325.
30. Sieber as quoted in White, "Nikolai Sieber and Karl Marx," 8.
31. Rubin, *Essays on Marx's Theory of Value*, 131–58. The very possibility of abstract labor requires, of course, that physiological labor first be given a social expression of equalization or quid pro quo. Abstract labor and value are, however, divorced from any physiological elements. As Roman Rosdolsky writes in *The Making of Marx's "Capital"*: "Physiological labour is not yet economic labour" (London: Pluto, 1977), 513.
32. Marx, *Capital*, vol. 1, 133.
33. Rubin, *Essays on Marx's Theory of Value*, 153; Marx quoted on "homogenous human labor" in Rubin, *Essays on Marx's Theory of Value*, 148 (quote from original German edition of *Capital*, vol. 1).
34. Marx, *Capital*, vol. 1, 138.
35. Rubin, *Essays on Marx's Theory of Value*, 136–37.

36. For a full discussion of the Marx-Podolinsky relation, on which the treatment here is based, see Foster and Burkett, *Marx and the Earth*, 89–136.

37. Karl Marx and Fredrick Engels, *Collected Works* (New York: International, 1975), vol. 46, 410–11.

38. Sergei Podolinsky, "Human Labour and the Unity of Force," appendix to Foster and Burkett, *Marx and the Earth*, 281–82; Foster and Burkett, *Marx and the Earth*, 110–17.

39. Karl Marx and Fredrick Engels, *Collected Works*, vol. 25, 586–87.

40. Nicholas Georgescu-Roegen, "The Entropy Law and the Economic Process in Retrospect," *Eastern Economic Journal* 12/1 (1986): 8–9; Nicholas Georgescu-Roegen, *The Entropy Law and the Economic Process* (Cambridge, MA: Harvard University Press, 1971), 277; Joan Martinez-Alier, "Some Issues in Agrarian and Ecological Economics, in Memory of Georgescu-Roegen," *Ecological Economics* 22/3 (1997): 231; Foster and Burkett, *Marx and the Earth*, 135–36.

41. Nicholas Georgescu-Roegen, *Energy and Economic Myths: Institutional and Analytical Economic Essays* (Elmsford, NY: Pergamon, 1976), 33–35.

42. Richard Levins and Richard Lewontin, *The Dialectical Biologist* (Cambridge, MA: Harvard University Press, 1987), 288; Stephen Jay Gould in *A Glorious Accident: Understanding Our Place in the Cosmic Puzzle*, ed. Wim Kayzer (New York: W. H. Freeman, 1997), 91; Roy Bhaskar, *Dialectic: The Pulse of Freedom* (London: Verso, 1993), 49–56.

43. Kallis, "Socialism Without Growth"; Wadiwel, "Chicken Harvesting Machine"; Wadiwel, "On the Labour of Animals," 544; Yaşın, "The Adventure of Capital with Nature."

44. Jason W. Moore, "The Capitalocene, Part I: On the Nature and Origins of Our Ecological Crisis," *Journal of Peasant Studies* 44/3 (2017), 606; Moore, *Capitalism in the Web of Life*, 1–7, 19–20, 37; Yaşın, "The Adventure of Capital with Nature," 389.

45. Moore, *Capitalism in the Web of Life*, 80, 85–86. The notion of "bundled" human and extra-human nature on which Moore relies is a Latourian formulation. See Bruno Latour, *Reassembling the Social: An Introduction to Actor-Network-Theory* (Oxford: Oxford University Press, 2007), 17, 134, 139.

46. On the Latourian character of Moore's thought, see Andreas Malm, *Progress of this Storm: Nature and Society in a Warming World* (Brooklyn, NY: Verso, 2018), 177–96; John Bellamy Foster, "Marxism in the Anthropocene: Dialectical Rifts on the Left," *International Critical Thought* 6/3 (2016): 393–421.

47. Moore, "The Value of Everything?," 280.

48. Marx, *Capital*, vol. 3, 1020; Paul M. Sweezy, *The Theory of Capitalist Development: Principles of Marxian Political Economy* (New York: Monthly Review Press, 1942), 52–53.

49. Baran wrote in Paul A. Baran and Paul M. Sweezy, *The Age of Monopoly Capital: Selected Correspondence of Paul A. Baran and Paul M. Sweezy, 1949–1964* (New York: Monthly Review Press, 2017), 253.

50. Moore, "The Capitalocene, Part I," 610; Moore, *Capitalism in the Web of Life*, 51–58.

51. Although neither natural processes nor household/subsistence labor (mainly carried out by women) contribute directly to the creation of value in capitalist accounting, the two should obviously not be confused with each other. See Marilyn Waring, *Counting for Nothing: What Men Value and What Women Are Worth* (Toronto: University of Toronto Press, 1999) for a powerful critique that avoids such conflations. On Marx, social reproduction, and the expropriation of women's household labor see chapter 3 of this book.

52. Moore, *Capitalism in the Web of Life*, 54, 71.

53. Moore and Patel, *A History of the World in Seven Cheap Things*, 24–25.

54. Moore, *Capitalism in the Web of Life*, 35–36, 85.

55. Malm, *Progress of this Storm*, 179.

56. For the wider tradition in left theory in this respect, see chapter 8 of this book; Malm, *Progress of this Storm*, 2018, 23–40.

57. Graham Harman, *Bruno Latour: Reassembling the Political* (London: Pluto, 2014), 14, 18, 81.

58. Moore, *Capitalism in the Web of Life*, 2, 40–41.

59. Moore, "The Capitalocene, Part II," 29.

60. Moore, *Capitalism in the Web of Life*, 54.

61. Ibid., 71.

62. Moore, "The Value of Everything?" 261.

63. For a discussion of Marxian rent theory and ecology, see Paul Burkett, *Marx and Nature: A Red and Green Perspective* (Chicago: Haymarket, 2014), 94–103.

64. Moore, "The Value of Everything?" 262; Jason Hribal, "'Animals Are Part of the Working Class': A Challenge to Labor History," *Labor History* 44/4 (2003): 435–453.

65. Jason W. Moore, "The Rise of Cheap Nature," in *Anthropocene or Capitalocene? Nature, History, and the Crisis of Capitalism*, ed. Jason W. Moore (Oakland, CA: PM, 2016), 89; Moore, *Capitalism in the Web of Life*, 71.

66. Richard White, *The Organic Machine: The Remaking of the Columbia River* (New York: Hill and Wang, 1995), 3, 6, 108; Moore, *Capitalism in the Web of Life*, 14–15.

67. Stephen C. Farber, Robert Costanza, and Matthew A. Wilson, "Economic and Ecological Concepts for Valuing Ecosystem Services," *Ecological Economics* 41/3 (2002): 382–83; Robert Costanza, "Embodied Energy and Economic Valuation," *Science* 210/4475 (1980): 1219–24; Burkett, *Marxism and Ecological Economics*, 18–19, 38, 93.

68. John Bellamy Foster and Hannah Holleman, "A Theory of Unequal Ecological Exchange: A Marx-Odum Dialectic," *Journal of Peasant Studies* 41/2 (2014), 223–27.

69. Alf Hornborg, "Towards an Ecological Theory of Unequal Exchange: Articulating World System Theory and Ecological Economics," *Ecological Economics* 25/1 (1998): 130–32; Alf Hornborg, *The Power of the Machine: Global Inequalities of Economy, Technology, and Environment* (Lanham, MD: AltaMira, 2001), 40–43; Alf Hornborg, *Global Ecology and Unequal Exchange: Fetishism in a Zero-Sum World* (New York: Routledge, 2011), 17, 104.

70. Howard T. Odum, interview by Cynthia Barnett, 2001, transcript, Howard T. Odum Center for Wetlands Publications, Gainesville, FL, http://ufdc.ufl.edu, 37–39.

71. Moore was a younger colleague of Hornborg, as a research fellow at Lund University in Sweden in 2008–10. Hornborg has recently criticized Moore both for his posthumanism and for his residual Marxism. See Alf Hornborg, "Dithering While the Planet Burns," *Review in Anthropology* 46/1 (2017): 1-17.

72. On Moore's frequent references to Costanza see, for example, Moore, "The Value of Everything?" 261; Moore, *Capitalism in the Web of Life*, 64; Moore, "The Rise of Cheap Nature," 8; and references to Costanza et al., "The Value of the World's Ecosystem Services and Natural Capital"; Robert Costanza et al., "Sustainability or Collapse: What Can We Learn from Integrating the History of Humans and the Rest of Nature?" *Ambio* 36/7 (2007): 522–27; Costanza et al., "Changes in the Global Value of Ecosystem Services."

73. Hawken, Lovins, and Lovins, *Natural Capitalism*.

74. Marx, "The Value-Form," 134; Karl Marx, *Texts on Method*, (Hoboken, NJ: Blackwell, 1975), 212.

75. Marx, *A Contribution to the Critique of Political Economy*, 36, 45–46.

76. Karl Marx, *Capital*, vol. 3 (London: Penguin, 1981), 949.

77. Marx, *Capital*, vol. 1, 871.

78. Stefano B. Longo, Rebecca Clausen, and Brett Clark, *The Tragedy of the Commodity* (New Brunswick, NJ: Rutgers University Press, 2015).

79. Moore, *Capitalism in the Web of Life*, 86.

80. Karl Marx, *Grundrisse: Foundations of the Critique of Political Economy* (London: Penguin, 1973), 887.

81.　Marx, *Capital*, vol. 3, 959; Marx and Engels, *Collected Works*, vol. 25, 105—6.

82.　G. W. F. Hegel, *The Philosophy of Right* (Oxford: Oxford University Press, [1820] 1952), 11, 303; Karl Marx, *The Eighteenth Brumaire of Louis Bonaparte*, 1963, available at http://marxists.org. "The proverb comes from one of Aesop's fables, in which an athlete boasts of the many feats he has performed in many countries and especially of a jump he once made in Rhodes. He says that he can prove this by the testimony of eyewitnesses 'if any of the people who were present ever come here.' At this, one of the bystanders tells the athlete that he doesn't need eyewitnesses since the place where he is standing will do just as well as Rhodes itself: 'Here is Rhodes; jump here!'" T. M. Knox, Hegel, *The Philosophy of Right*, 327.

10. The Planetary Emergency, 2020–2050

This chapter is an extensively rewritten and updated version of an earlier article by John Bellamy Foster and Brett Clark, "The Planetary Emergency," *Monthly Review* 64/7 (December 2012): 1–25.

1.　John Bellamy Foster and Robert W. McChesney, *The Endless Crisis* (New York: Monthly Review Press, 2012).

2.　Karl Marx and Frederick Engels, *The Communist Manifesto* (New York: Monthly Review Press, 1964), 2.

3.　Robert Heilbroner, "Ecological Armageddon," in *Economic Growth vs. the Environment*, ed. Warren A. Johnson and John Hardesty (Belmont, CA: Wadsworth Publishing Co., 1971), 36–45.

4.　Susan Solomon et al., "Irreversible Climate Change Due to Carbon Dioxide Emissions," *Proceedings of the National Academy of Sciences* 106/6 (February 10, 2009): 1704–9; Heidi Cullen, *The Weather of the Future* (New York: Harper, 2010), 261–71; James Hansen, "Tipping Point," in *State of the Wild 2008*, ed. Eva Fearn and Kent H. Redford (Washington, D.C.: Island Press, 2008), 7–8.

5.　James Hansen, "Comments on Assertions of Pat Michaels at Grover Norquist's 'Wednesday' Meeting," September 5, 2012; http://www.columbia.edu.

6.　Will Steffen et al., "Trajectories of the Earth System in the Anthropocene," *Proceedings of the National Academy of Sciences* 115/33 (August 14, 2018): 8252–59; Myles Allen et al., "The Exit Strategy," *Nature Reports Climate Change*, April 30, 2009, 56–58; Myles Allen et al., "Warming Caused by Cumulative Carbon Emissions Towards the Trillionth Tonne," *Nature* 458 (April 20, 2009): 1163–66; Malte Meinshausen et al., "Greenhouse-Gas Emission Targets for Limiting Global Warming to 2°C," *Nature*

458 (April 30, 2009): 1158–62; Catherine Brahic, "Humanity's Carbon Budget Set at One Trillion Tons," *New Scientist*, April 29, 2009; Katherine Richardson, Will Steffen, and Diana Liberman, *Climate Change: Global Risks, Challenges, and Decisions* (Cambridge: Cambridge University Press, 2011), 212; Michael E. Mann, "Earth Will Cross the Climate Danger Threshold by 2036," *Scientific American*, April 1, 2014, scientificamerican.com; American Meteorological Society, "Heatwaves, Droughts, and Floods Among Recent Weather Extremes Linked to Climate Change," December 10, 2018, https://www.ametsoc.org/index. cfm/ams/about-ams/news/news-releases/heatwaves-droughts-and-floods-among-recent-weather-extremes-linked-to-climate-change/. An increase in global average temperature of 2°C is equivalent to a carbon dioxide concentration in the atmosphere of 450 parts per million (ppm). This would be too much for long-term stabilization of the climate, which requires no more than 350 ppm. However, keeping below the trillionth metric ton in emission is regarded as a prior constraint, since it is thought to constitute a point of no return (or irreversible planetary threshold) in terms of the possibility for effective human action. If carbon emissions could be stopped below a trillion metric tons, it is considered possible to get back down over time to 350 ppm. See http://trillionthtonne.org/ questions.html#5.

7.   Climate Central, *Global Weirdness* (New York: Pantheon Books, 2012), 165–67.

8.   See Mark Lynas, *Six Degrees* (Washington, D.C.: National Geographic, 2008).

9.   "Ending Its Summer Melt, Arctic Sea Ice Sets a New Low that Leads to Warnings," *New York Times*, September 19, 2012; "Arctic Expert Predicts Final Collapse of Sea Ice Within Four Years," *Guardian*, September 17, 2012; Carey, "Global Warming: Faster Than Expected?," 52.

10.   Intergovernmental Panel on Climate Change, *Global Warming of 1.5°C* (2018), Summary for Policymakers, 14–19; Intergovernmental Panel on Climate Change, "Mitigation Pathways Compatible with 1.5°C in the Context of Sustainable Development," 111–12; James Hansen, "Rolling Stones," January 11, 2017, *Climate Science, Awareness, and Solutions*, Earth Institute, Columbia University, http://csas.ei.columbia.edu/2017/01/11/ rolling–stones/; Nicola Jones, "How the World Passed a Carbon Threshold and Why It Matters," January 26, 2017, YaleEnvironment360, e360yale.edu; Mann, "Earth Will Cross the Climate Danger Threshold by 2036"; James Hansen and Pushker Kharecha, "Cost of Carbon Capture: Can Young People Bear the Burden?," *Joule* 2 (August 15, 2018): 1405–7; Jason Hickel, "Degrowth: A Theory of Radical Abundance," *Real-World Economics Review* 87 (2019), www.paecon.net.

11. Intergovernmental Panel on Climate Change, "Mitigation Pathways Compatible with 1.5°C in the Context of Sustainable Development," in *Global Warming of 1.5°C* (2018), 111–12, 121, 161–62.

12. Lena R. Boysen et al., "The Limits to Global-Warming Mitigation by Terrestrial Carbon Removal," *Earth's Future* 5 (2017): 463–74. On the dangers of geoengineering see John Bellamy Foster, "Making War on the Planet," *Science for the People*, Summer 2018, magazine. scienceforthepeople.org.

13. Glen P. Peters et al., "Rapid Growth in CO_2 Emissions After the 2008–2009 Global Financial Crisis," *Nature Climate Change* 2 (January 2012): 2–3.

14. "CO_2 Emissions Reached an All-Time High in 2018," ScientificAmerican.com, December 6, 2018; "U.S. Carbon Emissions Surged in 2018 Even as Coal Plants Closed," *New York Times*, January 8, 2019; "The Low Carbon Economy Index 2018," PwC.Co.UK, www.pwc.co.uk; *Time to Get On With It: The Low Carbon Economy Index 2018* (October 2018), www.pwc.co.uk.

15. Richard York, "Asymmetric Effects of Economic Growth and Decline on CO_2 Emissions," *Nature Climate Change* 2/11 (2012): 762–64; "Greenhouse Link to GDP Not Symmetric," ABC Science, http://abc.net.au.

16. Charles H. Anderson, *The Sociology of Survival* (Homewood, IL: Dorsey Press, 1976), 122–23; Herman E. Daly, "Moving from a Failed Growth Economy to a Steady–State Economy," in *Toward an Integrated Paradigm in Heterodox Economics*, ed. Julien–François Gerber and Rolf Steppacher (New York: Palgrave Macmillan, 2012): 176–89.

17. Carbon Tracker Initiative, *Unburnable Carbon*, 2, http://longfinance.net.

18. Bill McKibben, "Global Warming's Terrifying New Math," *Rolling Stone* (July 19, 2012): 55–60.

19. Clive Hamilton and Jacques Grinevald, "Was the Anthropocene Anticipated?" *Anthropocene Review* 2/1 (2015): 67; Ian Angus, *Facing the Anthropocene* (New York: Monthly Review Press, 2016).

20. Johan Rockström et al., "A Safe Operating Space for Humanity," *Nature* 461/24 (September 2009): 472–75; Jurriaan M. De Vos, Lucas N. Joppa, John L. Gittleman, Patrick R. Stephens, and Stuart L. Pimm, "Estimating the Normal Background Rate of Species Extinction," *Conservation Biology* 29/2 (April 2015): 452–62.

21. President Barack Obama, "Interview of the President by the CBC," February 17, 2009, http://whitehouse.gov.

22. Thomas Friedman exemplifies the purely technological approach. See Friedman, "The Green New Deal Rises Again," *New York Times*, January 8, 2019.

23. Ecological modernization (green capitalist) theorist Arthur Mol remarks: "In a number of cases (regarding countries and/or specific industrial sectors and/or specific environmental issues) environmental reform can even result in an absolute decline in the use of natural resources and discharge of emissions, regardless of economic growth in financial or material terms (product output)." See Arthur P. J. Mol, "Ecological Modernization and the Global Economy," *Global Environmental Politics* 2/2 (May 2002): 93. Yet recent empirical analysis shows that such "absolute decoupling" has little reality at the global level, that is, to the extent that a decoupling exists within nations it is due to the shifting of production and environmental effects from one part of the globe (usually the more powerful part) to another (the weaker part). See Andrew Jorgenson and Brett Clark, "Are the Economy and the Environment Decoupling?: A Comparative International Study, 1960–2005," *American Journal of Sociology* 118/1 (July 2012): 1–44.

24. On how the entropy law constrains technological solutions to environmental problems, see Nicholas Georgescu-Roegen, *Energy and Economic Myths* (New York: Pergamon, 1976), 12, 57.

25. On the Jevons Paradox, see Foster, Clark, and York, *The Ecological Rift*, 169–82; David Owen, *The Conundrum* (New York: Riverhead Books, 2011).

26. Karl Marx, *Capital*, vol. 1 (London: Penguin, 1976), 492.

27. Marx, *Capital*, vol. 1, 247–57, 742. For the relation of M–C–M ′ to the economic contradictions of capitalism, see Paul M. Sweezy, *Four Lectures on Marxism* (New York: Monthly Review Press, 1981), 26–45.

28. Foster, Clark, and York, *The Ecological Rift*, 207–11.

29. On the failure of absolute decoupling and even relative decoupling of the economy from the environment, see Tim Jackson, *Prosperity Without Growth* (London: Earthscan, 2011), 67–86.

30. Solar energy is abundant but is "inherently dilute." A great deal of energy is thus necessary to convert it into concentrated form and hence the net energy return on energy investment (EROI) is small. See Howard T. Odum, *Environment, Power, and Society* (New York: Columbia University Press, 2007), 207–9; Howard T. Odum and Elisabeth C. Odum, *A Prosperous Way Down* (Boulder: University Press of Colorado, 2001), 163–68. Nuclear energy presents serious dangers and does not constitute a feasible overall alternative to fossil fuels. See Kozo Mayumi and John Polimeni, "Uranium Reserve, Nuclear Fuel Cycle Delusion, CO_2 Emissions from the Sea, and Electricity Supply: Reflections After the Fuel Meltdown of the Fukushima Nuclear Power Units," *Ecological Economics* 73 (2012): 1–6.

31. Harry Magdoff and Paul M. Sweezy, "Notes on Watergate One Year Later," *Monthly Review* 26/1 (May 1974): 8–10.

32. Paul M. Sweezy, "Capitalism and the Environment," *Monthly Review* 41/2 (June 1989): 6.

33. Murray Bookchin, *Remaking Society* (Boston: South End Press, 1990), 93–94.

34. This was famously highlighted by Barry Commoner, *The Closing Circle* (New York: Knopf, 1971), 138–75.

35. Howard T. Odum and David Scienceman, "An Energy Systems View of Karl Marx's Concepts of Production and Labor Power," in *Emergy Synthesis 3*, Proceedings from the Third Biennial Emergy Conference, Gainesville, Florida, Center for Economic Policy, 2005, 41; Odum and Odum, *A Prosperous Way Down*.

36. The argument in the following pages develops on an earlier analysis in John Bellamy Foster, "The Ecology of Marxian Political Economy," *Monthly Review* 63/4 (September 2011): 1–16.

37. Thorstein Veblen, *Absentee Ownership and Business Enterprise in Modern Times* (New York: Augustus M. Kelley, 1964), 300–301.

38. See especially K. William Kapp, *Social Costs of Private Enterprise* (Cambridge, MA: Harvard University Press, 1950); Scott Nearing, *The Economics of the Power Age* (East Palatka, FL: World Events Committee, 1952); John Kenneth Galbraith, *The Affluent Society* (New York: New American Library, 1958); Vance Packard, *The Waste Makers* (New York: Simon and Schuster, 1960); Joan Robinson, *Contributions to Modern Economics* (Oxford: Blackwell, 1978), 1–13.

39. See Paul A. Baran and Paul M. Sweezy, *The Age of Monopoly* Capital, ed. Nicholas Baran and John Bellamy Foster (New York: Monthly Review Press, 2017), 38, 248, 267, 457; Franklin M. Fisher, Zvi Grilliches, and Carl Kaysen, "The Costs of Automobile Changes Since 1949," *Journal of Political Economy* 70/5 (October 1962): 433–51; Baran and Sweezy, *Monopoly Capital*, 131–38.

40. Thorstein Veblen, *The Theory of the Leisure Class* (New York: New American Library, 1953), 78–80.

41. Paul A. Baran and Paul M. Sweezy, "Some Theoretical Implications," *Monthly Review* 64/3 (July–August 2012), 57.

42. The issue of "specifically capitalist use value" was addressed in a commentary on Baran and Sweezy's analysis by Henryk Slajfer, "Waste, Marxian Theory, and Monopoly Capital," in *The Faltering Economy*, ed. John Bellamy Foster and Henryk Slajfer (New York: Monthly Review Press, 1984), 302–13. The concept was carried forward in John Bellamy Foster, *The Theory of Monopoly Capitalism* (New York: Monthly Review Press, 1986), 39–42. The explanation of this as a transformation of

Marx's general formula of capital under monopoly capitalism, in terms of the emergence of $M-C^K-M'$, was first introduced in Foster, "The Ecology of Marxian Political Economy." Unbeknownst to the author at that time, a similar reformulation of Marx's general formula as $M-W-M'$ had been introduced a number of years before in Patrick Brantlinger and Richard Higgins, "Waste and Value: Thorstein Veblen and H.G. Wells," *Criticism* 48/4 (Fall 2006): 466. For how this concept of waste (unproductive labor) influenced Baran and Sweezy's analysis see Paul A. Baran and Paul M. Sweezy, "Some Theoretical Implications," *Monthly Review* 64/3 (July–August 2012): 45–58; John Bellamy Foster, "A Missing Chapter of Monopoly Capital," *Monthly Review* 64/3 (July–August 2012): 17–21. The case for Marx's theory of socialism as one of sustainable human development is made in Paul Burkett, "Marx's Vision of Sustainable Human Development," *Monthly Review* 57/5 (October 2005): 34–62.

43. Packard, *The Waste Makers*, 46.

44. John Ruskin, *Unto This Last* (Lincoln: University of Nebraska Press, 1967), 73.

45. Herman E. Daly and John B. Cobb Jr., *For the Common Good* (Boston: Beacon Press, 1994), 463.

46. See Frederik Berend Blauwhof, "Overcoming Accumulation," *Ecological Economics* 84 (2012): 254–61.

47. Captain Charles Moore, *Plastic Ocean* (New York: Penguin, 2011), 129.

48. Diana Wicks, "Packaging Sales Goals and Strategies," *Chron*, http://smallbusiness.chron.com; "Product Packaging Can Cost Three Times as Much as What's Inside," *Daily Mail*, July 13, 2007, http://dailymail.co.uk.

49. "Global Hunger for Plastic Packaging Leaves Waste Solution a Long Way Off," *Guardian*, December 29, 2011, http://guardian.co.uk; Moore, *Plastic Ocean*, 41; Hannah Holleman, Inger L. Stole, John Bellamy Foster, and Robert W. McChesney, "The Sales Effort and Monopoly Capital," *Monthly Review* 60/11 (April 2009): 6.

50. Kevin C. Clancy and Robert S. Shulman, "Marketing with Blinders On," *Across the Board* 30/8 (October 1993): 33–38; Clancy and Shulman, *Marketing Myths That Are Killing Business* (New York: McGraw Hill, 1994), 140, 171–72, 221; Robert Buzzel, John Quelch, and Walter J. Salmon, "The Costly Bargain of Trade Promotion," *Harvard Business Review* (March–April 1990): 141–49.

51. Heather Fletcher, "$316B in Ad, Marketing Spending Arriving in 2018," Target Marketing, January 17, 2018, https://www.targetmarketingmag.com/article/316b-ad-marketing-spending-arriving-2018/. More expansive definitions (including marketing

research, product development, sales promotion, etc.) provide higher estimates. See "U.S. Marketing Spending Exceeded $1 Trillion in 2005," *Metrics Business and Market Intelligence*, June 26, 2006, http://metrics2. com. Subsequent estimates with respect to marketing have been more conservative, but there is no doubt that global marketing was now over $ 1 trillion a year. At the global level, using the more restrictive definitions, marketing is seen as surpassing at $1 trillion. "GroupM Predicts Global Marketing Expenditures Will Surpass $1 Trillion," August 2, 2016, groupm.com.

52. Galbraith, *The Affluent Society*, 121–28. The one in every twelve dollars figure for marketing is based on the Blackfriars 2005 marketing estimate, representing roughly that portion of GDP that year. On the role of marketing in the maintenance of monopoly capital, see Michael Dawson, *The Consumer Trap* (Urbana: University of Illinois Press, 2005).

53. Robert S. Lynd, "The People as Consumers," in President's Research Committee on Social Trends, *Recent Social Trends in the United States*, vol. 2 (New York: McGraw Hill, 1933), 858, 867–88.

54. Juliet Schor, *Plenitude* (New York: Penguin, 2010), 40–41.

55. Schor, *Plenitude*, 38.

56. Marc Perton, "Jobs: 'You Have to Buy a New iPod at Least Once a Year,'" May 26, 2006, http://endgadget.com.

57. Roland Geyer, Jenna R. Jambeck, and Kara Lavender Law, "Production, Use, and Fate of All Plastics Ever Made," *Science Advances* 3/7 (July 19, 2017), http://advances.sciencemag.org.Ecocyle; "Environmental Facts," http://ecocycle.org/ecofacts; Annie Leonard, *The Story of Stuff* (New York: Free Press, 2010), 195; "Beverage Containers," *Report Buyer*, http://www.reportbuyer.com.

58. Pete Smith et al., "How Much Land-Based Greenhouse Gas Mitigation Can Be Achieved Without Compromising Food Security and Environmental Goals?," *Global Change Biology* 19 (2013): 2290–92; UN Food and Agricultural Organization, *Global Food Losses and Food Waste* (Rome: FAO, 2011), 4–9; Food and Agricultural Organization, "Key Facts on Food Loss and Waste Reduction," http://www.fao.org/ save–food/resources/keyfindings/en/. Food loss/waste, it should be noted, occurs at a similar level in poor countries, but the losses are not primarily due to waste, that is, discarding food, but rather to inadequate food storage facilities associated with underdevelopment.

59. Federal Highway Administration, "3.2 Trillion Miles Driven on U.S. Roads in 2016," February 21, 2017, www.fhwa.dot.gov, "Average Annual Miles Driven by Age Group"; American Automobile Association, "Americans Spend an Average 17,600 Minutes Driving Each Year," September 8, newsroom.aaa.com; Yves Engler and Bianca Mugyenyi,

Stop Signs: Cars and Capitalism (Vancouver, BC: Red Publishing, 2011), 13, 108, 115–16; Lester R. Brown, *Outgrowing the Earth* (New York: W. W. Norton, 2004), 92. The reference to a "car–first" transportation system is from Michael Dawson, "Electric Evasion," *Counterpunch*, October 15–17, 2010, http://counterpunch.org.

60. See Baran and Sweezy, *Monopoly Capital*, 389; Michael Kidron, *Capitalism and Theory* (London: Pluto Press, 1974), 53; Michael Dawson and John Bellamy Foster, "The Tendency of Surplus to Rise, 1963–1988," in *The Economic Surplus in the Advanced Economies*, ed. John B. Davis (Brookfield, VT: Edward Elgar, 1992), 63.

61. Kapp, *The Social Costs of Private Enterprise*, 231.

62. Karl Marx, *Capital*, vol. 3 (London: Penguin, 1981), 180.

63. To our knowledge the term "ecological debt" first appeared in Anderson, *The Sociology of Survival*, 143. The direct inspiration, however, was Commoner, who had employed the concept of "environmental debt," in *The Closing Circle*, 295; Odum and Odum, *A Prosperous Way Down*, 139, 173, 175, 179. Odum used the concept of "emergy," which reduced all forms of energy to energy of one kind (measured in solar emjoules) as a means of analyzing embodied energy, in *Environment, Power, and Society*, 278; John Bellamy Foster and Hannah Holleman, "A Theory of Unequal Ecological Exchange," *Journal of Peasant Studies* 41/1–2 (March 2014): 199–233.

64. Odum and Odum, *A Prosperous Way Down*, 149.

65. Ibid., 183; Odum, *Environment, Power, and Society*, 58, 276, 389–91.

66. Howard T. Odum, "Energy, Ecology and Economics," *Ambio* 2/6 (1973): 222.

67. Global Footprint Network, "World Footprint," http://footprintnetwork.org; BBC News, "How Many Earths Do We Need," June 16, 2005.

68. Howard T. Odum and J. E. Arding, *Emergy Analysis of Shrimp Mariculture in Ecuador* (Narragansett: Coastal Research Center, University of Rhode Island, 1991), 33–39.

69. Tom Athanasiou and Paul Baer, *Dead Heat* (New York: Seven Stories Press, 2002).

70. Hansen and Kharecha, "Cost of Carbon Capture: Can Young People Bear the Burden?," 1406.

71. Foster, Clark, and York, *The Ecological Rift*, 439–40.

72. This was true of the Soviet Union as well, the analysis of which, however, does not concern us here. See John Bellamy Foster, *The Vulnerable Planet* (New York: Monthly Review Press, 1999), 96–101.

73. Odum, *Environment, Power and Society*, 274.

74. Simon Kuznets, "National Income and Industrial Structure," *Econometrica* 17, supplement (1949): 217.

75.   Ibid, 212–14, 229.

76.   Ibid, 216–19, 227.

77.   Thomas Dietz, Eugene A. Rosa, and Richard York, "Economically Efficient Well-Being: Is There a Kuznets Curve?," *Applied Geography* 32 (2012): 21–28.

78.   "Environmental Cost of Shipping Groceries Around the World," *New York Times*, April 26, 2008; Sally Deneen, "Food Miles," *The Daily Green*, http://thedailygreen.com; Intan Suwandi, R. Jamil Jonna, and John Bellamy Foster, "Global Commodity Chains and the New Imperialism," *Monthly Review* 70/10 (March 2019): 15; Report Buyer, *The Food Miles Challenge (2006)*, http://reportbuyer.com, 2; Daniel Imhoff, "Thinking Outside of the Box," *Whole Earth* (Winter 2002): 12.

79.   See in particular Amory B. Lovins, L. Hunter Lovins, and Marty Bender, "Energy and Agriculture," in *Meeting the Expectations of the Land*, ed. Wes Jackson, Wendell Berry, and Bruce Coleman (San Francisco: North Point Press, 1984), 68–69; Michael A. Altieri, "Agroecology, Small Farms, and Food Sovereignty," David Pimentel, "Reducing Energy Inputs in the Agricultural Production System," and Jules Pretty, "Can Ecological Agriculture Feed Nine Billion People," in *Agriculture and Food in Crisis*, ed. Fred Magdoff and Brian Tokar (New York: Monthly Review Press, 2010).

80.   Marx, *Capital*, vol. 3, 216.

81.   Mindi Schneider and Philip McMichael, "Deepening and Repairing, the Metabolic Rift," *Journal of Peasant Studies* 37/3 (2010): 461.

82.   Odum, *Environment, Power, and Society*, 189–90.

83.   Odum and Odum, *A Prosperous Way Down*, 87. For a discussion of how Cuba has transformed food production, see Richard Levins, "How Cuba Is Going Ecological," *Capitalism, Nature, Socialism* 16/3 (2005): 7–25; Sinan Koont, "Food Security in Cuba," *Monthly Review* 55/8 (2004): 11–20.

84.   Samir Amin, "World Poverty, Pauperization and Capital Accumulation," *Monthly Review* 55/5 (October 2003): 1–9; Prabhat Patnaik, "The Myths of Capitalism," MR Online, July 4, 2011, http://mronline. monthlyreview.org; UK House of Commons, *A Century of Trends in UK Statistics Since 1900*, Library Research Paper 99/111, December 21, 1999, http://parliament.uk, 13; U.S. Census Bureau, *Statistical Abstract of the United States, 2012*, Tables 28 and 29, http://census.gov.

85.   Wen Tiejun et al., "Ecological Civilization, Indigenous Culture, and Rural Reconstruction in China," *Monthly Review* 63/9 (February 2012): 29–35; Wen Tiejun, "Deconstructing Modernization," *Chinese Sociology and Anthropology* 49/4 (Summer 2007): 10–25.

86.   Marx, *Capital*, vol. 1, 283.

87. On the scale of today's planetary rift see Foster, Clark, and York, *The Ecological Rift*.

88. On the relation between capitalism's internal economic contradictions and its external ecological ones, see Kent A. Klitgaard and Lisi Krall, "Ecological Economics, Degrowth, and Institutional Change," *Ecological Economics* 84 (2012): 247–53.

89. Herman E. Daly, "Further Commentary," in Jackson, *Prosperity Without Growth*, 267–68.

90. Marx, *Capital*, vol. 3, 959.

91. Max Weber was quite likely the first major thinker to stress that modern industrial capitalism was predicated on a fossil fuel–based environmental regime. See John Bellamy Foster and Hannah Holleman, "Weber and the Environment," *American Journal of Sociology* 117/6 (May 2012): 1636, 1646–50.

92. On the nature of planning for a socialism for the twenty-first century, see Harry Magdoff and Fred Magdoff, "Approaching Socialism," *Monthly Review* 57/3 (July–August 2005): 19–61.

93. On the important concept of plenitude, see Schor, *Plenitude*, 4–7.

94. Intergovernmental Panel on Climate Change, *Global Warming of 1.5°C*, 17; Steffen et al., "Trajectories of the Earth System in the Anthropocene," 8256–57; Minqi Li, *The Rise of China and the Demise of the Capitalist World Economy* (New York: Monthly Review Press, 2008), 187.

95. István Mészáros, *Beyond Capital* (New York: Monthly Review Press, 1995), 174, 893–94.

96. Baran and Sweezy, *Monopoly Capital*, 141.

11. The Long Ecological Revolution

This chapter is adapted and revised for this book from John Bellamy Foster, "The Long Ecological Revolution," *Monthly Review* 69/6 (November 2017): 1–16.

1. Francis Bacon, *Novum Organum* (Chicago: Open Court, 1994), 29, 43. On the Baconian "ruse" and Marx's response, see William Leiss, *The Domination of Nature* (Boston: Beacon, 1974). In Latin, as in most languages with gendered nouns, "nature" (*natura*) is feminine, bringing out the patriarchal aspects of Bacon's views. For a powerful ecofeminist critique, see Carolyn Merchant, *The Death of Nature* (New York: Harper and Row, 1980).

2. Karl Marx, *Grundrisse* (London: Penguin, 1973), 334–35, 409–10. Oddly, Michael Löwy quotes this same passage from Marx as a "good example of the sections of Marx's work that bear witness to an uncritical admiration for the 'civilizing actions of capitalist production,'" and the overcoming of

natural boundaries. Though plausible on its face, Löwy's position reflects a deep misunderstanding of Marx's argument, part of a dialectical critique of the Baconian "ruse"—that nature is to be conquered by a kind of subterfuge—and of the general attitudes of bourgeois science. Equally important is the theoretical context in which Marx wrote, namely the dialectic of barriers and boundaries first introduced in Georg Wilhelm Friedrich Hegel's *Logic*. Based on this dialectical understanding, Marx insists that capital is ultimately unable to overcome natural boundaries, even as it temporarily surmounts them by treating them as mere barriers. This overarching contradiction leads to perpetual, recurrent crises. Michael Löwy, "Marx, Engels, and Ecology," *Capitalism Nature Socialism* 28/2 (2017): 10–21. For a comprehensive treatment of Marx's argument, see John Bellamy Foster, "Marx's *Grundrisse* and the Ecological Contradictions of Capitalism," in *Karl Marx's Grundrisse*, ed. Marcello Musto (London: Routledge, 2008), 100–102. See also István Mészáros, *Beyond Capital* (New York: Monthly Review Press, 1995), 568.

3.   Karl Marx, *Capital*, vol. 1 (London: Penguin, 1976), 636–38; *Capital*, vol. 3 (London: Penguin, 1981), 754, 911, 949; John Bellamy Foster, *Marx's Ecology* (New York: Monthly Review Press, 2000).

4.   Karl Marx and Frederick Engels, *Collected Works* (New York: International Publishers, 1975), vol. 25, 460–61.

5.   John Bellamy Foster, "Late Soviet Ecology and the Planetary Crisis," *Monthly Review* 67/2 (June 2015): 1–20.

6.   Clive Hamilton and Jacques Grinevald, "Was the Anthropocene Anticipated?" *Anthropocene Review* 3/1 (2015): 67; Ian Angus, *Facing the Anthropocene* (New York: Monthly Review Press, 2016).

7.   E. P. Thompson, *Beyond the Cold War* (New York: Pantheon, 1982), 41–80; Rudolf Bahro, *Avoiding Social and Ecological Disaster* (Bath, UK: Gateway, 1994), 19.

8.   For the larger theoretical implications of the question of the relation of social relations to forces of production, and its connection to recent disputes in Marxian theory, see John Bellamy Foster, Harry Magdoff, and Robert W. McChesney, "Socialism: A Time to Retreat?" *Monthly Review* 52/4 (September 2000): 1–7. The concept of "social metabolic reproduction" is central to the work of István Mészáros, beginning with his *Beyond Capital*.

9.   The notion of a long ecological revolution is meant to draw on Raymond Williams's earlier notion of a "long revolution." For Williams, cultural and ecological materialism were always intertwined, reflecting the long convergence of the Romantic and Marxist traditions. See Williams, *The Long Revolution* (New York: Columbia University Press, 1961); Williams, *Politics and Letters* (London: New Left, 1979).

10.   For critiques of ecological modernization theory, see Richard York and Eugene A. Rosa, "Key Challenges to Ecological Modernization Theory," *Organization and Environment* 16/3 (2003): 273–88; John Bellamy Foster, "The Planetary Rift and the New Human Exemptionalism," *Organization and Environment* 25/3 (2012): 211–37; Jeffrey A. Ewing, "Hollow Ecology: Ecological Modernization Theory and the Death of Nature," *Journal of World-Systems Research* 23/1 (2012): 126–55.

11.   Trillionthtonne.org.

12.   Peter Frase, "By Any Means Necessary," *Jacobin* 26 (2017): 81.

13.   Leon Trotsky, *Literature and Revolution* (New York: Russell and Russell, 1957), 251.

14.   Connor Kilpatrick, "Victory Over the Sun," *Jacobin* 26 (2017): 22–23.

15.   Leigh Phillips, *Austerity Ecology and the Collapse-Porn Addicts* (Winchester, UK: Zero, 2015).

16.   Phillips, *Austerity Ecology*, 9, 23, 32–33, 39–40, 59–63, 67–68, 88, 132, 217–34, 246–49, 252; Leigh Phillips, "Why Eco-Austerity Won't Save Us from Climate Change," *Guardian*, November 4, 2015. In attacking the notion that Marx developed an ecological critique through his theory of metabolic rift, Phillips claims incorrectly that the concept of metabolism in science is restricted to chemical operations within the body, in isolation from its "exchange" with the environment. He also rejects recent scholarship (beginning with Hal Draper) suggesting that the famous phrase "the idiocy of rural life" in the standard English-language edition of the *Communist Manifesto* was a faulty translation. In nineteenth-century usage, the German word *Idiotismus* retained the meaning of its Greek origin, *idiotes* (a private or isolated person) and is more correctly translated as "isolation"—conveying the idea that rural workers were isolated from the *polis*. Phillips simply declares that since Marx was not afraid of being politically incorrect he would not have shied away from calling rural workers "idiots" (in the contemporary English-language sense). Here one can only quote Spinoza's famous phrase: "Ignorance is no argument."

17.   Phillips, *Austerity Ecology*, 60, 76, 85, 252–63. It should be noted that "Prometheanism" has two historic meanings. The first, derived from Lucretius, associates the Promethean myth with the Enlightenment and seventeenth-century scientific revolution. The second and more common contemporary meaning, used here, denotes extreme productivism or industrialism. Marx referred to Prometheus in both senses, lauding Epicurus as the Prometheus of the Enlightenment in antiquity, and later criticizing Proudhon for his mechanistic Prometheanism. See Foster, *Marx's Ecology*, 10, 59, 126–30.

18.   Phillips, *Austerity Ecology*, 89, 190, 255.

19. Ibid., 202–3.

20. Leigh Phillips and Michal Rozworski, "Planning the Good Anthropocene," *Jacobin* 26 (2017): 133–36; Phillips, *Austerity Ecology*, 67–68; Breakthrough Institute, "The Year of the Good Anthropocene: Top Breakthroughs of 2015"; Breakthrough Institute, "Leigh Phillips, Science Writer and Journalist," http://thebreakthrough.org/people/profile/leigh–phillips; *Ecomodernism Manifesto*, 7.

21. Peter Frase, *Four Futures: Life After Capitalism* (London: Verso, 2016), 91–119. Frase's notion of "Loving Our Monsters" is taken from Bruno Latour's article "Love Your Monsters: Why We Must Care for Our Technologies As We Do Our Children," Breakthrough Institute, Winter 2012.

22. The most popular geoengineering solution, the injection of sulfur particles into the atmosphere (sometimes euphemistically called "solar radiation management") is widely regarded in the scientific community as a solution more dangerous than climate change itself, since it would do nothing to stop the buildup of carbon emissions in the atmosphere, while creating whole new planetary dangers. The moment such sulfur injection stopped, climate change would resume on higher levels than ever before, as determined by the higher carbon dioxide concentration in the environment. The dangers of this form of geoengineering include a drier planet with more severe droughts and monsoons, possible erosion of the ozone layer, and disruption of photosynthesis. Further, it would do nothing to mitigate ocean acidification. Cloud brightening, endorsed by Frase, raises similar objections: if done over the Atlantic, it could contribute to the desertification of the Amazon, introducing new global ecological problems without alleviating any of the underlying causes of climate change. Nicolas Jones, "Solar Geoengineering: Weighing the Costs of Blocking the Sun's Rays," Yale Environment 360, January 9, 2014, http://e360.yale.edu; Christopher Mims, "'Albedo Yaughts' and Marine Clouds: A Cure for Climate Change?," *Scientific American*, October 21, 2009.

23. Frase, "By Any Means Necessary," 73–81; Phillips, *Austerity Ecology*, 105.

24. Daniel Aldana Cohen, "The Last Stimulus," *Jacobin* 26 (2017): 83–95.

25. Christian Parenti, "If We Fail," *Jacobin* 26 (2017): 114–27; Parenti, "A Radical Approach to the Climate Crisis," *Dissent* (Summer 2013); Parenti, *Tropic of Chaos* (New York: Nation Books, 2012); Andy Skuce, "'We'd Have to Finish One New Facility Every Working Day for the Next 70 Years'— Why Carbon Capture Is No Panacea," *Bulletin of the Atomic Scientists*, October 4, 2016; Skuce, "The Quest for CCS," Corporate Knights, January 6, 2016, http://corporateknights.com; Vaclav Smil, "Global Energy: The Latest Infatuations," *American Scientist* 99 (May–June 2011): 219. On BECCS, see Lena R. Boysen et al., "The Limits to Global-Warming

Mitigation by Terrestrial Carbon Removal," *Earth's Future* 5 (2017): 463–74; John Bellamy Foster, "Making War on the Planet: Geoengineering and Capitalism's Creative Destruction of the Earth," Science for the People, Summer 2018, magazine.scienceforthepeople.org.

26. Angela Nagle, "We Gave Greenpeace a Chance," *Jacobin* 26 (2017): 130–31. One might think that Parenti's references to the Venus Syndrome would leave him open to charges of "catastrophism." But such criticisms are seldom leveled at those taking ecomodernist stances, precisely because they tend to present ready-made technological solutions that minimize challenges to the status quo.

27. Branko Marcetic, "People Make the World Go Round," *Jacobin* 26 (2017): 106–7; Jonah Walters, "Beware Your Local Food Cooperative," *Jacobin* (Summer 2017): 137–38.

28. Marx and Engels, *Collected Works*, vol. 25, 105.

29. Ibid., 461–63.

30. Fred Magdoff and Chris Williams, *Creating an Ecological Society* (New York: Monthly Review Press, 2017), 247.

31. Carbon capture technology is most likely to be effective in the form of bioenergy with carbon capture and storage (BECCS).

32. The conception of freedom as the recognition of necessity is fundamental to Marxist theory. It was first introduced in Hegel's *Logic* and was incorporated into the materialist conception of history by Engels in *Anti-Dühring*. See Marx and Engels, *Collected Works*, vol. 25, 105–6.

33. John Bellamy Foster, "The Ecology of Marxian Political Economy," *Monthly Review* 63/4 (September 2011): 1–16.

34. Paul A. Baran, *The Longer View* (New York: Monthly Review Press, 1969), 30.

35. On military spending, see John Bellamy Foster, Hannah Holleman, and Robert W. McChesney, "The U.S. Imperial Triangle and Military Spending," *Monthly Review* 60/5 (October 2008): 1–19. On marketing, see Michael Dawson, *The Consumer Trap* (Urbana: University of Illinois Press, 2005), 1. The total quantities of both military spending and marketing have increased massively in the years since these works were written.

36. Magdoff and Williams, *Creating an Ecological Society*, 283–329. On the possibilities presented by an ecological revolution, see Fred Magdoff and John Bellamy Foster, *What Every Environmentalist Needs to Know About Capitalism* (New York: Monthly Review Press, 2011), 124–33.

37. Magdoff and Williams, *Creating an Ecological Society*, 309–10.

38. On the concept of the environmental proletariat, see John Bellamy Foster, Brett Clark, and Richard York, *The Ecological Rift* (New York: Monthly Review Press, 2010), 398–99, 440–41.

Index

socioecological metabolism, 132;
on soil nutrient cycle, 209
Liedman, Sven-Eric, 33–34
Lindley, John, 72
Linebaugh, Peter, 48
Linnaeus, Carl, 142
Lipietz, Alain, 199
Llorente, Renzo, 131, 139–40
Locke, John, 38, 52, 155
Looking Backward (Bellamy), 178, 181
Lucretius, 23, 32, 132, 151, 176
Lukács, Georg, 208, 214–15
Luxemburg, Rosa, 91
Lyell, Charles, 47, 141–42
Lynd, Robert S., 254

Macdonald, Bradley J., 132, 149
Magdoff, Fred, 283, 286–87
Magdoff, Harry, 247–49
Maitland, James (Earl of Lauderdale),
154–56, 163, 171
Malthus, Thomas Robert, 156, 161,
175, 199
Manchester (England), 27–28
manure, 22, 58, 60, 69–70, 74, 117–
120, 146, 150, 209
Marcetic, Branko, 281
Marcuse, Herbert, 195, 196, 215
Marshall, Alfred, 162
Marshall, John, 53, 57
Marx, Eleanor, 92
Marx, Karl: on agriculture, 12–13,
262–63; on alienated speciesism,
145; on animals, 130–32, 146–49;
in Anthropocene epoch, 212–17;
on British agriculture, 57–59,
120–23, 127–29; on British colonialism in India, 56; *Capital* by,
88–89, 178; on capitalist expropriation, 47–48; on corporeal issues,
31–32; on cotton and slave trades,
49–51; on Cunningham, 175; on
Darwin and evolution, 141–44;
on Descartes's dualism, 135–41;

on ecological limits, 61; on environmental hazards in production,
102–3; on exploitation of women,
78–79; on expropriation, 39–42;
on expropriation of nature, 43; on
food and nutrition, 29–31, 104–6,
109–13, 150; food-regime analysts
on, 114–16, 119; on forms of profit,
41; Frankfurt School theorists on,
190–91; on humans and nature, 7,
265; on hunger, 104; on Ireland,
64–78; labor theory of value of,
160–63; Lauderdale Paradox and,
158–60; Liedman on, 33–34; on
metabolic rift, 18–23, 33, 101,
204–12; Morris on, 179, 184; on
Native Americans, 52–53; on natural economy, 45–46; on nature, 269;
on nature, criticisms of, 191–204;
on Plutarch, 133–34; on property,
38–39; on slavery, 53–55; on social
labor, posthumanist critiques of,
221–28; on sources of wealth, 172;
on transition to capitalism, 36; on
use of machinery under capitalism,
246; on value relations under capitalism, 219–20; on wastes, 256; on
woman question, 92; on working
conditions, 27–29
Marxism, 198; ecological, 272, 286
Marxist ecofeminism, 212
materialism: Epicurean, 18, 23, 24, 32,
133–34; Greek, 165, 176–77; Marx's
materialism, 7, 18–19, 23–24, 31,
33, 105, 130, 132–36, 138–140, 142,
144–45, 151, 191, 193, 195–99,
203–06, 212, 217, 269
McChesney, Robert W., 187–88
McConnell, Campbell, 162
McKibben, Bill, 243
McMichael, Philip, 113–16, 119, 127,
263
Mechi, John Joseph, 118
Menger, Carl, 163–64